EX LIBRIS

Helen S. May

ARCTIC ADVENTURE

BY PETER FREUCHEN

ESKIMO

ARCTIC ADVENTURE: MY LIFE IN THE FROZEN NORTH

THE AUTHOR IN 1921, PHOTOGRAPHED IN GODTHAAB, GREENLAND, IN THE ONLY
ESKIMO STUDIO IN THE WORLD

ARCTIC ADVENTURE

My Life in the Frozen North

BY PETER FREUCHEN

ILLUSTRATED WITH PHOTOGRAPHS
AND MAPS

FARRAR & RINEHART
INCORPORATED
On Murray Hill   *New York*

TO

RICHARD FARNSWORTH HOYT

A GREAT FRIEND

Born July 3, 1888
Died March 7, 1935

LIST OF ILLUSTRATIONS

Map of Greenland   *front endpaper*

The author in 1921   *frontispiece*

Myself at 19 and 21 years of age   7

The *Danmark* frozen in at Danmarkshavn. Members of the *Danmark* crew   11

Feeding my dogs during the summer. Our house at Danmarkshavn   13

My cabin at Pustervig. Crowded quarters   17

Myself after the year at Pustervig   20

Henrik and Tobias, our Eskimo helpers   23

Two views of the *Danmark*   27

Entrance to the ice cave, *Gnipa-Grotten*. The edge of the icecap against Ymers Nunatak   29

Knud Rasmussen   33

An iceberg in the Thule District. The seacoast at Thule   39

Thule Eskimos cutting up a walrus. Head and skin of the walrus   43

Alakrasina with her son, Kale. Three Eskimo children at Thule   53

Map. The Northern Part of West Greenland   59

Resting our dogs before Devil's Tongue Mountain. Dogdriving in Melville Bay   68

Itukusunguaq and his wife   91

Rasmussen playing host at a coffee feast. A native hunter in his kayak   99

Rasmussen and old Arnajark   115

Natives harpooning a seal. Hauling a walrus out of the water   131

Aloqisaq, who did our washing. Native boy at Thule all dressed up   143

Two views of our house at Thule—summer and winter   151

Navarana   164

Navarana's mother with two of her children   169

Navarana setting her fox traps. Body of a wolf   177

We entertain visitors and traders. Jacobine Nielsen and
Navarana   183

Map. Route of the First Thule Expedition   189

Breaking camp on the icecap. The start of the First Thule
Expedition   193

My team fording a stream on the icecap. A perpendicular
wall of ice   198

Two of our dogs holding a musk ox at bay. Musk oxen in
fighting formation   211

Rasmussen and myself   217

The icefoot at the base of the mountains. Sliding down the
glacier   225

Myself after prolonged hunger and exposure   229

North Star Bay in the summer. Mountains between Thule
and the icecap   235

The *Danmark* at anchor. Our boat, the *Cape York*   259

A wedding party at Thule. Polar Eskimos summering at
Thule   273

Our new motorboat. Dogs waiting to be rescued   280

Reading my newspaper one year late. At my desk during the
long Arctic night   284

A typical house in Upernivik. Lively trading at a post in
South Greenland   290

Headquarters for the Fifth Thule Expedition. Peary's expedition house at Pim's Island   293

My summer tent made of skins   311

Missionaries at Thule. Rasmussen with a group of natives   315

Navarana and myself at Thule   327

Lauge Koch. Dr. Torild Wulff in a kayak   333

Rasmussen with my son. Mequsaq dressed for travel   337

Navarana with our two children   345

Sailing for Denmark   351

Captain Peder Pedersen, Knud Rasmussen, and myself. The
Danmark and our motorboat at anchor in the harbor   359

Pipaluk and myself   369

Map. Field of the Fifth Thule Expedition 373

Members of the Fifth Thule Expedition to Hudson Bay and Baffin Land 377

Father du Plane, Hudson Bay missionary, with a native. Captain Cleveland at Repulse Bay 383

Rasmussen and Dr. Birket-Smith. Akrioq chewing lines in our cabin 391

Myself on Danish Island. Kratalik and myself 397

Anaqaq, a Netchilik Eskimo. Inuyak, my personal servant 401

Dr. Therkel Mathiassen, Helge Bangsted, and Dr. Birket-Smith 405

Arnanguaq, her husband Akrioq, and Kraviaq 413

The boat in which Inuyak and I went to Chesterfield Inlet for a doctor. Hudson Bay natives constructing a kayak 415

Reindeer Eskimo wearing protection against snow blindness. Reindeer Eskimo starving. Netchilik woman. Netchilik man eating meat 421

A skin boat, rowed only by women. Tapartee and his wife 427

Atakutaluk, who ate her husband and children 433

Eskimo women carrying fuel home. Netchilik woman and two Hudson Bay children 439

Akratak and Boatsman 443

Contrasting costumes of Avilik and Reindeer women 461

Ten-year-old Mequsaq arriving in Copenhagen 464

Greeting Pipaluk in the harbor at Copenhagen 466

Map of Area Inhabited by Eskimos—Fifth Thule Expedition *back endpaper*

ARCTIC ADVENTURE

PART I

1

I HAD been in the harness all day and now that no traces held me back, it was easy just to walk, just to put one foot ahead of the other. Acute hunger seems to sharpen the other senses and, while my movements were automatic and I was too tired to sit down and rest, my brain was unnaturally alert.

It was my first spring in Greenland, 1907. Three of us, Gundahl, Jarner and I, had left the base of the Danmark Expedition to northeast Greenland, to familiarize ourselves with the landscape and collect such stray geological specimens as we could find. We had chosen to pull the sledges ourselves. You get to know the land much better that way than by sitting on the sledge, occupying yourself with the dogs and looking straight ahead.

Food and kerosene had been cached for us along the way, but when we reached the cache we found that a bear had been there before us. Even the canned goods were gone—the animal had chewed open the tins and eaten everything. He had examined the kerosene tank and, finding that it was of no use to him, given it a slap with his big paw, crashing it open. We knew that we could expect to find neither musk oxen, rabbits nor ptarmigans. The bear who had visited the spot some days before had not bothered to wait for us.

There was another cache for us to return to at the Koldewey Islands, enough food to last us several days while we studied geological formations. But even if we could, by hurrying, cover twice as much ground as we had anticipated, it would still take us three days to reach the Islands. We set out. There was nothing else to do.

We made slow progress. It was our fifth day now without anything to eat. We were weak and when we camped that night we cut some pieces of wood from the sledge and built a fire in order to melt ice for drinking water. After the tent was up there seemed nothing to say. It was useless to try to forget our present situation; we were too far sunk to try to think of anything else. We were so wretched that we were irritated at the sight of each other's faces.

In desperation I took my gun and walked away. I saw traces of rabbits, a few foxes and ptarmigans, but nothing living. I trudged uphill and downhill—there was no use going back to look into the haggard eyes of those two poor fellows.

At length I saw a rabbit. Unless I had been terribly hungry, I doubt very much that I would have spotted him. A cute, white little thing among the bowlders. Unfamiliar with men, he paid me slight heed and allowed me to come near. When he decided to run I fired, and he disappeared over the top of the hill. When I finally reached the spot where I had last seen him, the rabbit lay dead only a few paces distant.

I felt as if I had been hauled suddenly out of the sea after all hope of rescue was gone! I took the dead rabbit in my hands, hefted it—rabbits often weigh eight pounds up north—and realized what it would mean to us—a fine stew for three men and a chance, after what seemed months, of feeling that heavenly filled-up sensation.

I was so weak after the excitement subsided that I sat down on a stone to rest. I thought about eating the rabbit. Should we eat it all today, or keep some for tomorrow? Better eat all of it at once, and then walk as fast as possible for the cache. Chances were that we would find something else on the way. I sat and made plan after plan, each born of the fact that I had a rabbit and an hour ago I had had none.

At last I got up, and started back toward camp. The rabbit was heavy and, hanging on a string over my shoulder, interfered with my progress. I thought, "If I cut it open and take out the guts it will be much lighter." But back of that was the idea of eating the raw liver and heart, and not sharing it with the other two men who lay starving in the tent. I was ashamed of my treason, and hurried on, but soon I had to sit down again and rest, and temptation returned doubly strong.

Since I had killed the rabbit, and walked so far to get it, wasn't I entitled to half of it? If I ate it, wouldn't I be much stronger and able to do a greater share of the work? Yet if I ate a mouthful of the rabbit I might not be able to stop until I had devoured the whole of it. Suppose I did eat it all?—I would never have to tell Jarner and Gundahl that I had killed a rabbit.

It was not possible for me to resist as long as I sat still. I jumped up again.

I remember the voices that talked within me. With eight pounds of meat dangling from my shoulder, all the gnawing pangs of hunger returned tenfold. I commenced to sing in order to drown out any thoughts prompted by my stomach. Half singing, half crying, fighting the temptation to steal the food from the two men in camp, I walked on, hardly able to put one foot before the other. Whenever I sank to the ground from exhaustion I could think of nothing but my stomach.

I told myself that I could at least take the legs and chew on them. And surely nobody would want the ears—I could eat them. Finally I decided to eat it all, and then confess to myself that I was not fit for Arctic exploration, and give it all up. Then I felt calmer. I said to myself: "No, I'll wait until I reach the next hill-top." But when I reached the next hilltop something made me decide that this was not the place to eat—I would try to make the next.

And so, playing this trick upon my stomach time after time, I reached a hill from which I could see our tent in the valley below, a tiny white spot against the rocks. There my two friends waited patiently and trustingly for my return. I felt as if I had been rescued, but I was more ashamed than I had ever been in my life. I am sure that if I had not seen the tent at that moment nothing could have prevented my selfish betrayal of my comrades. And I could never have felt any pride in myself after that.

It was like reaching a friendly shore after the hazards of an uncharted sea, and my strength returned. Jarner and Gundahl saw me coming and greeted me with weak, but excited yells. I was close to tears, but I tried to conceal them while my two friends prepared the meal. We had camped in a patch of cassiope, that fine fuel which the Arctic produces—a small plant which covers the ground like a carpet and can be burned, either wet or dry, and will hold a fire for twenty-four hours in its ashes.

Jarner and Gundahl acted as though they were celebrating Christmas. I lay inside the tent, tired and faint, and every time I heard them exclaim over the quality of the meat and the excellent hindquarters, and say, "Freuchen gets the best piece because he found the rabbit and killed it," I felt that I was having my ears boxed. Even as we were eating, I could not feel as jubilant as they.

In the Arctic one's job is accomplished against a backdrop of continual struggle—continual struggle for existence. A great deal depends on the individual. If he gives less than his best he is finished, and his failure may be fatal to the men of his outfit as well as to himself.

I have heard it said that Arctic explorers are inferior men

who would be lost in the civilized world. This may be true of some of them, but character and an iron will are frequently demanded of a man in the North. I have seen bravery there among explorers and more generally among the natives, a quiet bravery seldom found or required in civilization. It is taken for granted. And I learned that no man should go into the Arctic before he is sure of himself. As for me, I was lucky. I saw my tent in time.

I had not been particularly sure of myself when I first went to the Arctic. No burning inner purpose, no desire to contribute anything to the knowledge of the earth's surface took me there. In fact, as I look back upon it I can see that I was just a green young man, weary of a routine existence and fascinated by tales of Arctic adventure and heroism. I knew nothing about the demands that would be made on me. All that came later.

As a child my inclinations were to follow the sea. My home town was a sailor's town, and I spent most of my youth on the sea. I owned my first sailboat when I was eight and, had my teachers troubled to look for truants, they would have found me in it.

Natural history alone fascinated me, and there seemed scant future in its study. Such research is for the dilettante or the young man of means, and I knew I would have to make my own way. Yet my interests were so varied—others might call them casual—that I rebelled against settling down to the mastery of any lucrative profession until approaching maturity forced a choice on me.

And so finally I enrolled in the Medical School at the University of Copenhagen and became a better-than-average pupil. My student work at the hospitals was satisfactory and my professors and instructors liked me. I studied diligently and my hands, which had been calloused, grew soft and white. I took advantage of the occasional invitations which came my way, learned to dance and transformed myself, on the surface at least, into a thoroughly pleasant and respected young man—one's daughter was always safe with Peter Freuchen.

I suppose I was as satisfied with my lot as the average young man is, yet once in a while I would put on my old clothes and, taking the back streets, stroll to the port and talk with my old friends.

One day while I was working at the hospital, an accident occurred at the docks, and the victim was brought in. For several minutes he had been thought dead; then a bystander discovered that he was breathing. The poor man was bruised and broken beyond recognition, his skull fractured, his ribs crushed and his

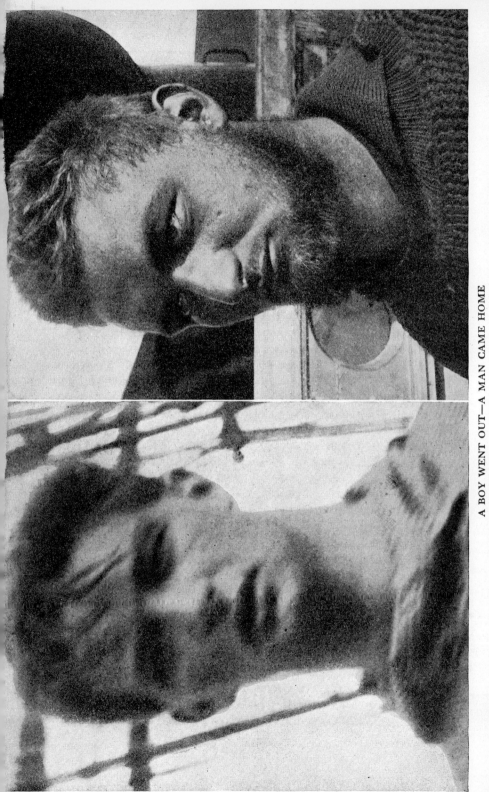

A BOY WENT OUT—A MAN CAME HOME

Myself at the age of 19, starting for Greenland with the Danmark Expedition

Two years later

ligaments ripped loose from their moorings. But undeniably his heart was beating feebly.

All the doctors said he would not live, he could not live. They said it then, and they continued to say it for months while he doggedly refused to fulfill their prophecies. Six months later his recovery was pronounced complete.

It was, everyone said, a miracle of modern medicine and surgery. A human being had been wrought from three buckets of blood and flesh and bone. Surgeons flocked to Copenhagen from all over the Continent to look at him. He was discussed, examined and photographed and prodded. Finally the doctors reluctantly turned him out into the world again. We all watched him go. We all watched him stop at the corner, and then start hesitantly across the street. And we all watched him as an automobile—one of the first in Copenhagen—ran him down and killed him.

That made me burn with impotent fury. I decided I was not cut out to be a doctor, and I left school immediately.

At that time there was a movement on foot to map the north-eastern part of Greenland, which had not yet been explored. A big expedition was to be sent out from Denmark, financed by state and private funds, under the leadership of Mylius-Erichsen.

I wanted to make my break with hospitals, study and the ironies and irritations of life in Copenhagen, so I decided to enlist if the authorities would have me. At first my services were refused, but I kept on pestering Mylius-Erichsen until he promised me a berth.

2

The usual delays impeded the departure of the expedition, and in the interim of waiting I was sent on to South Greenland to help arrange for provisions and to buy dogs.

I landed at Sukkertoppen, the largest settlement in South Greenland, and I found the town itself disappointing. I saw nothing but familiar old Danish houses. Later I discovered the native dwellings, undiscernible at first because they were down in holes, the huts made of peat and turf completely buried in the snow. It was surprising to watch the natives swarm up out of the ground like human ants.

I learned that a native who lived a few hours distant by boat had a number of dogs to sell, and I hired a half-breed Eskimo to take me there. We went by skin boat. The sea is open the year around in South Greenland, and in those days everybody used these vessels—they call them "women's boats" because the oarsmen are all women. It would have been a disgrace for a man to ride in a skin boat except as a passenger or a steersman.

The performance of the skin boats is a delight. They float like giant gulls on the sea, bobbing up and down without shipping water other than the spray from the crests of the waves. Even this might eventually swamp them if it were not for an ingenious device the Eskimos have contrived. Every skin boat is surrounded by the hunters in their kayaks. These kayaks are light destroyers; the skin boat, the heavy transport. The men travel along easily, amusing themselves by hurling their arrows at birds or occasionally attempting to harpoon a seal. In the high seas the kayaks deploy to windward of the skin boat and receive the spray from the waves. Fullcoats protect the men completely, and they can laugh at the water.

During a storm the kayakman must be able at will to turn his craft bottom side up and then right it again in order to protect himself and his tiny bark from the punishment of the waves. If the man sits upright and the avalanche of water drops on him, his spine may be broken. Therefore he must, at the right moment, roll over and take the force of the wave on the keel of his boat.

On my way to buy the dogs I sat in the stern of the skin boat watching the tactics of the kayakmen with utter fascination. But I was not accustomed to sitting idle while women worked, so I insisted upon taking an oar, to the great amusement of both the men and the girls. A few hours of the pace set by the women left me gasping, and it took no great amount of persuasion to make me relinquish my oar to the embarrassed young woman who had been trying to coach me.

The stamina and strength of these girls is astonishing. They sing through the whole day's rowing. Their songs are usually improvisations to fit the occasion, sung to some familiar Danish tune. They laugh and joke and tell stories as they row, often kidding the passenger who does not understand what they are saying.

Many of those in my boat were elderly women. Whenever we stopped to rest a young kayakman of about fifteen rowed close to the skin boat calling to his mother, one of the oarswomen. She bent over the rail, lifted up her coat and gave him suck at her breast as she would to a baby of a year or less. Later on I found this a practice common among the natives. The youngest child, or the boys in a family, continue to suckle for many, many years. I later knew one young man who was nursed by his mother until he married. It is a matter of pride with Eskimo women, a pride in their youth, and the pleasant knowledge that they still have babies to care for, even if the baby is a grown man. When a woman is no longer nursing a child she is old.

We rowed out across fjords and around huge rocky promontories. Nothing is so breath-taking as a Greenland fjord in summer. All about are magnificent snow-capped mountains, and the air is crystal clear and still as death. The sheer, towering cliffs are reflected in the vast mirror of the water, and the majestic, floating icebergs on the surface glitter with eerie colors. And the song of the girls—the hearty, childlike laughter of the natives. All of us young and full of life.

The trip took us thirteen hours and I thought surely the girls would be completely exhausted. Yet when they were told that there was to be a dance that night in the post manager's workhouse, they whooped with joy. After a day's rowing, a night of dancing would be just the needed relaxation!

One of the girls I had noticed particularly during the trip. Arnarak was her name, and she was lovely. She said she had special clothes for the dance, so I accompanied her to her father's house. He was a big hunter, and I was received as a guest of honor.

The girl dressed and then discovered that she had to reset her long, beautiful hair. She loosened it, and it gave me a shock to see it flow straight and black over the floor as she combed it. The sun falling upon it through the window gave it the blue-black look of a raven's wing. I was in an agony of love, and my sailor's heart nearly burst with pride that I should be the one taking her to the dance.

All might have gone well had she not been so eager to make an impression upon a young white man. To prove to me what a remarkably clean girl she was, she hauled out from under the ledge a big pail of human urine used for tanning hides and washing. Carefully she lowered her beautiful hair into the pail and thoroughly shampooed it, while my love cooled and my admiration sank as low as the tide in the English Channel.

By the time we reached the workhouse my spirit was gone. It rose again, but in quite another manner. Arnarak had reset her hair in an elaborate knot that wagged above her when she danced. Unfortunately I was tall and she was short. The ceiling in the small workshop being low, I was forced to bend over her while

Top. THE "DANMARK" IN DANMARKSHAVN, NORTHEAST GREENLAND, WHERE IT LAY FROZEN IN THE HARBOR FOR ALMOST THREE YEARS.

Bottom. MEMBERS OF THE CREW ON BOARD THE "DANMARK" LOOKING OUT FOR SEALS. *Left to right,* PETER HANSEN, BENDIX THESTRUP, CAPTAIN TROLLE, GUSTAV THESTRUP, "STORE" KNUD, BISTRUP, CHARLES POULSEN.

dancing, rather forcibly reviving a memory I wanted very much to discard.

But we had come to dance (square dances which the natives had learned from their Danish rulers) and we did, to the music of an accordion played by an Eskimo. He knew only the few songs he had heard played by the Danish sailors who visited Greenland, but the volume and the zest he drew from the wheezing instrument made up for his limited repertoire. Another native called the dances in Eskimo, which then was baffling to me and left me pretty much to my own devices. I succeeded in mixing up the figures royally. At last I discovered a trapdoor in the ceiling leading to the attic. I lifted it and could at least dance upright for the rest of the night, the dancers revolving around me as a center. Of course my radius was limited, and the odor of raw hides from the attic vied with my partner's urine-scented tresses, but I managed to have as much fun out of it as the rest of the boys.

Beautiful Greenland days!

3

Returning to Denmark, I had expected to find the expedition prepared to depart for the Arctic, but everything was still a shambles. The crew had encountered insurmountable difficulties in stowing our supplies, the boat required unexpected repairs, and we were constantly delayed by visitors demanding to view the boat, the dogs, the instruments and the brave men about to risk their lives for science.

The hundreds of curious onlookers made it almost impossible for us to get started. When an ordinary boat leaves the harbor nobody gives it a thought. But if a particular ship embarks for an unknown port with a possibility of death for some or all of the men on board, the mob crowds about like flies over carrion.

The expedition was the largest that had ever been sent from Denmark to the Arctic, and our imminent departure was heralded by reams of publicity which attracted to our decks both the Crown Prince of Denmark (now the King) and a German prince.

We left Copenhagen on the 24th of June, 1906. Never had a boat sailed out of a Danish harbor in such confusion. At the last moment we discovered that we were minus a number of absolute necessities and, since we did not have space for half of what was already on board, I learned a lot about how not to start

Top. FEEDING MY DOGS DURING THE SUMMER.

Bottom. OUR HOUSE ON SHORE AT DANMARKSHAVN, 76° 40′ NORTHERN LATITUDE, THE FIRST WOODEN HOUSE EVER BUILT IN NORTHEAST GREENLAND. NOTE THE CARIBOU ANTLERS FOR DECORATIVE EFFECT.

an expedition. Most of the boys could hardly be termed sailors, and unfortunately when they were needed most, during rough weather, many of them suffered from seasickness.

After a short visit to Iceland we left civilization behind and met the big ice between Greenland and Spitzbergen. Our first problem was to penetrate it in order to reach the uncharted and, at that time, unknown coast of North Greenland.

It is always a treacherous job. The ice will open a passage; then without warning it closes in on you, and you may stay there for weeks. Often it is possible from the crow's-nest to spot open water close at hand, but how to reach it? I never learned a method of combating the ice. We stuck fast for days in a stretch of open water completely cut off from shore by the ice pack, fretting at the delay and making elaborate and useless plans for cracking through it.

But the pack ice always furnished excellent hunting, and polar bears often pay one a visit. The smell of bacon is sure to attract them. Whenever the cook had fat over the fire we stood ready, guns in hand. Seals, too, were plentiful in this water, and we killed a few. They were especially welcome to the dogs that had long since tired of a dried fish diet.

After days of delay the ice split open before us and we knifed through it, reaching Greenland's east coast at a point farther north than white men had ever touched before. We established camp there for three years. The boat was to serve as living quarters for the majority, but a makeshift house was built on shore to accommodate four persons.

We did not know how to build snowhouses. Traveling during the winter, we lived in tents and all but froze to death because of our inadequate equipment. However, we were young and devoted to our task and eager for hardship. We thought we could stand anything. Mylius-Erichsen was a poor leader because of inexperience, but he was a grand fellow and possessed of rare common sense.

Several men who later became famous explorers were along, and among them I made friends. They taught me a great deal. One of these men was Dr. Alfred Wegener, our chief meteorologist. I acted as his assistant during this expedition and was responsible for weather observations and such limited meteorological research as we attempted. Most of our work, in retrospect, seems puerile. Now, with the aid of radio and modern scientific instruments, we have only to look at a chart to inform ourselves of the velocity of the wind and the weather conditions anywhere on the globe. But then we recorded every change in temperature, every vagary of the barometer to study it later at leisure and compare it with similar charts of other localities.

Dr. Wegener was one of the leading men of his day, and he specialized in the inversions of temperature which are now elementary knowledge to every airplane pilot. To ascertain the inversions we placed thermographs on the mountain peaks and I climbed up each day to get the readings. We also sent up kites and captive balloons carrying instruments. Science was then unconsciously paving the way for the aeronautics to come.

It was also our duty to establish a substation or two in order to make corresponding observations with the central post. For various reasons one of these stations was to be located as close to the icecap—the big glacier which covers the whole interior of Greenland—as possible. I was selected for that station, and was to have with me at all times one companion, this unfortunate to trade places with another at monthly intervals so that no one man should have to live with me for too long. Also I would have news from headquarters several times during the year, since I was to remain at the substation that length of time.

In the fall of 1907 we went in to build the cabin. We had to wait until the water froze so that we could transport lumber for the shelter by dog sledge. As the amount of lumber was limited the house was correspondingly small. When first completed it measured about nine by fifteen feet, but as the winter wore on and the cold increased, the interior of the house decreased in size, a layer of ice forming on the walls and ceiling as a result of respiration. Toward the last the room became so small two men could not pass each other without rubbing elbows.

After some time my company became so unbearable to everybody, I guess, that no one volunteered to join me in my isolation, and I was given the choice of returning to the boat or staying out the winter alone. If I stayed I would not see a human soul, as we were far north of the remotest Eskimo settlement. But I was just past twenty, full of a lust for novel adventures and, like a fool, I offered to stay out the year alone.

My main object was to make daily observations—one at the base of the mountain close to the ice, another halfway up, and a third at the top, about three thousand feet above sea level. The cliffs were almost perpendicular and were hazardous to climb, and I realized that the only way to negotiate the trek during the dark winter months would be to learn every crevasse, every foothold, every ledge so well while daylight lasted that a mere matter of darkness should not deter me later. And it didn't.

My cabin, constructed of stone and lumber, was located in a narrow cleft which, at best, was gloomy. Then the sun dropped below the horizon in the middle of October and darkness shut down around me. For many days I could see the almost horizontal rays of the sun red upon the face of the cliffs, and for more than a week I climbed into the sunlight as I walked to the top of the mountain. When at last there was no more light even at noonday, the Arctic night and the wolves were my sole companions.

No man should be left alone in the Arctic if it can possibly be avoided. So many situations may arise which, almost insurmountable to one man, are no trouble at all for two to overcome.

I had to be constantly on the lookout for wolves. One after another they ate all seven of my dogs, and finally became so bold as to prevent supplies from coming in. Sledges were sent in once a month, but bands of wolves attacked the travelers as they slept in tents. Fearful stories were told me when the dog drivers finally got through. Once a battle royal broke out during the night, and a Greenland Eskimo on the expedition jumped up fearing the dogs were tearing each other to pieces. He grabbed a stick and hammered away at the center of the disturbance. To his consternation a great, savage head emerged from the scrap. It was an enraged wolf that he had been beating, and the Eskimo had to defend himself as best he could with his club until help arrived.

Later on, when there was no trace of light on the land, two sledges drove straight into a pack of wolves, which promptly fell upon the harnessed dogs. The drivers could not risk the use of their guns for they could see nothing, and the wolves managed to tear three dogs free of their traces and make off with them. Then they attacked every sledge that tried to come in to me, and as the ice was pressed into high, dangerous ridges by now and the route further complicated by a heavy snowfall, it was impossible to keep up the traffic between me and the boat.

The small amount of coal I had brought in with me—the one factor that had kept the house from growing in upon me—was soon exhausted, and I had only a limited supply of spirits to burn for cooking. The coal stove merely cluttered up the room, and I finally heaved it out in disgust.

In the end the wolves, rather than the loneliness, bothered me most. They became an obsession with me. I have never been

Top. MY CABIN AT PUSTERVIG WHERE I SPENT SIX MONTHS WITHOUT SEEING ANOTHER HUMAN SOUL.

Bottom. THE CROWDED QUARTERS INSIDE THE HOUSE WHEN I WAS LUCKY ENOUGH TO HAVE COMPANIONSHIP. *Left to right,* MYSELF, THESTRUP, WEIN-SCHEINK.

so frightened in my life. After my last dog was killed there was nothing to warn me of their approach, and often I wakened to hear them pawing on the roof of my cabin.

I caught three foxes and two wolves in a most unusual way. I set a trap on my roof, let a chain attached to it down through an airhole into the cabin, and tied a crossbar to the other end of the chain so that it could not slip out. Then when the wolves approached, attracted by the smell of my cooking, and fell for the bait in my trap, I heard a fearful noise as the stick rattled against the ceiling and the trapped animal scrambled across the roof fighting for freedom. Then all I had to do was to step out the door and shoot him.

But the first time I trapped a wolf I had neglected to make the chain short enough, and when I crawled outside the wolf charged me. His teeth were far too close for comfort. I knew that I could not get out of the cabin so long as that animal was on my roof, even if I carried my gun with me, for I could not crawl out the tunneled passage, whirl and aim before he would be at my throat. I sat down and wiped the cold sweat off my face and for several moments could think of no solution. I was a fine trapper—caught in my own trap. Suddenly it occurred to me that all I had to do was to haul a few feet of the chain down through the hole and secure it, shortening the wolf's roving radius enough to keep him away from my door. The plan worked beautifully, and I killed him. But this was hardly sufficient revenge for my dead dogs.

As a matter of fact, I don't believe there were many wolves about; the two I killed were thin and scrawny, and probably had lived off the few hardy musk oxen that attempted to last out the winter. And when the musk oxen were gone they must have decided from the look of my figure that I would make a juicy meal. I could see their tracks all about and, if I stopped to listen, hear them padding round and round about me, their feet crunching faintly in the darkness.

As the winter wore on, the unnatural fervor of my hatred for the wolves increased. My food was running low, and the darkness and the cold and the constant discomfort set my nerves on edge. I jumped at the slightest sound, and the moan of the wind peopled the dark corners with evil spirits.

One day while I was on the mountainside I approached a huge rock which I always used for a landmark. As I was about to pass it a wolf that had evidently been asleep behind it jumped to his feet and yawned. I was in such terror that I leapt off the trail and dropped backward over the cliff. Fortunately for me I landed in a snowdrift, but it was a miracle that I did not kill myself or, at best, break a leg and be left to the questionable mercy of the wolves.

But I have a God-given gift which I had never appreciated before, and no one else has appreciated since. I love to sing. And my voice is so terrible that no living thing, not even a wolf, can endure it. From the day I made my discovery I never stepped out the door unless I was singing at the top of my lungs. I went up and down the mountain shouting out my joy in life over the snow and the Arctic night. The wolves were defeated. They tried hard enough, but they were no match for me. In fact, I can truthfully say that I made my living with my voice, a statement which nobody who knows me would believe.

Finally, just before the Arctic dawn, the ice became so thick inside my cabin that I could no longer stretch out on the ledge which I used for a bed. With no fuel whatever left I was in miserable shape, crawling up and down the mountain each day in what seemed to me more like a dream than reality. In my little hut I gave names to the different utensils, and often found myself babbling to my teakettle and to the pots and pans.

It was a fine day for me when I first saw the faint purple outline of the horizon to the south, and I knew that before long the sun would be back. I shall never forget my joy at the return of color. The prismatic beauty of the northern lights was so heady that for long minutes I could stand there and forget even the stinging cold.

And then at last, after four months of darkness and six months of absolute isolation for me, a lucky sledge ran the gauntlet of wolves and got through with food and fuel and, what was just as important to me, a companion for the short time before I went back to the base.

Unless a man has lived apart from human beings for a long period he does not know what he is saying when he cries that he wants to get away and be alone with his thoughts. Those thoughts can be extremely sterile and unattractive. It was heaven just to hear the new man complain about the weather or talk of the most commonplace events—anything was better than the silence or the sound of my babbling to myself or singing to the wolves. To know that if I should speak or ask a question it would evoke a reply made me tag him about like a lonesome hound.

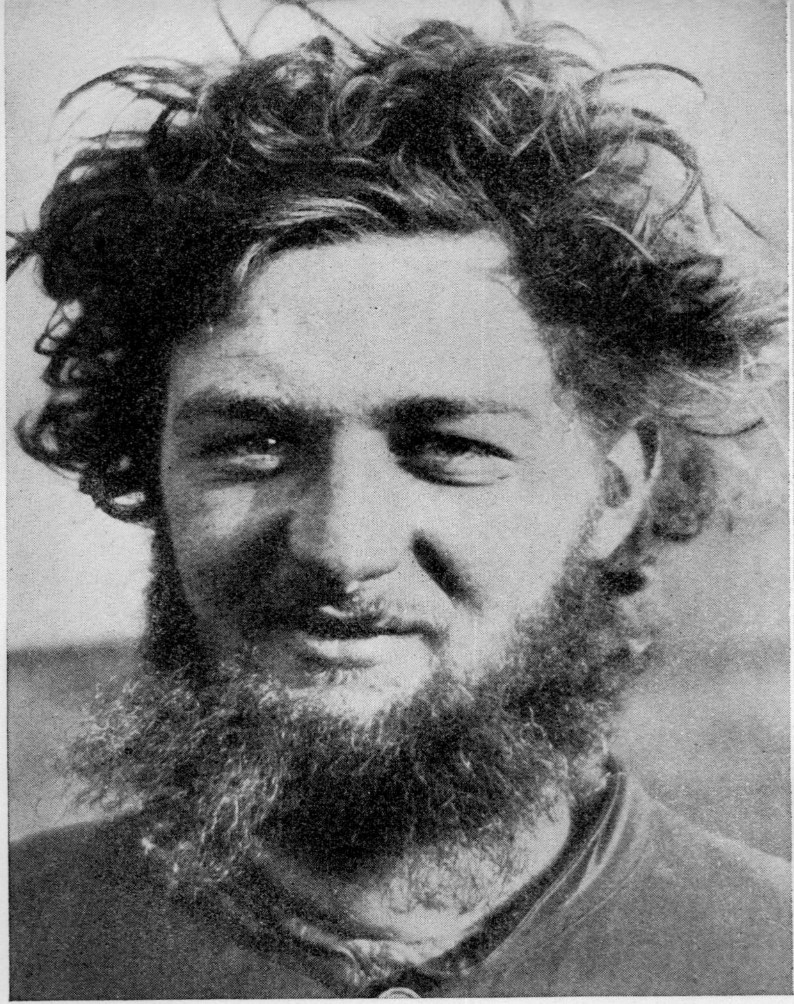

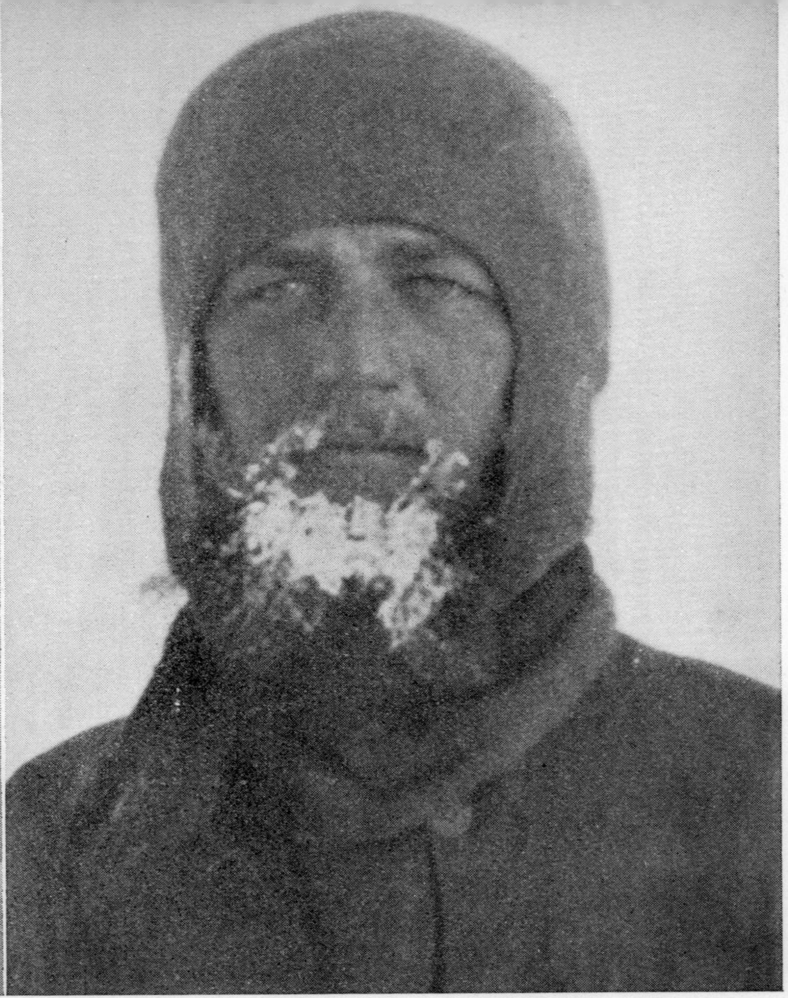

MYSELF AFTER THE YEAR AT PUSTERVIG

When I finally returned to the ship I learned that three of my companions were dead—Mylius-Erichsen, the leader, Lieutenant Hagen and an Eskimo, Joergen Broenlund.

4

In the early spring of 1907 these three men had gone off to the north on a long mapping expedition, and they had not returned by the time the ice broke up. We at the ship that summer realized that their plight must be a difficult one, but we knew that Broenlund was a fine hunter and felt sure that the fall would bring them back alive. Sledges were sent north to leave supplies at points agreed upon beforehand, and in this way their journey back to the base at least would be provided for. But it was not until the winter of 1907-08 that any trace of the three was discovered.

The diary found on the body of Broenlund told the grim story: The men had run into an unexpected fjord. It took them so long to traverse it that they were delayed in accomplishing their ultimate objective, which was to verify the existence of what was then believed to be the Peary Channel between Greenland and Pearyland. But Mylius-Erichsen wanted to complete his task, and went on, hoping the ice would stay in just a week longer than it had the year before. The ice went out, and with it all hope of the party's return until fall.

They had to depend upon hunting for their own and their dogs' food, and game was scarce. Their suffering must have been excruciating before they died, for they fought all summer long against the weather and ultimate starvation. Perhaps their worst piece of luck was the loss of their sewing kit, which made it impossible for them to repair their clothing. Broenlund had repaired his own boots with a nail, and his diary told how the other two had descended the glacier in their stocking feet in an effort to reach the coast.

Hagen had died November 15th, and Mylius-Erichsen ten days later. Broenlund, who must have been near death at the time, managed to struggle on to the food depot ten miles distant. Poor man, he was too weak to open the cache, and he died beside plenty of food and fuel.

Broenlund became a hero in Greenland. Monuments have been erected to his memory in Godthaab and in Copenhagen. His bravery was admirable, and though he had no reason to risk his life for science, his last trip to the depot, where he knew his body would eventually be found, was accomplished only to save the maps and tell what his companions had done.

The realization of the sacrifice these men had made impressed me greatly. Three men I knew well and admired suddenly were no more. That night as I lay on my ledge I understood for the first time the earnestness of what I was doing. My life, as well as my friends' lives, was endangered every moment of the day and night. I had merely admired explorers and their adventures before but had never understood the real significance of it all.

It was on this first expedition that I came to love the Eskimos. There were three of them with us: Joergen Broenlund, who died, and two other boys, Henrik and Tobias. From them I learned how gentle and fine primitive people can be. None of these boys had ever been away from home before, and life with members of the expedition was a drastic change from anything they had known. Their knowledge was limited, but they were to a great degree responsible for the success of the expedition. They acted as dog drivers and hunters, and on our trips we were given many opportunities to marvel at their skill.

Henrik was a little fellow who had not amounted to much at home. With us he got his first opportunity to prove his worth. He became an excellent bear hunter and walrus killer, and when later on he received the Order of Merit from the King of Denmark he reached his full stature, at least in the eyes of his own people.

What he lacked in size he made up in courage. The first time he ever killed a bear he was alone in his tent. He wakened suddenly and to his great surprise saw an enormous bear standing with his immense head inside the flap of the tent. Henrik's rifle lay alongside his sleeping bag but he was so frightened, he told us later, that for a moment he did not know what to do. Surely any move he made to pick up the long weapon would attract the attention of the bear. But this was no time for indecision. Henrik grabbed for the gun and fired without sighting. The bear fell dead, but the skin of the head was ruined as the exploding powder had scorched it.

Tobias had enjoyed great fame as a hunter at home, but when he got the chance to come with us and see more land than he could have reached with his kayak, he left his wife and son and skipped out. He never once fell short of what was expected of him. His greatest concern was that he was unable to read. He

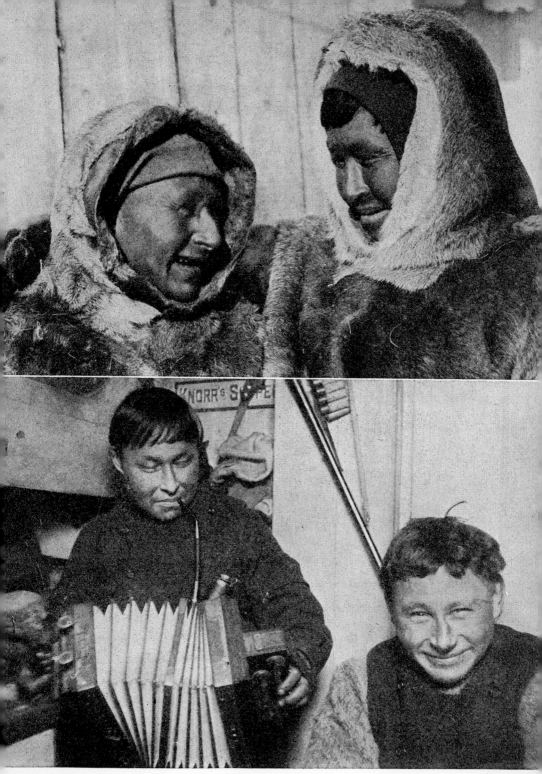

HENRIK AND TOBIAS, OUR ESKIMO HELPERS. HENRIK, THE BOY WITH THE CROOKED
NOSE, WAS MANY YEARS LATER TO BE EATEN BY WOLVES

and I became fast friends, but I have always felt that I tricked him, unintentionally, into the admiration he felt for me.

The two of us were camped one night on a bank close to the sea, and in the morning, half asleep, I peered out to have a look at the weather. Just over the bank stood a polar bear, sniffing uncertainly in our direction. Wide awake at once, I jumped back and whispered:

"There's a big bear standing right outside on the ice!"

Tobias leapt to his feet and seized his gun as I did. We needed bear meat badly for we were a long way from the ship and short of provisions. Both of us aimed and fired simultaneously. The bear struggled for a few moments, and then lay down and died, realizing he hadn't a chance against two hunters.

I went back into the tent to dress and Tobias ran down to the bear. In a moment he called:

"Come down and look at the wounds!"

There were two small holes not two inches apart.

"Which one is yours?" asked Tobias.

How could I know? It was enough for me that I had hit the animal at all, so I pointed my finger at the nearest hole and answered, without knowing how much hung upon my guess:

"That's the spot I aimed at."

"Yes, that must be yours," Tobias agreed. "I was too high. I knew it. You are a fine shot."

Later on when we cut the bear up we found the lead from the lower hole in the heart. There isn't a doubt in my mind that it was Tobias' bullet, but I had already taken the credit for it. He assured me of his lifelong friendship, and he has never failed me. For my part, I always feel that I did him an injustice.

Henrik and Tobias were interested in finding remains of native houses and graves and various other indications of habitation in northernmost Greenland. We excavated whole settlements, and found skeletons and tools that revealed a genuine Eskimo culture not unlike that in existence in southern Greenland. We also found skins and remains of fur garments in the stone houses, which would seem to indicate that not so long ago a later handful of hardy pioneers had attempted to wrest a living from the territory.

In 1823, Captain W. Scoresby, Jr., reported that he had seen Eskimos, perhaps thirteen in all, along the east coast, but at a point farther south than that covered by our explorations. At the sight of him the natives had fled, leaving their dwellings and fires

for him to examine. Scoresby had not attempted to make any
further contact with them.

Many years later other explorers visiting the same region
reported no signs of life. The cause of their extinction was doubtless starvation, for we discovered many human and canine bones
inside the houses. When no food is at hand an Eskimo finally turns
to his dogs and devours them. After the dogs are gone he is without means of traveling to secure more food, and so the eating of
the dogs only staves off death a short while.

All over the valleys and the mountains were strewn thousands
of caribou antlers, but we found not one live caribou. We knew
that in the 1870's, farther south along the east coast, a German
expedition had seen great herds of caribou whose antlers, the
Germans had said, reminded them of a forest as the animals moved
along against the skyline.

I learned the reason for this extinction of the caribou later
in West Greenland, but we could see from the kitchen middens
that once caribou had been a favored staple. Peculiarly enough,
though, there was not so much as a single musk-ox bone in the
leftovers of the late natives.

It is unbelievable to think that they would not have eaten
musk ox had the animals been there at the time. In countries
like the Arctic, where food is scarce, natives cannot afford the
luxury of sacred animals, and the absence of musk-ox bones shows
—to me, at least—that the musk ox immigrated into East Greenland after the extinction of the Eskimos in that country. Other
signs seemed to bear out this assumption.

After viewing these remains, Henrik and Tobias expressed
themselves as preferring to live in the colonized section of the
Eskimo world rather than associating with the white man only as
skeletons in a museum.

During our last six months in the Arctic we lived on little
but tomato soup and fishballs. Both those dishes are excellent, but
one can easily get too much of them. We had, however, been careless with our supplies, and we now had to pay for it.

There had been considerable fear for our safety in Denmark.
Ice was very bad in the summer of 1907, and it had been impossible even to make contact with a colony farther south along the
east coast of Greenland. Seal hunters had reported vast quantities
of ice in polar waters and, as a result, the Danish government had
sent out a ship to look for us, but it had failed to get through.

In 1908 the government promised a reward to any seal hunters who could make contact with us. One day three boats, so small that only Norwegian hunters would dare take them into the ice pack, appeared outside our harbor. While our ship was in the harbor and would not be free of the ice for months, nearly everyone on the expedition—I was away from the ship at the time— hurried out to visit the foreigners. And a little disappointed our men were, too, when they were fed fishballs and tomato soup on all three boats. The seal hunters considered it "Sunday food."

They brought us news from home, however. Not good news, but something to talk about. Seal hunters are excellent at killing seals, but as reporters they are—well, seal hunters. They told us that the King was dead, and we mourned our loss. Many months later we learned that it was not our king, but the King of Sweden, who had died.

The captains of the sealers were told that three of our party were lost. By the time they reached the mainland they had forgotten the names of the three lost men, and my mother was informed that I was one of the ill-fated number. So widespread was the story that some of my countrymen began to speak well of me.

5

At last our expedition was over. For me it had been an initiation into my future life, and it added to science more specimens and information of the Arctic than any other had secured. The price had been the lives of three of our comrades.

We left our harbor after building a large cairn to the memory of Mylius-Erichsen, Lieutenant Hagan, and Joergen Broenlund, who had given their lives.

Our reception at Copenhagen was heart-warming. We managed to arrive on a Sunday forenoon so that the crowd could get a good look at us. The King, the Prime Minister, and heads of the university greeted us, and for days we were tendered lavish banquets and interviewed by the press.

And yet there soon came a day when we were no longer news to anybody, and we had to adjust ourselves to routine work again. We scattered all over the country, and I have not seen many of my companions since then.

I went back to the university and took up chemistry and surveying. Yet I found it almost impossible to sit quiet and study, and it was difficult to accept the boys in my classes as equals. They understood nothing but school pastimes and pleasures and I, I an

TWO VIEWS OF THE "DANMARK" DURING OUR LONG STAY ON THE EAST COAST OF GREENLAND

Arctic explorer, thought their outlook on life entirely too frivolous.

I was still in the position of having to make my own way, and the easiest method seemed to be to write and lecture. My writing was trivial to say the least. I wrote three novels for a cheap magazine. Each one was the story of a beautiful girl who fainted on a lonely marble balcony. An old witch (or perhaps a handsome young gypsy man) found her and, placing a trembling hand to her bosom, produced a letter which involved the girl in a desperate intrigue. Five kroner—almost a dollar—a page was what I was underpaid for these masterpieces, so I gave up.

Although my lectures were based upon insufficient knowledge of my subject, they paid much better and soon, instead of my lectures interfering with my studies, my work at the university was interfering with my lectures. As a result, I took my examination in chemistry and said good-bye to university life.

Meanwhile, I had met Knud Rasmussen, a truly wonderful man, who was to be my best friend. Knud Rasmussen was born in Greenland. His father had been a missionary there for twenty-eight years, and his mother was part Eskimo.

After we had become friends we decided to give a series of joint lectures. But our debut was not as auspicious as it ought to have been. The scheme was for one of us to project lantern slides while the other lectured. We had bought, on credit, a well-advertised projection machine and, as Rasmussen was to give the first lecture, he gave me the signal to begin my contribution. Something dark and messy plastered the screen. I grew overheated and swore, but that made the lantern slides no better. And Knud Rasmussen lectured on apprehensively, not knowing what to expect next, flashing me signal after signal like a madman. Finally an inspiration was born of his desperation, and he explained to the fretting audience:

"Anyone can take pictures in Greenland in the summer when there is light, but these slides are something special. They were filmed in the dark of an Arctic winter! I am happy to have the privilege of showing the Danish people exactly what it is like up there during the long night."

When I flashed a Greenland dancing party on the screen, Knud explained:

"That is a bear hunt by night. It is extremely dangerous to attack wild animals with no light to shoot by."

I found a fine slide showing a group in a skin boat. He spun

Top. ENTRANCE TO THE ICE CAVE, "GNIPA-GROTTEN," WHICH EXTENDS FOR MILES UNDER THE GLACIER ON THE EAST COAST OF GREENLAND.

Bottom. THE EDGE OF THE ICECAP AGAINST YMERS NUNATAK. MY FIGURE AT THE BASE GIVES SOME IDEA OF THE THICKNESS OF THE ICE. THESE WERE TWO OF THE PICTURES WITH WHICH WE ILLUSTRATED OUR LECTURES.

a yarn about a hunter out in the cold and gloom of winter standing watch over a blowhole in an attempt to catch a seal for his starving children. The audience was deeply moved and applauded him roundly when he finished. But when I began my lecture they had had enough of midnight photography and loudly demanded to see how Greenland looked in the daytime. All of which caused us to give up our conservation program and hire a real projectionist.

We played every community in Denmark, and the experience was invaluable to us. It was at the completion of this tour that I embarked upon a new profession, one which I have never quite deserted and probably never will. I became a newspaperman. The cause was Dr. Cook.

In the fall of 1909 the whole world was stirred by a cable from Scotland which stated that Dr. Cook had arrived there on his way from the North Pole to Denmark. He was reported to be on board a Danish government steamer which had picked him up in colonized Greenland. By the time the news reached us, Dr. Cook was out to sea again, and it would be four days before he reached Copenhagen, four days in which the world could not communicate with him. Prominent journalists rushed from all over Europe to reach our capital before his arrival.

I received a call from *Politiken,* the biggest paper in Denmark, asking me to help a reporter there with the details of Dr. Cook's arrival, since the newspaperman was unfamiliar with the Arctic. How they happened to select me I never knew, but I was vastly pleased. In fact, more pleased than successful because, in my embarrassment, I answered yes to almost every question I was asked. This was the biggest news break of the year, and any slant we could invent was a story. The editor called for more and more material and finally, in the depth of night, asked for some special details concerning astronomical dates.

Dr. Cook claimed to have been at the North Pole on April 21st. In my confusion and weariness I stated that April 21st was the spring equinox, and we wrote a lyric gem about Dr. Cook's arrival at the Pole on the very day the sun, for the first time in the year, shot its rays across the everlasting ice. Since we had no facts to give the public, I was asked to supply them.

The next day all the rival papers had the laugh on *Politiken* for postponing the equinox from March to April. I was sick about it. My reputation seemed to be ruined and my career as a member of the press at an abrupt and ignominious end before it had well begun. I wanted to walk out without a word, but I knew that I must explain that it was my fault and take the whole blame. Nobody else should suffer for my mistake.

I went to the editor, Henrik Cavling, one of the most fascinating men I have ever met. I began to apologize, I told him how sorry I was, I offered to write a public explanation so that I, and not his paper, should receive the ridicule. He listened to me for a while, and finally interrupted.

"I don't know what you are talking about! What is it?"

I repeated my explanation.

"Oh! So you're the man who wrote that the equinox was in April," he said.

"Yes, sir," I admitted.

He thought a moment. "Well," he finally said, "why can't we take the stand in our paper that, in our opinion, the equinox at the North Pole *is* in April?"

I told him that it couldn't be done.

"Well, then, how does it concern *Politiken?*"

I explained how the other papers were laughing at us, but he cut me short:

"My dear young man, there's nothing to worry about. It's a mere accident that the month is called March instead of April; and, after all, what is a month compared with eternity? Young man, tell me your name once more. I like you, and I have a notion you're the type we can use on the paper. There is plenty to write about, and you, at least, have the gift of fantasy."

That was my initiation into the press.

By the time Dr. Cook reached Copenhagen scores of journalists had arrived. He met them all on board the boat and granted an interview. I listened with a group of men, one of whom was William Stead, who later was drowned on the *Titanic*. When Cook had finished talking, a young chap asked me what I thought about the explorer. I told him that I was no judge.

"But I thought you had been up to the Arctic. You must know something about it."

"Yes," I admitted, "and I have a hunch his whole story is a damned lie."

"I thought Cook was a faker from the very first, and I'm going right after him!"

The young man's name was Philip Gibbs, and his paper the *Daily Chronicle*. He challenged the authenticity of the story and his paper backed him. I gave him what help I could because it was impossible for me to contradict Dr. Cook in Denmark. After all, he was our guest of honor, and I was all but unknown. I approached several editors, but they turned me down. Finally one of them took my article to consider, and kept it so long that, before I could see him again, the story had lost its timeliness.

Meanwhile Dr. Cook was made an honorary doctor by the University of Copenhagen. The trusting Danes never suspect anyone. It did not occur to them that a man could go north, come back and tell anything but the truth. And to support his story, the astronomy professor at the university talked with Dr. Cook and reported that Cook knew so little about astronomy that it would be impossible for him to concoct false observations. It never occurred to any of them that there might have been no observations at all.

Politiken tendered a banquet to all the foreign correspondents and at the table a telegram was delivered informing us that Admiral Peary had recently returned from the Pole and was prepared to deny all Dr. Cook's statements. Confusion reigned, but we had a fake guest of honor on our hands and we were in no position to expose him and in so doing make ourselves ridiculous.

The well-known story came out of itself. Dr. Cook sailed for America and soon afterward his so-called "observations" were denied by the University of Copenhagen. Unfortunately the university had made no provision for recalling honorary degrees.

At any rate, Knud Rasmussen and I had a new subject for lectures, and we took to the road again. But Knud was restless. From his youth he had loved to wander. After a short life at the university he had returned once to Greenland with Mylius-Erichsen, my own late leader of the Danmark Expedition, and later he had made another trip to visit the natives who live farther north than any others in the world. He had wintered at Cape York, together with Count Moltke, a close friend of both of us, had learned to like the Smith Sound Eskimos and decided at some future time to return and live among them.

The time now seemed ripe for that return. Those Eskimos had proved their value to Admiral Peary, who had introduced guns and modern tools into what he had found a Stone Age culture. Now that Peary had conquered the Pole and no one else was scheduled to make the attempt, there was no one to continue furnishing the natives the goods to which they had become accustomed. It is true that occasional whalers visited them, but some

KNUD RASMUSSEN

years they did not, and the prices they paid and demanded were most unfair.

Denmark was at that time in possession of only the colonized section of Greenland on the west coast south of Melville Bay. Any foreign nation that pleased could take possession of the rest of the territory, but no nation could afford to maintain officials for such few natives as were represented by the Smith Sound Eskimos. Therefore, it would only be in combining state rule with big game hunting far out to sea that any other nation could appropriate that far north territory. And what such an arrangement might mean to the Danish Eskimos was unpleasant to consider.

It was Knud Rasmussen's idea to go up there, appropriate land, and live in the northernmost inhabited section of the globe. And he proposed that I go with him.

I thought about it for several days. I had myself to think of, and my own future. I realized that I had an equal opportunity with other young men to make a living in the civilized world. I might complete my studies and become a doctor. Or I could become a sailor. I might, since I had made a start, make a name for myself as a newspaperman. I might do any number of prosaic things.

But I decided against all these possibilities. The spirit of adventure was my heritage. My grandfather, somewhat of a roamer himself, had implanted in me traditions for seeking out the strange and the different.

I told Knud I would go with him—and I have never regretted my decision.

PART II

1

THE decision to go to Greenland, which had seemed so important to make, was only a decision. Knud Rasmussen had married a brave, fine girl and she would suffer, since she could not go along. And we had to raise the funds.

We first tried to get money from the state, but ran up against the bureaucrats who asked such asinine questions and made such stupid objections that we knew our chances in that direction were nil. The bankers listened patiently, but requested a statement that government officials sympathized with our plan. And sympathy is difficult to extract from a responsible minister whose lesser officials are sulking.

But we had many friends, and one of them wrote a letter to a prominent Dane who lived in Baku, in the Caucasus. The gentleman had never seen either of us—perhaps that was the reason for his contribution—but he put up money enough to fit out a small boat and buy a little grub and a trading outfit. We were ready to leave.

We had another invaluable friend, the Danish engineer, M. Ib Nyboe, who acted as our representative and counted neither hours nor money in his efforts to aid us. He and Adam Bierring from Baku were responsible for the whole expedition and the acquiring of that section of Greenland for Denmark.

During these negotiations I saw a good deal of human nature at its worst. My respect for the human race lessened. I saw snobbishness and envy and penuriousness where I had looked for broad-mindedness and understanding. I was disappointed in people who had told me how they admired men with the fortitude to conquer the wilderness—this was at banquets. They now advised me to stay at home, take a job and behave myself. Which meant to me, stay at home and be dull and never do a thing you have not seen thousands of others do in exactly the same way.

We were thrilled to be on our way, even though a heavy debt rested on our shoulders. We were young and still believed that life would reward us with a reality equal to our dreams. One day we found ourselves close enough to the southern coast of Greenland to view Cape Farewell. That point is seldom seen, for ships ordinarily keep far away from the coast in order to avoid the ice. Even when the immediate water is clear, the polar ice lies to the south as far as the eye can see; the prevailing wind is from the southwest, and it may blow the pack in before a ship has an opportunity to get clear. We saw the huge mountains on shore, an ominous foreboding of the sternness of the land. The sea ran high and the rocks offered no solace. They are black and towering, and there is no pity in them. As I stood at the wheel I realized for the first time that I had burned my bridges and was up against something which would demand the utmost from me.

We ran into the ice and out again. We all worked desperately; the crew—six men besides Rasmussen and myself—understood that a wreck would benefit them no more than it would us.

We landed first at Godhavn where I bought some dogs and a few supplies we had neglected to purchase at home. Knud Rasmussen refused even to look at the dogs, for he had an uncle living at a remote settlement who had a reputation for being the best dog breeder in Greenland, or perhaps in the world.

At Godhavn an elderly Eskimo woman named Vivi came to us and asked permission to join us as housekeeper. She had relatives up north among the Smith Sound people, as her mother had come from there. She was the daughter of Hans Hendrik, a renowned Eskimo who had followed eight American and English expeditions to the far north. We told Vivi we were sorry, but that we were too poor to pay her wages; besides, we did not know what we were running up against. We were going to have to live off the country and try to earn a livelihood by hunting.

She answered that her own condition was so desperate that any change would be for the better, and she wanted no wages. That seemed to settle the argument, and we decided to take Vivi with us. Then it developed that she had a son about ten years old, a boy she had acquired at some place or other because, as she explained, "I got stuck during long time by ice conditions." We shipped him too.

Next we stopped to visit Knud's Uncle Carl. He lived in a settlement named Qeqertaq, and ruled like a king. He was an old native of superior mentality who had made himself rich and was the trader of the community. We secured dogs and dog food and clothes from him, and Knud told him to take whatever he wanted from us in return, for we had no money.

What a time we spent there! We had some gin with us—prohibited in Greenland—but we distributed it liberally, and the games and dancing lasted for days. Uncle Carl was famous for his skill as a marksman, and he always asked his guests to hang their pipes for targets on nails atop the fence posts around the dog yard. He was never happier than when he had to furnish his friends new pipes because he had shot their old ones to bits. Uncle Carl also had a two-piece orchestra—himself on a violin and his daughter on an accordion. They played for us in the sunlight all through the night.

Qeqertaq is situated in a fjord dotted with floating icebergs, and our captain was no particular admirer of the anchorage. Yet we dared not depart before the hospitality was at an end— Uncle Carl felt that any criticism of the fjord was a direct reflection on himself. As a result, we stayed longer than we should have. On the last night a big wrestling match was staged for our benefit. The loser was given a glass of gin—the winner had the honor and joy of victory. I found this a typical example of Eskimo sportsmanship.

From Qeqertaq we sailed off into parts unknown.

In order to penetrate farther north the voyager must traverse Melville Bay, a stretch of water considered by whalers to be the most dangerous in the Arctic. Ice blocks crowd the water the year round, and we feared for our ship, which was not meant to be an ice jammer. At times we had to saw docks in the ice pans and stay inside them in order to avoid the gigantic pressure from the hummocks. And we continued to forge ahead, since so long as one remains on the Greenland side of the bay the current puts him to the north. It is a well-known fact that in Arctic waters the current follows him who keeps land to starboard.

We got across Melville Bay without mishap, but as soon as we had passed through this stretch which we had dreaded so much we ran into a fierce gale that whipped our sails, and our weak motor was no match for it. Where we were driven I have never discovered, and it is a miracle that we were not thrown up onto the Parry Islands or that we got through at all. In the middle of the storm our boat was tossed against an iceberg and our rudder cracked. I ran out to try to take in the foresails, but at that moment the iceberg eased over and tossed great cakes onto the deck. Chunks of ice broke from the berg and, churning about in the water, cracked off our propeller blades like the daintiest chips.

And there we were, powerless in the gale, when the wind increased suddenly, as it often does in the far north, and blew us straight into a snug little harbor, North Star Bay.

We were seen by the natives and they ran out to greet us. They had spotted us the day before tossing about in the storm but thought we had surely been wrecked by now, and they had tried to figure out where they might find some of the wreckage and lumber which would drift in. "If we had known Knud Rasmussen was on board," they said, "we would have realized he would make harbor."

We unloaded our goods and settled down. We had not planned to make this our station, but we had no alternative; afterward we found it to be the best location in the whole district. It was possible to bank our small boat at low tide and screw two new blades on to the propeller, and after a few days we watched it sail away leaving us, two lone white men, in a little world of North Greenland Eskimos.

We built a house on shore; it was not very big nor very comfortable, so we spent as little time in it as possible. Still, during the long winter months when it was banked with snow it was warm enough inside. And it was always crowded with guests.

I soon became acquainted with a number of these wonderful people who were to be my lifelong friends. Not once have I ever had reason to distrust one of them. They had already received a fine impression of white men through their dealings with that great educator, Admiral Robert Peary, and had learned much from him.

We had brought a globe with us, and it stood on a box outside the tent in which we lived during the summer. I saw a group of Eskimos gathered around it listening to something an ancient native was saying, something I did not understand. As I was young and conceited, I approached them to explain in my broken Eskimo. Knud Rasmussen listened for a moment, and then said:

"You don't need to interrupt him. He was just lecturing to them about natural conditions in the Antarctic."

Then I heard the old man—this was in 1910—tell the younger men that far, far south penguins could exist, and that seals and birds were afraid of nothing, because there were no wild animals to prey upon them as they did here in the North.

I have recalled this many times since when I have heard

Top. AN ICEBERG IN THE THULE DISTRICT IN WINTER.

Bottom. THE SEACOAST AT THULE WITH A SKIN BOAT AND DOG TEAMS ON THE THAWING ICE.

people asking silly questions about why there are penguins at the South Pole and none at the North, etc.

A few days after our arrival in North Star Bay a steamer put into port. It was the *Beautic,* commanded by the famous Captain Bob Bartlett and chartered by Harry Whitney and Paul Rainey.

Whitney was no stranger in these waters, as he had once wintered at Etah. He was the man who had rescued Dr. Cook, when that curious person came home from his "North Pole" trip. Cook and his two fellows had no dogs and had walked all the way from Cape Sparbo at Jones Sound, and they were completely done in. Harry Whitney was, at the time, at Anoritoq. He saw three microscopic dots far out on the ice and went to investigate. Whitney took Dr. Cook on his sledge and brought him to shore.

Cook was very weak, and if it had not been for Harry Whitney, who nursed him back to health, and a gale which broke up the ice immediately, the doctor would never have been able to foist his trickery upon the world. While Whitney never believed in Dr. Cook, he did not then take the trouble to go for the instruments which Cook said he had left at Etah. Neither did he question the two Eskimo boys, Itukusuk and Apilak, who had accompanied Dr. Cook. He merely took it for granted that nobody would believe Cook's story—he did not take into consideration the gullibility of the civilized world concerning events in out-of-the-way places.

Later on I got hold of the "instruments"—a common sextant, which could tell nothing. Itukusuk sold it to me, glad to be rid of it, because Cook had paid him only a few boxes of matches for a year and a half's work. Besides, Itukusuk had lost his wife during his absence to a stronger man. I gave him an alarm clock for the sextant, which he immediately took apart and divided among his many friends and relatives.

Whitney asked us to visit him on his steamer, and I made the terrible faux pas of mistaking the valet for Whitney. The valet was faultlessly dressed and Whitney lolled about in an old pair of amply patched stoker's pants. Whitney had five young walruses on board and the natives, whom he had put ashore as a special favor, told me with ill-concealed envy that the walruses drank condensed milk, a whole box every day. He also had a young musk ox and a full-grown polar bear which had been taken from the water in a net. The bear had been lowered into the coal bunker and was now as black as any of his cousins in the Canadian woods.

Whitney and I had a fine talk, interrupted all too soon by Captain Bartlett who told me to get the hell into my miserable boat because he was going to sail out of this God-damned hole.

Ashore our first problem was to secure meat for our dogs. That is, in fact, the greatest problem of the North. Eskimos take great pride in their dogs and keep far too many of them. Humans and dogs eat exactly the same things, but the amount consumed by the natives is trifling compared with what the dogs demand.

It is an Eskimo custom to present everyone with a portion of meat at the killing of a big piece of game. Which means, of course, every *man* except the man who owns no dogs.

I became aware of this practice the first day we went out after walrus. They were at that time to be found directly across the fjord, and, as we had brought a sailboat along, it was comparatively easy for us to get over. Some of the men in kayaks take after the big beast and hurl their harpoons into him. The harpoon is in reality a spear with a loose point. On striking the walrus the handle falls off, but the point which penetrates the skin is attached to a line ending in a bladder to keep the walrus afloat after it is dead. Also fastened to the line is a kind of drift anchor of hide stretched across a square wooden frame, which prevents the walrus from traveling too far. After the harpoon is secured in the animal, the killing must be done, for the harpoon point is only caught beneath the skin. This is accomplished by spears which penetrate the walrus's lungs and intestines, but it takes time, skill and bravery as the natives cannot hurl the heavy spears from great distances, and if the spear sticks into the walrus without killing it, the man has to row close enough to the prey to yank the spear out again, an extremely dangerous maneuver. Consequently, it is much better for the killing to be done from a larger boat, from which guns can be fired and a fast kill made. Afterward, the boat is of great use to tow the carcass ashore.

It is always great sport to haul a walrus to shore and cut it up. As often as possible we let the tide beach it and then await low tide to carve it. Every man receives his share, and he knows from long precedent exactly what portion is his. The man who first puts his harpoon into the animal is the owner or procurer of the walrus and gets the credit for it. As reward he takes the head, the left flipper, the guts, and especially the heart. Number two takes the right forepart, but none of the insides; number three the left rear portion, and so forth. If there are more men, the whole thing is divided into more parts. If twelve boys are around, twelve parts are given out. I was lucky the first time to get a forepart, because I had killed the animal after someone else had harpooned it.

I thanked the hunter as I found myself suddenly the possessor of several hundred pounds of meat. Later on at camp he told me not to thank anyone for meat:

"Up in our country we are human! And since we are human we help each other. We don't like to hear anybody say thanks for that. If I get something today, you may get it tomorrow. Some men never kill anything because they are seldom lucky or they may not be able to run or row as fast as others. Therefore they would feel unhappy to have to be thankful to their fellows all the time. And it would not be fun for the big hunter to feel that other men were constantly humbled by him. Then his pleasure would die. Up here we say that by gifts one makes slaves, and by whips one makes dogs."

Rather a nice way of living!

We spent the fall of 1910 collecting meat. The big killings are made in the spring, so we had to depend largely upon the natives for our supply. Unfortunately, the place in which we had settled was not the best locality for game, but we learned to overcome this drawback. The Eskimos are great visitors, and as soon as a man has finished his caches he begins to make the rounds. Then the simplest method of bragging is for the host to stuff his visitor's dogs so full of meat that they can eat no more. We took our dogs visiting.

Several of the men, we found, possessed more meat than the others. They had secured it by clever politics. As I have said, at the division of a kill meat is given only to the man who can prove his manhood by exhibiting his dogs. Certain fathers, taking advantage of this custom, made presents of a few of their poorest dogs to their half-grown sons, so that the son could pose as a man. Some of the less fortunate often made veiled hints concerning the practice, but they never dared discuss it openly as that would indicate dissatisfaction with their share. If they did so, the hunter would inevitably toss his own portion to the complainer, shouting, "Here is something for you," and then appeal to the rest of the receivers to give their portions to him too, thus bringing dishonor, and a great deal of raw meat, upon the man and his house. Nevertheless, the man with sons certainly had an advantage.

Top. THULE ESKIMOS CUTTING UP A WALRUS.
Bottom. HEAD AND SKIN OF THE SAME WALRUS.

The dogs we had brought with us from Danish Greenland still had full sets of teeth, and we were asked by the natives to cut them off or dull them. In the south the dogs run wild the whole summer—and winter too, when not in use—and forage for themselves, eating anything except wood and stone and iron. But where we lived the rules were different. Here the dogs were tied up so that we could leave anything about without fearing its destruction.

It is impossible to tie dogs with sealskin lines if the animals have the full use of their teeth. Therefore the long sharp teeth which the dog uses for tearing and slashing must be dulled. This is accomplished easily with puppies by using a stone or a file to flatten them. But ours were full-grown dogs, and the operation had to be performed with a hammer. To handle the poor animal for this operation, he must be stupefied—hung by the neck until he is unconscious. This state is reached when his excrement drops from him. Then he is hurriedly let down, his jaws pried apart and held by two skin lines, while his teeth are flattened with a hammer. This is, of course, a cruel operation, but it apparently does not hurt the dogs very much. Time after time I have seen them jump up and shake their heads a little, then run off to eat or fight or whatever comes into their minds.

Consequently, the dogs cannot eat frozen meat in winter, and it is always a matter of great concern to thaw it for them. They are fed mostly on walrus hide cut into large chunks just possible for the dogs to swallow. They are also fed in a group so that, in order to get enough, each animal must wolf his food without waiting to masticate it. While to the casual observer this seems unnecessarily cruel, the scheme is entirely practical. Since the animals are unable to chew the meat, it requires a long time for digestion and remains in their stomachs for several days, thus giving the dogs an impression of having been filled up recently.

On sledge trips we feed our dogs every second day, and at home, during the winter when they are doing no work, every third day. Later on when it is warmer they require less food, and in summer, when they are tethered along a brook or at some pond, they need to be fed no oftener than once a week. The dogs realize that when they are at last let to food they must store up for a long interval. They are never as good on trips the days after they have been fed as when they are expecting food at night and are hungry.

This custom preserves the wild nature of the dogs, of invaluable aid on bear hunts, but has come about chiefly because of the rigorous nature of the land.

Remember that the Thule District—as it was named because it is the northernmost in the world—is not teeming with game. Sometimes days pass with nothing to eat, and if dogs are accustomed to food only every other day they can go without for four days and feel no worse than we do when we miss a single meal. For the same reason men eat only at night when traveling or hunting. In the morning they fill up with water before leaving home, and make up for the fast at night when back from the day's work.

2

After our house was put in livable shape, we left Vivi in charge and set out separately into the surrounding country in order to let the natives know we were there, and to procure meat for the winter. We also were prepared to make scientific investigations, and collect specimens of various sorts for the museums at home. But since the financing of a scientific expedition is at times most difficult, we had determined to finance our own by trading with the natives, furnishing them with goods, making a living for ourselves, and at the same time making the northern, as well as the southern, part of Greenland Danish territory.

One of my tasks on this trip was to procure some caribou skins. Since the best way to do this is to shoot the animals oneself, I set out with my dogs in company with a grand old couple, Asayuk and Anarwree.

They were childless, and she dominated him completely. Nevertheless, Asayuk was the most intelligent man I met up there. Ingenious, mild, soft-spoken, and boasting the longest hair of the tribe, he took the lead of our little caravan. His wife was famous for her sharp tongue, but was respected for her ability as a hunter and sewer. She had a reputation of having "got everything"—which meant that she had killed bear, walrus, musk oxen, caribou, seal, and all manner of birds.

We were to go inland to a nunatak inside our home glacier, and I was reminded of my experiences on the east side of Greenland. Here the crevasses were just as deep and broad, but Asayuk found a way in and out between them, seemed to know instinctively where they were and took us safely to the land we sought.

Since my first expedition I have had a feeling—and it still is with me—that I shall end my days in a crevasse on the icecap.

Every time I return to it I know that some day it will claim me. But each time I mount the glacier—and I have been on it many times—I think that it need not be this time.

High up in the nunatak we came upon old abandoned huts. Asayuk told me of desperate men who had run away from home and gone into the mountains to get away from their fellow men. They became ghosts or were taken by the Inland people, the Eqidleet. He told me from his own experience of one such person, a man who was driven mad by a woman.

It is funny, but it is told, he said—and Asayuk was known to speak only the truth, that there are men born who care for one particular woman, and it takes them seven years to forget her. A certain young man had taken a girl from her family and lived with her at Inglefield Gulf. He made himself conspicuous by speaking of her when out hunting with other men. When they stayed out overnight and all slept together, he regretted that he could not be at home with his wife, and even mentioned her name without shame on several occasions. At last some of the dignified hunters remonstrated with him. It is well known that a man who reveals such dependence upon a woman is likely to offend the seals, as they do not care to be hunted by inferior persons. Therefore, he was told either to stay at home and sew and care for the lamps or employ his mouth for the talk of men.

But the poor boy persisted. Then one day a big hunter with many children to care for lost his wife. And while the hunter could have taken a widow experienced in housekeeping, he thought it would be amusing to take the young man's wife and see if he dared fight for her.

The frantic young husband did his best, but he was not permitted to kill the hunter as that would have been too great a loss to the tribe. He was advised to use his arms and strength, or depend upon the speed of his dogs to recapture her. Instead, he did nothing but sit upon a stone for three days and cry like a baby. Even his wife said to the other women that he had left his dignity behind in the tent where they had lived.

When the young man saw her laugh and chide him for his weakness, he determined to live no longer with his people; he went inland and became a qivitoq—a ghost who may never return home.

He was seen once from a distance, but as those who saw him felt he was about to approach, they fled. He had not been heard of for many years until a hunter went upcountry for caribou, and found his dead body in a small hut.

Asayuk had known the young man and told me that he was only a boy, but he remembered that the other men had kidded him because he was never willing to lend his wife or borrow other men's wives.

This is the story of a man who died because of his belief in one, and only one, woman!

I went to look at the abode of this Arctic Romeo, and saw that he had had scant room for mourning. His hut was made of stone and peat, and the animal bones about the floor indicated that he had kept alive for a considerable length of time. Asayuk told me that no one had wanted to bury him and his head had lain on the ground for several years until some of his relatives relented enough to put it in a grave. We saw the grave; cruel Nature had been sufficiently touched by his love to grow flowers of many colors about his stone pile.

Our detour to look at the grave displeased Anarwree, who always told us when and where to camp and prepare our meals. She had ample reason for her displeasure, for she killed three caribou while we got only one apiece. She regretted that she had come with us at all, because she soon discovered that I was as bad as her husband about sitting around and talking. But in spite of her tongue she made it pleasant for us, and mixed us a paste of thawed caribou marrow and brain which was delicious as chewing gum.

She also took us to a lake where, after hurriedly preparing spears, she killed a number of salmon. I later sent them to the museum in Copenhagen, and learned from the authorities that they were indeed real salmon, which must have found a means of ingress from the sea under the glacier.

After our successful trip we decided to visit Anarwree's brother at Inglefield Gulf. It was a long trip, especially in summer, but the brother had a number of small children who would enjoy the delicious things we had to bring them and, furthermore, Anarwree was anxious to bear the news of the white men settling among them. Knud Rasmussen was known to everyone and almost recognized as a member of the tribe, but no one had heard of me, and it gave Anarwree a certain eminence to accompany me. Visits in the summertime are almost without precedent, and

Anarwree and I set out alone. We left our sledges at a spot on the glacier close to the land we headed for.

At that time caribou were scarce and the mystery about which I had wondered in East Greenland was solved. Years ago they had been abundant and the natives did not know how to kill them as they had no bows and arrows. Then, in 1864, authorities tell us that foreigners came over from Admiralty Bay in Baffin Land—Asayuk had been one of the immigrants, a mere child at the time—bringing with them weapons to hunt the caribou.

The foreigners were delighted with the abundant hunting, but later on the "Great Nature" became displeased and killed off the caribou. There was an extraordinarily warm spell during two successive winters. Rain fell as in summer, and the thaw set in. The waters hit the cold earth, which did not believe in giving up the frost while it was still dark, and froze immediately, covering the ground with a solid sheet of ice for the remainder of the winter. The caribou could not paw through to the grass and moss, and most of them starved to death.

But the Great Nature had meant to kill all of them, and therefore repeated its novel behavior the next year, and this time only a scattered few caribou remained. These were so famished that they approached the natives' houses and their hunger drove them into the teeth of the dogs.

Next summer carcasses were found over the whole country, and in the winter it was impossible to catch any foxes as they had gorged themselves on caribou meat. Still the foxes did not go unpunished. They apparently felt that winter would always furnish abundant food for them, and the following summer they neglected to make caches in the bird cliffs. When winter and the great cold came around again the foxes ran into the hills hoping to find food there, but it was all gone. As a result they came back to the Eskimo settlements and fell into the traps.

The fall had set in, and while it was not yet very cold, Anarwree and I found that we could walk across Olriks Bay on the young ice. As soon as ice turns white it will hold a man's weight if he steps carefully.

We stopped at a cache and helped ourselves to meat. It was obvious to Anarwree that the cache had been made by a certain man named Sigdloo, who always left his meat in a stone grave. As she had not thought Sigdloo anywhere near this country, it caused her no little concern, and that night, which we spent in a stone hut we had discovered on the way, Anarwree took the occasion to question her foot ghost about it. This she did by tying a string around her foot and asking it a question: if the answer was yes, she could lift her foot; if it was no, no power on earth could get her foot off the ground.

She could not get her foot off the ground, and she said she could tell by this that someone had been killed. She did not dare attempt to determine who it was that was dead, for it might well be one of her relatives, whose bereaved family should certainly not be visited in time of mourning. If we approached unaware of the disaster, we could not be blamed; therefore there was no point in asking the ghost too many questions.

Vastly excited, we resumed our journey next morning. I was stiff from having slept on the barren ground, but felt rested and in an hour or so completely thawed out. We passed a big lake famous for its fine salmon. The natives from roundabout were fishing. Formerly, when caribou had been abundant, fishing was a job for women and children, for it was unsportsmanlike. "Fish don't fly away," the men declared.

We walked and walked across a vast plain, dotted with small stone huts, kramats, where hunters had dwelt on their trips, and a few ruins of more permanent residences which had been lived in by natives who had no kayaks and must spend the summers collecting food away from the sea.

There is always ice in the big lake at Inglefield Gulf, but during the summer only a large pan of it remains, floating about and shifting from side to side with the wind. Along the shore the shallow water affords a grand playground for the children. Young salmon gather here too, seeking refuge from the large fish. The children run out into the shallows and gather the baby salmon up with their bare hands and eat them raw. They think it most amusing to feel the fish squirming about their mouths and throats.

It is amazing that the children can spend whole days in the ice-cold water without apparent harm. At least they receive the benefit of a long bath, perhaps their last, for when they stop playing with fish their opportunities for baths are gone forever.

By this time we could cross the lake on the new ice, and we felt sure that we would reach the village before the sun dropped below the horizon for the night. Suddenly we saw two people in the distance coming toward us. While no one has enemies in this country, it is always a little problem to meet strangers—they may be embarrassed or not want to meet you—and we stopped to discuss our next move. While we talked the other two advanced at a fast pace; we could see that they were a man and a woman. Anarwree identified them as Odark and Meqo, the latter not his wife. Anarwree informed me of this, but when we met no comment was made to this effect.

Odark's first questions were to determine who I was and what I was doing here. He was vastly pleased when he learned that I was the partner of Knud Rasmussen, who was his best friend. After some discussion he and Meqo decided to return to the settlement and entertain us. They felt that there was a party in prospect and did not want to miss out on it.

We found Odark's two brothers, his cousins and countless relatives at Inglefield Gulf—in fact Odark was related to everyone. After the welcome we were fed with cooked caribou, dried narwhale and rotten seal meat. After which the conversation ebbed, though I felt that not all had been told that there was to be told. Nothing is dearer to an Eskimo than to sit quiet, knowing that he has some sensational news to drop into the conversation if he so desires.

Anarwree was at a disadvantage as I was present and she could not talk about me. But she could, and did at great length, discuss our ship and the different sailors who had been with us. Our house was subjected to minute discussions as was Vivi, who had originally come from Inglefield Gulf and was remembered by everyone. The fact that Vivi now spoke a different dialect was subjected to some friendly criticism. But after two days these subjects were squeezed dry. It was only then that we learned what had happened in Inglefield.

Three sleeps before we had arrived Odark and Sigdloo had killed a man and annexed two of his wives!

Odark and Sigdloo had both been with Harry Whitney on his trip and from that glorious journey they had brought home loads of stuff sent them as gifts by Admiral Peary whose companions they had been on his polar expedition. Sigdloo, as his special prize, had a cracker barrel so large that he could not keep it inside his tent. Whenever he wanted crackers he went down to the beach where he had left the barrel.

In the same community lived Uvisakavsik, a great hunter and important citizen, but one who had lost the respect of his people after he had returned from America, where Peary had taken him following an expedition to the Pole. It was evident to everyone that the man had taken leave of his senses. When he came ashore he lost no time in telling the most incredible yarns.

He said that he had seen people living in big houses on top of each other, like auks in the bird cliffs. His audience let that pass. Perhaps Uvisakavsik had made a mistake. But he also told them that he had seen more ships in the harbor of New York than there were icebergs in the fjord. Smiles flicked the corners of his listeners' mouths. How could anybody get wood enough to build so many ships? Then he related that he had seen real houses move on two iron bars, houses bigger than any tent, with walls of glass. Inside the houses sat many smiling people not in the least worried over their fate. Suddenly the whole house began to move away, and Uvisakavsik had seen no fear on the faces of the unfortunates trapped inside. While he had meditated this marvel he had seen several wagons roll past. There were neither dogs nor horses hitched to them, nor was there any smoke coming from them to account for the movement, as there was from ships.

His people listened patiently and questioned. No animals to haul, no smoke to indicate machinery inside. That did not sound so good.

Uvisakavsik kept on. He had viewed so many houses that it was impossible to see past them into the country. The paths between these houses reminded him of clefts in the mountains. Even the roads were made by human beings and covered with a smooth material which was neither cold, like ice, nor transparent.

His audience was plainly uneasy now. This was too much. And when he persisted, on top of everything else, that he had talked into a little handle that carried his voice through a tiny thread to Peary who was, at the time, several sleeps away, and that Uvisakavsik had spoken clearly to him without being forced to shout, his sentence was settled.

Wise old Sorqaq, medicine man of the tribe, stepped forward and addressed the newly arrived man solemnly:

"Uvisakavsik! It appears that you have been far away and no longer know the truth. Go to the women with your lies!"

After that he was never believed. A big liar, an undependable man!

Shortly after, he was forced to take the consequences of his lying. Rather than suffer the opprobrium of his people he went farther south for a while. But after some years he returned, still retaining some of the white men's habits. He wanted a flag, and having a pole, he planted it in the ground and hoisted a bearskin to wave in the wind.

Sorqaq held a séance and discovered that this was shocking to the bears, who would keep away from the coast until the skin was brought down. Still Uvisakavsik could not be persuaded to strike his colors.

He had one wife, but he thought it would prove his strength if he had two, so he took another one, in spite of the scarcity of women in the tribe. Not to be outdone, the other hunters decided to keep two women in their houses, which made Uvisakavsik determine to have three. He could easily afford three and, since he was very strong, could steal the wife of a man weaker than himself.

At this propitious moment the Whitney expedition came through and took with it a boy whose wife Uvisakavsik had admired. There were left in the community only two men who were unafraid of him—Sigdloo and Odark. Odark's wife was already dead, and he lived with his brothers close to the bad man's camp. Sigdloo had formerly been on friendly terms with Uvisakavsik and the two men had exchanged wives for a while. Any woman who lived with Uvisakavsik was considered fortunate, because he always had plenty of meat for the winter.

But at length Uvisakavsik became unbearable. He had not been with the Whitney expedition and had received no gifts. Yet he had developed a taste for white men's food during his trip with Peary, and the only means by which he could satisfy this craving was visiting Sigdloo in his tent. Sigdloo would not have grudged him crackers, but Uvisakavsik insisted upon boasting and lying while he ate. He told of the meals he had eaten in the white men's country, of seeing piles of bread higher than the meat pile, and of certain places where no meat was eaten at all. He had seen coffee and tea served several times each day with as much sugar as anyone desired. Then he said he had seen berries hanging from trees high above his head, and he had only to shake the trees and the berries fell into his hands. Of course, everyone knew that there were tall trees, but saying that berries grew on them was absurd.

Sigdloo told him to come and have tea and crackers as often as he desired, but not to think he could make a fool of him. Uvisakavsik was insulted and said that this was the last time he would ever come to Sigdloo for crackers. Next time the crackers were to be served in his own house.

Sigdloo did not understand this, but the following day when

ALAKRASINA WITH HER SON, KALE

THREE ESKIMO CHILDREN AT THULE

he went after crackers, Uvisakavsik warned him to keep away as he had appropriated the whole depot at the beach. And the next day when Sigdloo wanted some of his belongings, he heard a bullet whistle over his head and had to drop down behind his own boxes. Each time he attempted to get up a shot sang over his head and he had to lie still a long time before he dared crawl home.

Shortly afterward Uvisakavsik waylaid Alakrasina, the wife he had loaned to Sigdloo, and warned her not to return to Sigdloo again. Thus the situation reached a climax, and that night, as the sultan was sitting at home with his women, Sigdloo went to his friend Odark and poured out his misery. Odark did not say a word in reply but at once accompanied Sigdloo back to Inglefield Gulf.

The next day was fine and all the hunters went out to sea in their kayaks. Uvisakavsik harpooned a narwhale, and each man took his portion except Sigdloo, who refused to accept any part of it.

"A man is scared," said Uvisakavsik. No one answered.

In the evening Uvisakavsik was observed once more helping himself at the cracker barrel.

The following day the hunters went out again in kayaks. Sigdloo, waiting an opportune moment, raised his gun and fired at Uvisakavsik. But he was not accustomed to shooting men—or perhaps his gun disapproved—for he only wounded him in the right shoulder. The wounded man made as if to aim his gun, but before he could get it to his shoulder Odark shot him through the head, and he toppled out of his kayak and drowned.

Odark appropriated one of Uvisakavsik's wives, Meqo, known as the best sewer in the tribe and an extremely humorous woman. No one had ever seen her angry. Sigdloo took back Alakrasina, who was no great prize, but he preferred her to his former wife, whom he had traded to the dead man. Her name was Ateetak, and she was, I thought, the only handsome one of the lot. Meqo, the much-wanted, was one-eyed. The third was taken by a smart young fellow, Apilak, who had been with Dr. Cook and had lost his wife during his absence. Apilak was an especially fine young man, but was always involved in a tangle of love affairs.

This was the story Anarwree and I heard, and we were served meat killed by the murdered man. The murderer, Odark, was one of the finest men I have ever met. He had been Peary's right-hand man at the North Pole, and he told me that Captain

Bartlett had given him permission to shoot Uvisakavsik. When collecting a crew of natives for his expedition, Bartlett had said he had no use for Uvisakavsik and would not have him on his boat. To Odark, this seemed sufficient excuse to shoot him. He realized, however, that white men disapproved of killing one another, and he had been afraid when he first saw me that I had come to take him away.

3

Anarwree was in a hurry to get back to Thule. The brother of Uvisakavsik lived in our community, and she knew that the news we brought with us would be a sensation.

The way home was easier as ice now covered the fjords and the lakes. But the uneven surface of the ice was difficult for me, especially as the Eskimo men who went back with us, as is customary in the Arctic, had gone on ahead leaving me to my own devices. They do not do this in a manner of purposeful neglect, but are afraid of hurting a man's feelings by offering help which he may consider a criticism of his ability to take care of himself.

I already felt completely at home among these people. They were very dear to me. Each day everyone came to visit us, and etiquette demanded that they should all be offered something to eat. They had nothing to do in bad weather but sit around and talk over the daily happenings, and they always contributed to our meat supply with their fresh catches. This kept us cooking at all times of the day.

At last, on the 19th of October, came the day when the sun dropped below the horizon for the winter. One might think the natives would regret its going, but they rejoice instead. The long summer, with the sun always circling overhead, is tiresome. We live in tents then, and it is impossible to make these dwellings dark at any time. It is broad daylight when you wake up, and broad daylight when you go to sleep. Your eyes ache for darkness, and as soon as the sun disappears the women cry out in pleasure:

"Oh, joy and happiness! Now at last the sun is away. Now comes the winter when we shall hear from the other fjords, and we ourselves shall go and visit. Now comes the time of walrus hunting and the seals will be at the blowholes. Joy and happiness!"

The winter season must be taken advantage of from the start. For a short period before the snow falls it is possible for the hunters to walk in their bearskin soles on the ice in perfect silence.

The hunter can then listen to the yammering of the seals at the blowholes, and walk near enough to spear them before attracting their attention. This is the best and easiest method of hunting seals throughout the whole year, but it can be done only when the ice is free of snow. It is comparatively safe too, and consequently many natives prefer hunting seals to risking their lives hunting bear.

In the fall about half the polar bears go to sleep for the winter. On the way up the valley to the icecap they passed along the shore directly across the harbor from our house. Bears are extremely clever and know the country well enough to cut across the promontories in order to avoid the long trip around the cape, especially at the time of year when the ice is not yet solid.

The young people, or those who can leave someone behind to hunt seals, usually go south to Melville Bay in the autumn to hunt bears. Knud Rasmussen had a passion for this sport, and he traveled down there every year. He was always first to go, to charge into adventures that had slight appeal for me. This year he and his party were hurled up on Bryant Island by a gale. The island is only a barren rock, and they were forced to remain there for three weeks, eating nothing but the meat of one extremely fat bear. The only variety was achieved with soup prepared from the bear meat, fat soup too. The odor of bear meat nauseated him for months afterward.

As soon as the ice was well formed, Eskimos from distant parts began to arrive at Thule. I found it extremely interesting to meet them, for the natives are by no means all alike. You will find good ones and bad ones, old and young, men and women. We had to take all of them in, and they all made it a point of coming to visit us at least once a year.

The district we were to serve with our trading post reached as far north as any natives lived, and as far south as Melville Bay. At the time of our arrival only a scant two hundred persons dwelt in this territory, and these were scattered far from one another up and down the coast. With our arrival they had to learn how to trade.

Only four families lived at our settlement. We did not want more, for they wasted too much of our time in visiting. Also the district was not the best along the coast for fox and other wild game, and we needed fox pelts to pay for our trading. We could have bought skins and meat from the natives, of course, but our idea was not to pay too much for native products which would not demand a good price at home.

Knud Rasmussen, an artist in many lines and the most beloved man I have ever known, had a way of doing things which was not only economical for us but made the seller grateful beyond expression. For instance, he wanted a pair of boots. Instead of going directly to one of the natives and asking a price, he merely let it be known that he needed boots, and examined the footgear of all the men who came visiting.

"I'm such a fool," he said to one of them, "but ever since I was a kid I've been particular about my footgear. It seems to me your wife makes nice boots. If you had only had skins, I certainly would have asked you to have her make me a pair."

"Me, skins!" the offended man cried. "I have plenty skins, so many that they bother me. I don't know why my wife tans all these skins during the spring, but she can't be stopped."

After some days the proud man showed up with his wife, exhibiting a pair of boots. Knud looked at them closely, and then in a distressed tone said:

"I am very thankful for these! I see how you want to please me, but I am terribly sorry. I told you that I am particular about footgear, and I need them especially fine. These are fine boots, but not fine enough. I shall pay for them, but don't be offended if I don't wear them."

The Eskimo leapt to his feet. "Oh, now I had some fun! He was fooled—he thought these were the boots we were going to give him." His wife did not quite appreciate his humor, but as a loyal member of his household she, too, laughed.

"It was only a few pieces of skins hurled together between two bites," he said. "Don't think we thought of giving you such things. She did not know your measure, and these are to find your size."

He laughed again, but his humor had about it the stench of bad acting. After a while the couple went home, and the man must have had plenty to tell his wife about the dishonor she had brought upon his household. She made the boots over, and when her husband brought them back the soles looked as if they were grown to the vamp. The stitches were not visible, and the poor girl's fingers were bleeding from the task.

A few days later many men came with their wives bringing matchless boots. Knud accepted them as gifts, and his manner of taking them was so gracious that the ladies were never more proud than when they saw him wearing a pair of their boots. If his feet got wet, they were disconsolate.

On the other hand, I always had trouble getting boots because my feet were unusually large. The women never took measurements; they simply looked at you, went home and made the boots. If the boots did not fit, nothing could be done about it.

Under their system, the blame for everything always rests upon the husband, who is ruler and dictator of the household. Therefore you cannot go to a woman and order anything from her. She belongs to her husband, and he is the one to be asked. After he consents, she must carry out the task for you, but not before.

This may give the impression that the poor women are the underdogs. Quite the opposite is true, yet a rigid etiquette is preserved. A couple is a unit; the man is the mouthpiece, the woman the brains—unofficially, of course. If you want an Eskimo to do something, it is always good politics to interest his wife in the task first—then you may be sure he will do it.

4

We decided that I should try to cross Melville Bay that winter and secure from the government post at Tassiussak a number of things which we had neglected to bring with us from Denmark. The time of year was favorable because, in spite of the darkness, we had a bright moon and calm skies. Knud was to remain at the post during my absence.

It may seem strange to the average reader that Knud Rasmussen and I so constantly occupied our time with traveling in a land where travel was so hazardous. Perhaps the principal excuse for our excursions was to break the monotony which moves in like the Arctic's gray, impenetrable fog. Then one does not need much excuse to travel, or do anything out of the ordinary, conditions permitting. While we seldom went recklessly into danger, we were always aware that it might suddenly confront us if we moved outside our house, but even certain peril was better than sitting about with no prospect of change in routine ahead of us.

Besides, the more we traveled the more natives we made our friends and the better was our prospect of making our trading post a financial success.

I had new clothes, including my first, and last, foxskin coat. (Foxskin is considered very warm, but it is not tough, and unless

Kane Basin

ETAH

INGLEFIELD LAND

Nege

INGLEFIELD GULF

SAUNDERS I.

THULE

PARKER SNOW BAY

CAPE YORK

Melville

BRYANT I.

THOM I.

Bay

CAPE SEDDON

The
Northern Part
OF
West Greenland

Baffin
Bay

WANDEL
LAND

BJOERNEBORG

NUGSSUAQ
STUISALIK

TASSIUSSAK

UPERNIVIK

NORTH

PROEVEN

SVARTENHUK

GIGDLORSSUIT

Northeast
Bay

UMANAK FJORD

NUGSSUAQ PENINSULA

DISKO
ISLAND

GODHAVN

Disko
Bay

KRISTIANSHAAB

G R E E N L A N D

G. A.

one is careful he is apt to rip a hole in it which may result in death on the trail.) I also had new bearskin pants and several pairs of well-fitting boots. The evening before I left a young Eskimo girl came to the house bringing a pair of mittens she had sewn, saying that "someone" had left them at her home. I wondered, but I could not understand the reason for the gift. Later I learned that she had made them in order to thank me for some pieces of bread she had eaten one day while visiting us. I did not remember ever having seen her, but young girls are not especially conspicuous in that tribe. Fathers do not want to waste their fine animal pelts on grown girls. It is up to their future husbands to dress them, since a husband is always anxious to have his wife look well and not disgrace him. Many wives wanted to trade especially fine foxskins to us for the manufactured goods which we owned, only to have their husbands forbid it. They preferred their women to use the foxskins for their own adornment.

This girl was dressed in dogskin pants, so disgraceful in appearance that they considerably restricted her visiting. Yet nothing would persuade her to request better material from her mother. She also wore an old coat of her mother's, and most of the time she carried a little brother about with her in her hood. The mittens she brought me were none the less warm, and I bought her some fine presents in the south.

To travel long distances with new people is always interesting. I had with me four men, with old Asayuk as the leader. Though he had never been south of Melville Bay, he had heard so much about the route that he was positive he could guide us there. His dogs were not fast, but they were steady, and he could use his whip with great skill. And at night he delighted in telling us the most fascinating and outlandish yarns.

My way took me up across the icecap for a long distance, as the sea was still open around a few of the capes. After ascending the glacier I wondered how Asayuk could find his way. I learned later that, as the prevailing wind is from the southwest, the ridges in the snow—the so-called sastrugi—all point the same way; if the general direction toward one's destination is known, it is easy to hold to a straight course.

Cape York, on the route south, is the scene of many of the greatest events and much of the folklore of the Arctic. It was there that the natives first saw white men, and they still recount tales which have taken on the dignity of tradition. The whalers formerly called at Cape York every year, but now they do not come any more for whaling no longer pays in those waters. Consequently, the community is not so important as it once was, but it is still an excellent hunting locality.

At Cape York lived a very remarkable man and a great hunter—Angutidluarssuk. His house was small and did not reveal a single sign that he was the best provider in the country. He could hardly walk, yet when the occasion demanded he could run like a deer.

One day as a number of us were standing about a blowhole in the ice, a bear approached us. Our dogs were tethered far away in order not to disturb the seals, so we all took off after him on foot. Out in front of us shot old Angutidluarssuk. Before the bear could reach open water the old man had it cornered. Instead of killing it, however, he waited until a little boy, who had never got a bear because he had no dogs, caught up with him. Angutidluarssuk let him spear it first. The boy was unable to kill it, but his harpoon was the first in the beast and the prey was technically his. Angutidluarssuk had killed the animal by the time we caught up with him and those among the first to arrive shared in the skin. But the boy, whose pants were scraped almost clean of hair, got a whole new pair, and the rest half a piece each. There is enough hide for three pairs of pants on a bear. The meat was divided among all the others, and that evening as we camped on the ice and cooked the meat there were no words fine enough to praise the young man whose first bear it was.

In Cape York I stayed with Qolugtinguaq, the man who had accompanied Astrup on his Melville Bay mapping venture. In fact, Qolugtinguaq told me that Astrup had intended deserting Peary's expedition and going off on his own. But he had neglected to consider the fact that it requires a real man to head an expedition. He hated to get up in the morning and always got a late start. When he had reached Thom Island he was so petrified with fear at his own daring that he sat down and cried. Qolugtinguaq felt sorry for him, but lost respect for the white man and was pleased when Astrup decided to return to Peary—he did not want the natives in the south to see such an inferior specimen of the white race.

None of the natives liked or respected Astrup. He became furious and hysterical over trifles. Qolugtinguaq was at the time a very young man and had only recently been married. His wife was hardly more than a child, and Astrup treated her as if she were a menial. When she wanted to run about and play her husband did not forbid her, but cooked for himself or else went to some other man's house for his food. But "Assolo" Astrup demanded that she stay at home and wait upon him, and even struck her occasionally for not hurrying to him when he called her.

I asked Qolugtinguaq why he had allowed another man to strike his wife, and the dignified man answered:

"It is hard to oppose a white man. If I had objected to his striking my wife it would have shown how devoted I was to her and have made me ridiculous. Also, a man who is angry at a mere child is not even worth the censure of other men."

As a snowstorm had made the ice bad, we spent several days at Cape York passing the time in eating and visiting. Angutidluarssuk was noted for the lavish parties he gave and the excellence of his provender. One day as we were all sitting about a native's hut waiting for the meat to be cooked one of the men mentioned in passing that it was too bad the gale was so fierce that it prevented him from driving out with his dogs to secure some "oil-jammed" birds.

Apparently word of this remark spread fast, for shortly after we heard a voice outside shouting:

"Everyone is invited to Angutidluarssuk's house to eat giviaq."

Our mouths watered over the prospect, and we hurried to the party. It was difficult to walk in the gale, especially as the village at Cape York, Ingnanerk (The Slope), is situated on the face of a cliff. In spite of that, everyone from the village was gathered there ahead of us. The women had shed their boots and climbed back of the ledge where they chattered incessantly.

Angutidluarssuk sat at his place and asked us if it had been difficult to reach his house. He told us of a man who had fallen down the cliffs once a long time ago.

"Aye, aye, he thought he could jump from one step to the next. But he stepped on the air. And that was the end of Kimik, the man who walked on air."

This witticism fell rather flat, and he tried again to start the conversation rolling. But none of us was much interested in talking. Finally a great idea came to him: how about having a bite to eat?

That being what we had come for, we said we had never given it a thought, but if he offered us something we knew this was the place to find the best food in the world.

The old man laughed. "Well, there are some people who don't know much. I never have a thing fit to eat, and I am only happy when I eat in your houses. But, as I am a bad entertainer and you have witnessed my poor attempts, you may as well know the whole truth—I have nothing to offer. Still I understand Pita likes to view our squalor, and he may as well have his chance now."

After saying this, the old man picked up a sealskin line and went outside. The rest of us sat about telling each other what an extremely talented man he was, and one man related how Angutidluarssuk never slept during the summer season when the seals basked on the ice. He came in with his sledge loaded only to go right out again, and only rested when the weather was so bad that it drove all the seals into the water.

A few moments later we heard Angutidluarssuk's voice:

"Somebody would be of great help! This weak man cannot even haul in his own food."

Several youngsters leapt to their feet, ran out, and returned tugging at a line. The rest of us hauled too, exclaiming over the great weight of the thing on the other end of the line and doubting that we could possibly get it in the house. Finally a big poke of sealskin, frozen and covered with snow, came through the door, followed by our host, taking off his coat so that it would not thaw and become wet. His head was sprinkled with ice and snow, and he smiled his broadest, all-inclusive smile. As he entered he explained that he had gone out after some small birds as everyone had been talking about food:

"The thought then came to somebody that there was a poke of birds in a cache near here. And as the weather was favorable for bringing supplies, one took the dogs and went for it."

Of course, before he had even invited us to the party he had driven to the cache for the poke, and left it just outside on the ice.

We told each other that this was too much hospitality. Here was something we could talk about for years, and we were sorry he had to waste his food upon such poor, undignified folk. The great Angutidluarssuk! Who had ever heard of his equal?

Angutidluarssuk straddled the poke on the floor and grabbed an ax. We kept silent, for nothing is more interesting than watching someone else work for one's benefit, and Angutidluarssuk chopped up part of the poke. All of it was frozen solid. After half the thing was split to pieces he sat down and took a portion of the mess—birds and feathers—in his hands, broke it to bits, removed most of the feathers and commenced to eat.

"As I said and as it was foreseen," he said, "the taste is awful! Hereby everybody is asked to get out. My poor dogs will refuse to eat this, and my reputation is ruined forever."

At this signal everyone jumped at the savory delicacy. Those who had wives handed portions to them on the ledge. An eloquent silence, broken only by the crunching of bones, ruled over the whole house.

I must tell you that we were eating little auks. These birds, hardly bigger than starlings, live in such great numbers in the cliffs near-by that the mountains seem alive. They come in early summer and hatch their eggs. At that time the country is quite different—the flutter of wings, song and babbling are over the earth all day long. When night settles down the birds fly out to sea and return to the cliffs at daybreak. They lay only one egg each among the stones. These birds play an important part in supporting life in the whole district. Their skins are used for clothing, and shirts made of them are soft and warm. Auk meat, too, is delicious. But they serve principally as a lure to the foxes that haunt the same cliffs and collect caches of the birds during the summer to last them through the darkness.

But here we were consuming a special delicacy—auks pickled in oil. This is done by killing a seal and skinning it through its mouth without splitting the skin. Not every hunter can do this, but when it is accomplished satisfactorily it makes a magnificent poke, because most of the seal blubber still clings to the skin.

The person intending to fill the hide takes it along with him to a spot where the birds are thicker than fish in an aquarium and, with a net attached to a long stick, he catches the auks as they fly past, often bagging enough in one day to fill his sealskin, which is then latched and covered with stones. The sun must not reach it or the oil will turn rancid. During the summer the blubber turns to oil and soaks into the birds, which decompose slowly without interference from the air.

This makes a dish which tastes like nothing else in the world, and one loved by old and young alike. The white feathers turn pink, and may be easily plucked out. The birds are often eaten frozen, as we ate them, but some connoisseurs say they are better warmed up. In fact, frozen meat never tastes as strong as it does when it is thawed out. When frozen the diner must chop the birds out of the poke with an ax, but after they become soft they may be eaten with grace and elegant manners. The gastronomist takes them by the legs and bites the feet. Then with a deft twist of his hand he removes the feathers—or most of them. After that he skins them, from the bill back, and, having turned the skin inside out, sucks the most delicious fat out of it. Finally he swallows the skin at one gulp, and then begins on the meat.

After our hunger was dulled we had time to laugh and joke, and search among the remains for the viscera, especially the heart and the blood around it, which is frozen very hard and glues the teeth together as it thaws.

Angutidluarssuk and his charming old wife were glowing from their social success. The women on the ledge began to ask for more and now, when their husbands took them second helpings, they were particular, and sometimes refused: "No, I don't want this one. Give me that piece over there and cut off some of the feathers." They compared their birds and told stories of catching them in flight last summer, and as their spirits rose they became more demanding, some of them asking for water. Finally Qolugtinguaq jumped to his feet.

"What!" he exclaimed. "Can Angutidluarssuk furnish everything? Can he bring the spring into the house? It sounds to me as if the auks are back in the cliffs.—Oh, I see that it is the women who jabber so loud. Let the men come outside so that the women will have room to do their talking!"

This quieted the more hilarious spirits for a moment, and some of the women were overcome with embarrassment. But not for long, since everyone was happy and the party had devoured more than a hundred pounds of meat.

One of the most talented visitors belched and nearly lifted the roof off the house, and all the others followed his example to prove to their host the enjoyment of his feast. Some others belched in quite another way, and this caused screams of merriment.

Angutidluarssuk was now a great man of the world, beaming at his good fortune in having pleased his guests. As soon as he made sure that his friends had eaten plenty, he plunged the dipper into the water bucket and passed it around. Every man filled his mouth, then bent forward to wash his hands in the water trickling from his lips, and wiped his mouth and hands on a fine blue foxskin. Angutidluarssuk said:

"Your hands may smell of my awful stuff and my shame endure longer than necessity demands!"

Now came the time for storytelling, but we were satiated

with pleasure; besides, we had a real job before us to reach home again. As we left, Angutidluarssuk's old wife said:

"Somebody in this house is sorry that the children cannot come and have a bite"—knowing full well that all the children would visit her tomorrow.

After we reached the house of Qolugtinguaq I learned more about the old woman, Itusarssuk, and why she was so fond of children. She was one of the great ladies of the community, a worthy soul, gentle and kind and meek. Realizing this, it came as a shock to me to discover that she had once killed four of her own children.

A long time ago she had lived on Herbert Island alone with her former husband and their children. She suffered the terrible fate of watching him drown. He had been out in his kayak for many hours and had fallen asleep. Itusarssuk could see him, but he was so far out to sea that her voice could not reach him. Suddenly, as she looked at him, a wave upset his tiny craft. She saw him threshing around in the water for a few minutes, and then drift away, face down. She was alone and could do nothing to rescue him. She was left to provide for her five children.

The summer was not far advanced, and they had not yet brought their spring catch to the island, so she had little to eat. There are almost no auks on Herbert Island, and she had to kill and eat the dogs, hoping that some help would arrive. Once she saw a dead whale float by the island, but she had no way of getting to it. Another time she saw two bears on an ice pan, and in the far distance specks that were kayaks from other islands. But among them were no relatives of her husband, and they did not come to her.

She had to make her own house for the winter, and it was hard for her, being only a woman. The children cried for food, and when their eyes were not upon her, she cried too. Finally they ate their clothes made of animal skins, and when nothing more was at hand she knew that she had to end the pain for the small children, so she hanged them. The oldest girl, about twelve years of age, helped her mother hang the younger ones. After three of them were dead, the eight-year-old boy refused to die. He said that to die looked very unpleasant, to judge by the expression in the children's eyes. And he said that he would look out for himself until he was ready to die.

After he had run away, the girl herself fastened the noose around her neck, and said that perhaps after a while she would not feel the hunger. Her mother tightened the line, and soon the girl's misery was ended.

Itusarssuk's strength was entirely gone, and she could not even cry any more. After a while she took the bodies down and buried them. The girl's hand was raised, and refused to allow the mother to place it alongside her body. This was because she had never been possessed by a man.

Iggianguaq was the boy. He lived the whole summer on grass and the excrement of rabbits. Occasionally he killed a young gull, and he and his mother both held onto life. In the fall when the ice formed, Angutidluarssuk, then a young man, arrived and took her to his home. He never beat her, for he realized that she had had a hard time when she lived for so long with the specter of death.

This was the story told me of Itusarssuk, and was the reason she could never punish a child for anything he did, but took care of all the young people of the settlement.

5

The gale abated. Next day, though the wind was still strong at Cape York, the experienced hunters knew that a few miles offshore the weather would be fine and calm. So, loaded down with meat for our dogs, we resumed our journey toward Tassiussak.

At that time it seemed to me a human impossibility to start out in a storm. The sledges were full of snow, and the helpers had to hang onto the supplies until they were lashed to the sled. It was difficult to get the dogs under way. The poor beasts, so close to the ground, had to face the stinging snow from which we could protect our faces.

But old man Asayuk swung his whip and off we went, and after an hour's drive we reached the calm, only to be confronted with a new difficulty—the darkness.

So long as one can follow old tracks he is safe, but we had to seek out new routes and try to avoid bad ice at the same time. Our course took us almost due east in the beginning, but the stars helped little. The ice was still thin in places, the current shifting it to and fro, leaving great areas of open water so that we constantly had to shift our course. We tried to remain close to shore, but at times open water stretched between us and the dark mountains, so the wise old guide found it better to keep outside. Occa-

Top. RESTING OUR DOGS BEFORE DEVIL'S TONGUE MOUNTAIN.

Bottom. DOGDRIVING ACROSS A STRETCH OF SOFT SNOW IN MELVILLE BAY.

sionally two pans of ice had separated for a long stretch, and then we could only follow the gap until we found a place where they came together.

I trusted Asayuk and followed him blindly, but the other three men felt that they could shift for themselves and got so far behind us that, after we had crossed a crack in the ice, the two pans yawned apart before they could cross over, and we were separated. Still, none of them seemed to mind, for they knew that we would very likely come together again soon.

The dogs tired easily, for they do not like to run on ice which is not covered with snow. Salt-water ice is always wet and covered with a layer of moist salt. This eats into the dogs' paws, causing stubborn sores which are slow to heal. The dogs also needed water. Unlike men, dogs can satisfy their thirst by lapping up a mouthful of snow.

After a while even Asayuk did not know where we were. Then unexpectedly I saw an iceberg looming up directly ahead, and my head dogs fell into open water. Icebergs in the Arctic are always surrounded by clear water or very thin ice, even in the dead of winter. I was frightened and dared not run forward to help the dogs out as the ice would not have supported me. Meanwhile Asayuk had disappeared. With the help of my harpoon stick I got hold of the traces, but they were in such a mess that it was impossible to haul in the swimming dogs by the lines. Then I tried to pull the sledge backward, and by using all my strength got the animals out of the water.

After I had assured myself that I was in a safe place I untangled the traces. The sealskin lines had been in the water and instantly froze solid, and I had to use my bare hands to get them straight. The dogs, wet and shivering, tried to climb off the ice onto the sledge, and it was almost an hour before I was ready to start off again.

And I started. But where?

The whip was now frozen and unwieldy, and the dogs were uneasy, as I was a poor driver and they had no confidence in me.

Where I went I do not know, but I trusted to the instinct of the dogs—in this instance a misplaced trust. Soon I felt a sickening movement, a tug at the runners, and discovered that the left sledge runner had cut through the ice. When I tried to get off the sledge my foot broke through.

One is helpless on new thin ice. If you fall into an opening between two chunks of solid ice, there is always a possibility of cracking off the edges until finally you encounter a piece strong enough to support your weight. But there is nothing to be done when the thin ice once begins to give way beneath you. I tried to make the dogs pull ahead, but they could not move the sledge. I was lucky enough not to have everything, sledge and all, suddenly vanish. Presently I discovered that the right runner had cut through also and that I sat upon a sledge resting entirely on the crossbar. The dogs were sick of the sticky ice, and I could not get to them or even get off the sledge.

There was nothing for me to do but wait. My mittens and boots were wet, yet I was afraid to move to keep myself warm. All about it was dark and quiet as the grave, and I could only sit, hoping that after some hours the ice would be thick enough to support me. I had not the faintest notion of what had become of my fellow travelers, nor did I care much at that moment. Finally I became so cold that I dared stand erect on the load—I might as well die one way as another—and swung my arms and even moved my feet, but each time I did so I could feel the movement of the sledge settling into the ice.

I had no way of knowing how long I stayed there. But at last I could bear it no longer and decided upon a desperate plan— to cut the dogs loose so that they could save themselves, and then with my harpoon try to walk out of the thin ice. This would have been certain suicide, and I was saved from it by the long and despairing wail of a distant dog. I figured that the sound had come from one of the other teams. I answered by pulling in one of my dogs and beating him until he whined and his teammates let out a ululation of sympathy which could be heard for miles in the calm night. Then I listened attentively; after a few moments there was an answering howl.

The exercise had sent blood coursing through my legs and arms again. I felt better. It was something to know that another human being was somewhere about, even if we could not come closer to each other. Again I tried the ice with my harpoon, but it broke through; if the ice cannot support the weight of a harpoon, it is not ready for a man.

After what seemed hours I saw a tiny flare in the darkness— the light of a match! But I could not answer it. Again I swore because I did not smoke and carried no matches. I saw six matches flare and die, and I could only beat a dog each time and try to make myself heard. But I received no answer, and the signals ceased. More than anything I wanted to hear a voice, but the only sound was the crashing of the ice pans as they were thrown together by the currents below us, currents which might send us all to hell at any moment.

More hours passed, and I almost lost the spirit the sight of the matches had given me. My only consolation was in knowing that someone else was in the same predicament as myself—and that helped little.

And then, from far off, I heard a shout. I eased myself to my feet and answered:

"Naw! Naw!"

I yelled louder. Nothing happened. Then I heard the voice again. Apparently the man was trying to explain something to me, but I did not understand Eskimo any too well and his voice was almost drowned in the voice of the sea. I sat down again. From time to time I stood up and shouted, and sometimes received an answer, sometimes not.

Evidently he slept fitfully as I did. Finally it seemed to me that his voice was a little louder, and I screamed until my throat contracted. I had not breath enough to keep up a constant bellowing, but I was so excited that I could not sleep any more.

Several more hours passed, and at last I could distinctly hear the voice shouting, the voice of my friend Asayuk:

"I am coming."

How his message warmed me! And yet it took many hours before he came near.

"Na-a-a-w, Na-a-a-w!" I shouted at intervals. I knew by his answer that gradually he was drawing near, and I could not understand why he was not faster, since, I thought, he must be either afoot or driving his dogs. And yet it was requiring hours for him to cover a distance which at most could have been half a mile.

Finally he was within talking distance, and I knew the reason: he was in the same state as myself. I yelled:

"How is it, then, that you are coming nearer to me?"

"I am drifting!"

Fortune then, and not any of our efforts, was bringing us together. We could hear ice crashing around us, but we did not care much. Asayuk told me he had been in the water, but was not seriously wet. Then I thought I could see him, but I must have been mistaken, for he said he could not yet see me. He asked me to light a match and I told him I had none.

He decided that he would sacrifice his last matches and let

me try to walk over to him. I was to tie my harpoon line to my leg and thus have a means of returning to my sledge.

It worked as we had planned, and the ice did not crack beneath me now. But I could not see Asayuk when I was at the end of my line. I added my whip to the harpoon line and from the end of this I could just make out his dogs, and I dared drop my guiding line and struggle out to reach him. He assured me that we could easily find my tracks back to the sledge as it would soon be daylight—by which he meant a dull red glare on the horizon to the south, against which it is possible for a few hours to see the silhouette of a man.

We were overjoyed to be together, but had no time to waste in congratulating ourselves, for we must immediately try to get off this wretched ice. I helped him pry his sledge runners loose. We accomplished it by unloading and distributing the load over a large area of ice, and then pulling the sledge up. We reloaded and got his dogs going. They were wet through and thirsty, and could scarcely crawl. Then we drove to my sledge, but we dared not go too near as the ice would not permit it, and we had to approach with the utmost care.

As we worked we saw a huge iceberg loom up and seem to sail by, though we did not know whether it was the berg or our own pan of ice that was moving. Most probably we were doing the sailing, for eight times as much of the iceberg's bulk lies beneath the water as one sees above, and when the current grasps an iceberg it barely moves. Yet in spite of their torpor, I have seen icebergs plow through heavy surface ice as if nothing at all were in their way. Then suddenly they will stop and sometimes remain anchored for years in the same place. Icebergs are full of mystery.

At last we were ready to travel—but again, where to go? Asayuk went out to investigate the ice. As I saw him disappear I remembered Peary's confidence and reliance in the man when all the other natives were fearful of their fate. Peary would never give up, and somehow Asayuk always made it possible for him to proceed.

Unfortunately he did not do the same now. We must wait, he said, and meanwhile we had better eat some meat and frozen bear fat. It was fine, and gave us courage.

We could feel that we were drifting. Asayuk said that we could not expect to remain long where we were, and should place our sledges a short distance from each other so as not to put too great a load upon one section of the ice.

The wise old man was an authority on natural science in his own country. Not a secret was hidden from him. He explained to me that salt-water ice is tough and flexible—it can bend under a sledge and not break. You can see the ice bending under your team, a wave rises between the dogs and the sledge, and the sledge will skim along in the trough of the wave. The great danger is in driving so fast that the sledge runners cut through the crest.

He also told me that so long as ice is black there is no trusting it, but when it turns white it can usually be depended upon. Therefore traveling in the dark of winter is dangerous because the dog driver cannot detect the shade of the ice.

As I sat waiting I realized that already I had spent almost twenty-four hours on the ice. I had not eaten a single meal, nor drunk anything.

Added to this, it was Christmas Day!

I had hoped to reach Tassiussak this evening, and would have done so if we had not landed in this predicament. I thought of my many happy Christmas evenings in Denmark, where my mother and father had made it a never-to-be-forgotten occasion. They had observed all the traditions of the day, and if I had been there now I would have been eating stuffed goose and steamed puddings—and all the fat I wanted. Somehow the fat and the food were all that really mattered now—the gifts would have been pleasant, but they did not seem important. I knew that my family would be thinking of me, doubtless visualizing me at some gay gathering. I felt miserable and the victim of a rotten deal.

The fact that I had brought it all on myself never occurred to me. When I turned my head I could see the silhouette of Asayuk, silent and immutable as if carved in wood, against the dull crimson glow to the south. Lucky man, he did not think at all, but sat patiently awaiting the moment to move on. But I had to remember and torture myself with the thought of all that goose fat. And the box which Knud had sent along for me to open on Christmas was on one of the three sledges now lost from us.

I watched the silent stars glow brighter over our heads—that meant colder weather and the ice strengthening. I have no idea how long I celebrated Christmas in this futile fashion, but at last Asayuk said he thought we could go on. I don't know what had decided him but I thought I would go crazy if we did not do something besides sit and wait for the ocean to freeze over.

We got our dogs in order, and Asayuk insisted on walking

ahead, stepping in his padding, soft-footed fashion, cautious of his way and testing the ice now and then with a spear. He walked, and I envied him. My feet were numb, but I had to sit still and follow him with my team, cracking my whip to the aft in order to prevent his dogs from running ahead of me to catch up with their master. Presently he came back, jumped on his sledge and drove off in a straight line. I followed close behind and I could finally see that the ice was a bit more solid.

Asayuk stopped a couple of times but never let me know what was on his mind. He only smiled when I asked him, and drove off again. Suddenly I heard him yelling at his dogs to stop, and I noticed at the some moment that my own team were leaning into their traces. They might have smelled something—a bear possibly— and this was dangerous. If it was a bear, they would bolt after it, and there would be no stopping them. But we quelled their eagerness, and the weight of the sledge, heavier when there is no snow on the ice, dampened their enthusiasm. And then I saw a huge mountain looming up out of the darkness.

"What is that?" I shouted at Asayuk.

"Yes, what country can it be?" was all the answer I got. But it was something solid and substantial, and it looked particularly beautiful to me.

Unfortunately we found a broad streak of open water between us and the shore. We followed it for a distance, and then Asayuk decided that we would have to go to the opposite end of the island. It was Sagdleq, he said, which is the native name for Bushman Island in the northern end of Melville Bay.

At the other end of the island, he said, there was a cave where all the comforts of the world were to be had. If we could only reach it we would be safe. The wind was rising again, but since it came from the land I felt that the island might protect us from its full blasts in approaching the shore.

We finally reached a point opposite the cave. And we saw people there ahead of us—the other three members of our party, who had found this place and been there for three days. We could still not reach them as high tide laid a broad band of water between us. The ice, by rights, should have driven in to shore, but there were so many icebergs stranded here that the ice was firmly fastened to them and did not drift.

We shouted back and forth to our friends, and they told us how comfortable they were. There was nothing for us to do but await low tide—and since it was not yet at its height, I knew that it would be at least six hours before we could land. Our dogs were in miserable shape, baying and trying to crawl onto the sledges whenever we stepped off.

Asayuk endeavored to make a float from a number of ice pans, and ferry across. It took us several hours to hack loose first one pan and then another. After we had maneuvered the first one under the second, we found that it would not float with a sledge on it, so we had to cut a third and get that under the two already fixed. At last it was ready, and it looked fine. Asayuk tried it first, and his dogs all leapt on with him. Naturally they did not know enough to spread themselves about the pan, but all huddled together on one corner, which tipped the float so much that the lowest pan slipped out from under and shot up like a cork. The next one did likewise, and Asayuk plunged into the water with his dogs threshing about him. I finally managed to get hold of him, but he had discovered that during our efforts to construct a ferry the tide had ebbed and he could now stand on the bottom, the water reaching only to his waist. The dogs swam back and broke the ice before them in trying to crawl up. The whole thing was a terrible mess.

I was thoroughly wet by now, and Asayuk stood before me with the water dripping from him. Worst of all, his sledge had been in the water too, and the bottom of the load was soaking wet. But he was born to the North, and he took it like a man.

Then I saw a man loom out of the darkness. He was Mitseq, one of our boys, and he had found a spot at a short distance where the ice reached shore at low tide. We walked there and found a perfect passage.

We hustled into the cave and found everything in the greatest confusion. Even the fire was out, and there were no matches. We decided that we would attend to the dogs first, and ourselves later. The animals went madly for the snow, and had tangled their traces into unbelievable knots. Trying to untangle twelve dogs in complete darkness and Arctic weather is a job for any man.

But at last it was done and we could take stock of ourselves. The three boys had been in great trouble. They, too, had been separated and had had to waste their matches in locating each other again. In searching for us they had been lucky enough to run into Sagdleq in the dark. There they had stayed for the first night, and after that the moon was gone and the ice so treacherous that they had decided to remain until either the ice was thicker or we turned up. In which event they could go on or, at any rate, go bear hunting so that they would not return home empty-handed. But at last we were all together, and the reunion was pleasant.

But what can you do in a black cave without a light? There are different methods of making a fire, of course, but here we attempted the simplest one. We extracted the lead from a cartridge and divided the gunpowder, pouring half of it back into the cartridge. From the boxes we cut a number of sticks and arranged them in a pile over the other half of the powder, then discharged the blind cartridge directly into the powder on the ground. There was a blinding flash, and the sticks caught fire. After they were blazing steadily we added blubber, of which we had plenty, and soon were warming ourselves.

Old man Asayuk had to take off his wet clothes before the fire and had nothing to put on, as his sleeping bag was also wet. I offered him mine, and he was too miserable to refuse. We pushed the sledge into the cave, and stuffed his stiff body into the bag. Finally he thawed out, and we made hot soup for him and got him feeling well enough to smoke a pipe—and then everything was fine.

There was a fire for light and for cooking, and at last we could open our Christmas box and feast to our rescue from the ice.

The cave was dry and cozy. Outside the storm roared, but it did not concern us. Our dogs were safely tied on a thick blanket of snow which would dry them out perfectly. While the boys had been waiting for us they had cut portions of food for the dogs, and the animals at least were taken care of for three days.

We added more blubber to the fire, and the boiling bear meat, covered with a thick, succulent layer of liquid fat, made us forget our troubles. When we had finished the food, our palates craved more delicate nourishment, and Asayuk suggested that we make tea. I filled the pot with ice and hung it over the fire, and soon the steam rolled forth in a white, hospitable stream. I poured Asayuk's cup first, he being the oldest and most dignified member of the party. Once more there was a tingling in his feet, and he began to feel better.

He sipped the tea, spluttered and made indignant protest. I defended my way of brewing it, but when I tasted it I had to admit that the flavor was peculiar. I turned to the three boys, and they explained that, since they had no pot for boiling meat, they had been forced to use the teapot. This naturally had not improved the flavor of the tea, but furthermore, Itukusunguaq had left the mittens which he used for handling dog food on top of the pot, and one of the fingers, well soaked in rotten blubber, had fallen into it. I had not seen it in the darkness.

Asayuk was furious and demanded fresh tea, but the boys kidded him and told him to take what was coming to him or make it himself. The latter he was unable to do as he was without pants. But soon the first brew was drunk, and when I rinsed out the pot to make more I found, besides the mitten, two chunks of dog meat. That is never good for tea. In fact, tea is a refined drink even requiring clean water.

Coffee is a drink for old women who talk so much that they can't use their tongues for tasting. If you have bad water, make coffee and make it strong. Nobody will notice the difference. But tea must not be brewed unless the water is good and the pot clean.

6

Sleeping in a cave in midwinter is not the most comfortable thing in the world, for the largest wall is made of wind, and the floor of stone or ice. Asayuk was in my sleeping bag, but I could not justly complain of that since Mitseq had brought no bag at all with him. We pushed our sledges inside and laid our skins on them. A rule often forgotten is that one must have a good, warm layer beneath him in order to rest well. If you have but one caribou skin for the night, put it under, not over, you. We piled up our skins and talked and drank chocolate and ate crackers and loads of food from the Christmas box. I remembered that this was my mother's birthday and told the men about her. Our fire blazed high, and presently I felt so warm that I took my coat off—the beautiful foxskin coat of which I was so proud. Twelve fine blue foxskins had gone into it, besides the white hood and blue tails about the face.

While I sat there and worked to get the ice out of my whiskers, the cave suddenly rocked with thunder, and a great stone was hurled out of the wall. Had it struck us, we should have been killed. I leapt to my feet and away from the fire, for I realized that the heat had caused the stone to drop. I explained this to Asayuk, but he said that the spirit of the mountain demanded darkness for his slumber because it was winter. He would not harm anyone, and if we left some meat for him when we departed, everything would be all right. I protested, but Asayuk read into the fact that none of us had been hit the proof of the friendliness of the spirit. If the spirit had meant to kill us, he could have done so quite effectively by closing the mouth of the cave.

I tried to explain the scientific reason for the blast, but Asayuk looked at me as a man does at a child who is unable to grasp the eternal verities. He explained patiently that he had heard the same explanation once before from Verhoeff, a stone-wise gentleman who had followed Peary. And Verhoeff had disap-peared and never been found—the spirit of the mountains had taken him to show him what was the truth and what was not the truth.

After the excitement was over I went back to my coat; it was frozen stiff, and I could not get my arms through it. It had been wet from my sweat. Unfortunately I tried to force my way into it, and my left arm broke through the thin skin. I found a needle in my kit and stitched it together, but I woke up during the night with the frost biting into my shoulder. Everyone else was asleep, and there was nothing I could do. I tried to put my mittens in the hole, but they only made it worse. When I finally fell asleep I dreamed that my shoulder had turned to marble.

In the morning I was unable to move my arm at all, and even after it had been warmed beside the fire I did not have com-plete use of it. We mended my coat again, but I was not used to the thin foxskins and my movements were apparently too vigor-ous, for it ripped over and over again, letting more and more of the frost into my shoulder. After struggling with it for two days I could sew no more. Asayuk patched it with a piece of sealskin which kept the wind out, but let the frost in, and during the whole trip I was conscious of the pain. The torn foxskin gave me a souvenir which I bear to this day. Even as I sit writing this, I feel the rheumatism in that damned shoulder, and seldom get through a day without a reminder of it. And all this because I was bighearted and let Asayuk use my sleeping bag.

We spent three days in the cave. The young men fretted and worried and kept a constant lookout for reassuring conditions of the ice, but it was not safe to go on. At least we knew where we were, which was something.

On the south side of Melville Bay from Bushman Island down to Cape Holm there is an open fissure which is always treacherous. During the late winter months the water is frozen over, and no one considers the danger seriously. Many times since then I have driven down that fissure. It is called the "Mouth of the Sea" by the natives, as it opens up every springtime. But at this time of year, especially in the near total darkness, it was impossible to use the "mouth." Outside the "mouth" is a shallow stretch of water which is easy to spot because of the many icebergs grounded there.

This particular bank of icebergs has in former times played an important role in Arctic life. At one time there was considerable communication between the Eskimos north and south of the large bay. When they traveled over this route it was difficult for the women to spend such a long period of time on the ice. When times were bad and game scarce, the poor women were not allowed to pass their water on the ice lest they insult the seals, and were forced to go ashore. But that, of course, was impractical so far from land, and as a result they were permitted to ascend the icebergs to urinate. The name of this particular bank of icebergs is called "Crowree"—a place to leave one's urine.

While we waited for the opportune moment to move on I continued to sleep on my sledge, but I was young and foolish and nothing would have made me admit that I went through hell every night and spent most of the time running up and down the cave to keep warm.

Minik was a great nuisance to all of us. He was an unhappy lad with a bad disposition. As a boy he, with his father and four others, had been taken to America. All except Minik had been stricken with an epidemic in New York and died. He had been adopted by very decent people and been given every opportunity, but he was a born good-for-nothing. He felt that rules did not concern him, and laws were made for him to disobey. After countless attempts to get him interested in something—anything—he was given the opportunity to choose a profession. His choice was to steal money and run away. He was apprehended at the Canadian border, sent back to New York, and finally brought home to Greenland on one of Peary's relief ships. He returned to the North with no property or money—he had been given plenty in America but had spent it all during the trip for liquor and such. He was absolutely destitute when I first saw him. We had taken him into our house, and soon found that he did not remember a thing he had learned in America, and could barely read or write. At least he never did.

I do not tell this as a proof that it is impossible to educate Eskimos, for even in Greenland Minik was regarded as unintelligent and irresponsible. But he believed that the world had been bad for him and blamed others for his lack of character. In America he had longed for Greenland, and now that he was in Greenland he wanted to be back in America.

7

When we left our cave we had no choice of a place to go. Old Asayuk had to be dried out thoroughly, and the nearest settlement was Savigssuit, Meteorite Island, the island from which Robert Peary took the famous meteorites which had formerly been the source of all the knives and tools of the natives.

There were only three houses on the island, and we approached them while everyone slept. The ears of the natives, however, are attuned to all noises, and they hurried out to see who was coming.

A certain ritual has to be observed when arriving at any place in the Arctic. From the ice the visitors shout out:

"Sainak Sunai! Sainak Sunai! (Wonderful pleasure and happy to be here!)"

"Assukiak, assukiak! (Same to us, you are right!)" is the people's answer. They know immediately who is approaching.

It is a fact that everyone is known by his voice. It was annoying and troublesome to me at first when I met someone only to receive the answer: "Oanga (It is I)." And when I would repeat, "But who are you?" "Oanga!" was all he could be induced to say. No one would mention himself by name, and in a country where four months of the year are spent in total darkness—and most of the visiting is done during these months—it is difficult to recognize the natives by their voices. But I learned very soon. I had to.

We arrived at Savigssuit at a peculiarly embarrassing moment. A wife-trading for the night had just taken place, and the men could not decide whether or not to return to their own homes and entertain us properly. The three men of the village had encountered bad luck on their last hunting trip, and they attributed it to the fact that some of the women had offended the bears. Therefore, to fool the cunning animals, the men had decided to change wives for a night so that the bears could not possibly know which hunter to avoid.

The wise man of the community, Ulugatoq (the man with the big cheeks), finally solved the whole problem: nobody should go to sleep at all for the night, but we would all spend it together feasting and singing. And so we fed our dogs and gathered at

Ulugatoq's house, the largest in the place. After the host had assured us that he was unable to serve anything that was edible, he happened to recall that someone had left a piece of meat outside. "It might," he said, "still be there, as it has been refused by the dogs several times." This, of course, was such a hearty recommendation that our anticipations rose to the sky.

A short time later Ulugatoq returned, and we helped him bring in a great quantity of narwhale skin, or mattak, which is one of the delectable dishes to be had in the North. This piece had been preserved for two years, and the thawing and freezing had cured it beautifully. The epidermis was almost free from the leather underneath, and the blubber turned green as grass.

Standing over his precious food, Ulugatoq chopped the skin in two with his ax, and then cut out the blubber to be used as oil for the lamps, stretching out the process as long as possible in order to give everyone the opportunity to tell him how fine his party was going to be. He complained of the dullness of his tools, stopped to sharpen them and, when finally ready to proceed with the apportioning, sat down and looked up with an embarrassed smile:

"How can I serve such a thing for the big white man? I better take it away and ask him to help himself from the sublime food he has brought from his own brilliant countries!"

Everyone assured him that no one in the world would enjoy his food more than I and, like a miserable man being carried to the electric chair, he chopped the skin into pieces as large as the palm of his hand. Meanwhile Asayuk informed me that Ulugatoq was a famous social light, and that his standard of behavior made him a lion at parties. I was witnessing a sample of his man-of-the-world manners, and I told him how amazed I was to find such a person in the North. He smiled cunningly, and sampled the food himself.

"I was right!" he said. "This food tastes of nothing but dog excrement and urine."

After this recommendation Asayuk had to step onto the ledge to take off his boots and pants, and the women hung them over the lamps to dry. The rest of us grabbed the food spread out on the floor. It was delicious. The bouquet was excellent, and the spicelike flavor of the blubber tantalizing. The skin of a whale is lined with a thick layer of epidermis. The leather hide, of course, is unedible, but one may cut it into small bits a little larger than a lump of sugar and hold it between his teeth. The whole thing is vastly refreshing, and scientists have stated that there is no better cure for scurvy in the North than mattak.

We ate and ate and belched to show our appreciation, and after the mattak was finished we went to work on the frozen meat underneath the skin. Narwhale meat must be eaten raw and frozen, for when it is cooked it develops the strong whale flavor that is so unappetizing. After we had finished, the wife gave us, as a special treat to impress upon us the wealth of the house, individual serviettes of birdskin cut from a discarded shirt of the host. When our fingers and faces were clean we sat back to await the concert.

At Savigssuit lived Iggianguaq, son of Itusarssuk. As already related, he was spared when his sisters and brothers had been hanged. He was a small but vigorous man, and noted for his excellence as a hunter. He explained that he was really larger than he looked: he had been stunted from having insufficient meat in his childhood. And he had learned from this that pups must be fed well from the very start so that they may develop into big strong dogs. Later on they can endure privation.

Everyone knew that Iggianguaq was the best singer in the community, in fact, the only singer. Arctic music unfortunately requires a team—two must sing together. Iggianguaq said that he was in no mood to sing, and would have to go out to untangle his dogs. However, he made no move to go, so we renewed our entreaties. I told him that his reputation as a musician had reached as far as North Star Bay, but he merely sat still, looked at me fishy-eyed, and asked if I thought North Star Bay was very distant. Realizing my mistake, I said:

"It would give me great pleasure to hear you sing."

He answered: "Peterssuaq! In this country, though you are big and tall, you are but a newborn baby. You seem not to know that if a man does not feel like singing he cannot be made to do it. And I do not sing tonight!"

Naturally, I took this as final, but Ulugatoq dragged a drum from under the ledge, tightened the skin on it by licking it with his tongue, and handed it to the reluctant performer. Iggianguaq took it and cried:

"Oh, why do you give it to me? I don't know how to sing! Must I use a drum for it? I really don't know, for I never tried before."

Everyone encouraged him: "Qa, qa, come on. Let us just

this once hear a really fine song. Oh, how happy we are that we have this famous singer in our midst!"

He looked bewildered and embarrassed; then it occurred to him that he could not sing alone, and he invited Mitseq to accompany him. Mitseq, not to be outdone by his southern contemporary, demanded an equal amount of coaxing. After an interminable discussion of which one was to play the ayayut, they at last began to sing, a modest little tune that amounted to nothing.

Only one man sings at a time, dancing as he sings. We would hardly call it dancing, for he is not permitted to move his feet. He sways from side to side shaking his head, emphasizing the rhythm of the song with his voice, body and face. As he sings he invariably becomes more and more excited and forgets everything about him. Across from him stands his partner, stiff and stern, gripping the ayayut in both his hands, awaiting his turn.

The chorus sits grouped about the singers and joins in little by little. In this the women may also take part, and finally the whole room surrenders to the song. There are seldom any words, nor is there even music from our point of view, for they utilize half and quarter tones which torture the uninitiated ear. The singer repeats his rhythms several times, each time ascending the scale a little until his song ends in a wild shriek. The whole audience is possessed by the song, and emotions are whipped up to a frightening pitch. Realizing this, the artist must always end his song with something to make his audience laugh. He bends closer and closer to his partner and stops beating his drum, or quickens its pace, at the same time diminishing its accent, and his partner grips his little stick and brandishes it before the singer, waiting for the proper moment. Then when the singer has nearly finished, the partner grasps the stick with both hands, rotates it round and round, while he takes up the wail:

"Ay! Ay! A-ay—aa-a-a-a-ay!" The singer yells the same vowels, and as soon as he is completely exhausted both men laugh, and the audience laughs until the house rocks.

The ayayut, the only Eskimo instrument, is made from the skin of a walrus throat stretched over a frame of bone to which a handle is attached. The frame, rather than the skin, is beaten, and the drumstick is usually of bone or wood. The drum is only a means of setting the tempo, but its solemn booming in the tiny houses adds to the spirit of the scene. Before the singing begins all the lights but one small candle are extinguished. The two men stand in the middle of the floor, and the audience sits in the darkness, their bodies swaying from side to side and back and forth, hypnotized by the voices and the dull throb of the drum—boom-boom-boom—boom-boom-boom—always three beats in succession, its volume dictated by the different passages of the song.

When the first man has finished, the next takes his place and sings one; then the first man sings three and the other three. Again the first sings seven, and the partner follows him until both are so exhausted they can no longer stand. At this point someone else is always so excited that he jumps to his feet, grasps the drum, and challenges another man to match him. They remove their coats as the air is usually hot and close by this time, and stand naked, their fine tanned bodies rigid with muscles, their long hair switching from side to side. After hours of this they often slaver at the mouth, but no one seems to mind, since almost everyone is equally moved.

At such moments one realizes the hidden forces in these people, and it was at this Arctic sing that I decided to learn as much as I could of the secrets which lay dormant in their souls.

After two pairs of singers had been worn out two women jumped to their feet and asked to be permitted to sing. They acted as if something long buried in them could be released only by yielding to this moment of ecstasy, and the men asked if I would mind.

"You see," said old Asayuk, "we are only a few of us here, and we are all friends. Of course, it should not be, but we understand it is not to make us ridiculous, and the poor women seldom have an occasion here to sing."

My permission was granted, and Kuyapikasit and Sivaganguaq began to sing and dance. They were two passionate women, neither especially young, but both vital and fervent. Sivaganguaq had once been married to Tatarat, a lame man, but after the accident which made him lame she had been taken by so many men that her husband suggested one of them keep her for good, and Ulugatok had brought her home.

Sivaganguaq had a nickname—Ingminik—which means "spontaneous," but it was not used in her presence for it had been given her as the result of an incident in her life so scandalous that she would never live it down.

Her home had been at Cape York when the whalers used to call there to trade with the natives. The whalers were all strong men and, being without women for many months, were always crazy for girls. The Eskimo men, realizing this, brought their wives aboard the ships and managed the women's accounts. While the women went below to entertain the sailors, the husbands stayed on the upper deck. Afterward, the faithful wives would come up to their patient husbands bringing with them the rewards of their charms, and there was always a certain amount of good-natured competition between friends, exhibiting the amount of sugar and tea and crackers they received. "Look at what my wife got!" one would say. "It doesn't look as if your wife is in favor down there. Oh, my wife is such a wonderful woman!"

But it was always a little strange to the natives that the white men misjudged the values of the women. A splendid, and very popular, girl might find slight favor among them, while it often happened that the whalers went wild over a woman who amounted to nothing, could hardly sew and was traded from man to man because she was of no account at all. White men are funny!

One season, however, Ulugatoq had gone off on a long journey, leaving Sivaganguaq alone with the children, and while he was gone the Upernadlit—"those who arrive in the spring"—sailed into Cape York.

Sivaganguaq was in a dilemma. She was a woman of strict morals and, as her husband was not present to take her to the ships, she dared not go out by herself and bring shame to their house. But the children, seeing other mothers return from the ships laden with sugar and tea and crackers, could not understand why their mother denied them such luxuries. The poor woman sat at home bemoaning her fate, and presently the ships weighed anchor and sailed away. All the neighbors came home with their sledges overflowing with delicacies and the women with so much to talk and hint about that the desolate Sivaganguaq and her unfortunate children wept together.

A few days later another whaler swung along the edge of the ice and signified his willingness to trade with the natives. Still Sivaganguaq had no husband to take her aboard, but she had three dogs and she decided that this time nothing was going to cheat her of her just due.

She did well, and returned with bags full of the most delicious food, as well as a mirror and a pair of scissors, and she found that she had received more in a single visit to one ship than a number of her neighbors had in two.

But after a few days her nemesis in the person of a severe and offended husband returned. He had hurried in order to beat the spring thaw, and certain gossipy persons on the route had ielated to him the horrible thing his wife had done to his honor as a man. Of course, he must avenge it, so he called her out of his house and beat her before all the natives in the settlement. Sivaganguaq was a polite woman, so she did him the favor of screaming and crying for mercy. But later she told everyone that she had been deathly afraid he would not beat her, for if he had not it would indicate that he placed small value on her. But now she was sure of his love, his honor was vindicated, and both of them were delighted with the gifts she had received from the boat.

Nevertheless, the name Ingminik followed her through life.

She could sing like a bird, her screams and yells trailing off like the cries of an eagle, and such a passion for song and excitement I would never have suspected in any of these silent, patient women who sit all day long on the ledge sewing and cooking.

The night was spent in listening to the eerie Arctic music, and my ears rang with its discords. When I awakened I was cold and found that I had not undressed but had slept where I had been sitting, and the guests had either gone home or now lay deep in dreams about me.

It is impossible to keep the nights separate from the days. If anyone is tired he goes to sleep, and when he wants to get up he does so, regardless of the time. The beauty of it is that no one needs to wait for a meal to be served; there is always plenty of dog meat hanging outside the door, and the owner never cares how much anyone appropriates.

I walked out of the house. It was day; along the horizon to the south I could see a dull glow. I decided to walk up to the spot where the two famous meteorites had been located before they had been taken to the Museum of Natural History in New York.

One of the young natives accompanied me to the spot, though no one could miss it, as the great Peary always did a job thoroughly. In order to get the meteorites down to the ship he had built a road on which to haul them, a road that will never be used again. The road is made of stone and is quite a landmark, and takes anyone interested directly to the spot where the stones dropped from the heavens.

The meteorites had been reported a number of times. Captain Ross, who discovered the natives here for the first time in 1818, heard of them, and the Eskimos who lived in Danish Greenland knew they were here. Even the King had heard the rumor, and announced his wish to have them brought to Denmark.

At that time there was at Upernivik a missionary who wanted

a post that was better than the one to which he was entitled. Unfortunately in those days many of the priests who went to Greenland did so only because their qualifications allowed them to go nowhere else. But they knew that, after a certain length of time in the North, they would be rewarded with appointments at home which would elevate them to a level with the best of the theologians.

His Majesty made known his desire to have the meteorites. Christoffersen, the priest at Upernivik, undertook an expedition to fetch them, but he underestimated their size and took along only a sledge, trusting the dogs to be strong enough to haul them. He underestimated his own capacity for traveling too, for after two days on the road he decided he had had enough and consumed all the liquor he had brought along to insure his comfort on the trip. As a result, he had a long, quiet sleep, then turned back and reached the parsonage safe and sound, only to become known to the gracious King as a man with the best intentions.

The natives said the two meteorites carted away by Peary were not the only ones in the country, and Ulugatoq told us that, though he did not know exactly where it was, his father had told him of an island called Savik (Iron), which he used to visit as a boy. There he could chip iron from one of the stones. I tried to locate the spot but was never able to do so.

When we were ready to resume our journey Asayuk came to me and said that he could not accompany me farther as he had been warned in a dream that he had a number of enemies among the natives south of Melville Bay; he went on to explain that the people from the south had been ill treated by his forefathers when they had last come north to trade. I finally got the story out of him:

The Tassiussak Eskimos lived where they could purchase wood for sledges and kayaks from a tribe farther south to whom it was carried by ocean currents, and these people had formerly driven north to trade their wood for sealskin lines, bearskin and dogs. This would have been a great favor to the northerners, but the southerners were unmitigated beggars, and asked for everything they saw.

Asayuk's forefathers' people grew impatient with the methods of the southerners and decided to be rid of them once and for all. It was the time of year when the birds lay their eggs in the cliffs at Saunders Island, and the only way to reach the eggs was by means of ropes let down from the top of the cliffs. The northerners managed to send all the southerners down the cliffs for eggs, and then dropped the lines, leaving the troublesome strangers marooned on the face of the cliff. This seemed an effective method of doing away with them, while at the same time obeying the letter of an agreement not to kill any traders.

Sitting in their tents the northerners heard the poor beggars wailing in the cliffs for several days, and then at last the noise ceased. Everyone thought they were dead. The perpetrators of the plot went to the cliff to view the bodies and found all the strangers gone. Apparently despairing of help, the southerners had at last decided to chance the descent of the cliff rather than submit to starvation, and by some miracle, or perhaps with the aid of a magic formula, they had reached the ground safe and driven off with their dogs. Since then, oddly enough, there had been no word from the southerners.

I tried to convince Asayuk that this had all happened so long ago that no one would remember or, in any case, blame him, but he was convinced that the many discomforts he had already suffered on the trip were proof that he was not wanted. He also said he had remembered that his wife, Anarwree, did not know where to find his cache of auks from which she was supposed to make him a shirt, and when I promised him shirts to burn from the store at Tassiussak, he was all the more anxious to return.

"If this is true," he said, "one would not want Anarwree to waste her time sewing birdskins."

I realized that he was lost to the trip and let him return along with Minik, who complained that he had to have his food more regularly. I was glad to see him go, for he was a troublemaker.

8

Our course took us inside another island, Cape Melville, and we made good time, spending our nights in the open sledges as the weather held good. There are so many icebergs after one has passed Cape Melville that it is easy to find shelter from the wind.

Sleeping on the ice requires a certain technique which must be learned and followed exactly. One must protect his head from the cold. To do this a big skin is laid half under the pillow and bent forward so that it will hang down over the sleeper's head and the aperture into the sleeping bag. Beneath the bag is placed the skin which the driver sits on during the day, and his bearskin pants are tucked between it and the sleeping bag to keep them from freezing. His boots are also stuck halfway into the bag, only the feet protruding, to keep snow out of them. On the other hand, the coat is never taken inside the bag. If warmth penetrates it, the snow on it will melt, wet the coat, and next morning it will be frozen solid.

I had secured at Savigssuit a coat made of caribou skin to replace my foxskin garment, and this I took off last each night, rolled it up and used it as a pillow or else spread it over the sleeping bag.

There is quite a trick to getting into a sleeping bag when it is forty below zero. It takes a long while for the bag to warm up, but even if a fellow cannot sleep because of the cold, he can at least lie quiet and feel slightly rested in the morning, when comes the task of dressing again in the open.

The first move is to secure the pants from beneath the bag. Often they are fairly comfortable, for the warmth from the sleeper's body has permeated them. Then you put on the boots. These are usually frozen stiff from the day before, and are easy to get into, though you may have to stomp around a bit to start circulation in your feet. And then comes the worst job of all—especially for me—to get the coat on.

My nose is prominent, and invariably frostbitten in the morning. A coat of caribou skin is heavy of itself, and must be pulled over the head like a turtleneck sweater. Each day on the road a little more ice gets into it, and it feels like rough sandpaper as it is dragged over the face. The sleeves are usually frozen solid and must either be hammered soft or a whipstock or harpoon handle shoved through them to make a passage for the arms. After the coat is on a while it always thaws out and falls about the body as friendlily as it did the night before. Help from a companion should be avoided in struggling into the coat, for he will ruin your strategy. After all, you are the only one who really knows your own coat.

And yet, in spite of all this, traveling in winter has its charms. There is the sweet odor of meat over the fire at night, the natives working swiftly and quietly, their stout bodies a very part of the great wilderness, the dogs tied safely near-by, and towering above in gigantic, white silhouette, the protecting iceberg. Our nights were fine and peaceful.

On the fourth night out of Savigssuit we were awakened by strange noises from the dogs. Eskimo dogs never bark unless they scent a bear, and then the noise they make is a cross between a growl and a bark. Because of their ferocity toward bears, the dogs must be tied at night when traveling; otherwise, if the dogs have happened to smell a bear during the night, the owner will wake in the morning and never see his animals again.

Our three dog teams signaled for bear, and like puppets on strings my two companions shot from their sleeping bags, dressed, cut their dogs loose and dashed after them. I dressed as fast as I could and followed them, because not far off I could hear the yips of the dogs, the roars of the bear and the shouts of the men.

When I reached the scene Mitseq shouted to me that he did not have enough dogs—it was too dark to shoot—and that he would have to go back to camp for mine and for his spear. He dashed off and I stood by with Itukusunguaq. When the bear got away from the dogs, Itukusunguaq merely followed and waited. Shortly all my dogs arrived and immediately leapt into the fight. Each time the bear tried to escape several of the dogs jumped onto his back. At times he circled agile as a cat, but he could never get more than one dog under him at a time, and the rest of them would be all over him like ants. He could, of course, wound this one dog terribly, but while he was doing so he would have thirty-five others biting, snarling and tearing at him. So he would hurl the dog into the air and try to defend himself in some other way. Once I saw my king dog tossed high above my head and thought he would be killed when he landed, but he gathered himself into a ball as he lit, and without a second's hesitation tore at the bear again to give him what he owed him.

The two brothers, Mitseq and Itukusunguaq, decided they would have to spear the bear in order to kill him—it was unthinkable to shoot into the swarming hive of animals. Itukusunguaq offered me the first opportunity. I refused, since I valued my life, and told him I would rather an expert did the killing. He charged into the mess and hit the bear. Heretofore the bear had not seen us at all, considering the dogs his only antagonists. But now he felt the spear and saw the long handle protruding from his hindquarters.

Bears are "so constructed that they do not like to have a spear in them." That is the Eskimo way of expressing it, and even if it is understatement, it is true. This one forgot about the dogs and pulled the spear, handle and all, out of his body. How he managed it is almost inexplicable, for the stick is made to break easily, leaving the spear in the flesh. But he did so and left us weaponless as our guns were still of no use. Again the younger

ITUKUSUNGUAQ, ONE OF MY COMPANIONS ON THE FIRST TRIP TO TASSIUSSAK, STANDING WITH HIS WIFE OUTSIDE THEIR SUMMER TENT IN THULE. THIS WAS BEFORE A MISSIONARY HAD INFORMED THEM IT WAS A SIN TO GO ABOUT UNDRESSED IN THEIR HOME

brother, Mitseq, ran to the sledge for the other spear and his mittens which he had forgotten in the excitement. In no time at all he was back, and now it was his turn to try to kill the bear, weakened a little by loss of blood. Mitseq landed a blow squarely between his ribs. The bear surrendered at last; he went down with thirty-six dogs snarling over his body. But the dogs annoyed him even in his last moments, and he raised one huge paw to wipe them off his body. Then he rolled over, driving the spear farther into his ribs, and died quickly.

Strangely enough, dogs recognize a fallen enemy. They can be savage and dangerous even to their masters while they are in combat, but the moment the bear is defeated they loose their grip and lie down to await their reward—the warm, fresh meat.

It was only when the excitement of the kill was over that we had time to realize how cold we were, and how much colder we were going to be before we had finished skinning the bear. The temperature was fifty below, and in the darkness the skinning was a ticklish job, the white pelt covered with snow.

Whenever one of us could endure the cold no longer he would thrust his knife into the muscle of the recently slain beast, carving a hole large enough to bury his hand in the warmth of the meat. It is amazing how long meat will remain warm. I have had to leave animals exposed overnight a number of times in temperatures worse than fifty below, and next morning found all except the outer layers still unfrozen. The brain, especially, often takes days to freeze.

Next day we had an added burden of bear meat, but our stomachs were full and we did not care. We had fine, well-fed dogs, and though our course took us over good ice and bad ice, we could already see the crimson flush of day eating higher into the southern sky, and the moon rose to show us the way. The beginning of January is great.

After some days the sky became dull again. The stars grew fainter, and we noticed the ominous drift of snow on the ice—the natives call it "floor sweepings." Soon the wind struck our faces.

This is always the question at the beginning of a storm: how long should one try to keep going? You can stop early and make an igloo and meet the gale prepared. But then you have to be ready to swallow the blame that follows if the gale grows no worse. I made a rule to keep on until the dogs balked. In this instance we had no choice, for we were in the only section of Melville Bay where there are no icebergs. At the lee side of the icebergs there are always huge drifts of snow which one may cut into blocks for snowhouses.

So we kept on, and we had to drive much too far before Itukusunguaq stopped and told us that we might make camp. We tied our dogs as quickly as possible, took our knives and saws and went to work. In the Thule District the natives use common wood saws to cut out the blocks of snow. When later I visited Hudson Bay, where I learned to build real igloos, the natives there saw me work with my saw and smiled, and did the work with their knives twice as fast.

I could not help comparing this with my experiences on the east coast of Greenland. There we had considered a snowstorm as a brother of the devil. We lived in tents and kept in our sleeping bags as much as was humanly possible. I remembered that the cook got out of bed in the morning to prepare breakfast, and the rest showed their noses above the covers only when there was hot food to warm them up.

Now I heard Mitseq say that he was happy to have a snow-storm as it would compel us to make a house. He wanted to dry his mittens and his stockings. He was much better off now, for in Savigssuit he had annexed a sleeping bag.

We brought our blubber lamps into the igloo. Ours were made of copper plate and were much more durable than most lamps, which are of soapstone and apt to break if dropped.

We made the house as comfortable as possible and covered the ledges with skins. The lamps we placed on a tripod anchored in the snow and over the fire we stuck long sticks into the walls to serve as a rack for the clothing, which is first brushed free of snow with a tilugtut, a wooden saber, one of the most practical tools to carry on a trip in the Arctic.

At last everything was brought inside and the door closed from the inside. The last man out cuts a block of snow large enough for the hole which serves as an entrance. This is carted inside, and then, after everyone is in, plugged into the opening. Snow is chinked into the fissures along the sides. The occupants are then in a cozy room and the howling of the gale is only a pleasant reminder of their own comfort. The dogs never make trouble so long as the snow drifts. They merely curl up, their noses buried in their tails, and let the snow furnish a warm, comfortable blanket.

When I had learned this means of defense against a storm, the delay seemed merely a pleasant respite from routine. I realized how little I had known as a young boy, brimming with an enthusiasm masquerading under a disguise of scientific research, and understanding nothing of the essentials of living in this kind of climate.

We remained inside the igloo for three days. It is fine to lie down and listen to the gale, but a time comes when it is better to poke your head out and find that the wind has abated and the drifting ceased.

We had to excavate our sledges, and the dogs popped up like subterranean beings discovering that air as well as snow can be inhaled. They stretched and ran about to get the rigor out of their bodies, and then pulled to the extreme lengths of their traces to relieve themselves of three days' accumulation. Dogs are, in their own way, very hygienic animals.

It is sometimes quite a job to pull up stakes after a snowstorm, but we knew where we had left everything, and merely had to dig down to it. The snowhouses are rather difficult to enter with all the goods as the entrance is very small, but leaving the house is another matter. Then one may cut an exit as large as necessary.

The very last thing to be done when leaving a snowhouse is to walk inside and empty one's self. One is thus protected both from the cold winds and from the dogs, for nothing is dearer to an Eskimo dog than fresh human excrement. In fact, it is often necessary to protect oneself from them with a whip or, if the act is being performed by a number of persons simultaneously, to describe a circle, each man facing out. The most comfortable method, of course, is to get a boy or girl to stand over you, whip in hand.

Our dogs were rested, hungry and full of energy, and sped over the snow. Poor beasts, they live only from one meal to the next, and they believe that the faster they run the sooner they will be fed. But Melville Bay is wide, and the darkness made it wider, as we could never know what manner of ice we were running into. It required days for us to cover the same territory we could have traversed in hours had it been daylight. Since that adventurous trip I have made the journey more than thirty-five times, and now I know every cranny and habit of the big bay, but I shall always remember that first journey.

After some days the dogs had forgotten their rest and slowed down to their usual speed, which is not convenient for the driver if he runs alongside, for he can neither run nor walk, but must run two paces, walk one, and repeat over and over again.

Suddenly our dogs sniffed the snow and turned at a right angle from the course. Running full speed it was impossible for us to turn them. I jumped on my sledge and did my best to keep it right side up. Ahead of me I saw Itukusunguaq struggling with his dogs to stop them, and finally he brought them under control. I drew alongside and the three of us ran ahead of the dogs with our whips to head them off.

"What is it?" I asked. "A bear?"

"We don't know," Mitseq answered, "but it is not a bear."

"But why are the dogs so crazy?"

"It is something we cannot tell."

I found some matches and struck one. We examined the snow and found ahead of us a great trough like no track I had ever seen.

"What is that?" I asked.

The boys were still at a loss. Mitseq suggested that it might be better to turn back. We were outside our own territory and perhaps the spirits of this part of the world employed such tracks as this to mislead the unwary traveler.

Of that I had no fear. Then Itukusunguaq, the oldest of us all and an experienced man, shouted at the top of his voice:

"Paunguliaq! It is a wanderer! Some people on this journey are three lucky boys. It is a wanderer!"

With no more explanation both boys shrieked with joy, leapt to their sledges and cracked their whips. There was nothing for me to do but follow, and I did so, confused and a little angry. I felt that the boys should show a little respect for their employer instead of screaming a word I did not understand and then rushing off. They could not know whether I wanted what we sought or not.

I had not much time to think, since my dogs were streaking through the darkness, and it was all I could do to stick on the sledge. Occasionally I caught a glimpse of the track we followed. I could see no marks of any claws in the snow, only a depression as if a boat had been pulled along with the oars dragging. I noticed, too, that the thing had never changed its course for any obstruction, but had passed directly over ice hummocks and all. I was mystified.

By great effort I caught up with the boys and shouted at them again. Their only answer was:

"A paunguliaq! A wanderer!" But from their faces I could see that we were on the track of something as exciting as a gold strike.

Then suddenly I saw the thing—a huge, black mound apparently without head or tail. The dogs swarmed over it—we had to use our whips to get them off. I approached closer to discover that it was a huge walrus apparently driving straight across the ice to find open water.

Itukusunguaq was the first to draw his gun, and he shot the beast in the head. It died without a struggle. We stood beside almost a ton and a half of meat, an unparalleled and undeserved cache.

Before we could slice it we had to fasten our dogs. This was done by chopping two holes which slant towards each other in the ice and meet at the bottom. The hitching strap was then hooked through this, and no dog in the world could break from such a mooring.

The weather was absolutely calm. We got our flat blubber lamps and started a fire for light, and then made ready to carve up the walrus. I noticed that Mitseq was acting strange, but it was dark and cold and I thought this was merely his way of expressing joy. Still he stood back and waited. "Naw—naw—naw," he said. "Let us hurry and take our knives to it. Come on, come on!"

I suspected no trick, so I drove my knife into the animal. A yell and raucous laughter saluted me. Mitseq whooped, grasped my arms with his hands and grinned at me. I still did not understand, but finally they explained. By driving my knife into the walrus I was the second man to use a weapon on the beast, and as there were only three of us along, I would receive the smallest portion.

The first two men always take the front portion, but the very first man to wound the animal gets the head and all the intestines. The third man receives the whole hindquarters and gets even more meat than the killer himself. The third man in this instance was Mitseq, and he was babbling with pleasure. Of course, no Eskimo would permit another man to be without meat on such a trip, but ownership is ownership, and he would thereby have the pleasure of giving it to me—which is worth much to an Eskimo.

We camped on the spot that night, gorged ourselves on the meat, cached the rest and let the dogs drink deep of the gallons of blood inside the carcass.

Itukusunguaq told me that such a "paunguliaq" is the dream of every dog driver. The paunguliaq is a walrus that has been caught above the ice for some reason or other. Walruses have almost no nails on their flippers and must trust to their blunt noses to keep their blowholes open. They can stay beneath the ice only so long as it remains thin enough for them to break it. During the winter many of them remain close to the icebergs where the ice is always thin and trust to the sea floor to furnish them food. But occasionally they find the surface growing too solid, and then they ponderously drag their great bulk across the ice to a more advantageous wintering place. A walrus has an amazing instinct for scenting open water, but once in a while he may select the wrong route, as this one obviously had. But no matter what direction he chooses he sticks to it and allows no obstacle to deter him. He waddles across somehow, though his method of locomotion must be a terrific handicap abovewater. Often he must stop to sleep along the way, but the cold apparently does not bother him much. Both front and rear flippers of this animal were frozen badly, and the layer of fat under the skin was unusually thin. The stomach was entirely empty—the poor walrus had evidently been a long time on his last trek.

He was big and he came in handy for us. We had to leave the meat, and we could not be sure that a bear would not get to it before we returned, but we piled it up and stuck a harpoon into the middle of the pile. And on the tip of the harpoon we hung a small bundle of hay taken from our boots; this would swing in the wind and keep foxes away.

9

It was still many days before we reached Danish territory, and during the last miles we followed tracks already made by native sledges. These tracks we hailed as Columbus must have hailed the first birds flying about and the twigs floating in the water when he approached America.

But we had to be careful. None of us had been here before. Mitseq and his mother and father had driven south once many years ago, and had intended going all the way, but when his family had reached the first small settlements they had found the natives such unashamed beggars that they were stripped of trading materials long before they could reach their destination. They had to turn back and go home emptyhanded. Nevertheless, Mitseq had gained much information about the routes—when Eskimos give each other information they omit nothing—and he was certain he could guide us to Ituisalik, the first Eskimo village under Danish rule.

He did. He read the sledge tracks which the trappers had made, and learned from them that the sledges of these people were small and seldom loaded. He could tell that the dogs were harnessed in short traces and were fed fish, and that the drivers' whips were short and had thick, heavy lashes. Later I learned how to read the tracks, but then such information gleaned from them seemed miraculous.

Finally many tracks converged into what could almost be termed a road, and the dogs grew excited and broke into a run. We jumped onto our sledges and cracked our whips to gather speed for our last dash. We wanted to look impressive as we drove in. At last we could hear the dogs of the settlement howling their distrust. The natives were warned, and we saw two boys suddenly shoot out of the twilight as if discharged from a bow. They were Kale and Isak, the young sons of the great Itué, called Simon the Bearhunter by all the Danes from near and far.

More men and women and children rushed out to meet us and we stopped to greet them. Mitseq and Itukusunguaq were embarrassed by the practice of taking off the mitten and extending the right hand to be shaken. They had already mentioned it to me, and the much-traveled Mitseq had explained that it was to indicate that if the right hand was tired the strangers would help to support it.

Still, it seemed awkward. I, too, had almost forgotten this manner of greeting. All of us talked together in the usual manner, but suddenly an enormous voice from the shore reached us:

"Halt! Stop and listen to the one who speaks here! This is the country owned by the King, and he has ordered me to stay here and look out for those who enter his royal land. Nobody may come with dogs unless he has read this paper and answered yes to it."

It was Itué who spoke, the famous ruler of Denmark's northernmost territory. He had been unable by circumstance and neglect to learn to read, but as he saw a white man among the strangers he brought forward a lantern with a candle in it and told me to read the paper which he handed me. Though nearly worn out, it was still decipherable, and I asked if I might not wait until I had cared for my dogs and come into his house. Knud

Top. KNUD RASMUSSEN (*first row, right*) PLAYING HOST AT A "KAFFEE MIK" (COFFEE FEAST) TO SIMON THE BEARHUNTER (*on Knud's right*).

Bottom. A NATIVE HUNTER IN HIS KAYAK WAITING FOR SEAL OR WALRUS. NOTE THE HARPOON AND HUNTING BLADDER.

Rasmussen had advised me to proceed in this manner, since it would permit Itué to demonstrate his authority.

"Oh, no! Oh, no!" he answered. "This country is ruled by two men—the King and me! And neither of us can permit you to stay here if you do not read the paper and say yes. And it must be said loud and clear!"

I glanced at the paper. The text was written in Danish and English, and was merely a warning not to bring diseased dogs or Eskimos suffering from venereal or other contagious diseases into the territory.

I looked it over carefully and handed it back to Itué.

"Yes!" I shouted like a stentor. "I am your man. I will obey."

As if these were the magic words of the Sultan of Baghdad, Itué's manner changed. His strong, stern face suddenly broke into a smile and his mitten was snatched off. He grasped my hand as if we were lifelong friends who had been separated for years.

"I guess you are Peterssuaq," he said. "We know of you and you are our friend! Kunuk [Knud Rasmussen] is back, we have heard, and has brought you along. So you belong to us!"

I visited his house, a small but extremely clean hut with whitewashed interior and a ledge groaning under feather cushions. It was evident that Itué and his family were above the use of skins for comfort or decoration. On a shelf were several colored cups and gewgaws, and pictures with religious motifs covered the walls.

Itué's wife, a slim, neat woman, and his whole family greeted us. There was about them an air of prosperity which I had not observed before in any of the natives. Their speech was colored with an accent unfamiliar to our ears, and we had trouble in understanding them at first, but we got along famously.

Itué informed us that we were not allowed to leave our dogs without a night watch, and delegated his two sons as watchman. This was a salaried job, of course, and, not unlike the majority of businessmen, he felt that his own relatives were better fitted for the work than anyone else.

He also impressed upon us that we would most certainly need a guide the rest of the way to the trading post at Tassiussak, and none other than Itué himself would guide us. He was an excellent host, but he complained bitterly the whole evening that he had no coffee to offer us and had had none himself for the past week. Finally I donated some of our own coffee, and he chose to see in our arrival the generous benevolence of the God to whom he had prayed ever since his coffee had run short.

Only three families lived in this community, and the other two resided in a house even smaller than Itué's. He, of course, was the big man of the community, but there was one who ran him a close second, Pele. Pele was not noted for his strength, but he was of tremendous importance in this northernmost Danish district because of his ability to read. This accomplishment made him both preacher and teacher. These dignities not only gave him a handsome salary—thirty-six kroner a year, or about sixty cents a month—but made him God's spokesman on this part of the earth. He had the floor every Sunday and the privilege of informing everyone what displeased him and God. Many little grievances could be aired during his sermons—perhaps all his audience had not been like Jesus the Beloved and shared their game with everyone in the community including the minister. Occasionally one of the publicly chastised members of the congregation would attempt to discuss the matter personally with Pele after the sermon, but he always held his ground and remarked loftily that his message had come direct from God the Almighty One, and who would dare enter into petty bickering over God's Word?

As if this were not enough distinction for one man, Pele was official letter-reader of the whole countryside, and once when there came to the place a stranger who boasted that he, too, could read letters—and did, upon two occasions without consulting Pele—the minister of God had him exiled for his audacity.

Pele's wife was a blind, elderly woman, the sister of Itué's wife. Before her marriage, the mighty Itué had had to support her. Itué, however, saw an out for himself by ordering Pele, who was Itué's nephew, to marry her. Pele was said to have objected strenuously, but there was nothing he could do about it. The couple had three small daughters and now lived very happily together. It was surprising to witness the facility of the blind woman in sewing and cleaning skins.

The hearty natives from the north were used to much more food than was offered by these southerners. Kruaq—frozen meat and blubber of the narwhale—was served but there was almost no blubber attached to it, and the meat was cut into small pieces with a woman's knife wielded by one of the sons. And then, what seemed unique to us, the major portion of the meat was taken out of the house again. This was recounted later by Mitseq and Itukusunguaq as the strangest experience they ever had.

The southerners were also great competitors at parlor games, and the two brothers from the north were invariably losers. By the time we were ready to leave they had almost no tobacco, knives or small accessories left.

Nor did we sleep comfortably. The ledges were shorter than ours and, as I am very tall, my head protruded beyond the support, even when I curled up like a cat. There beneath my nose was the huge container of family urine—a sure indication of wealth and affluence—and the stench was that of some specially noxious form of ammonia. My eyes ached terribly by morning, and I was delighted to start early in an attempt to reach Tassiussak the same evening.

We stopped to eat with Itué's brother, Markus, who lived alone with his wife and children far from any settlement. Markus' family also relieved my boys of a number of their possessions, and I knew that unless we hurried they would soon be naked.

We drove through an impressive landscape, down a long valley between high mountains which housed millions of birds. But it grew slowly darker and clouds washed across the sky. Itué was afraid we would be unable to reach Tassiussak if he could not see the moon, for the current is swift there and shifts the ice about treacherously. We would, he said, have to stop with either Solo in Sarfak or Abel in Saitoq. Since I knew neither of the men, it made no difference to me where we stopped.

We reached Sarfak safely, though the current ran close to the land and, as I was the last to cross the passage, I had barely made it when the ice entirely disappeared behind me.

Sarfak was in an unusual state of turmoil. The arrival of visitors in a community of four or five houses is always an exciting event, but we had come on a very special occasion. Solo himself explained it after we tied our dogs:

"We are having an important election; the King has ordered us to hold it today, so I cannot delay until tomorrow and treat you as you should be treated."

It was the first real election to be held in Danish Greenland. The new law gave the natives the right to vote for members of the commune council, and as this was the very first election it was especially solemn. They considered me a man of great intelligence because I could read, and Solo asked me to help them out of their difficulties and supervise the proceedings.

Sarfak, with its five houses, was quite an important community and entitled to select one member of the council. Farther north at Ituisalik and similar places, four villages joined forces to elect one representative. Since Itué was the most powerful man of his district, he railroaded his brother Markus into office with little trouble. However, the more southern, and therefore more civilized, Sarfak had a different problem, especially since the balloting was to be done in absolute secrecy.

The hunters were uncertain as to what was expected of a member of the council. They only knew that the office paid no salary and the members were entitled to only fifty ore (ten cents) for one meal each month on the day of meeting. As it would often take several days to travel back and forth, the hunters quite naturally, and sensibly, decided they could not waste their time at lawmaking. But the King had spoken, and somebody had to be elected.

There was in Sarfak, however, an ideal man for the office— Abelat by name. He had formerly been a big hunter, but was now old and useless. His knees were weak and his eyes could no longer see to hunt. Occasionally he could walk to the seal nets close by and catch a seal, but he was definitely on his relatives' dole, so he was instructed to become a member of the council.

Abelat had neither political talents nor ambitions, but he was forced into the latter at any rate. His son, Gaba, was supporting him, and Gaba thought this might be a way of getting the old man off his hands for a few days each month. Abelat had cried and protested, but he knew full well that there was nothing else he could do, for he was old and accustomed by now to bend to the will of others.

So Abelat was made the candidate for councilman. To avoid further confusion, no one was permitted to run against him. But there were to be five voters, excluding Abelat himself, and it was easy to see how confusion would arise in spite of anything that could be done. Especially as it was impossible to depart from the clearly expressed letter of the law which demanded that the election be held in secret.

Solo's house was the largest and therefore the one most worthy of such an unusual honor. We all trooped inside and searched it carefully for plotters, though what or who might be hidden in it I never could understand since it was a single room with no furniture, no tapestries and no alcoves.

After we were assured that everything was as it should be we went outside and Solo, the greatest hunter of the place and thereby entitled to all privileges, prepared himself to enter the secret ballot booth. This brought up an unforeseen problem. The law plainly stated that the voters should write the name of their candidate on the ballot, and only two of the voters were able to do this. I suggested, as a way out, that since there was only one candidate, the uneducated voters should merely make a cross on the ballot and I would later translate these crosses to the name "Abelat," and thus come within the law.

Solo wiped his hands carefully and, grasping a box of matches, crawled through the tunnel into the house to do his duty to king and country. Inside he lighted a candle, voted with the pencil and paper which had been provided, blew out the candle again and came outside. The others followed him one by one, each returning to the out-of-doors much heated and excited by the ceremony. Finally, after they had all accomplished their duty, Solo repeated three times in a loud voice—still according to the dictates of the law: "Does anybody else want to vote?"

There was no one else to answer, so the election was pronounced at an end, and we all went inside to discover two names and three crosses. Abelat had been elected unanimously!

This surprising result was greeted with shouts of delight, and we were told that in honor of the day Solo would celebrate and make coffee. Itué was greatly pleased and told me later that, after having witnessed this performance, he regretted very much that he had not held a real election at his house. He would certainly do so next year now that he knew how.

Everyone at the feast was happy except Abelat, the newly elected council man. He refused to drink coffee and sat and cried because it was discovered that he did not know how to act at the meetings, and could not even read the old laws, much less write any new ones.

Though Solo looked more like a pig than any man I have ever seen, he was friendly and hospitable. He asked whether we intended to add to the celebration by serving some of the food which Itué had told him about, and we reluctantly brought forth our frozen bear meat.

The weather was still bad next day but I insisted upon traveling as far as possible. We reached Saitoq where the most famous hunter in the district lived. His name was Abel, and he was a truly great provider. A husky man and ugly of face, he was full of laughter and carried himself with a fine, natural dignity. He would not allow me to attend to my dogs. "My boys will see to that," he said.

His house was large and notable for its cleanliness. His wife, Tippo, was no beauty—her face was as flat as her body—but she was brisk and efficient, and I knew now how important it was for a hunter to have a clever wife. The couple had four daughters and all of them, because of our arrival, were dressed in their fine anoraks and boasted the most elegant pants and kamiks I had ever seen. Such finery is difficult to obtain in the Arctic, and requires great skill and patience to manufacture. An old aunt of the hunter lived with the family, and was as much honored as the wife. She was evidently in part responsible for the wealth of the house.

We were served coffee and bread baked in a pot over the blubber lamp. It is very good. The dough is mixed and allowed to rise in the conventional manner. Then it is placed in a covered pot and hung high over the flames for hours. After it is thoroughly baked on one side it is taken out of the pot, turned upside down and again placed in the pot. After two more hours the bread is completely baked, and it is as delicious as cake, with no crust whatever.

I slept in Abel's house that night and was regaled with an account of the great event of the day before—the election, of course. There had, it seemed, been an irregularity in the proceedings, and it had been necessary to repeat the election. One of the voters had gone into the booth to cast his vote, and had not come out again. Everyone had waited and waited, wanting to give the man plenty of time and not rush the thing through. But after several hours they grew worried lest the importance of the voter's duty had robbed him of his powers and the others entered the house to find out what the trouble was. They found the voter fast asleep. This, of course, had necessitated a whole new election, for its secrecy had been violated.

Gaba was elected councilman here. I found it a little difficult to differentiate between the various Gabas in the beginning. Later I learned that a number of years previous a mighty man named Gaba had departed this earth, though by various signs impossible to ignore it was obvious that Gaba was not totally absent, and in order to please his spirit all boys born within a period of ten years were named Gaba. In Kook there were five men of the same name. There they were called Gabassuaq (The Big Gaba), Gabalark (The Bad Gaba), Gabakasik (The Poor Little Gaba), Gaba Parkringasok (The Pale Gaba), Gaba Angmaglortok (The Round, Fat Gaba), and so on.

Abel brought in my sleeping bag and let me sleep on the floor this night, which was much more comfortable. I watched the entire household get ready for bed, and I could not help noticing that the women all wore absolutely white shirts, laundered perfectly. Urine as a cleanser may not conform to our notions of hygiene, but it certainly is excellent for washing clothes. During the night I watched the contributions to the immense urine pail left in the middle of the floor. The family got up one or two at a time and added to the much valued tanning and washing fluid.

In the morning I was waked with steaming, black coffee. Itué had already drunk two cups, and I took mine in my sleeping bag. The hostess in this part of Greenland always serves a saucer as well as a cup, and etiquette demands that the cup be so well filled that it spills over into the saucer. As a matter of fact, coffee must be sipped from the saucer rather than the cup if one would conform to Eskimo standards. One merely holds the cup and pours coffee from it into the saucer which is held daintily with three fingers outstretched. The sugar is hard, lump crystal and is not put into the coffee but held in the mouth like candy. At parties one is much admired for his dexterity at sipping coffee, sucking sugar, and gossiping over the latest scandals at one and the same time.

Abel decided that he would follow us to Tassiussak even though the weather was not favorable, and Itué told me that Abel never failed to get through.

The clouds hung low round mighty Nulok Mountain and the ice did not look inviting, but Abel knew how to avoid the worst places. Down in this part of Greenland the many islands cause very bad ice. The tide runs in and out with such force that it is apt to wear out the ice from below. Hunters use short traces on their dogs, so that they may turn the sledges quickly. We with our long traces were at a disadvantage, for the dogs always run in the sledge tracks ahead of them. Since our traces were so long our sledges often cut across bad ice on the sharp curves and we broke through. Abel, however, proved an expert guide and took over the command of the party from Itué, who would have permitted such highhandedness from no one else. Once I fell into the water, but it was so cold that the water froze before it had penetrated my skin clothes.

After a number of hours we reached the point from which we could look down into the sheltered settlement of Tassiussak. A swarm of natives streamed out to meet us. There were six or seven houses here and their lights made the impression of a city of considerable size. My two boys, Mitseq and Itukusunguaq, were impressed.

We were asked about the trip and a tall native inquired after his "countrymen" to the north. He was Tobias, the schoolteacher, and his voice proclaimed his dignity. He had been taught far to the south, in Godthaab, the capital of Greenland, and had received a degree from the high school there. After we had talked for a few moments it was suggested to me that I had best get along to the trading post as Nabaja—Mr. Nielsen—knew we were coming and his wife would most likely have coffee ready for us.

10

In meeting Nielsen we made our first acquaintance with a family which, for many winters to come, was to be our host year in and year out. We took possession of their house as if it were our own and filled it to overflowing with our friends. Yet never did I see anything but smiles on their faces nor feel anything but extreme pleasure in their greeting.

Nielsen was married to a half-breed woman, Dorte, an extremely clever person. They had four fine children who were soon like brothers and sisters to us. We were given coffee and cake which tasted better than any cake I have ever eaten before or since. What a meal Mrs. Nielsen could lay upon the table! I was given the second room to use as my own, Nielsen gave me my mail, and I was in paradise.

In the evening a ball was given in my honor. The largest room was jammed with all the villagers, and an ingenious member of the tribe played an accordion. Only a tiny space, as small as a modern night club floor, was left for the dancers, but their enjoyment was boundless. Everyone was prepared for such a jam, and there were no flimsy dresses to catch and tear. The girls laughed and screamed with delight, but my two boys were extremely embarrassed. They had never witnessed such a celebration, and they realized that they did not yet know enough to criticize. Yet there was nothing I could do to induce them to take part in such a shameless exhibition as traipsing around the floor with a girl.

"Especially as I do not know which one to take after the dance and where to take her! We only do our women plays in the dark where people can hear but not see," was Itukusunguaq's comment.

Coffee and hardtack were served. Nielsen sat in the interior of the house and was bored. His dancing days were over, he said, and only occasionally would he venture into the ballroom to pay his respects to his wife and the teacher's wife. However, after several hours his resistance weakened and he went to the cupboard and produced a bottle of gin. He took a swig to assure himself and everyone else that it was not poison, and to make assurance doubly sure, took another quick one. Then he paced up and down the dance floor with a glass in one hand and a bottle in the other. Whenever he spied a favorite he would stop and pour a drink for the much-envied fellow. Tobias was first. Abel and Itué second and third, and then a few others were favored with the divine liquid. The rest gazed longingly at the bottle, and one particularly daring man prayed humbly. "Nabaja!" he said; that was all.

The trader turned to him and explained that a certain loan was yet outstanding. When this was paid, it was just possible that a drink could be had upon occasion.

We danced until my shirt was wringing wet and my feet scorching. Nabaja's daughter, Jacobine, squealed with pleasure and was so delirious that she kissed me for being the cause of all this. A Gaba was there also. He was the only man in Tassiussak on parish relief, which was given him in the form of rye meal and blubber. Tonight he had forgotten his misery and was never off the dance floor, skipping and tapping about as if he had never done anything else. He received two portions of coffee and crackers, as I gave him mine. When Nabaja passed with the bottle there was no disappointment in his eyes—his dreams were all of food. This was his night as well as mine.

Ten o'clock was Nabaja's bedtime, and he had a most effective way of ending the party. He did not go to each one and tell him that the host was sorry he must be going, but merely stood in the center of the room and raised his hand. He did not speak a word, but his guests melted away like chickens before a fox. The last man to hury out was Gaba the Poor, who wanted to savor the feast to the last.

Nabaja and I went outside and walked up and down in front of his house. He paced there for hours each day like a lion in a cage. He suggested that we remain outside for a while as his wife would make us some real coffee and, besides, it would give the air in the house a chance to clear. When the natives dance in their heavy clothes they perspire, and this intensifies the odor of urine in their pants and boots. His windows were sealed for the winter, and fresh air could only circulate through the door.

Nielsen attempted to instruct me in my dealings with the natives. "So long as you are going to stay here for many years, you might as well profit by my experience," he said.

His wife never threw away coffee grounds. They were always kept frozen outside the house and, after they had been used once, were fine for coffee to serve customers who came to trade. The customers were delighted with it, and often brought a piece of meat or a bird to express their appreciation.

After this warming over, the grounds were still not discarded, but used to furnish refreshment for dances and parties. Meantime, of course, the residue had been frozen again. But thawed out, and a pinch of salt added, it was always splendid for dancers. After this third brewing, the beans were given to poor women who could use them a couple of times more before they ate the grounds with a spoon or chewed them like tobacco.

Greenland teaches economy.

I slept until late the next morning and then came out to watch the natives trade. Their methods were quite different from those of the Smith Sound Eskimos who are scattered over a tremendous territory. South of Melville Bay they are grouped together in settlements, seldom travel far, and derive their principal income from blubber and sealskins, since they have no fish or fox pelts to sell. As a result, they buy supplies for a day or two only, and invariably demand coffee before anything else.

The coffee beans they purchase raw and roast them to a crisp. To make them go a long way, the Eskimos mix the beans with rice or barley, or whatever. This form of coffee turns them into near-addicts. When they are without coffee, they say they feel worse than when they are starving.

The natives buy small quantities of coffee at a time, and the trader must rely on the accuracy of his scales to make both ends meet. He purchases his coffee in bags weighing 218 pounds, but he sells it by the ounce. And if he deals out a bean too much with each ounce he will cheat himself of more than two pounds to a bag.

Nielsen's store contained a number of objects, such as woolen shirts and fine pots and pans, which were utterly fascinating to my boys. There were also a great variety of knives, tobacco, sugar, tea and matches in quantity. Mitseq and Itukusunguaq were crazy to satisfy all their desires, but I warned them to hide their treasures when we started for home, as otherwise they would be begged out of everything. Consequently they packed their goods in boxes and nailed them down securely so that they would not be tempted to open them and show off their prizes. My own purchases consisted principally of matches, for we had either forgotten to bring a sufficient quantity with us or they had gone back on the ship to Denmark.

11

We gave our dogs a few days' rest, enjoyed ourselves thoroughly, and then said good-bye to the Nielsens over a last cup of coffee. The weather was fine, the ice much better, and we knew that we could get back to Thule in a hurry, not stopping at all until we reached Ituisalik.

We found Itué in the midst of great tragedy. He had gone home the day after we arrived in Tassiussak, carrying fourteen pounds of coffee. Now, only one week later, it was all gone. He was humble and apologetic about it, so I paid him for the next year's piloting to Tassiussak at this time. If I had not he would have been unable to buy more coffee until the seals came up on the ice and he had more blubber and skins to trade.

His son Kale, a splendid young fellow, and Markus' son Tobias thought it would be great sport to follow us for a couple of days on the trip north. We knew that their motive was other than mere sport; they had heard about our cache of walrus meat, and they wanted part of it. They were also anxious to get a bear and have us divvy up if we bagged one. As for them, they never divided portions. They did not cut up the skin for pants, but sold it in one piece to the trader.

We were anything but eager for them to come along, but we could not say no since we did not want to get a bad reputation. The Eskimos south of Melville Bay, unlike our own, are terrible beggars, fill their cups with sugar, eat everything in sight, and have abominable camping manners. The worst thing about them, perhaps, is that they never tie up their dogs at night and these dogs, still possessing all their teeth, eat the traces. Our sealskin lines were especially tasty to them for they were not tanned in urine.

But they were impressed by the great people who came out of the mysterious north every year. We built a snowhouse and the two poor boys had no sleeping bags but showed up with, of all

things, feather pillows. These are, of course, no good for sleeping
in snowhouses, so instead of sleeping quietly they never tired of
pestering us with questions about the north. What kind of country we had up there they could not fathom. They had dreamed,
they said, of being like the people to the north, and it was this
spirit which had made them follow us as far as we could tolerate
them.

Unlike the Polar Eskimos, the southerners are also braggarts.
We might not call them by such a harsh term, but Mitseq and
Itukusunguaq were embarrassed for them when they told stories
of adventures in which they admitted they themselves played
heroic roles.

We liked Kale, but when he asked us about the bear we had
killed on the way down, he compared it with a number of bears
he had shot himself, and went into great detail about his heroism
in getting his own first bear. Itukusunguaq listened patiently for
a while, but finally even his stoical politeness was tried.

"How many bears have you killed in your time?" he asked
Kale.

Kale figured carefully, and admitted to five. This was too
much for Itukusunguaq. Grinning at Mitseq, he said:

"Well, well, here is a man who has killed five bears!"

"Naw! Naw!" exclaimed Mitseq. "Can you imagine!"

This sarcasm went over Kale's head, but Itukusunguaq
finally told him in disgust that he had better keep quiet until he
had something to boast about.

I could see the atmosphere in the igloo growing thicker by the
moment and made a futile thrust or two to lighten it. But hostility
was in the air, and I had not much control over my own boys.
Mitseq, a young upstart, commenced criticizing the habits and
customs of the southerners:

"I feel sorrow for their minds down there. They completely
forgot to give me something back for the things they begged from
me."

Kale said they never paid for what they accepted as gifts, but
Mitseq replied that he had not accepted one thing from them
without paying high.

I tried to explain that different people have different
customs, but both Mitseq and Itukusunguaq affirmed that the
southerners asked for gifts in such a manner that no real man
could deny them and retain his self-respect. With the way things
were going I was exhausted by the time they all fell asleep.

But next morning when we emerged from the igloo our dog traces were gone. I was disgusted and told both Kale and Tobias to return home as we could not afford to have them with us any longer. Their own traces were eaten, and we had to make them new ones from our harpoon lines before we could get rid of them. The leftovers which we were going to throw away the cousins begged to keep. This was even more disgusting to Mitseq. "If one's dogs had to run in traces caught by someone else, one would rather they were all dead, and never raise his whip again," he said.

Finally we were alone and delighted when we saw Kale and Tobias disappear in the low-hanging mist to the south. Lucky we were to be rid of them, too, because an hour later we sighted a bear and killed it. Had they been with us they would have been entitled to portions, and would doubtless have asked for the whole skin. And, said Mitseq, we should have been forced to give it to them in order to avoid the name of "those who are close about bearskins," a horrible stigma indeed.

At last the light was returning. It was almost the end of January and we were as pleased to greet the coming of day as we had been to see the sun disappear months ago. One morning we could detect the colors of our dogs. During the long night we recognize them by their individual shapes, and now it was almost a surprise to remember that some were red, others black and white and spotted. Day by day the period of light lengthened and its intensity increased. We were traveling north, of course, but the sun rapidly gained on us. The weather was good and the weather was bad, but we did not care, for we were nearing home. We found our walrus meat almost intact. A bear had been at it, but he had evidently not been very hungry.

After we passed Cape Melville we recognized landmarks, and realized how foolish we had been in our choice of a trail on the way down. Had we been able to see, no rough ice would have endangered us, and we could have avoided all the traps we had fallen into. But at least we had the pleasure of making fun of ourselves now.

At Cape York we met our friends, and visitors from the north told us that Kunuk was preparing to cross to Ellesmere Land to hunt musk oxen, and was only awaiting my return to take charge of the post in his absence.

The ice round Cape York was now excellent and we made it home from there in two days. After we had rounded Cape Athol we caught sight of Umanak, the mountain which dominates our fjord, and were at home in less than three hours.

Knud Rasmussen's welcome was heart-warming. He should have been an organizer of parties. In fact, he was the Arctic Elsa Maxwell, for he was never happier than when he could celebrate something or other, and I never knew a man who could find so many occasions for celebration. All the natives were summoned and our stories and laughter rang out until morning.

Yet in the group there was one face I missed—that of a certain young girl. I inquired about her, the stepdaughter of Uvd-luriark, and all the natives were amazed and wanted to know why. I explained that I had brought something to pay her for the mittens she had given me. Everyone snickered, and I realized I had done something that was simply not done: I had mentioned and asked for a girl.

But next day I met her as she walked on the ice with her little brother slung on her back. When she saw me she hid behind an ice hummock. I started round to find her but she ran as fast as she could go. She was hampered by the child on her back, and it was easy for me to catch her and hold her.

"Why do you run away?" I demanded.

"I don't know."

"Are you afraid of me? You need not be!"

"No, I am not afraid, but someone told that you had inquired for me yesterday before everyone. Therefore I was embarrassed!"

"I forgot your name—what is it really?"

"Oh, I am nobody, just the most ugly and foolish girl in the tribe."

"I don't think so, but what is your name?"

"I don't know."

"You mean you don't know your own name?"

"No, I never heard it."

"Nonsense," I persisted. "Of course you know your name. Why won't you tell it to me?"

"Others can tell it to you, but it is not important."

"I brought something back for you, something you will like."

"Oh, no, don't give me anything," she begged. "Give it to somebody worth giving things!"

And while I looked about me in desperation for a means of breaking through her self-abnegation, she made a quick movement and disappeared in the dark.

Later on I asked one of the girls at our house about her

name. She, too, refused to tell me, explaining politely, "You are making yourself ridiculous asking for a young woman's name."

We had in our household three women—Vivi, whom we had brought from the south, Arnajark, an elderly woman, and Aloqisaq, a strong woman who had recently lost her husband.

Arnajark had been Knud Rasmussen's servant during the previous winter he had spent with these people, and was utterly devoted to him. She found it difficult, however, to compete with Vivi, who had been baptized and carried her nose in the air as a result. Whenever Vivi found herself left out of a conversation she revenged herself by taking out her psalm book and screaming her faith at the top of her lungs. She could always impress the natives with this performance, but her learning was sketchy when put to practical purposes.

One day Knud Rasmussen asked Arnajark to count the foxskins in the attic. Vivi overheard his request, and laughed: "These people cannot count at all. They only know up to twenty, and there are many more skins than that."

Knud called her bluff, and told her to go count the skins herself. Vivi tried to get out of it, but he would not let her off. She spent hours in the attic, and then came down to ask for a pencil and paper. After many more hours she returned with a paper so littered with numbers that we could not make any sense out of it. If we had owned as many foxskins as she had computed, we would have been millionaires.

He looked over the figures, and then asked Arnajark to go up and count. In a half-hour she was back.

"There are now four piles with ten coats in each," she said. "Then there is one pile with three coats, and six foxes left over."

A coat is ten foxskins, and the stupid woman had figured correctly. We actually had four hundred thirty-six skins.

We lived contentedly in our little house, and never shall I be so happy again. Perhaps most men could not have endured the isolation, but I had everything I wanted—friendship, trust and a busy, active life. We did not cheat the Eskimos, for they were our friends, and they came to use for the fulfillment of their wants. Arnajark was put in charge of the natives—or rather, she put herself in that position. Vivi did the cooking, and a fine cook she was too, and much respected. Arnajark chose the place closest to the window so that she could be the one "who calls out when a visitor arrives, and tells who it is."

Everyone in the village visited us daily. When a man did not

KNUD RASMUSSEN OUTSIDE OUR HOUSE AT THULE WITH OLD ARNAJARK

come, we could be sure he was out hunting. Strangers came from great distances to trade goods and stories. Our stock of trading material was limited as we had little money to fit out our post, but everyone was happy to have us whether we had anything or not. "Now we are like the southerners and have a store near-by," the natives would say. Some even questioned our prices: "People never appreciate things if they can buy them for nothing." And others insisted upon paying more than we asked so that they could boast of the value of their belongings.

Of course, there were a few who had visited far to the south and seen real stores beyond Tassiussak. They said that if we were real traders we should have a scale to weigh our goods. Didn't genuine stores always weigh everything?

Knud, never at a loss, could answer this criticism: "You see, all our goods have been weighed before they were packed."

We saw our supply of goods diminishing, and Arnajark warned us: "Don't sell too much. It will never do for some people to have more than we do. How may we take any pleasure from life if we trade our precious things for nothing but foxes, which run loose in the mountains winter and summer?" That was certainly, from her point of view, good logic.

Aloqisaq was the strongest woman I have ever seen. She, as I have said, was a widow, but her husband's story is one of the most amazing I have ever heard. It is a true story, yet I wonder whether any doctors will credit it.

Agpaleq, the husband, was an old man before he owned his first gun. He was so childishly delighted with it that he wanted several different size cartridges, "just to fool the gun."

One cold, fall day he went out after caribou. He took two boys with him to carry back the meat he was sure he would get, and all the way he boasted about his fine gun. How much better this was than sneaking up on a caribou with a bow and arrow!

They spotted two caribou across a creek, and Agpaleq had such confidence in his weapon that he determined to get them both with one shot. Carefully he loaded the gun, and then dropped a smaller cartridge down the barrel. The caribou stood one just above the other, and he felt sure that the small lead would carry higher and hit the upper caribou. He instructed the boys to hide while he inched forward to get in position.

At last he was in the right spot, and he eased the gun to his shoulder. He never remembered pulling the trigger. The gun, however, went off with a fearful crash, exploded in his hands, and a splinter of it flew back and crashed in the left frontal bone of his skull. The boys rushed forward thinking him dead, but he commenced to move and talk crazily and to roar like a bear. When they looked more closely they could see his brain beating in the open wound.

They dared not stay with him and went home to call for help, but found only his wife and one other woman when they arrived. Aloqisaq, however, packed their heavy tent on her back and walked out to her husband. I know of no man who could have performed the feat, and it was only her great strength which saved them both.

He was still alive and inquired why she had come. He remembered nothing that had happened. Aloqisaq pitched the tent over him—she dared not move him yet—and there they stayed for several days eating the meat she had brought with her. When rescuers arrived to bury the body they found Agpaleq still alive, though his feet had been frozen and gangrene had set in, and, most amazing of all, part of his brain had poured out of the wound.

This I was told by other witnesses than Aloqisaq. These people are familiar with anatomy, and are certainly able to recognize brain matter when they see it. They all assured me that at least a cupful had come out, and they had cleaned out more with a spoon. After which Aloqisaq sewed the skin together.

Agpaleq's recovery was slow, but almost complete. The accident resulted in peculiarity of habits rather than invalidism. During the remainder of his life he could sleep for a week or more at a time, and remain awake an equal length of time. When asleep it was almost impossible for him to be awakened, and it became quite the custom for his neighbors to walk into his house and help themselves to whatever they might desire, including his wife. Agpaleq slept soundly through it all and never knew what practical jokes were played on him.

He also became almost unbearably dirty, soiled himself and never cared. Prior to the accident he had been neat and clean, but afterward he was always smeared with grease or blood or both. His hands were filthy, his toes rotted away and filled the house with the most noisome stench. He could still hunt in his kayak, for he retained his heels and half of his feet, and was useful until the time of his death. After which his wife came to us and brought her son with her.

I came home late on the night after Aloqisaq and the boy

had arrived, and Knud suggested that I fit the lad out with a shirt.
I was tired from a day of walrus hunting, but I complied. The lad
seemed frightened and embarrassed, and would not say a word.
I told Knud this, and he translated it to the natives in the house
at the time. They all roared with laughter, and I was finally told
that he was deaf and dumb. Aloqisaq tried to excuse herself for
bearing him, but said that she had not discovered his affliction
until he was two years old, and then she loved him so much that
she could not bring herself to kill him.

I adopted him as my own, taught him to speak, and he stayed
with me for many years.

Aloqisaq had formerly been with Peary's expeditions and
had learned how to wash clothes. This was a life-saver for us, as
Vivi already had enough to do. Aloqisaq got along famously with
her work until one day I tried to find a suit of underwear I
especially liked. I searched all over for it and finally asked her if
she knew what had become of it. Shyly she said she would bring it
to me next day. Upon further inquiry I learned that she had not
thought it dirty enough when I discarded it, so she decided to
wear it and make the washing really worth while.

12

When Knud was finally ready to leave for Ellesmere Land I
decided to accompany him part of the way. A number of years
ago Asayuk had found musk oxen across Smith Sound, and since
then the natives made a yearly pilgrimage to secure meat. We sent
out word to the north and south that we would both be gone
for a while and set out with Uvdluriark, our good helper at the
post.

The ice was solid and we made Cape Parry the first day.
Knud's dogs were fine, but vicious, and he could hardly approach
them himself. But this served a double purpose—it made them
excellent for hunting bears and keeping old women off his
sledge, for when an old woman asks to ride it is impossible to
deny her. One may be sure that if he refuses to let her ride she
will spread scandal about him and his team.

The first night we slept in a cave, and next day reached Netsilik, a famous Arctic community around which countless legends
and traditions have grown up. No other place has so many murders to its discredit, and upon the big stones outside the houses
may be seen the footprints of the famous conjurer, the angakok,

who is believed to have come here to escape from the devil, Tornarsuk. He had such power and strength that his feet made a deep impression in the stones for the skeptics to view.

At Netsilik lived old man Sorqaq whose fame had reached me before I came to Greenland. He had once been the greatest hunter and angakok in the tribe, and had never ceased to resent the invasion of natives from Admiralty Bay who had brought with them the kayak and the bow and arrow, and had so colored the lives of the people who had been here before them. Sorqaq never adopted the new ways, and consequently the newcomers had usurped a great deal of his glory. He was still, however, the best dog breeder of the tribe, and boasted a team of black dogs the superior of any man's. This had eased his passage into old age, and he did not complain.

When we arrived at Netsilik he was ailing. He had been out on a long hunting trip with a number of younger men to the far north—Lady Franklin Bay—where the houses Greely erected in 1883 were still the source of lumber and sledgewood for the natives. Sorqaq, as always, was far ahead of his companions, and they, suddenly surprised to see him driving back toward them, had questioned him. He admitted that he had come to an iceberg and driven his dogs around it, but forgot to straighten them out when he reached the other side, and they had completely circled it and backtracked on their course. This had been a crushing blow to the old man, who remarked:

"Such things are foolish. I never was foolish before. I must be growing old!"

He had decided to return home, because, he said, he had in his time seen many old men make fools of themselves, and he did not wish his own sons to laugh at him. When he was well enough to go hunting again, he determined always to go alone.

Mayark was my host at Netsilik. Knud told me that he combined more good and bad traits than any other man in the North. That evening we had a long talk, and Mayark advised me to marry since everyone knew that no man should be without a woman. He, it seemed, had just the girl for me. Over my protests he brought her forth.

In a whisk Arnanguaq was completely undressed, and her master stood her before me and pointed out, like a slave trader, her especial qualifications, leaving nothing to my imagination. It was a great recommendation, of course, that she was cross-eyed, which would make her the more valuable to me—I would not have to waste my time fighting over her. Her body was not without its virtues, and her manager would have us marry immediately.

I was both young and bashful, and was more embarrassed for the girl than for myself. Without giving too much offense, I tried to explain my reasons for not wanting to marry her, and finally lay down to sleep. Later I heard the girl whisper to her protector: "Do you think I should stay here, or get out and let him come to me?"

She went away, and I did not go to her.

My reputation as a doctor unfortunately followed me. But I was glad to be of such service as I might. I was asked to go to Ulugassat (Northumberland Island) to take a look at Sigdloo's wife. Sigdloo had been "number three man" with Peary, was one of the murderers of Uvisakavsik, and had taken Alakrasina, the worst of the murdered man's wives. She was an ill-tempered, hysterical female, and now, it seemed, her right arm was paralyzed. What could I do for this?

She had been Uvisakavsik's favorite wife until he grew tired of her. While she had lived with Uvisakavsik she had become pregnant, but foolishly denied it to the other women. Even long after they could see her condition she refused to admit it, and bragged that Uvisakavsik was such an excellent provider that she was merely growing fatter.

When her time came she had given birth to a boy, but to give truth to her lie she had strangled the child.

After her marriage to Sigdloo her arm commenced to wither and lose its vigor—it was the arm with which she had killed her child. I recommended massage, but at this she scoffed. While she had learned to sew with her left hand, she was such an unpleasant woman that Sigdloo had tried to get rid of her and given her away to other men. They always sent her back, and finally in order to avoid her, her poor husband spent most of his time with his neighbors. His beautiful hair and pleasant manners made him popular with the ladies, while his prowess as a hunter and his reputation as a companion of Peary made him a favorite with the men.

Sigdloo met Knud at Odark's house, and asked Knud for his advice. Should he and Odark shoot the brother of Uvisakavsik in order to forestall his revenge? Or what?

Knud would not have been the man he was if he had not long ago foreseen this. He had already talked with Samik, the brother of the murdered man, and explained to him that there were to be no murders for revenge. If Samik killed a man, would not he then be murdered? And if someone killed him, what would become of his little boy? The child would be fatherless and would not have the opportunity to buy a gun from us for many years.

Knud had promised to tell the same thing to Odark and Sigdloo, which he did. They all agreed it would be best to do no more killing, as they both had wives. Besides, Knud pointed out, Sigdloo's gun, given him by Peary, had already been dignified by one murder, and that seemed to satisfy him.

At this time of year nearly everyone for many miles around was gathered at Pituravik and Karrat, an excellent locality for spring walrus hunting. Many of the Eskimos who had been with Whitney had neglected their winter caches, and were trying at this late date to make up for their derelictions. We stopped and talked and bargained with the natives, and while there Ukuyak and his wife came rushing up from the south. He, too, was one of the men who had been with Peary, and there was a hearty reunion of the four hunters, Sigdloo, Odark, Pualuna (whose two wives were frightfully jealous of each other) and Ukuyak, whose wife, Atitak, was very pregnant indeed. The other three agreed that Ukuyak, despite his youth and smallness, was far more clever than they, was never weary and always up first in the morning. His dogs were famous and his ability as a hunter unsurpassed.

Ukuyak was in a hurry to reach home in time for the birth of his child. Women in the Arctic never know when their children are due, but there were unmistakable indications that Ukuyak's wife did not have long to wait.

We set off for Neqé, our final destination, Ukuyak and his wife as well as several other travelers in our party. We were now in the northern reaches of Polar Eskimo land, which is divided into three sections defined by their relation to the southwest wind which prevails over the whole of Greenland. The Eskimos who live at Cape York and in Melville Bay are called Nigerdleet —Those Who Live on the Windy Side. Immediately north are the Akuarmiut—Those Who Live in Between. This section includes the land where our post at Thule was situated. And north of Cape Parry live the Oqonermiut—Those Who Live on the Leeside.

Those terms are definite and characteristic, but there are many severe gales on the Leeside. Without warning one intercepted us on the way to Neqé. There were no clouds in the sky, but suddenly far out to sea the snow was whisked into the air, and before we had time to make any preparations the storm was upon us, the atmosphere an unbreathable mixture of snow and blinding ice. My dogs were whipped off their feet and, in spite of my frantic efforts, gathered about the leeside of my sledge. My companions were blotted out by the storm, and I crouched there quite alone, wondering what to do. At last I crawled—it was impossible to stand—ahead and came upon the rest of the party. They were all gathered together holding a confab. When I was near enough to make them hear I yelled as loud as I could to ask their advice.

They had no time for my troubles. Atitak was in labor.

We tried to build an igloo for her, but the snow was so thin that as soon as blocks were cut they were worn out by the wind and blown to pieces. Somehow I got a glimpse of poor Atitak's face, and I saw on it all the pain and distress a woman feels under such circumstances. She seemed to expect me and Knud to do something for her. And yet what could we do? There was no hope of building a shelter, and it was out of the question for her to undress.

It was a desperate moment and we had to employ desperate measures. We placed Atitak on the leeside of the sledge, and a number of the men grouped themselves upon it to break the wind. We split the woman's pants only as much as was necessary. The bag of water had already broken, and I knew that the moment had come.

Eskimo women always stand on their knees when giving birth, their husbands supporting and embracing them from the back and helping to expel the fetus. This was Ukuyak's first child and he had no experience, so Qolugtinguaq, who had several children to his credit, took over the task and pressed the baby out in no time at all. Atitak snatched up the child inside her coat, wrapped some skins about him—it was a man child—and soon had him warm and snug. The storm abated somewhat, we emptied the load from Knud's sledge and bade him drive Atitak across to Neqé at once to get her inside a shelter. When we finally reached the village we found her well and gay, and the boy already slung in her hood.

Neqé is the gayest place in the Arctic during the walrus-hunting season. When we arrived the sea was open after the storm, but it would freeze over again in a short while.

I stayed at the house of Iggianguarssuaq and his wife, Inuaho. One day she came running into the house excitedly shouting something I could not understand. She beckoned me to come out, and then I knew. The sun had come back!

We could not see it, but its rays were pale gold on the cliffs. I had an almost unconquerable desire to climb the mountain and face the sun itself, but I knew it would be gone before I could get there.

Two days later we saw the sun low and swollen on the horizon. Everyone rushed out of his house to greet it, took off his coat and mittens, as is the custom, and thrust his bare hands high above his head. Thus we stood bareheaded and exposed, though it was still bitter cold, for as long as the sun favored us that first day. The children commenced to cry, but no one paid any attention to them, since everyone knew that he who exposed his face and hands to the sun on the first day of its appearance would be alive at least until next year at the same time. If he failed—no one would venture to predict what might happen.

While we waited for the ice we played all manner of games, including one not unlike American football. In former times it had been a more strenuous game: the ball, made of the head of a seal stuffed with grass, was placed at an equal distance between two villages, and the inhabitants of both villages charged upon it. Combatants had often been killed, but rules had now been formulated which prevented such slaughter. Men and women both took part, the girls with their babies in the hoods and the children having the time of their lives.

As a matter of fact, the children in this tribe were early introduced into the life of the community. One little girl of perhaps fourteen months, who could not yet walk, was a passionate smoker of her parents' pipes. Her mother and father were delighted with her precocity and never failed to show her off.

At Neqé also lived a remarkable old lady, Kullabak, who was the talk of the village. She had been married to a very poor hunter who had fortunately died, and she had moved in with a much younger and better hunter. But before she could make this advantageous change, she had to do away with her son.

I never saw the boy, but from what I was told he must have been a holy terror. At any rate, no one blamed her for the drastic measures she had resorted to.

The boy's debut in terrorism had taken place at Cape York where he collected a load of rotten birds' eggs and hid them high up on a hillside. Then one day he became loudly hysterical and shouted: "A ship! A ship! A big ship is coming!" Magic words, of course, to natives who were seldom visited by outsiders.

They all hurried up on the hillside to get a look at the boat. Meanwhile the boy crouched behind a rock, and when his friends were close enough he jumped out and pelted them with his peculiarly offensive cache. This naturally reflected upon Kullabak's house, and she had tried to apologize, but being a lone woman without a husband there was not much she could say to reëstablish herself.

So she asked Mayark to help her get rid of the boy, and Mayark took him up onto the glacier and pushed him down in a crevasse. That, by all rights, should have been the end of him. Kullabak went into traditional mourning, but her mourning was pretty effectively interrupted when the boy came walking into the house. By some miracle he had escaped death in the fall, and had followed the crevasse to its portal near the sea.

After that no one dared touch him, and the boy played all manner of tricks to revenge himself. He was a big, strapping youngster, but he had no hunting gear of his own and had to borrow what he wanted from the hunters while they slept. One day, while Mayark was away on a hunting trip, he went to Mayark's house and told his wife that he had followed Mayark some distance and that when they had parted, Mayark had told him that he might stay in his house and take all a husband's privileges. Mayark's wife was an obedient, loving wife, and not until her husband returned home did she realize that she had been tricked. All the villagers had the laugh on Mayark.

The boy also helped himself from various caches and never took the trouble to close them. His mother was at her wit's end, and finally decided that if she wanted to save the honor of her house she must do something desperate. One night while he was asleep with his head protruding beyond the end of the ledge, she made a sealskin-line noose, slipped it over his head and pulled it tight.

Thus ended the criminal pranks of one young man, and his mother was highly honored for her good deed. Now she was remarried, and her great, booming voice was always an asset at parties.

13

Knud Rasmussen left me at Neqé when he went on north for musk oxen. Two brothers were to have accompanied him, but at the last minute the elder discovered that his dogs were in no condition for the strenuous trip. His wife, however, had been counting on the trip and the musk-ox skins resulting from it and, rather than disappoint her—he was much in love with her, her husband sent her along with his younger brother, Inukitsork.

This so-called wife-trading among the Eskimos is an interesting custom. Most persons believe it results from a lack of morality, but this is decidedly untrue. I have never met a people with a more strict moral code, though it is a different code from that of the white race.

An Eskimo's love for his wife is quite apart from the urgencies of his sex life. If a man desires a woman and has no wife of his own, he may borrow another man's wife. It would be impossible for him, however, to go to a married woman and suggest that she sleep with him without first consulting her husband.

There is also a purely practical and economical advantage in wife-trading for the hunter. If he goes alone, he must spend a great portion of his time building an igloo, cutting ice and melting it. At night he must return to a cold shelter, and he has no means of drying and tanning his skins. Instead, his evenings must be spent mending boots and drying clothes, and he must carry plenty of spare clothes with him. However, if he brings a woman along, all this is quite different. He builds her an igloo, and she takes care of everything else. She has the house warm when he returns, and his food steaming hot. His boots and mittens are dry and soft and mended, so that he need not cart along many changes. And while he is out hunting the woman dries the skins on a frame inside the igloo, scrapes them and removes all fat and meat, so that they can be folded together and he may return home with thirty or forty instead of the ten raw skins he would otherwise be able to haul. This is perhaps the greatest advantage in having a woman along—besides this, she can hunt rabbits and take care of the meat caches. Oh, there are many fine things about a woman.

Now, it may happen that a man needs skins, and his wife is unfit for travel. She may be ill, or pregnant or caring for a tiny baby. How much better for him, then, that he arrange to leave her with a friend while he is away and, in exchange, take his friend's wife along with him.

The Eskimos believe that the human animal can be trusted in any relationship save the sexual one. Men and women may have the best intentions regarding abstinence, but when the cravings and desires come upon them they are helpless. Realizing this, they make and demand no promises of each other, but so arrange their lives that they can never be criticized for what they do. When the hunters come home, the wives return happily to their own husbands, who listen with amusement to the stories the women have to tell of the trip.

Furthermore, I have never heard any obscene talk or unclean stories, because everything that is human is natural, and the refinements and perversions of sex have never occurred to anyone.

After Knud left we learned of a horrible disaster which had befallen our friends Pualuna and Qolugtinguaq.

At Sarfalik, where they lived, a little glacier slopes down to the sea, and from days of old children have used it for coasting. The sea is never frozen over there as the current is swift around the point. It is especially exciting for the boys and girls to slide to the very edge of the glacier: the girls scream out at the danger and the boys feel proud and strong in turning and averting disaster at the last moment.

Qolugtinguaq had a fine son, a really beautiful boy, who had just killed his first seal—the first step toward becoming a man. Pualuna's two daughters had reached the age at which they began to look at a boy with quickening interest. Meeting at Sarfalik after a long separation, the children, who were cousins, were delighted to see each other. The boy took the girls to the top of the hill and put them on his toboggan—a sealskin. The girls held up the forepart so that they could stick on, and they slid down the glacier over and over again, the girls yelling and the boy roaring with delight. Each time they came nearer the brink, but their parents stood by and, remembering that they had done the same thing as children, did not interfere with the pleasure. Instead, they hailed the children and shouted, "Fine! Fine!" which, of course, made the boy all the more daring.

And then, with the parents looking on, the boy decided to show the girls his best stunt, and not turn the sledge until he reached the very edge of the ice. He either forgot, or lost control, for the three children shot into the water and were never seen again.

When we heard the news we were all silent, though such disasters are far from uncommon where the natives live always on the very brink of disaster and sudden death. One of them finally said:

"Why are we situated in a corner of the world like this? We all know it is the most wonderful of all countries, and life is better here than anywhere else, but we must pay for its beauty time after time. Those who are old would rather die than make the Great Nature so hungry for human beings that it takes our children."

All the people felt a real and abiding sorrow. Semigaq, an old woman, told us that she had been expecting some disaster after the birth which had taken place out on the ice—everyone had talked while the woman was in labor and had not done what was to be done after the birth. And Qolugtinguaq had assisted the woman instead of her husband. Added to this, the newborn child had been dropped on the ice, and it stood to reason that such things could not go unpunished. Qolugtinguaq had been warned before, she said, that he should not interfere with other people's affairs.

Poor Qolugtinguaq! He took his dogs and, at the end of the prescribed mourning period, drove away.

"I am going far to forget my sorrow," he said. "I felt last night that I did not care for my other children, and I had better leave!"

Months later we heard that he had been seen by bear hunters in Melville Bay, and next year that he had traveled far south and was living at Ikerasarssuk. He lived for a while with an elderly, good-for-nothing woman who bore him a child. The child was black, according to rumor, and died at birth. After Qolugtinguaq finally returned home, and I mentioned the incident to him, he said that he was not surprised. "I was in a fog the whole time," he said. "Perhaps she is not the only one who had babies. I have been at many places and there were many women everywhere."

Eskimos always remain in mourning for five days. The women sit with the pants of the deceased on their heads, never sleeping, never lying down, so that if the departed children return they may find their way home. The children did not return, and after the five days I went to visit the bereaved people.

Alinaluk, Pualuna's first wife and the mother of the two girls, stood upon the slope where her children had coasted to their deaths.

"Don't pity me," she said. "I cannot bear it. I am born to un-happiness and am empty of tears. Talk to me of many things, but do not pity me."

Her sorrow was touching, and her people tried to comfort her. Pualuna's second wife cried ceaselessly, as though she could not understand that the days of mourning were over. That night Pualuna came home bringing a barbed seal, and gave me a piece of skin for lines. He told of his experience in musk-ox hunting, and of having lost six dogs. Then he looked at the weeping woman and the one without tears. He sighed and asked me to be patient with his women: "They are great followers after women's ways, but I am not in a mood to blame them." That was his only reference to what had happened.

In the other house Torngé, Qolugtinguaq's wife, sat sewing when I entered.

"Hereby somebody comes visiting," I said.

"Oh, is somebody out to look at people? Unfortunately you did wrong coming in here. Nobody at all is at home—only women, and you had better get out as soon as possible."

"Are you alone?"

"The Terrible has gone out hunting," she said. Dutiful wives always refer to their husbands as "the Terrible," "the Dreadful," "the Frightful," etc., to signify how frightening and impressive their husbands are.

Torngé asked if I desired anything to eat. I said no, and we sat silent for a while. Then she said: "No one wants to talk in this house. No words are to be heard here and only tears to be seen. That can be no pleasure for a mighty man."

When I left she said: "I thank you for coming." The fact that I could say nothing to comfort her was proof to her of my own grief and sympathy.

After her daughters' death Alinaluk never smiled again. She still had one baby daughter who was learning to walk, and a few weeks later she asked her mother-in-law to look after the child as she wanted to drive to Etah for some things she had left there. She took seven dogs and drove off. Everyone knew she was an excellent driver, but she never returned. After a while one of her dogs came back, the dog which belonged to the baby.

It was said afterward that she had been taken by the Inland people, the mysterious and fantastic inhabitants of the big glacier. These people are, of course, the Canadian Indians who, after many, many years, have assumed a mystic reality in the minds of the Eskimos.

Pualuna drove desperately across the countryside in search of Alinaluk, but found no trace of her. Possibly she had descended from the glacier at Cape Alexander and driven into the sea to join her children. Perhaps the dog had had the good fortune to slip out of his traces before being dragged to the bottom with the rest of the team, but the Eskimos believed she had sent the dog back to prove that she had been kidnaped. No one ever believed she had been drowned. No, she must have been taken by cannibals from Ellesmere Land, Inland people, or ghosts. The fact that the little daughter commenced to cry on the very evening of the day her mother departed was a sure sign that the woman had met a terrible fate.

Tribal custom forbade mourning for poor Alinaluk. If she were not dead, it would certainly bring evil to her. Only the little girl, Maktak, cried and was never happy again. Her condition might have been the result of the stepmother's treatment of her, of course. Her stepmother was a kind, goodhearted woman, but did not regret the fact that there was now only one wife in the house.

It seemed to be written that this should be a season of dreadful accidents. While we waited at Neqé for the ice to improve I learned more of the people and their folkways than ever before. After all, this was a large community and something seemed to be happening at every hour of the day.

Among the natives was the man Angudluk who was lame as the result of once freezing his legs. He could go out in his kayak in the summer, or drive his dogs if there was someone along to untangle his traces. His wife, who was a clever driver, often accompanied him and, when the two were in a party of hunters, collected her share of the game.

One day while the two of them were out together they left their thirteen-year-old son at home. A favorite pastime of the children is to hang themselves by their hoods. When the hoods tighten about their necks blood is kept from their heads and they eventually lose consciousness. The other children in the house take them down as soon as their faces turn purple.

The state of unconsciousness is so delightful, the children say, that they play this game at every opportunity, over and over again. They played it on the day Angudluk and his wife were away.

Angudluk's son was the largest child in the group. One after another he hung the smaller children up and lifted them down when they were purple, and laid them on the ledge to recover. When all of them had had their turn he helped them to hang him up. Eventually he grew purple in the face and kicked his legs as the signal to be taken down. The children tried to lift him off the hook, but he was too heavy. They made every effort and still could not lift him, and, as he soon stopped kicking and threshing about, the children forgot about him and ran out-of-doors to play, leaving him hanging in front of the window over the door.

When the sledges came home the mother cared for the dogs and Angudluk, cold from sitting all day, hurried inside. He crawled through the tunneled entrance and saw the feet of his son hanging down over the doorhole.

There followed another five-day period of mourning. No one was allowed to leave Neqé, and all the sledges were turned front end toward the houses so that no one could be suspected of leaving.

We saw the sad little funeral procession. Only the best skins were used as a coffin. The father drove the dogs up into the hills, and some of them turned stubborn and bolted. Everyone had to stop and punish the dogs, whose howling added to the dolefulness of the occasion. The poor family, whose privations were stringent enough already, left many gifts for the boy, especially a little gun he had wanted, a big knife, and the pipes and tobacco belonging to the whole family—he would be there a long time and need all these things. All the mittens which had been used in constructing his stony grave were left also.

When the time of mourning was over the ice was perfect for walrus hunting. Some six miles from shore was a thin layer just strong enough to support a man and brittle enough to permit the walrus to break through without difficulty.

One moment the expanse of ice will be smooth, and the next the huge head of a walrus is seen poking up through it. Then the hunter must move quickly and hurl his harpoon into the head before it is withdrawn. The best points to strike are the tough, thick upper lip or the neck. But the harpoon must penetrate deep enough for it to turn and stick.

As soon as the animal is wounded it disappears and tries to get away. But the line on the harpoon is intended to prohibit this. In summer, the end of the line is attached to a bladder, but in the winter there is a noose on it. The hunter carries a spike mounted on the end of a big stick almost as tall as himself. He must quickly hitch the noose over the stick and thrust the spike into the ice. Then, when the walrus bolts, the line draws tight. The man must throw his whole weight against the spike, and often I have seen men severely hurt as the line snapped against it.

Top. NATIVES HARPOONING A SEAL, IN ORDER TO PULL IT ACROSS AN EXPANSE OF WATER WHERE THE ICE HAS SEPARATED.

Bottom. HAULING A WALRUS OUT OF THE WATER NEAR THULE. NOTE HOW THE BEAST HAS BEEN TIED TO THE ICE AT THE LOWER LEFT.

After the animal is exhausted the hunter may tie it to the ice in the same manner as dogs are hitched. The enraged beast usually cracks up the ice all around, but the hunter can now use his spear to kill it when it comes up.

I stayed at Neqé for several weeks and learned to know the people well. The young people always talked most, and the older ones criticized them for it, for it is not well for young people to tell of their exploits in the presence of their elders.

And yet, inexperienced as I was in their ways, I could tell that all was not well with these people. Another strange incident occurred which made everyone realize that evil spirits were at work.

At Pituravik, a settlement near-by, there is a brook which flows in winter and summer alike. No one understands the cause of its not freezing over unless there are volcanic forces at work beneath the glacier. The brook is called "Sersinerssuaq" (the constant stream). The natives take great pride in it and regard it as a minor miracle. Suddenly this year the water turned brown as coffee. The taste was unchanged, but no matter how long one allowed the water to stand in a pail it remained brown.

There could be no doubt that something had to be done to exorcise the devil at work.

14

The old man, Sorqaq, who was also hunting in the district, announced that he would attempt a journey to the nether world to ascertain the reason for the tragedies. Sorqaq was believed to have put an end to the last epidemic before it had destroyed the whole tribe. He had met the devil and conquered him—perhaps he could do it again.

At any rate, his preparations for the descent proved his honesty. He fasted until his interior was completely cleaned out, examining his excrement until he was satisfied with his state. After three days he announced himself ready for the journey, and the time of departure was set for the following night. The old man meanwhile climbed high into the mountains seeking solitude to formulate his speech to the spirits and to train himself to swim through the rocks—which he would most certainly have to penetrate in order to meet the devil.

A huge igloo was constructed by adding many blocks of snow to the largest house in the settlement. Several men worked at it, and the snowblocks were cut by the elders who realized the seriousness of the undertaking. After it was finished the inside was draped with a tapestry of old tent skins. Sorqaq inspected the stage which was to witness his marvels, said nothing, and departed for further meditation.

Presently the natives were requested to gather and were led to their places by Krilerneq, Sorqaq's assistant. Krilerneq himself was an old man, but with the aid of a cane he was as strong and spry as anyone. His eyes burned with his fervor, his gestures were quick, his walk nervous.

Like a stage star making an appearance in an ancient vehicle, Sorqaq was the last man to enter the house, and he was announced three times before he finally arrived. He greeted us all by saying that we were a pack of fools to have come: what he proposed to do was nothing, and furthermore he could not even do it.

We all accepted this as the modesty it undoubtedly was; then he walked up to me and asked me to leave:

"This is nothing for a man like you to look at. I am only a big liar, and even if these idiots are stupid enough to believe in me, I never expected you to stand for it. I am only a foolish old man, and what happens here has nothing to do with the truth."

"Even so, I should like to listen to your wisdom."

"Well, well," he replied, "if a man is born white he may still be born stupid."

I assured him of the truth of that statement, but he shook his head sadly and went over to the ledge.

"Oh, only a little lie is on my tongue," he murmured. "A funny little lie that I may give sound to and try to fool you with!"

He peeled off his clothes, which were taken by Krilerneq, and sat stark naked. Krilerneq then took up several sealskin lines and bound him tight, tying his arms beside his body and binding his legs together, the thongs cutting deep into his muscles. The old man held himself rigid during this process. Occasionally a deep sigh escaped him.

When there were no more lines at hand, Krilerneq placed his drum and a large section of dried sealskin beside him on the ledge. The lights were extinguished, and the only illumination came from one tiny flame. We could barely make out each other's faces; we could see nothing distinctly.

Then Krilerneq took his place among us to make sure that no one approached the angakok, for it would mean death.

After a few minutes of utter silence we heard Sorqaq's voice in song. It was weak and quavery, but slowly grew stronger and seemed to emanate from different parts of the igloo. After a moment we heard the voice of the drum, as if beaten by a padded stick, and slowly its sound, too, grew in volume, until the house was filled with the song, the crashing of the drum and the rattling of the dry skin, now over our heads, now beneath our feet!

The noise was almost unbearable and I took hold of Krilerneq's arm, pretending fright. Actually I wanted to ascertain whether or not he was contributing to the noise. Obviously he was not.

How long the din lasted I am unable to tell. I remember that when it finally calmed I felt as if I had been dreaming. By now all of us had joined in Sorqaq's song, but slowly it seemed that the voice of the angakok was fading away. At last I definitely felt that it reached us through the walls of the igloo, perhaps from above or below. And then suddenly we could hear him no more.

None of us realized what had happened or when it had happened, but when Krilerneq turned up the flame so that it was possible to see a little clearer—there was no Sorqaq on the ledge.

The drum was there and the skin was there, but that was all. I was intoxicated by the heat and the odor of bodies and the song, and perhaps I did not examine the igloo carefully enough. But I did look at the tapestry to see if he could be hidden behind it, and he was not.

All of us sat there singing as we had before. Ecstasy was upon the face of every man and woman. Their cheeks were swollen, their eyes bright and shining. Their mouths hung open, and their bodies were naked from the waist up in order to endure the heat. They swayed back and forth to the rhythm of the song, and their heads marked the double beats. No one seemed to see anything, but merely to use his eyes as beacon lights. In the middle of the floor was Krilerneq writhing and twisting like a dancer.

Beside me sat a young girl, Ivaloo. Her naked body was pressed against mine, and her strong young scent swept over me. I tried to speak to her, but she did not hear. Instead, her eyes followed Krilerneq directly in front of us. Her long hair sprayed loose from the knot on her head, and swung from side to side as she sang. The rhythmic swish of her hair made me as senseless as the rest of them.

Ivaloo was married to a clever young hunter, and while he was away she played the whole day long with her friends. Now she was no longer a child, but a grown woman endowed with the witchcraft of her tribe. Her face was a mask, and occasionally her voice rose above the song in a wild screech, her eyes always upon the swaying Krilerneq whose madness drove the audience into the hysteria of cattle before a pack of wolves.

When I looked into the faces of these people I could scarcely recognize them as the calm, quiet friends who came down to Thule to trade with us. Whence has come this leaning toward mysticism? No one knows the origin of the Eskimo, but it is not difficult to trace them to a moderate climate; many of their traditions derive from the worship of trees, snakes and frogs. Perhaps they were Asiatics originally and have drawn from the Far East their reliance upon the supernatural. Here I saw them caught up by a spirit which they could not possibly understand, the prey to emotions and passions which in everyday life would puzzle them.

Suddenly one of the men, Krisuk, went out of his head. Unable to contain himself to the regular rhythm of the service he leapt to his feet, crying like a raven and howling like a wolf. He ran amuck, and the audience had to defend itself against his attacks. He rushed at me, I pushed him away and he fell over Ivaloo. With a quick move of his hands he tore her boots and pants completely off, but she, almost as wild as the man, screamed not in fear but in ecstasy. They began to yell in a tongue I could not understand—certainly it was not the usual Eskimo language. Angakoks are not permitted to employ the commonplace terms for things and people, for it would bring disaster upon the objects mentioned. But everyone seemed to understand what was said— and if there is such a thing as speaking in tongues I heard it then.

No longer able to bear the confinement, Krisuk dove straight through the wall of the igloo, leaving a hole for air which was much needed. We could hear his shrill voice far out on the ice. Someone shut the door, and soon everyone in the room was stripped.

The song continued and I fell completely under the power of the spirit. No longer was I able to observe dispassionately what occurred. Ivaloo lay naked across me, and I could feel someone else chewing my hair, clawing my face. The noise, the odor of bodies and the mystery of the moment caught me completely unprepared.

Then suddenly all was changed. Krilerneq, who had been the leader of the madness, announced that Sorqaq was trying to return.

He beseeched us all to take our original positions and told us to sit up and sing. No thoughts should concern us but those of the angakok who was at this moment fighting his way up through the granite beneath the igloo. We were as yet unable to hear him, but Krilerneq, who had himself made the pilgrimage a number of times, said that he could feel his imminent arrival, and complained over the suffering he was undergoing. Krilerneq, being the assistant, shared the travail of his friend who had to swim through the rocks as if they were water.

During this interval Krisuk returned—a quite different and chastened Krisuk. He was naked and shivering, and his ecstasy of a few minutes ago dissipated. Looking for the warmest spot in the igloo, he dived between two fat, perspiring women, causing them to squeal when his body touched their hot bellies. Ivaloo, crawling over me, complained because the intruder had returned, and called him all the names she could think of, but was interrupted by Krilerneq who suddenly declaimed in a sonorous and terrible voice:

"Quiet! Quiet! The shadow is ripened. The shadow is ripened."

Angakoks are not permitted to pronounce the word "man"—in their mouths the term must be "shadow." They must also say "ripen" instead of "come" or "arrive."

We all listened, and as from afar off we could hear Sorqaq's voice. Krilerneq extinguished the light completely, since no one must look upon the angakok "muscle naked"—he has been forced to leave his skin when descending into the ground—lest he die.

And now there was pandemonium. None of us knew which was up and which was down. I remember it all as a black fog which engulfed me.

Krilerneq told us that Sorqaq was coming closer and closer, and we, too, could hear the angakok's voice. Krilerneq explained to us that Sorqaq was having difficulty in finding the house as someone had left it in his absence and returned.

But magically we knew at last that he had returned—from the sky or from the depths his "shadow" had "ripened." The igloo reverberated with the noise of his drum and the rattle of the crackling sealskin sometimes over our heads, sometimes under our feet. I raised my hand to try to grasp the skin and received such a blow on my arm that the bone was almost shattered. Hell itself had suddenly come to earth.

And then it all stopped. Krilerneq murmured a long rigmarole, and the igloo was quiet save for the crying of the children. They may have been crying the whole time, but no one had known it. Krilerneq's droning voice prayed to the supposedly present angakok to learn what secrets he had learned concerning the cause of the accidents.

Sorqaq's voice answered: "Three deaths are still to come. The Great Nature is embarrassed by the white men who have come to live with us, and refuses to betray the real reason for its anger. But no great disaster will come to us if the women of the tribe refrain from eating meat of the female walrus until the sun sets again in the fall."

The angakok had done his duty and the performance was over. I have no idea how long it had lasted. Someone brought fire from the next igloo and lighted the lamps.

There was Sorqaq sitting on the ledge still wrapped in his many strands of sealskin. I did not have the opportunity of examining him to see whether he had been free and bound again. He was extremely weak, covered with sweat, and spittle ran down his chest. Krilerneq warned me not to touch Sorqaq as the fire from the earth was still in him, and would be until he moved again.

He sat quiet until Krilerneq removed the lines, then fell back and lay in a coma. At last he opened his eyes. His voice was weak and his mouth dry. He tried to smile as he saw me.

"Just lies and bunk, the whole thing!" he said. "Do not believe in anything. I am no angakok. I speak nothing but lies. The wisdom of the forefathers is not in me!"

He fell back again, and we all assured each other that we had indeed witnessed an amazing thing and been in the presence of truth itself.

Next day I tried to talk with the natives about yesterday's performance, but they were mute. Ivaloo and my hostess, Inuaho, said it made them realize I was a white man—an Eskimo would not want to discuss things which were never mentioned, only done.

Slowly the gathering at Neqé thinned out. The walrus season was nearly over, and it was time to go to such nomadic homes as they had. The men, officially, decide where to go, but never make a move without consulting their women. If they are out of sinew with which to sew, they must go where narwhales are to be captured. Those who need bearskin for pants must move near Melville Bay. If foxskins are needed, they must remain near bird cliffs.

In the following years a new system evolved. Formerly Cape York was the only trading post, but since we had established a post at Thule many of the Eskimos settled down in near-by communities. Their demand for civilized goods and implements grew greater year by year.

Eskimo communities are seldom large, since they have no official chief or commander, but at each community there is one great and mighty man. He is invariably the best hunter, and the rest are little better than his servants. He has, of course, no real power over them, but he is always up first in the morning, the first man out on the ice, the one who makes all the plans for hunting trips—and the lesser men respect his wisdom and intuition.

Two such great hunters never remain in the same community. They may be the best of friends, but no one place is big enough for both of them. Only Angutidluarssuk, the greatest of all the hunters, paid no attention to boundaries. Wherever he happened to be he was commander, and provided more fresh meat than anyone.

This year the three brothers of the murdered Uvisakavsik chose the same location. While there was peace in the tribe, brought about by Knud, they nevertheless felt there could be no harm in sticking together.

The murderer surrounded himself in another community with his brothers and brothers-in-law. One might as well be careful.

15

It was almost spring when Knud returned to Neqé from the north, loaded with skins and enough musk-ox meat for the whole tribe. His cries and his laughter preceded him and resounded over the whole place. We all felt that we were better off when he was with us. His was a tangible force to which we might cling in the wilderness. We played games in his honor, and he was always foremost in every kind of sport. Unfortunately we had a near accident.

A boy walked far out to sea and hid behind an ice hummock. Then he jumped up holding a bearskin over his head with which to tease the dogs.

Such excitement I have seldom seen. Here was an opportunity to prove to the womenfolk who had the best dogs. The animals were hurriedly hitched to the sledges—probably thirty teams in all—and we were off, shouting our bear signals and laughing and lashing the dogs. My team got tangled up with two others, but finally we neared the camouflaged young man.

The boy was to keep the bearskin over him until the first team was almost upon him, then discard it and save himself. But he wanted to give an especially fine performance, and ran about with the pelt still over his head, dogs hanging onto it ferociously. Many of them bit through it, and the blood streamed from him. I finally got him free and drove him home while the others remained and watched the dogfights which resulted. As soon as the boy's wounds were healed he was at it again.

Among all his myriad activities, Knud was writing a book concerning the traditions, myths and folklore of the natives. Born in the Arctic and familiar with the language, he was better fitted than anyone else for the work.

Before we returned to Thule he wanted to talk with a certain old woman, Semigaq, who was wise in the ways of her people— and a great gossip besides. "Where is my old sweetheart?" he asked, going from house to house. No one would answer him until he inquired at a big gathering held at one of the homes. One of the men answered:

"You see, it is like this: Old Semigaq has very few relatives here and she is alone most of the time. She went out to trap foxes some time ago, and her traps are a long way from here. She walks with a little sledge, using it both as a support and as a conveyance for her pelts. We all like Semigaq and pity her because of her age. When she did not return after the last gale we talked it over and had great pity for her, but we decided that instead of going to find her, we had better use all our pity for her now and then never feel sorry for her any more."

This haphazard method of caring for old, lonely people was not in accord with our scheme of things, and we hurried out to look for her. The snow had begun to drift and my dogs were difficult to manage, so after a while I decided to seek shelter in a cave along the cliffs where Semigaq was known to keep her traps. I drove my dogs up over the ice foot and into the cave, and there I found the poor old woman.

She had not been especially comfortable, but she was at least still alive. She had caught, and eaten, three foxes which she was very sorry had been dead when she found them, since she had torn the pelts in skinning them. She had wanted them for her grandson. She had no sleeping bag, but was thankful for her sledge; she could sleep on that. Her strength was exhausted, but her appetite was enormous, and the casual observer might have thought she had only been out for a walk and got a little chilly.

She had not, however, wasted her time during the storm. All her life she had been a great angakok, and here in the cave she had heard many voices and talked with the spirits of people long dead. She had gleaned much information about the living which would enable her to shame them.

When I brought her back to the settlement Knud Rasmussen was angry because of the natives' treatment of her and ordered all the women to sew her a new dress. She was overwhelmed with new clothing, and said that she could never remember having looked so well.

Next day we started for home, and old Semigaq, perhaps because we had rescued her and expressed more concern over her than had her own people for many years, decided to go with us. She climbed on Knud's sledge and refused to get off, sitting upon, and smashing, his camera. When he seemed perturbed over this she immediately took the offensive and scolded him for fooling around with things which could not bear the weight of an old and half-starved woman.

Many sledges followed us to Thule. The natives were on the way to their summer places, and wanted to trade with us. We had few things left with which to trade, but everyone was satisfied. "It is nice to live in a country with a store," they said.

One of them came to us and complained: "Your stuff is too cheap! When we had to wait for many years for the whaling ships, and when we had to give all the foxskins we owned for a knife, we were more pleased by the possession of the knife. Now every boy can own a knife, and they are too common."

Old man Panigpak, a man with a reputation for ingenuity and long trips, came from a great distance to trade. He secured what he wanted and, as I had a few knives left, asked for one of them. In exchange he took five fox pelts from his bag and gave them to me.

"You are mistaken," I said. "A knife does not even cost as much as one fox!"

He smiled in his mild way: "I am sorry. My tongue is going to protest against a white man. Perhaps it may fall out, but nevertheless I am right and must speak. You cannot know that I have been without a big knife for a whole year and have been missing it terribly. That is why I give you so many skins."

We continued the discussion in our sitting room. In line with Eskimo logic, goods possess a value according to the need of the buyer rather than the scarcity or abundance of the supply.

"A thing may have no value," he said, "but I need it, and I pay for what I need."

I could not make him understand me. His idea was to let the purchaser decide the price. Many others said that they would certainly have appreciated their goods more if they had been more expensive—a psychology which some of our modern, fashionable stores realize to be sound for persons of our own race.

16

The inhabitants of Thule must travel to the coast in order to catch little auks, and since there is one special season of the year for it, nearly all of us went together. Vivi and Aloqisaq went along with us, but life in the open did not agree with Vivi, the southerner, and she returned home.

I stayed with the family of Uvdluriark, whose young step-daughter, Mequpaluk, had given me the mittens. She repaired my boots and mended my clothes when necessary. She was a handsome girl, but her own clothes were so shabby that her body showed through in many places. It was strange to see her in a household which, aside from herself, was so affluent. But her father would have it no other way. "When she is married," Uvdluriark grinned, "it is up to her husband to dress her." She was an excellent worker, and her devotion to her younger brothers was touching. Whatever I paid her for her services she always gave to them, and would never eat at my house without hoarding the scraps for the small ones at home.

Knud Rasmussen remained at home and entertained his old ladies with afternoon teas while they regaled him with stories. Semigaq became a member of our household, and made herself useful by consulting her various ghosts concerning the future. Most of the time her guesses were lucky.

Knud, who had carried her to Thule on his sledge, had to furnish her with sleeping skins. In the first place, she owned almost nothing, and in the second, she fancied that the man who brought her should take care of her. "Perhaps you have no skins," she said, grinning toothlessly.

He gave her his own sleeping bag.

He regretted it later, for she filled it with more lice than any of us had ever seen. Still, lice are not too terrible. In fact, it seems to me that only people who have never had them really fear them. I will admit that in the summer their attacks are troublesome. But in the winter, when one lies in his sleeping bag and it is too cold to sleep, they are not particularly annoying— they keep one company of a sort.

They can be disposed of easily by having the women look you over. It is considered quite elegant and in the height of fashion when one feels a louse biting to indicate the spot with his finger, bend over, and let a woman pick it out. It is also possible for her to reveal her emotions toward the man in so doing. If she crushes the insect between her fingers or drops it in the lamp flame, she is merely being courteous. But if she cracks it between her teeth and eats it, that is a sure sign she looks with favor upon the man.

But Knud had a real problem. Semigaq was obviously in our house to stay, so he commanded her to bathe. She had the dignity of many years upon her shoulders and had done many foolish things, so she meekly surrendered to the bath. Then he ordered her hair combed.

This was out of the question, as it had not been untangled for many years, and was caked with dirt and oil and whatever else may collect in an old woman's head. Knud grabbed a pair of scissors and cut it all off. She yelled and screamed that she would not remain in a house which permitted such indignities, but there was nothing she could do. When he had her finally cleaned up and a woolen cap powdered with boric acid tied over her scalp, she was young and happy and gay once more. Her greatest regret was that she could not be with the rest of us at the bird cliffs.

The song of the auks is sweeter than anything else to the natives. "Pi-u-lee, Pi-u-lee-pi-u-lee," they cry, flying out to sea in living clouds at night, and early in the morning assembling in the cliffs once more, singing the whole day long. Each time a man swings his net through the air he captures seven or eight of the small birds. The net is then quickly turned so that they may not escape, and they are hauled in. The auks are killed by placing the finger on the chestbone and moving the heart a fraction of an inch. The bird dies instantly, and a delicious collection of blood clots around the heart, to be eaten later when the meat is frozen.

But many birds are eaten immediately. They have just migrated from the south and their skins are lined with a thick layer of fat, so that those fond of good food pluck, rather than

ALOQISAQ, THE STRONG
WOMAN WHO HAD
SAVED HER HUSBAND'S
LIFE, WHO ACCOMPA-
NIED PEARY ON ONE OF
HIS EXPEDITIONS, AND
FINALLY CAME TO US
TO DO OUR WASHING.
HER TEETH ARE WORN
DOWN TO THE GUMS
FROM CHEWING SKINS

NATIVE BOY AT THULE
ALL DRESSED UP AND
WISHING HE WASN'T

skin, the birds and boil them in a pot. I was too lazy to do this, but little Mequpaluk plucked them for me. Never would she eat any of the fresh meat herself. She said she had plenty of the skins to chew at home, and they were good enough for her.

The old women chew the skins day in and day out to remove the fat so that they can be used for clothing. After many years their teeth wear down to the gums, and it is difficult for them to digest their food, but their jaw muscles are in fine condition as long as they live.

The dullness of their teeth makes it possible for the old women to chew the delicate auk skins without cutting holes in them. The skins are so small that a grown man seldom has clothing made from them, though it is said that occasionally a young woman without babies is so fond of her husband that she chews sufficient skins to make him a shirt.

There is no such thing as a wage system in the Arctic, and the old women sit together and chew. Their chewing never stems their flow of talk about old times and adventures, while their laughter and chatter rivals the pandemonium of the birds in the cliffs.

Many times I fell asleep waiting for the birds. And when I woke the sun was still high in the sky, the birds chattering gaily. That was a happy life. I shall never forget it.

When we were ready to return home the ice was bad, and I had to take Uvdluriark's stepdaughter along with me. It was then that I discovered what an extraordinary person she was. There was no laziness in her; to work was her pleasure. When we halted to rest the dogs, she always untangled the traces before the animals had a chance to lie down. Whenever I needed anything she foresaw and, if possible, fulfilled my need. She was the only girl I ever met among the Eskimos who really cared for flowers and birds.

We drove home in the night, though it was daylight. We could see the moon, but it was pale and unreal before the sun. I looked at it and remarked that when the moon was only half as large it was easier to examine it with my field glasses. She looked at it carefully through my glasses. I have always been too proud of my little knowledge, and I started to tell her about the mountains on the moon which she could see through the glasses. She stopped me:

"Mountains? The man, you mean?"

I smiled down upon her from the great height of my learning, and told her that there were indeed mountains upon the moon.

"But then," she asked, "what about the man up there?"

"There is no man in the moon."

I was surprised that anyone should really believe the myth, but she explained that her grandfather, who was a wise old man, had told her there was a man in the moon. Her mother believed it too. How could one believe anything the angakoks said if they lied about the man in the moon?

This she asked in a very modest way, and as sincerely and simply as possible I assured her that they were wrong—there was no man in the moon. From that day forward there was a secret bond between us. I was to her the man who knew everything, and I tried in every manner possible to live up to the great faith and trust of her clean and innocent soul.

When we reached home we parted—she to run to her mother's tent where she spent more than twenty hours a day caring for her small brothers and keeping house.

I was to go to Saunders Island, outside Wolstenholme Sound, where there is excellent walrus and bird hunting in the summer. Knud was going to haul our clumsy boat to the water on his sledge, and I planned to sail it to the island. While I was loading it, a good friend of ours, Ululik, came down to inquire where I was going. I told him, and he proposed that I take with me a number of fine, small skins. His daughter was going to have a baby soon, and he wanted her to have the skins for the child. His mother-in-law, Krulee, had been busy chewing the skins out on the coast.

I asked him how the old woman was, and remarked that I had not seen her for several days.

"Oh, no," said Ululik blandly. "We left her there!"

"What do you mean, you left her?" I asked.

"She stayed there to catch more birds during the summer, and we will see her next fall if she is still alive. She was quite fat and can endure much privation, for I even left some blubber for her. She can stay in the cave very nicely."

I was startled. Here was Ululik, a kindly, decent fellow, leaving his old mother-in-law to die if she could not contend with the weather and the animals and starvation. Her only defense was that she was rather fat when last seen.

I hitched up my dogs again and started off after her. We could not permit such treatment of old people while we lived here, and I felt that I must teach them a lesson.

The ice was bad now round the cape, and I fell into the water time after time. In spite of the difficulties I kept going, and finally found myself on an ice pan which I intended to use to ferry across an open stretch that extended from Cape Athol far out to sea. I used my harpoon stick for an oar, and got along nicely until suddenly a little breeze came up and, in spite of my frantic efforts, I could see that I was being swept out to sea. The movement of the ice was not fast, but the breeze was constant, and all about me the ice began to crack up and drift out. At last I realized that my only chance was to permit myself to drift and hope that I would drift close to firm ice.

The dogs knew that something was wrong, and gathered round me. I let them crawl upon the sledge to get their aching feet out of the water, and bundled myself up as I had done many times before.

One has plenty of time to contemplate his past life in such hours, and somehow it seems more real than the present circumstance, for the seriousness of my plight dulled the impressions I drew from it. I merely knew that there was not one chance in a thousand of my being rescued, and I had plenty of time to grow accustomed to the idea.

The drift quickened, and I looked about my little floating island with lagging interest. All around me in the water were the thousands of small birds—the little auks that make the mountains gay during the day. Now it was night and I discovered that never for a moment did the small birds lose their vivacity. They dove and came up again. I could stand directly over them and see them swimming below and feeding on the black wing snails. They played and fought until it was time for them to return to shore. I envied them their wings, for I must stay here and either die of starvation or drown.

Seals popped up around me. One big bearded fellow flopped onto the ice pan close beside me. I shouted at him, and at first he was petrified by the unexpected voice, but his curiosity made him stay. After a while he became used to me and found out that sound does not necessarily kill. When he finally disappeared I was more lonesome than ever.

Morning brought no change in my situation. I could not even observe the drift, for the small pan on which my sledge rested was the only piece large enough to support me. So I had to sit and wait, and it was much worse than if I had been able to fight against my fate. There is something particularly grueling about sitting quiet in the sunlight while the birds sing all about you—and know you are only awaiting death.

After a time I could tell that my piece of ice was moving—south, always south, and farther from shore. I tried to keep two points on shore in a line, and at last calculated my drift. I noticed, too, that my pan was slowly revolving, imperceptibly wearing itself out in collision against small chunks of ice.

I never grew tired of observing. I was sure that I was going to die, yet hope never ebbs so low that one entirely gives up. I watched my position, and it was just as nerve-racking as figuring out a difficult problem in calculus. I could not let it alone. I told myself that I should sleep until I was close to the next cape, and then try my luck there, but it was impossible. I came closer and closer, and I could see the ice ahead of me dashed against the cliffs and broken into a million pieces. That was what I had to face. Yet my pan was not destroyed against the cliffs, but slid past outside.

At the end of two endless days hunger replaced fear. The farther south I drifted the more I relied upon my ability to land at Conical Rock on the island outside Agpat. If there was clear water and no wind I would try to get out of the sledge and make the dogs swim to shore, towing me. I had heard of a like instance, and at any rate it would be worth the attempt. But the tide came in and stopped my progress altogether. And I sat there, my ice pan revolving slowly, slowly, never quite stopping.

I must have fallen asleep, for I remember nothing until I looked up and found myself just opposite Conical Rock. There was no possibility of reaching it, for between me and the rock was a jam of small cakes of ice.

South I went, always south. Even though weak, I was clear-minded and could use my eyes. And yet I was not the first to sight rescue.

As I sat staring out to sea I noticed that my dogs pricked up their ears and looked toward land. I was almost afraid to follow their gaze, because I had been disappointed so many times. But I did look, and not so far from me were two natives standing near a sledge on the ice. I thought I had combed the coast all along my drift and would have spotted any sign of life long before I was so close.

And yet, there were people. I could see them clearly—seal hunters at the edge of the ice, and a kayak in the water. I was saved!

Later I could not understand why I did not shout with joy. I think it must have been that deep in my soul I had known that my time was not yet—I was to be saved for the icecap. My fatalism had told me that that was the place for me to die. And therefore I only raised my arms to let the men know I had seen them, and they returned my salute.

Then I sat down and waited until I drifted closer, and they went on with their hunting. I must have been crazy, but all my interest was in their success or failure. I was so pleased when a seal drew their bullet, and disappointed when it sank out of reach of their harpoons.

The men were Qidlugtok and Itukusunguaq, the latter my companion on the trip to Tassiussak.

They had taken land at Agpat where there were many barbed seals and birds to furnish meat and eggs. As if by prearrangement, the ice jam about me parted leaving clear water between me and the two men. Itukusunguaq paddled out in his kayak, tied their harpoon lines to mine and my lashing line, and rowed back with it. Then I chopped two holes in my ice pan to make the line fast, and they hauled me and my dogs in to solid ice.

The men greeted me but betrayed no great excitement, and went to work untangling my traces.

"Where are you going?" said Itukusunguaq, as if this were my usual mode of travel.

"It was possible that somebody came slightly out of one's course," I said. That was all the explanation they needed.

Later they told me that they did not like to ask what had happened, for they were frightened lest someone had died. What I had done looked a little adventurous to them.

They drove me to their homes and offered me boiled birds and dried meat. The sun was bright, and I soon forgot my terror of a few hours ago. When they learned that I had left Thule to search for an old woman they shouted with merriment, and the adventure became known as one of the most comical things the Eskimos had ever heard of. The two young wives asked me if I was *really* going for old Krulee, and when I assured them I was they laughed again, and said they were sure she would be very pleased. But they let me know by their expressions that they thought me a fool to risk my life hunting for an old woman.

I left them the next morning and went on, keeping to the land this time, even when it meant crossing the glacier. I got three seals and cached them at Parker Snow Bay, then ascended the glacier again, left my sledge close to the icecap and walked down to Krulee who was busy with her catch. The little auks were like bees in a hive, and spattered our clothes with their dung.

She thought I had merely come to visit her, and when I told her to make ready to return home with me she looked as if she had been rescued from the grave. Her joy was as obvious as that of a child who has been given a new toy, and she hopped about and clapped her withered hands, singing to the sun about the people she was going to see again.

Poor Krulee; she thought of no one but her small grandchildren, and she imagined they would be as happy as she when they met.

She did not have much to take with her. "My pot!" she cried—it was an empty meat tin. "And the bucket!"—a tin only a little larger. "My teakettle!"—an empty tin which had once contained condensed milk.

Her sleeping blankets were even less pretentious. There was no hair left on the caribou skins, and it had been years since they had sat upon a living animal. But one precious object she never took off—a genuine enamel cup which Knud had given her. She wore it on a string round her neck, and her old fingers would caress its blue border and her eyes sparkle when she looked at it.

Suddenly she remembered that she could not leave yet. No, indeed!

"Why not? What are we waiting for?" I asked.

"You see, Ululik left three sealskins for me to fill. I already have one and a half filled and I think I'd better finish the second before going home. You are young and strong, and you can take the catcher and do it much faster than I can."

She had not the strength to drag the sealskin pokes after they were stuffed, and had had to make the caches before the birds were in them, running back and forth with a few birds every few minutes, and removing the stones from the pokes each time, as the sun must never shine on the poke or it will draw out the flavor of the birds.

I could not resist her. I forgot my dogs; I forgot I was tired and wanted to get home. I sat there the whole day and caught little auks for the man who had left his mother-in-law to almost certain death and had ordered her, as her final task in life, to fill three pokes with giviaq for him so that he might give impressive parties with them during the coming winter.

We stayed overnight and in the morning had such a load that

it was with great difficulty we hauled the stuff to the sledge. I proposed to leave the tins behind, but she refused. They were her property. She found it difficult to sleep, and it was nice to have her own pot in which to cook a little food for an old mouth while the others slept.

I promised to give her some other pots.

"Oh, now I am happy," she cried. "When you give me the new one, I will have something to send my oldest granddaughter who is going to have a baby."

She talked of what she had thought while she had been there alone. She had wept a few times, but only to while away the time, and she had no ill word to speak of her son-in-law or his wife, her daughter. They were both, she said, very kind to her. I asked her why, then, they had left her.

"Oh, that was only because such ideas were put in their heads!"

Lovely old Krulee! I regret that I should be lying if I described the reception she received from her son-in-law as "enthusiastic."

17

When the time came for our spring campaign to Saunders Island, Knud Rasmussen stayed at home with his three old witches, Vivi, Arnajark and Aloqisaq, to unearth material for his book from them. The three women had been the best of friends but, now that they had lived in close quarters for a long time, each vied with the other in the telling of tales. Knud gave them little presents for their information—old tins, tea leaves, rags and papers,—and they stowed away whatever was left over from the table. Each woman collected this junk in a box; when it was filled no power on earth could prevent her setting out to distribute her gifts among her relatives. Knud Rasmussen could therefore determine from the amount of knickknacks in the boxes when the different women were about to set out on their journeys, and he extracted information frantically while he could, even though it meant passing up the bird season.

Saunders Island is the Arctic bird haven for auks, ducks and fulmars, those strange fowls which cannot walk because their knee joints are bent almost double. If they are placed on the ground or on the deck of a ship they are unable to take off again, and so they must alight only on the steep cliffs from which they can soar into the air.

TWO VIEWS OF OUR HOUSE AT THULE—SUMMER AND WINTER

The fulmars are the first birds to appear in the spring, long before the ice breaks up. Although the flavor of their flesh is bad, the hunters go after them. After a season of nothing but walrus and bear meat, any change is for the better. The birds soar so high that they are mere specks, but they drop like plummets when blubber is thrown overboard.

Those we got from the cliffs were fat, and the taste not too revolting, but their feathers had a typically nauseating odor. Fortunately the natives in the far north do not use them for pillows, but in South Greenland they do. I remember once at a dance Knud and I saw two lovely native girls whom we could not approach because the family bedding was stuffed with fulmar feathers. It is a drastic, but effective, protection for any girl.

When the time for walrus hunting arrived many more natives joined us at the island. Walrus come up from the south and pass Melville Bay as soon as the water is open. On their journey there are no clams or oysters for them, and they feed on the seals. When they arrive at Cape York, where they never halt, their stomachs are full of seal meat and skin. At Parker Snow Bay, the first place where they find a tasty menu, they stop for a few days. When they reach Agpat, they settle down to feed for a long time.

Many of us went out on our boat, which was a great boon in towing the carcasses, but for real excitement, you must hunt the great beasts from a kayak. You get no impression of their fierceness or strength if you stand on the deck of a big ship. But in a kayak the hunter is on the same level with the walrus.

Walrus, as said before, must dive to the bottom to secure their food. With their long tusks they plow up the dirt and shells, then take the soil and mud and shells between their foreflippers and swim upward. The dirt washes out in this process, leaving the stones, clams and oysters. Then they rub the shells between their thick, scabrous flippers and crush them. The heavier portions sink, the meat floats, and the walrus opens his mouth and swallows it. Consequently one never finds shells of any sort in a walrus's stomach. Many uninformed writers have expressed surprise at this.

The period of time the animals remain submerged is determined by the depth of the water. At Agpat they stayed down for seven minutes; at Pituravik, nine. They always remain for a short while on the surface, heading into the current, which permits the kayaks to approach from the rear.

The hunter must try to judge where the walrus will next

appear in order to be in the immediate neighborhood. The experienced native knows by the action of the animal while on the surface whether he is feeding, or merely idling about. At the moment the hunter sees the head of the beast emerge his arms dart like lightning. His kayak shoots forward straight as an arrow, and when he is close enough he hurls his harpoon directly at the animal. If he makes a hit, the bladder attached to the rope is dragged out of the boat as the walrus dives, and is often pulled completely under the surface for a long period.

As soon as the bladder is visible again, the men in the big boat rush toward it and the real battle begins. Nowadays guns soon end the fight, but in former times the hunters had to finish the walrus with their spears. That process was often cruel, and the beast floundered about in the water for hours until it had bled to death.

The stomach is always the prize portion, since it is usually filled with the most delicious clams and oysters, and the stomach juices serve as a tantalizing sour dressing.

If one has been eating meat and nothing but meat twice a day, a feeling of lethargy eventually overcomes him. But immediately he has eaten these clams it is as if he had taken a magic potion of pep and energy. If anything is left over, the two openings of the stomach are tied up and the rare article brought home to the women who use it for making soups.

It was at Saunders Island that I got my first walrus. I had been out in a kayak numerous times and was anxious to get one, but never had the opportunity. Now it was my turn, and I was lucky enough to be directly behind the beast when he came up for air, so I rushed ahead.

Never had any animal looked so enormous to me, but I could not turn back without looking ridiculous. I remember that I even hoped the beast would hear the splashing of my oar and dive, but that was not to be.

I was almost upon the walrus before I had any plan in mind. It was breathing deeply, preparing to go down again for more oysters. Now was the time. Suddenly my harpoon flashed through the air. Without waiting to see whether it had struck home, I whipped my kayak around and made off. My little boat trembled, and I hoped I was not being attacked. It was, however, only the bladder being dragged from the boat.

And the first thing I knew men were shouting and hailing me from the other kayaks and the boat. I had got my first walrus!

I was "newborn in the land"—as the natives put it—because harpooning a walrus is the first step toward becoming a hunter. I was *somebody* now. The Eskimos even have a special word for "killing the first walrus," so important is that event in the life of a man.

All of us went on shore to celebrate, and Knud, apparently scenting a party, arrived with his three ladies on his sledge. He had brought coffee and bread (he had actually planned on giving the party to celebrate the completion of his book, until I stole his thunder). But none of us cared about a book when such an important event had occurred: I had caught a walrus!

With Knud came Ivaloo and her husband. They had planned on summering at Etah, but the angakok had forbidden women to partake of female walrus meat, and Ivaloo could not go there. Both male and female walrus are abundant there, while here at Saunders Island only the bulls pass by on their way to the mating grounds to the north.

Ivaloo was a great beauty, and she was well aware of her charms. She and Tatianguak, the adopted son of the murdered Uvisakavsik, were newlyweds, and they said they wanted to remain close to us in order to avoid any grudge fights which might arise.

The young husband came to me several times and confessed that, since he was a very bad hunter, he had no business being married to such an attractive woman. He said he thought he had better leave her and let me marry her—perhaps I would give him a gun and wood for a sledge in exchange. I explained that whatever else we did in our colony, we could not indulge in wife-bartering.

He sat quiet for a few moments and then walked away. I watched him as he explained the conversation to Ivaloo who listened interestedly. It was obvious that the scheme had been hers. I remembered her actions during the séance at Neqé, when she had been wild and positively out of her head. Now she was coldly calculating the advantages of belonging to a white man. She had evidently told Tatianguak that the marriage might not last long, and she would eventually return to him a much richer woman.

Ivaloo was remarkable to look at with her clothes off, for on her shoulder and, extending along the upper side of her right arm to the hand, lay a huge red birthmark.

I was told that there was a very special reason for this—Ivaloo was one and the same person as her grandmother!

The old woman had been living in an igloo with the family near Parker Snow Bay when a snowslide crushed the dwelling. By a miracle everyone but the grandmother escaped. The whole family had suffered severely from exposure as the catastrophe had occurred at night and found them all naked.

The body of the grandmother was not discovered until the following spring when hunters found her right arm and shoulder protruding from a snowdrift. The gulls had eaten the flesh away to the bone.

Shortly after this event Ivaloo was born—and on her right arm and shoulder was a mark in precisely the same position as the scar left by the carrion birds upon the old woman. Consequently it was quite evident that Ivaloo was the old woman reborn.

Knud Rasmussen returned to the house with the three old hags, and we stayed on to collect eggs and catch walrus. Then one morning I was aroused by an ear-splitting yell. Everyone was apparently going crazy, shouting and screaming, dancing and howling. What they were saying I could not ascertain, but finally I heard the word "Oomiarssuaq!" and a few moments later made out the masts of a ship sailing round Cape Athol.

A ship at this time of year was totally unexpected, and I realized instantly that this one belonged to whalers, the Upernadlit, those who arrive with the spring.

Everyone leapt into our boat and proceeded to hurl the meat out of it in preparation for the trip to the vessel. It was amazing to discover that the natives still had fox pelts to trade—the women had kept some for their personal use—now that the trading fever possessed them.

The ship was gradually approaching, and I induced the natives to wait until it was near before we set out. I must admit that the sight of its masts against the snow and ice was a welcome one to me.

Before we got into our little boat I told the women that they could accompany us on only one condition—that they promise to keep away from the sailors. I explained that I had nothing to say concerning their morals, but that they might very well contract venereal diseases and contaminate the whole tribe. The women all accepted the conditions and we put our oars to the water.

The crew of a whaler is, perhaps, not made up of God's best boys, and they must be kept busy if they are to keep out of trouble. The wise captain has them polishing rails and scrubbing the deck even when such cleanliness seems unimportant. Captain Adams of the *Morning of Dundee* was a veteran of the northern seas, and on old friend of mine. Beside him on the bridge stood his seventy-four-year-old first mate. He had lived on a whaler for sixty years, and had never spent a summer at home since he was fourteen.

The two men were delighted to see us and pleased to know that we had settled down at Thule, even though it meant three hundred less blue fox pelts a year for them. They realized that in the Arctic every man must work for his own interests, and their greetings were hearty. It was fine to go down into a warm cabin and have the steward serve us a meal that included bread and chocolate and sugar (which we had exhausted) and hardtack. Captain Adams had brought mail for us, and we chatted for a long while. I remember that he said he needed eggs and asked if we had any. I pointed to a cache of more than a thousand and told him to take them.

"There are eggs on the islands!" the captain shouted. "Lower two boats and go after them."

A few men moved listlessly. "All hands!" came the order.

We heard a few members of the crew muttering about its now being "free watch." Like a shot out of a gun the captain was up in the rig and had slid down upon the deck. He stood there a giant among trolls, turning his gaze from one man to another.

"Who said 'free watch'? Which one of you lazy devils?"

No one had said a word, apparently, and the boats were lowered away. When Captain Adams returned to the bridge I pointed out to him that he had not told the men where the eggs were. He dismissed this oversight with a wave of his hand.

"Don't worry—it will give the men something to do to find them."

They found them all right, almost every egg in our caches. They returned with both boats loaded, and the unexpected harvest was ordered salted down.

We spent several pleasant hours talking, after our meal in the cabin. I told him that I had found a dead whale with his harpoon buried in it during the last summer, and we both cursed the American who had invented artificial whalebone.

I must confess that I had forgotten my natives entirely, and when I prepared to leave I remembered them with a start. They had, it seemed, been enjoying a hearty meal in the crew's quarters, and had had the time of their lives. When I called to them to get into the little boat the women were the last to arrive. They were grinning, either in amusement or fear—those that came at all. I demanded to know the trouble. One innocent soul, whose innocence empowered him to tattle on the others, informed me that Aloqisaq had lost her pants.

This was a rather delicate predicament for a lady—especially one who has no skirt—and I went down to the men's quarters to try to find out what had happened.

"Well," she said, "the pants simply disappeared." She could not understand how it could have happened. I questioned the sailors but none of them had the pants. I asked which bunk she had been in, but that got me nowhere as it appeared that she had not restricted herself to one bunk, and she could not identify her particular hosts. I gave up and handed her a big red handkerchief to tie around her middle like a diaper. She did not look very pleased—or very stylish—but it served. The *Morning of Dundee* sailed away north, and I never saw it again.

The natives discussed their trading with the whaler, and were all dissatisfied with their bargains. If they asked for a knife they received tobacco. Two of them were given broken pipes, and the others got what the captain thought he could best do without rather than what they wanted. Later I could point to this as a recommendation for our store, and the natives all agreed that we were superior traders. Still, it *was* fun going aboard the whalers. . . .

Mequpaluk, Uvdluriark's stepdaughter, ran down to the beach to receive us—she had been left behind, as usual, to care for the children and the dogs. I heard her remark that she had been crying because she wanted so badly to go with us—but now she was happy enough to get something for the children from our loot.

I must confess, regretfully for virtue's sake, that none of us fared so well from the visit as Aloqisaq, though she had to spend part of her earnings for an old pair of pants. She gave a big party that night to celebrate, and was offended because I would not attend.

18

I spent the evening in my tent reading the rest of my mail. I read the letters from my family over and over again. They were filled with local gossip and warmth and affection, and I felt as if I were no more than a few miles from them.

I saved the letter from the girl I had left at home until the last, partly to tantalize myself, and partly because I feared the news it might contain. I had not dared ask her to share my present life, yet secretly I had hoped she would. When I finally opened the letter, I could have cried with joy—she was coming up to join me, probably on the boat that was to bring us fresh supplies this summer!

She wanted to share my life, whatever it was. She wanted to live in my house, wherever it was, and become an Arctic woman. Together we would make life gayer and pleasanter than it had ever been anywhere in the world!

I was in the skies, and set about making preparations for her arrival. As a letter from Knud's wife told him that he was the father of a newborn daughter, both of us were so excited that we scarcely knew what we were doing.

But while we waited for our boat we had to keep up our daily tasks. Summer came. We hunted in kayaks and sailed to near-by communities in our little boat. And on one day during that summer Knud gave us the fright of our lives.

We were after narwhales which are amazingly fast. Knud was persistent to a fault, and when one came up on the left side of his kayak he threw his harpoon into the animal, though he knew that the whale should have been on his right side. When the whale dived it pulled the line attached to the bladder round Knud's body, capsized the kayak and hurled him into the water. He was an excellent swimmer, but the line was twisted about him, and he disappeared below the surface in the wake of the wounded narwhale. The rest of us sat in our kayaks, absolutely helpless. For once I knew what it meant to feel my blood run cold.

After an interminable interval Knud came up far away, gasping for help. We rowed frantically, but long before any of us reached the spot where he had appeared he was down a second time. I was afraid he was done for this time, but a second later he bobbed up again. This time he stayed up and we hauled him out of the water.

Not for a moment had he lost his nerve. He had merely hung onto the bladder, he said, as he figured his weight would quickly tire the narwhale and the animal would come to the surface.

"You'd better go home for a change of clothes," I said.

He eyed me reproachfully. "Don't you see that this is our chance for a big killing?" Later on I asked him if he did not at least want his clothes wrung out.

"Why?" he said.

"Because you're wet as hell!" I roared.

"By God, I forgot that!"

That's the kind of man who makes a real explorer.

But our ship did not arrive. The harbor at Thule usually remained open for only twenty-five days each year—from August 1st to 25th—and already it was the middle of September. We were nearly out of supplies, especially matches and nails, and must do something to replenish our store before the winter closed in on us.

We decided that I, being the sailor, should try to make a voyage across Melville Bay to the Danish settlement in our sailboat, stopping at Saunders Island to pick up supplies for the trip from our caches there. But as we reached the island, we saw a small schooner already there in the harbor. It was our ship; it had spent forty-five days in crossing Melville Bay!

My girl was not on it!

For me that was all that mattered. Born a lady, and reared in a large city, she had decided at the last moment that she could not face such an existence. I had known all along that it was asking too much of her, and I could not blame her for changing her mind. But at the time it was the worst blow that had ever hit me.

How empty my little preparations for her arrival! How much more empty the house than it had been before. My life loomed ahead of me like a river meandering aimlessly through a barren desert, and I had in a sense to reshape it into unexpected channels.

But I was still young, and my life had been an exceptionally clean one. In Denmark I had lived mostly with my parents, and since then I had been too busy to get into trouble. My mother and father had instilled in all of us the sense of our position, and taught us that the world and its evil ways were not for us. As a sailor the filth and horror of the harbors had been repellent and had kept me away from loose women. I suppose I had dreamt of "saving myself" for a pure girl—and now her failing me seemed especially ironic. She had, I was convinced, ruined my life.

The captain of the boat said he could not stay with us one hour more than was absolutely necessary, so we pitched in and worked night and day at unloading. The ship was small and our money was low, but our credit was still good and we determined to stick with the career we had chosen.

I hastily dashed off a letter to my mother—the only one I had time to write. There was in it nothing of the thrilling stuff one reads in adventure novels. I had neither time nor inclination to worry her with that. And then the ship sailed away.

It would be difficult for outsiders to understand that we were glad to see it go, but we were. As it disappeared round the cape we settled back into our routine of living, and found it satisfactory. We slept two days before setting out for bear meat, without which our dogs would starve.

There is no such thing as an easy, uneventful journey in the Arctic. Each time one leaves home he knows that he is taking his life in his hands, yet even these dangers become commonplace. Before we reached Cape York all of us had narrowly escaped freezing to death, I had fallen into another crevasse, and shortly afterward was plunged into the ocean when my sledge and dogs crashed through the thin ice. This time I was saved by the fact that enough frozen meat was lashed to the sledge to float it.

At Cape York we ran across Minik, the boy who had caused us so much trouble. He was living there in one of the houses reserved for the young people of the community.

There are such houses in most of the larger communities—dwellings which have been constructed many years before, and now in reality belong to no one. During the summer anyone may appropriate them. The roofs must be taken off so that the sun will have a chance to thaw the ice and dry the walls, and in the fall the stones and peat must be replaced. In these houses the boys and girls may live together without censure or obligation beyond the demands of the night.

The Eskimos take a wholly natural and practical view of sex. They consider no marriage happy unless a sexual affinity exists between the two concerned, and therefore they believe it most important for the man and the woman to test and establish this affinity before they undertake a permanent union.

Unfortunately two families of missionaries had come north. Both were natives from South Greenland, and were sincere believers in their doctrine and their God.

I never like to say too much concerning Christian missions among pagans. I have seen all manner of men and women missionaries, and many of them were unfit for the task they elected to perform. At home no one is able to judge whether or not these persons will make successful missionaries, and those who donate to the cause always believe in the benefits of carrying the word of God to the pagans—it is natural for anyone to assume that his charity is not wasted.

These two men were not so much responsible for their inadequacy as were those who had sent them. Few people realize how dangerous it is to bring new creeds to a race settled into an old and, to them, satisfactory mode of living. I have always felt that a teacher of a scientific subject has a simple task compared with that of the missionary. Any fairly intelligent person can pick a man out of the street and teach him a set of rules to follow in accomplishing a given problem. But a missionary—who is supposed to teach a little of everything—should be a man of great culture, general knowledge and sympathetic understanding. It is unfortunate that such a combination is rare among missionaries. Usually all it takes for them to secure appointments is a burning desire to preach about their God, and everything else be damned!

We must realize that missionaries are going to violate all manner of racial rules and traditions, and even trample upon what the pagans have always believed to be decency. Such a program requires tact and infinite patience.

Usually they set to work on the question of sex. It is strange how sex has always interested the church. Of course, sex has always interested everybody, and if the church is able to control it, the church is immediately an important factor in the life of a people. But I have always been a little embarrassed for preachers, who seem to wield such small influence over their own flocks at home, daring to interfere with the ways of an alien race.

I have often been surprised that missionaries dare do what they do. They certainly had their hands full at Cape York.

Arnanguaq, the young lady who had been offered to me last winter, was now living there. She was the joint mistress of four young men who lived in one of the youths' houses, and Knud asked me what we should do about it. I told him that I would not mix up in her affairs, but he said it was our duty to support the missionaries. He went to talk with the girl.

"Don't you think," she said, "that I would rather marry one single man? This is the only way I have of getting in touch with them." What a natural and innocent thing to say. And how clean, after all.

That same evening Minik came to me and said he wanted

to marry Arnanguaq. He had no house, but if he might move in
with us he could offer her a shelter for the winter, and in the
spring build her a home.

We thought it over and decided to let them move in with us—
thereby saving Minik, who was probably a good enough fellow
and only needed a break, and the girl. We would also be supporting the work of the missionaries, and each of us would feel like a
hell of a fine fellow. Minik left the next day with his bride. There
had been no ceremony.

Knud decided to go on south after more bear meat, but I had
had enough of the trip and started for Thule alone. The ice was
favorable along the coast and I let my dogs run as they liked.
The dwindling daylight on the high mountains was awe-inspiring.
Nowhere else in the world have I seen such a riot of color. I sat
alone on my sledge, my dogs pulling me swiftly—all of us a part
of a country that day by day revealed its soul more clearly to me—
a soul white and fine and without lies. The life was good, a man
had time and inclination to dream.

Here I was alone; there was no one else who could do exactly
the sort of thing I was doing. This knowledge flattered me
and made me believe that I owed it to myself to stay here and
foster my own happiness. Without that no one can accomplish
anything.

I reached home and was more satisfied than ever. I saw
Minik working at last, adjusting to conditions and trying to
make a living for himself and his wife. He had exaggerated his
own importance, he said, when he was one of six selected to go to
New York, and had been the only one of his people to survive
the journey. But now he was back in the North, and he promised
to begin over again and forget the outside world.

He and I built a small house beside our larger one. I moved
in with him and his wife, as, in the Arctic, it is difficult to separate night from day and the natives are apt to run in at all hours
to talk. Knud could stay up for twenty-four hours and then sleep
almost as many but I liked to go to bed at a regular time. We
agreed that our old house would be office, dining room, dwelling,
and trading post. Knud would sleep in the attic, and I would
stay with Minik.

Minik's wife was not, unfortunately, much of a housekeeper.
Her patience was inexhaustible, and there was not one ounce of
bad intention in her. As a matter of fact, there were very few
intentions of any sort in Arnanguaq, for she was as resourceless a

girl as I have ever met. She could never think of anything to do. It was not long before Minik began to remain longer and longer away from the house on his hunting trips.

One day he announced to us all that he was going north, and he was going alone. He did not know how long he would be gone. I made no move to prevent his going and he set off, leaving me alone with his young wife.

To circumvent any whisper of scandal Arnanguaq invited Mequpaluk to spend the nights with her. Each evening after the girl had done all her chores at home she came running down to the house. Her clothes were still disgraceful, her boots almost soleless, and her stockings furless. But she was always in the best of humor and our room became a cheerier place when she entered it. She had a trick of recounting her experiences so quaintly that everyone laughed with her, and each night we awaited her arrival with impatience.

Finally one evening when she came Arnanguaq was absent, and I told Mequpaluk that she had better stay with me. She looked at me a moment and then remarked simply:

"I am unable to make any decisions, being merely a weak little girl. It is for you to decide that."

But her eyes were eloquent, and spoke the language every girl knows regardless of race or clime.

I only asked her to move from the opposite side of the ledge over to mine—that was all the wedding necessary in this land of the innocents.

Next day she wanted to know whether she was to return to her home or not, and when I said no that was final. A few hours later one of her brothers came to ask why she had not come home. She said:

"Somebody is occupied by sewing for oneself in this house!"

The boy was startled but said nothing, and turned on his heel to race from house to house with the news. After a few hours sledges hurried north and south to tell what had happened and to hear firsthand the comments of the neighbors.

Again I was amazed at the discretion of these wonderful people. Not one of them spoke a word to either of us which would indicate that the girl had not always lived in our house. Visitors came as usual, and talked as if she had been my wife for years and they had been her guest many times.

The only dissatisfied person in the household was Vivi. She had recently celebrated her twentieth birthday—as her son was

NAVARANA

fourteen, she may have miscalculated slightly. She explained to me that she wanted very much to marry, and some lucky male might be encouraged if she subtracted a few years from her age. "Still," she added, sighing, "these ignorant people do not even know anything about age."

The next evening my little wife asked me to come down to the beach with her so that we could talk alone without a roof over us. She said that she had spent the day in speculation, and she had decided, now that she was married to a white man, to use one of her other names. (Also, Odark's wife, Mequ, had died recently, and the name "Mequpaluk" could not be spoken any more.) She had been too frightened, however, to change her name without consulting me.

I agreed that she should take another name, and from then on she was known as "Navarana" over all Greenland.

The first thing was to secure a wardrobe for her. Now she had plenty of furs to select from, and she hired several friends to do the sewing. There was no thought of actual payment as, Navarana told me, the sewers were delighted with the privilege of sitting in our house and listening to everything that was said. Their reward was in being able to tell what they had seen and heard.

We fixed up our room considerably and, when I came home with my first seal after our marriage, we invited all our neighbors to a feast. Still not one word was said of its being an unusual occasion.

Shortly afterward walrus were reported at Dalrymple Rock and, the ice being favorable, I left home with a number of the villagers to drive out and get a few. It was too far to return home each night, especially as it was light for only a few hours now, so we slept on our sledges. In the evenings we built big fires, cooked the meat and made hot soup, and one of the men had a great idea.

"Let us boil some eggs," he said, and was applauded for his ingenuity. This concerned me more than the others, since I was the only man who had eggs cached on the island. However, caches belong to the community, and I could not refuse to bring them out. The caches may not be carted away, but as much may be eaten on the spot as is possible.

Frozen eggs are among the finest of God's gifts. In freezing, the shell always cracks, but the white of the egg that escapes freezes and dries, and is delicious to the taste. The shell is removed after holding the egg between the palms for a few moments, and then the egg itself is eaten like an apple. The number each man could put away was almost unbelievable, especially as these were eider duck eggs, almost twice as large as hen's eggs.

After we had consumed many dozens, the pot was filled and dozens more boiled—and I was the one man who had gathered any eggs.

When I returned home I began to appreciate the woman my wife was going to be. She still wore her rags, but her new boots were finished, and she looked incongruous in pure white, long boots with bearskin emerging from the tops and giving way to pants which would scarcely hold together. But next day the pants were replaced with fine new ones, and then she boasted the best raiment in the tribe.

I related the egg episode to Navarana and she promised to put a stop to it. I was a little apprehensive lest my honor as a hunter be tainted, but she was far too clever for that. "Do you really think," she said, "that I would do such a thing to you? Oh, no!"

She merely remarked to her mother that she was afraid we would have no eggs when she came to visit us this winter. Her mother, a fine, intelligent woman, then dropped a kernel of suspicion into the community. "Perhaps," she ventured, "the walrus-hunting season may not last as long as usual this year, since someone has dropped eggshells on the ice and the walrus may take offense." The women carried this gossip to their husbands, who discussed it at length. Finally the elders of the community decided that, even if they could not be certain, it might be just as well to refrain from eating eggs while hunting walrus.

Thus I reaped my first material reward from marriage.

PART III

1

AN entirely new life opened up for me, one which bound me closer than ever to the Arctic.

Many years later I heard the term "going native," but it did not occur to me then that that was what I was doing. I did know that my marriage to an Eskimo girl made a final breach with the world I had known as a young man, but I had already left that world far behind. Navarana was immediately accepted as my wife wherever we visited in Greenland, and no one worried over the duration of our union. Not until long afterward, after our two children were born, did any of the natives admit to me that they had not at first taken our marriage seriously. Even Navarana's mother had thought it but a casual arrangement, and that Navarana would soon be sent home.

Navarana's own life had been a blood-curdling saga of the Arctic. As a small girl she had lived with her parents on Salve Island. One of those inexplicable epidemics that so pitifully ravage a primitive race struck the people, and on the island where they lived only Navarana, her mother and her small brother were spared. They had no meat to eat and were forced to butcher their dogs for food. When this source of supply was exhausted they ate their clothes and dog traces and anything available. The little boy was about three years old and was still nursing. The mother soon had no milk left, and the child in a frenzy of hunger bit the nipple off her breast. Then, seeing no hope of keeping him alive, she hanged him while Navarana looked on. The mother's grief, Navarana told me, was worse than the sight of the dead child, and she swore to her mother that she did not want to die, no matter how hungry she was, but would remain to comfort her.

Navarana told me that she ate grass and the excrement of rabbits and chewed on the tatters of old skins and, with the fall ice, Uvdluriark arrived on his sledge and took them both to his house.

After a couple of years Navarana went to live with her grandfather and grandmother. Her grandfather, Mequsaq, was a veteran of great dignity and experience, and he lavished all his affection upon her. While living with Mequsaq she had the good fortune to escape a siege of starvation which wiped out thirteen others at Cape Alexander. This had occurred the year Mylius-Erichsen and Knud Rasmussen were there for the first time.

The old man and his wife and Navarana at the last found only two others alive, Kullabak and her son, Kraungak. They took the boy along with them (there was not room on their sledge for Kullabak), and when they reached the next community, left Navarana and Kraungak in a shelter while they went out to look for walrus. They got one, rescued old Kullabak and saved all their lives. Navarana told me that she remembered only one incident of this experience: while she and Kraungak waited for the old people to return, the boy, whose feet were frozen, cut off one of his little toes with a knife in order to impress her. He said it didn't hurt, but she could never forget it.

I had thought I was well acquainted with the people of Greenland, but now their lives became doubly rich for me. Navarana told me countless tales I would otherwise never have heard. The Eskimos, great gossips about surface matters, are remarkably close-mouthed and conservative concerning anything that really matters.

When we drove north the natives we met treated Navarana with a deference and respect she had never known before. We met Minik on the way—he was returning home, after all—and told him that his wife was expecting him. He appeared none too enthusiastic.

Navarana's grandmother had died, and we wanted to find her old grandfather, Mequsaq, and suggest that he come to live with us. We discovered him living with some of his other relatives, but he was delighted that his beloved granddaughter was now in a position to offer him a home. He had been dreaming of this for years, he said.

Mequsaq had been born in Canada, and was a grown man when he first came to Greenland in 1864. He lost an eye soon afterward in a fight with cannibals during a period of starvation. He saw his own mother stabbed and carted off to be eaten, but he and his brother escaped, although it cost Mequsaq not only the loss of an eye, but a severe wound between his ribs, and another on his neck. This last was the worst of all, he said. Blood streamed from it for many days, though he tried to stop the wound with grass.

NAVARANA'S MOTHER WITH TWO OF HER CHILDREN

After the famine Mequsaq returned to Canada, but some years later he came back to Greenland with the splendid leader, Kritleq. This man was a great angakok, and his power was so magnificent that when he drove at night his followers could see a pale light over his head—the Eskimo substitute for Christianity's halo.

Mequsaq, not unlike many white men and women of his years, was much inclined to talk about "the old days." He was no longer motivated by fear, and dared now to mention persons long dead. His stories were inexhaustible.

Navarana gloried in her new eminence, and was delighted to be able to repay her grandfather for the countless things he had done for her. We had many provisions with us, and she was at her best when acting as hostess to a group of people. It is wonderful what responsibility and affluence can do in a short time for a person who has never before had anything. She was a little confused at first, but soon became mistress of every situation.

Navarana and her grandfather were always recalling something that had happened a long time ago. The first time she handed him the sugar box, she said:

"Do you remember when somebody got all the sugar in the house?"

This was enough to set him off. Navarana had been the pet of the household, he said, and he himself the greatest man of the tribe. He had come from the greatest distance, and he maintained his reputation by going on far journeys. Once he started north with a number of hunters, but they soon tired and decided to return home. But not Mequsaq. No, he would go as far north as the world went!

Alone he reached the spot on Lady Franklin Bay where Greely's expedition had first camped, and which they had left to go to their doom at Starvation Camp farther south. Had they remained near their store of provisions at Lady Franklin Bay, they would have found any amount of wild game.

Mequsaq suddenly found himself in possession of unlimited goods from the Greely cache. He piled as much as he could upon his sledge and brought home, among other prizes, a large box of granulated sugar. Navarana, then a child, took possession of the box and would permit no one to come near it. She ate it with a spoon and developed an acute stomach-ache. But even this did not stop her, and she ate until it was all gone. Only then did she say: "Oh, why did I not save a little until later?"

Many of the people who came to visit us remembered this episode. They all said that they had never expected, after the little girl's greediness, to find her the keeper of a whole box of sugar.

It grew darker, but we wanted to drive farther north to tell more of the natives that we would soon be going south to Tassius-sak for mail, and suggest that they accompany us. We had to round a cape where the ice was not yet thick. It began to give way under us and finally, when we reached a pan which seemed a bit safer than the last, we stopped. We sat on the sledge and peered ahead into the darkness.

"Are you afraid?" I said.

"Is a woman afraid when she is driving with her husband?" she countered. "Doesn't she trust her worries to him?"

Such talk encourages a newly married man and makes him feel that he amounts to something. I did my best, but the ice was so bad that we had to try another route, one that took us up over a section of the icecap. When we reached it the dogs were too exhausted to pull us and we both walked between the upstanders of the sledge. I whipped the dogs in order to impress upon Navarana that she had married a man who could bend dogs to his will. I swore and yelled, but our advance was embarrassingly slow. Occasionally the dogs stopped and I ran forward to grab the animals by the necks and beat them for their laziness.

I had been afraid to admit to Navarana that I was worried, but after some hours I was exhausted and we seemed to be getting nowhere. We should have been down on the other side long since, so I said:

"Let's go back. These dogs can't take the load across!"

"You don't want to turn back and admit to people that we could not cross, and listen to their laughter. The women will make fun of me for not getting where we wanted to go. I do not like to hear that."

"To hell with the women's kidding!" I shouted. "You can see for yourself that the dogs can't drag the sledge along."

She looked up at me shyly, as if afraid to say what she knew she must: "It is not impossible that maybe something could be done to make them try it?"

"What would that be? Show me what you suggest."

She mumbled something, and asked me not to think badly of her. Then she took my whip and started for the dogs. They perked up at this new voice of authority, and instantly Navarana had them on their feet. She was a fury turned loose. From the shy, sweet little thing of a moment ago she was transformed into a mad witch. The crack of the whip was like ice breaking; her voice echoed over the icecap, and the dogs leapt into their traces.

Away from the merciless lash they tore, the load as nothing to them. The animals instinctively knew that authority was in the hands of a person who knew how to command.

We dashed toward the highest point in the passage as if we were on the heels of a bear. So fast did we go that I could hardly keep up with the sledge, and I looked with admiration at my little wife with the big whip in her hand; she was more beautiful than ever, and I forgot everything in my awe of her.

When we reached the top she halted the dogs and handed me the whip:

"They only felt ashamed because they were driven by a poor woman, and hurried so that they might not be offended any more."

I knew that I had coddled my dogs too much, but I told her that in my country we did not use dogs for hauling and it was difficult to learn to drive them. She explained that she had gone hunting often with her grandfather, and she had learned to drive from him.

"But don't tell anybody," she warned, "that I took the whip while driving with you. I do not want the women to say my husband is not the best dog driver in the country."

What the women would or would not say was, for a long while, our court of last appeal.

Some time later I discovered that I had lost my big knife. We were hungry and unable to slice off pieces of frozen meat for a cold lunch. I explained to Navarana how much I missed the implement. We drove on, she sitting silent for a long while. Finally she said:

"Great dog driver! Are you terribly sorry over the loss of your big knife?"

"Well, you understand," I answered, "it is bad to be without one."

"I regret I did not know how much it meant to us. Do you want me to cry to show my fellow feeling?"

I was touched by her sympathy, and I explained that we had hundreds of knives back at the store. This one would be forgotten entirely.

"It is so hard to understand this way of life," she said. "Never had one thought anybody could live so well."

When we were ready to return to Thule old Mequsaq followed us with his seven dogs. They were excellently trained, but so vicious that no one could come near his sledge. No one but Navarana, who, though she had not seen the dogs for two years, could untangle their traces and fondle them as if they were puppies.

"One is not afraid of one's grandfather's dogs, of course," she said.

We camped in the open and Navarana made our bed with skins laid between the stone of the cliff and our sledge. She knew how to make it warm by gathering dry grass from the slopes which thousands of birds had fertilized during the summer.

But Mequsaq had nothing to protect him. I wanted to offer him some of our skins, but Navarana warned me not to do this. Nevertheless I did, and he refused me—he wanted to sleep on his sledge, he said, so that he would be certain to wake up if anything happened. Navarana explained that he had once made a vow never to cover himself when he slept out-of-doors. An accident had occurred one night which he could have prevented had he been awake. His only explanation was—and the only one I ever did hear from him:

"Somebody belongs to a time when we did not cover up when traveling. That is done inside houses! Of course it is cold, but if one thinks of something else, it is soon forgotten."

While we squatted around the campfire waiting for the meat to boil, Navarana told Mequsaq about the knife I had lost. The old man's constant smile disappeared. He stretched his old limbs before the blubber blaze, and said:

"To lose a knife is the death of many!"

He had seen people die of exposure because they had no knives to cut snowhouses. He had seen people starve before a walrus they could not carve up. A knife had been the cause of his first battle, and he told us the story.

It happened during his first year in Greenland, just after he had come over from "the other side," as Canada is called.

"A long time ago when few whalers came along," he began, "before there were ships that could move by giving out smoke, the people here were content with the small knives they made from the stones at Savigssuit . . ."

At Agpat (Saunders Island) there had been a great hunter,

Kayurapaluk. For many years he had trapped foxes and at last brought a great many skins to a whaler who gave him a big knife in exchange. It was a shining, steel thing, and he could cut more with it than all the other men together. He always took more meat than his share, and had more dog food than anyone else.

The other men gazed at the knife and admired it, and Mequsaq could remember that the children gathered round it to touch it with their fingers. Kayurapaluk basked in their admiration of the knife, but would not permit them to take it in their hands, as he wanted to be the only person to wield it.

Mequsaq, young and ambitious, wanted a knife like it. Everyone laughed at such boldness, because Kayurapaluk was a great angakok, and obviously the only man intended to possess such a magic knife. But Mequsaq found a friend to help him, and they spent many months trapping in the bird cliffs. They got dozens of foxskins as well as four bearskins, which were cured with the nails on them as the white men preferred.

They were fortunate enough to meet a ship which came up in the spring. The captain overpaid the boys and gave each of them a knife. They hurried away to prevent his discovering the overpayment and taking the knives back.

Later they joined Kayurapaluk for the summer and sported knives exactly like his. They liked to lend their knives to many of their friends, which made Kayurapaluk furiously angry.

And then one evening Mequsaq and his friend returned from a day in their kayaks and the children told them that Kayurapaluk had stolen the knives and thrown them into the ocean. What a loss! The poor fellows were as badly off as they had been before. So great was their grief that for days they did not utter a word. Finally Mequsaq said that he would not let such an outrage pass without retribution. They had nothing to lose now, and even if they were too young to challenge the great angakok, they would get even with him somehow.

A few days afterward some children were playing on the beach, holding a flapping gull in their hands.

"Let me cut off its head, as they will cut off the head of Kayurapaluk!" said one of them.

"Let me break all the bones in the gull, as they will break all the bones in Kayurapaluk!" said another.

"Let me thrust my harpoon through the gull as they are going to thrust their harpoon through Kayurapaluk!" said a third.

But Kayurapaluk was a great angakok, and overheard what the children were saying. Next day when all the men were out in their kayaks he paddled up to the two conspirators and said:

"I hear you intend to kill me! You had better not try! When we are out in kayaks I can take care of myself, and with those miserable knives you have you can harm no one."

They did not answer, but he had given them an idea—they would kill him with their small knives.

The summer faded and winter came. The sledges had to be hung upon the meat rack at night lest the dogs break loose and eat the traces. One morning Kayurapaluk went to take his sledge down, and had to reach high to get it. When he stretched upward, a streak of his belly was visible between his pants and shirt. The two young men watched their opportunity, leapt forward on either side of him, and ripped open his stomach with their small, ridiculed knives. Kayurapaluk screamed and tried to reach his weapons to defend himself, but his intestines poured out of him and he fell over. He tried to gather them up in his hands and run to his tent for his conjuring outfit, but as he ran his bowels slipped through his fingers, and he sagged to the ground unable to stem the flow of blood.

"It looks as if the small knives are not so bad in many ways!" he said. And then he died.

This edifying story Mequsaq told us as he waited for his meat to be cooked. When it was ready, he ate contentedly without giving his part in the cold-blooded murder a moment's further thought. I could scarcely believe him capable of such violence, he the grandfather of my wife and as friendly a man as anyone could hope to find. He looked no more terrifying than an old character actor in full regalia who pauses between scenes to reminisce about missed cues and the time he played with Sir Henry Irving.

Before we had finished our meal we heard sounds of dogs and men approaching, and soon a whole party of travelers drove up—several sledges, men and women and children. They were on their way to Thule to trade with us, and Navarana became a bit excited as the duties of hostess weighed heavily upon her. All the other women were superior to her in age and experience.

Nevertheless, she let it be known that she had tea to offer them with sugar in it, that she slept at the side of the white man, that she could open his stores of supplies, take out a pipe, carve her own tobacco, fill her pipe and pass the plug to whomsoever she desired before returning it to the box. Later she explained to me that she did this because there was a certain woman in the party who had always been especially cruel toward her. Navarana had been at her house a number of times and seen others fed, but had never been offered anything herself. She had been ordered to come and care for the children while the mother was out visiting, and had overheard herself discussed as if she were little better than a dog. So she dared to boast in order to impress this other women. Still, she had not been certain that I would stand for it, and she had been ashamed of herself.

We all slept well. I woke up in the middle of the night, and heard round me the healthy sounds of many people sleeping. It came over me that now the breach with the past was clean and complete. I had settled down in the Arctic, and I was accepted by my new family. I was happy. I fell asleep again with such a feeling of contentment as few persons ever enjoy.

When we reached Thule, Knud Rasmussen was there before us. He had, of course, already heard that I was married, and he met us with the warmest congratulations. He told me that there was no other girl, from Cape Farewell to Thule, who was good enough for me.

Knud brought with him the lame man, Tatarat, and his mother. I protested vainly that our house was already over-crowded, but since I had added to its congestion with a wife and her grandfather, my protests bore little weight. Besides, Knud needed the poor man to furnish him material for stories.

The other residents of the house complained of Tatarat's odor, and it must have been high indeed to elicit comment from people who dress in skins and eat nothing but meat. Knud decided to give his friend a bath. The lame man's mother tried to prevent it, but Tatarat made no serious objections. He had had, he said, many strange experiences, and he might as well try bathing for a change. I refused to touch him when I saw his body, which was not like a human body at all, but matted with long black hairs. Knud and Arnajark threw him into the tub and worked on him with brushes used, on pleasanter occasions, for scrubbing the floor. As his skin broke through the dirt, Tatarat's expression changed from one of surprise to delight. In later life he took several more baths and became a great propagandist for soap and hygienics.

Navarana was almost as happy as she could be. All her clothes were ready for her now, and she was easily the best dressed woman

Top. NAVARANA SETTING HER FOX TRAPS.

Bottom. WOLVES WERE VERY DANGEROUS AND HAD TO BE SHOT.

in the tribe. There was only one fly in the ointment: when certain women came to trade they recognized the skins they had traded to me in her garments, and they never neglected to tell her how happy they were at being permitted to furnish her with clothes. Mayark's wife remembered the circumstances of catching this fox, and Amémé told Navarana that she had been in a quandary whether to keep that one—"that one on the left sleeve"—for herself or sell it. Then she had caught one she liked much better, so she had sold this one.

This, of course, was not to be endured by any housewife, especially the wife of a hunter, and Navarana decided to trap her own foxes.

Trapping foxes had been a woman's job until Knud and I arrived among the tribe. The men could fight walrus and bears, and could hunt seals, since it takes great skill and strength to kill them. But now that fox pelts represented actual value, the men competed with their wives. The women, however, still had to procure skins for their own and their children's garments.

Navarana had already trapped a number of foxes, but had never before been permitted to keep the skins for herself. Now she had a team of her own dogs, and she visited her own traps and had great good luck. Very often I drove out with her and she taught me how to outsmart the animals. Sometimes we rode together from early morning until late at night, and she regaled me with tales of her own life and the lives of the natives whose joys and scandals few men of the white race are ever permitted to glimpse. She was also intimately informed concerning the various Arctic and Polar expeditions, from the point of view of the natives. In almost every instance the Eskimos chose to praise the worthy and denounce the unworthy.

Dr. E. K. Kane has a splendid reputation among them; Dr. Isaac I. Hayes, a very bad one. Peary is their idol, and Dr. Cook denounced for reasons that have nothing to do with his alleged trip to the Pole. He was usually kind to the natives, they said, but they never trusted him, though they could give no particular instances of his deceit.

Our fall passed without unusual incident. Old man Mequsaq kept busy. He owned no meat at Thule, and refused to take any from me, but he was related in some manner to almost everyone in the community and secured enough to feed his dogs. He liked to hunt foxes but would not do so at the bird cliffs where everyone else hunted. He must go to Saunders Island and trap them where the task required real ingenuity. He was lucky in trapping a number, but for some reason best known to himself he insisted upon giving away all the females and bringing home only the males. Since he always happened to trap more females than males, he made many of the neighbor women happy. I asked him why he did this, but he could not explain it, and Navarana, wiser than myself, begged me to allow him to do as he chose. He had been born in another country, she said, and in other times, and perhaps our ways seemed strange to him too. She was right, of course, but I was again surprised to find such tolerance and breadth of vision among the natives.

2

Knud and I liked to make the trip to Tassiussak together—and this winter Navarana would go with us. We had prepared a great many gifts for Christmas and I suggested that we postpone the voyage until the next moon. We discussed it at length, but finally decided that postponing the trip so long might make our return to Thule rather dangerous, so we must set out early in December or not at all.

Nevertheless, we had our Christmas party—and a fine one it was, even if we did celebrate it on December 13th. Knud rigged up an artificial tree, and the natives were dazzled by its lights and colors. We invited everyone in the settlement, and everyone came. Each one accepted his gift with the utmost solemnity. The native missionary and his family were at first somewhat skeptical as to our wisdom in changing the date of the holy day. But when they understood that if they did not approve they would receive no presents, they realized that, so long as the church must be flexible, it might as well bend a little to the left at this time. We ate roast goose out of tin cans, and cakes, and sang all the Danish Yuletide songs. Navarana told me that, after this Christmas, she could never again pity herself. When there are such good times and such joy in the world, all other worries and troubles become insignificant details unworthy of discussion.

Knud and I suggested that, since the trip would be a cold one, Navarana wear a man's costume. She was violently opposed to the idea at first, but when Knud assured her that in South Greenland the colony managers' wives all wore men clothes, she finally consented. The man's costume is much warmer, consisting of a long coat and bearskin pants reaching to the knees. The woman's pants are made of foxskin and are much shorter. Their boots extend to the crotch, making walking difficult, and running almost impossible. The men wear a string of fox tails around their knees where boots meet pants to fend off wind and catch drifting snow. Secretly Navarana's friends laughed at her when they first saw her in a man's outfit, but later she told them how comfortable she was, and within two years all the smartest girls in the tribe provided themselves with such a traveling costume.

We set out shortly after our "Christmas," with the new moon. When we reached Cape York we discovered Qolugtinguaq, who had returned from his voyage "to forget his great sorrow." He was once again the jolly old friend, and had fascinating stories to relate about the places he had visited.

The day before we decided to go on we were all awakened by an ear-splitting yell and an answering roar from the natives on the ice. A young fellow had been sent up from Cape Melville to tell everyone that a great narwhale stake was in progress at Imnalugssuak.

Now a narwhale stake is the dream of every hunter, but it is so colossal a thing that no one dares speak of it openly. Within an hour we were all racing toward Imnalugssuak. No one slept on the way down, and when we arrived we found the two small houses in the community jammed with people, and the excitement running high. The moon was brighter, and we left all of our women at the houses and drove out to the scene of the stake, about two hours away. On the way we passed great piles of meat and blubber, tusks and mattak. The natives had naturally taken as much meat as they could before sending the word to the surrounding country.

An entire school of narwhales had been caught by the ice. A sudden cold spell had hardened the ice around the spot where they were feeding, pressing them into an ever-decreasing space. At last there was so little space left that there was not enough room for all to breathe and they crowded and shoved against each other when they came up for air, splashing water up over the edge of the ice and thickening it further, until they were complete prisoners.

They dived and swam as far as possible in search of another hole, but always they came back for air. Every half-hour or more they came to the surface of the hole in great numbers, fighting and lunging about. It was not safe merely to shoot them, for the dead whales would be pushed aside under the ice shelf. We had to harpoon them and let them remain on the end of our lines until the school dived again. Then we could haul them up onto the ice and be ready for the return of the live ones. We could never tell in the darkness how many there were, but no matter how many we killed it seemed that just as many came back to the hole in the ice.

The poor animals had a bad time. They were not frightened of us—a harpoon under their hide was as nothing compared to their air hunger—and it was almost an act of mercy to kill them, since they would have strangled to death or, had they come out onto the ice, been frozen.

We made a wonderful catch, finally refusing to harpoon the small ones but waiting for the biggest tusks to appear. We collected hundreds in our store that year.

The narwhales continued to return to the hole for two days— one of those days the real Christmas. I stood beside the blowhole and watched the steam from their blood and heard the desperate breathing of the unfortunate beasts. The moon was over us, and the northern lights danced from one horizon to the other. Never have I seen such splendor of illumination. The men, tired but still excited, jumped about and yelled. We had built big fires beside the blowhole, but nothing could frighten the whales away. It was cold but calm, and none of us felt the sting of frozen toes or fingers. We cooked meat and mattak as we worked.

And then finally the school disappeared and did not return at all. The last time they came to the surface there were only a few small ones, and we decided not to kill them but await the bigger fellows, and these did not come back. Evidently they had found a crack in the ice somewhere else and saved themselves. But we already had more meat than we could use, and had only kept up the slaughter because the opportunity might never present itself again.

The tusks—the well-known spiral horn which was once sup-' posed to be that of the unicorn—could in those days be sold profitably in China and India. The Chinese used them for medicine. Since that time the Americans have brought their patent medicines to China, and the yellow people no longer eat pulverized unicorn horn for their ailments.

When I returned to the settlement I found Navarana installed in one of the houses like the grand dame she was. Later she told me that some of the older women—among them a few of her own relatives—had been forced to sleep outside on the sledges, and had complained. But Knud had insisted that she sleep inside and never in the future defer to her relations.

The rest of the trip was tiresome and uneventful. At Bjoerneborg we found provisions which Nielsen had cached for us during the summer, and Navarana commenced to worry over her debut in the outside world. Should she wear her man's costume or should she go back to her own decent way of dressing? We assured her we still had a long distance to travel, and the people she would meet would not be judges of style. Still the entrance into a new country excited her so much that she did not sleep at all the last night. She saw her first completely wooden house, and was sure that she would soon be in contact with people, all of whom could read and write.

When we approached the first settlement all the men ran out to greet us, shouting: "Kuisimangitut tikeqisut.—*The unbaptized are coming.*"

The Polar Eskimos did not know the difference between "baptized" and "unbaptized," but those who had visited in Danish Greenland had always been looked down upon by the baptized southerners because of their natural status, and so they resented it. Navarana had heard the term used belittlingly, and now that it was applied to her she tilted her nose in the air and sniffed.

"One gets the idea here that something smells of urine!" she remarked.

Their emancipation from the urine bucket was the Polar Eskimos' triumph over the southerners. The northern people carried it from their houses as quickly as possible, while the southerners used it for everything from driving ghosts out of their dwellings to washing their hair, and keep it inside until the stench brings tears to their eyes. Still, Navarana was a bit premature; before she entered any house she had used the retort which she had planned to give when anybody called her a pagan.

We stayed overnight with Itué and his family, and our arrival was the occasion for the customary celebration. The women were eager to meet Navarana, the girl who had married the white trader, and she was taken from house to house, three houses in fact as Ituisalik's population had jumped fifty per cent this year.

Next day we drove on and stayed overnight at Abel's house, where our first reception was duplicated. Here Navarana saw white linen sheets, and was horrified at the extravagance. But she had yet to meet Nielsen and his wife, the social arbiters of the whole district.

WE ENTERTAIN VISITORS
AND TRADERS AT THULE.
NEITHER ONE QUITE
TRUSTS OUR CAMERA

JACOBINE NIELSEN
(*left*), A TASSIUSSAK
NATIVE, AND NAVARANA

The Nielsens were prepared for our arrival by runners who had gone ahead to tell them of our coming. To my great surprise Navarana was greeted with a certain aloofness, especially by Mrs. Nielsen. Later I learned the cause of it:

The Nielsens had selected me for their son-in-law. Their daughter, Jacobine, was as yet unmarried, and in Danish Greenland marriage is much more of a business proposition than in the far north. My qualifications were nothing to brag about, but when there was only one unmarried white man in the community, I suppose I was a catch. Among the educated natives and half-breeds the parents arrange the marriages of their children, and the young people are fairly content. They know they must marry young, or else suffer the jibes reserved for spinsters and bachelors, those ridiculous figures of Eskimo folklore. The entrance of the bachelor or spinster is always the cue for laughter.

It took Mrs. Nielsen two days to get over her pique, but she soon became one of Navarana's closest friends. Until then she had been living in a splendid social isolation, as she was the only native woman married to a white man—now she could share this questionable distinction with Navarana.

Knud and I left Navarana with the Nielsens as we wanted to meet the district manager at Upernivik and inquire into the fate of a fellow explorer, Ejnar Mikkelsen, who had started for the Thule District via the north coast of Greenland and had never appeared.

The going was bad, as the water was swift between the various islands and wore out the ice from below, and our big sledges and heavy loads were a handicap in the south. We finally reached Krasserssuaq which, in former days, was said to have been the scene of disgraceful goings-on. According to tradition, there had been a native brothel there, and strange sexual cults and orgies had held sway. Now a native trader, Bistrup, was the only man there and we avoided his house, since we knew that he slept on fulmar feathers and would expect us to do likewise.

We camped in a cave during a storm that night, and met an Eskimo, Lars, and his son. They stopped and had coffee with us, but Lars was superstitious about sleeping in caves—because of the evil spirits—and insisted upon going on in spite of the storm.

Next day we went on to Kingitok, where Lars' family lived. Within a few feet of his house we found the bodies of the man and boy floating in a narrow stretch of water. We had to bring the tragic news to the widow, and we stayed with her that night.

She bore her sorrow bravely and in silence; we were more touched than we would have been had she cried and shrieked as most natives do to prove their grief. She moved away from the place later, and since then no one has lived at Kingitok, which in former days was a big trading post. The spot also has a certain eminence in history, as it was there that an ancient Scandinavian runestone was discovered—which seemed to signify that the Vikings had penetrated that far north before turning back.

In Upernivik we were the recipients of a brand of hospitality encountered nowhere except in the Arctic. The manager, Harries, and his wife could not do enough for us. It was grand to sleep in a bed between white sheets, and sit at table with white linen napkins on our laps. Every evening we danced, and the carpenter shop rang with our shouts and laughter.

I remember that we asked the manager why he did not join us. He thought we were young jackanapes to be wasting our strength on such frivolity, and told us so. Later Knud took me aside.

"Peter," he asked, "do you think we shall ever be so old that we will not dance whenever we have the chance?"

At the time such a possibility was too remote for consideration, but in 1921 I reminded Knud of his remark. At that time a number of young fellows on an expedition stopped with us at Thule, and asked permission to dance. Then we found it inconceivable that the boys wanted to dance every night they were ashore.

Three pleasant weeks passed, and the ice would not freeze. As we were out of dog food and must leave for home, we decided to use skin boats to transport us across to the good ice. We were also determined, once we reached Thule, to set out in search of Mikkelsen. We bought some oatmeal (both of us hated it so much that we knew it would last a long while), and some solder to repair our stove.

We set out, and the water was as calm and free of ice as it would be in summer. The sun was returning, and by noon it was already fairly light. Several of the natives accompanied us to bring the boats back.

One incident occurred en route to Tassiussak which boded ill for the success of our venture. While rowing we sighted an object in the water—and, approaching it, decided that it was a sleeping seal. One of our boys, Nasaitordluarssuk, had his harpoon ready before anyone else and hurled it at the very moment I discovered what it was. My shout was too late, and the harpoon struck the body—the body of a drowned man, Peder Lynge, a good friend of ours. He had gone out to shoot seals from the ice, and had worn new kamiks with slick soles. Apparently he had slipped and fallen into the water.

Now we had mistaken him for a seal and harpooned him—which, to a superstitious people, is worse than killing a man outright. The native minister refused to tell the wife, and we had to turn back with the body. The poor boy who had harpooned the body, was told to cut off the handle of the weapon and leave the point in the dead man, and he was forced to give the stick to the widow to be buried with Lynge. I recall it all as a very painful ending to our delightful stay at Upernivik.

We were told that we had better give up all thought of the search for Mikkelsen. It was clear to everyone that we were not meant to go.

This advice followed us, of course, to Tassiussak, and Navarana, unfamiliar with such superstitions, was warned to prevent my going. She was troubled and did not know what to do. Here was her friend, Dorte Nielsen, a wise, older woman, offering her advice which ran counter to her husband's belief. Navarana's admiration for me was great, but Dorte Nielsen insisted that all men were fools. What should she do?

On our trip back to Thule a child was born at Saitoq with a tooth already in its mouth. This was also a sign to the old women that the world was going to end unless something was done to prevent it. The poor natives were frightened lest the minister hear of their bargaining with the devil, but they managed somehow. The devil, once called upon, stuck around.

He approached in the evening from the ice foot in the shape of a black dog. The natives called our boys and Navarana to look at the devil, but they were unable to see him, and felt ashamed because the others, the baptized, could. Sometimes the devil was heard outside the houses, one night just outside Abel's door. One of the girls, braver than the others, poked her finger out through the hole in the skin window, but she pulled it back in a hurry; it felt, she said, as if she had plunged it into boiling water.

Worst of all, the devil ran into some of the houses and had sexual intercourse with the young girls. They could hear him approaching, but they dared not light a match as death would come to them if they did. The poor girls admitted their submission, because they dared not resist the devil. Or so they said!

All these terrible events were related to Navarana, and she was disconsolate because her lack of knowledge and understanding prevented her seeing the devil. We drove away regardless of the portents. Light had returned and with it colder weather, so we hurried to keep warm.

One day as we picked our way across Melville Bay we saw the head of a bear high up on a towering iceberg. We stopped, and could scarcely credit our sight because there were no tracks leading up to the lair. We climbed until we could get a view, and found that there was a pair, a mating couple that had apparently been living on nothing but love for many weeks. It was impossible to drive them down to our level, so I, being the tallest, was chosen to scale the wall and shoot them.

Supported by the others, I chopped holes for my toes in the iceberg, and ascended as gingerly as I could. I was soon beyond the aid of my supporters and had to use my hands and feet to cling to the ice cliff. I reached the little platform which served as an entrance to the cave and tried to maneuver my gun into position, but the male bear had no intention of permitting me to do this, and rushed me. He was so close that I felt as if I were in a cage with him, and I lost my hold on the ice and tumbled back onto the harpoon handles held by my friends. The bear above us retired to his cave and resumed his love-making.

We then decided that I should crawl back up with a rag fastened on the end of my harpoon with which to lure the pair out. This I did, and both bears charged the flag. Knud and Nasaitordluarssuk fired. I realized that I had no talent for playing the part of William Tell's son—the zing of the bullets was entirely too close for comfort.

There is an old superstition among the Eskimos that much evil will result from skinning and cutting up an animal on an iceberg, but there was nothing else for us to do as the bears retired to their cave to die, and it was impossible for us to get them out whole. The blood flowed like a brook and disappeared in a crack as we cleaned the animals. We hooked our lines around the carcasses and began to pull them out of the cave.

The moment we heaved on the meat there was a detonation like a cannon shot. It was all so sudden that I did not know what was happening. But the thunder rolled on and on. I felt as if I were treading air, and saw Knud tossed high above my head. Then I knew nothing until I recognized Navarana smiling down at me and I felt of myself to discover whether I was hurt or not. Aside from a few minor bruises I was all right.

The iceberg, Navarana told me, had exploded, and we had all been hurled from it and out onto the ice below. I looked at the berg, and it was quite different in appearance, for it had tipped over, and was now bottom side up.

The explanation was simple: Icebergs are formed under terrific pressure within the icecap. When they slide out to sea and this pressure is removed, the slightest thing may alter their balance and throw them into violent readjustment. The warm liquid flowing into the crack had done just that. As is so often the case, unreasoning superstition derives from an intrinsic truth.

The amazing thing was that none of us was hurt. The bears were half buried in ice, and our meat was much more accessible than it had been before.

It was too cold to sleep in the open that night, and we built an igloo. The next day, for the first and only time in my life, it was too cold to travel. Our breath fell like snow from our nostrils. I had seen pictured representations of such temperatures, but never before had I known it that cold. We had only a mercury thermometer, and that was rendered useless in this weather. The natives have a rather quaint expression for such extreme cold. They say "it is so cold the urine comes back to one." Which means that when a man passes his water, it freezes before it strikes the ground and builds a little pile of ice which mounts higher and higher as he adds to it.

We had our two bears for meat, and we stayed inside the igloo, though we felt ashamed of ourselves for doing so. Knud tried to pretend we did so because of Navarana, but she protested that this was an affront to her honor. No man would say such a thing about her! If the women at home heard the story, they would think her old and feeble. It was the worst thing they could say of her.

Nevertheless, I remember that no traveling was done that horrible day.

3

We reached Thule without further undue interruption, and found a great many customers waiting to trade with us before we set out on our trip to locate Mikkelsen. We took care of them as best we could, and then began our preparations for the expedition.

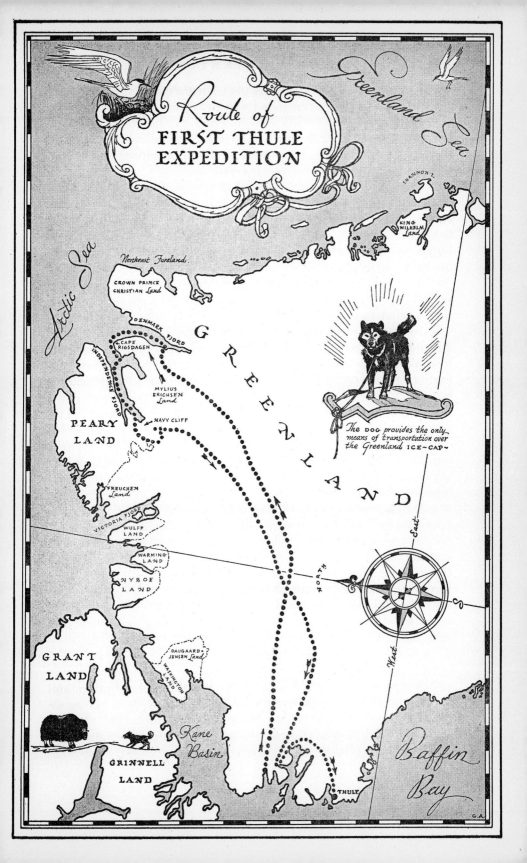

Greenland Sea

SHANNON I.

KING WILHELM Land

Arctic Sea

Northeast Foreland.

CROWN PRINCE CHRISTIAN Land

DENMARK FJORD

GREENLAND

CAPE RIGSDAGEN

INDEPENDENCE FJORD

MYLIUS ERICHSEN Land

NAVY CLIFF

PEARY LAND

FREUCHEN Land

VICTORIA FJORD

WULFF LAND

WARMING LAND

NYBOE LAND

GRANT LAND

DAUGAARD-JENSEN Land

WASHINGTON LAND

Kane Basin

GRINNELL LAND

THULE

Baffin Bay

Route of **FIRST THULE EXPEDITION**

The DOG *provides the only means of transportation over the Greenland* ICE~CAP~

East

North

West

G.A.

I wanted to determine our longitude as accurately as possible. I would have the good fortune, or so I thought, to observe an eclipse of one of the planets by the moon shortly before we were due to set out and thus check my calculations. I figured and figured, awaiting the day. I have never been very good at astronomy, but I was better than Knud, so I tackled the job. I checked my figures three times, and each time the task occupied a full day.

And then on the day of the eclipse a snowstorm blew up, and we saw nothing of the moon, let alone an eclipse of a planet by it. And so we would have to set out with our approximate longitude, as usual. Nowadays when I listen to time signals on the radio, I can't help but remember the futile hours I have spent with my crude instruments, and obtaining usually inaccurate results.

We were to take with us my father-in-law, Uvdluriark, and a fine young fellow, Inukitsork. They were the best men available and both volunteered to make the trip, not as hired men, but as Greenlanders whose unique privilege it would be to take a look at the other side of their country, and make their own observations.

Legend had peopled the back side of Greenland with all sorts of monsters, but Peary had reported that there were no inhabitants whatever. Matew Henson (Marripaluk), Peary's negro servant, had, however, done his best to replace the legend of, for instance, wild people who existed on stones, with exaggerations quite as singular. There were, he had told the Eskimos, rabbits large as dogs, and many other astonishing phenomena. Now was the opportunity to prove or disprove it.

We planned to follow the sea to the north coast, and then go east until we met Ejnar Mikkelsen, or came upon traces of him. We would return, well, when we returned. We might be forced to spend the winter on the other side, but what of that?

We took plenty of tools and ammunition, matches and some spare wood. Our first object was to get enough dog food for the first lap of the journey, and that was best secured at Neqé. Vivi went north with us, too, protesting the while. We had closed the post, leaving Navarana in the annex, and she was glad to be free of the criticism of the old hag. Before we returned Vivi had married a fine young fellow no older than her own son.

At Neqé we interrupted the social season of North Greenland. Hunting had been bad during the year, and now everyone was here to replenish his supplies. Knud immediately took command, sent the young boys out to get game for us, and had the women sewing all manner of new clothes for us, never neglecting to break the monotony of the work with parties.

At one of them, I remember, we ate qongulaq, the strongest dish the natives prepare. It requires a certain skill to make it, but the result is worth—to the natives—any amount of trouble. They pickle walrus liver in a bag of blubber, keeping all air away from the liver. They suspend the blubber bag in a stone cache or cave for a year or more. It must not touch the ground, and the sun must not reach it. When it is ready to be eaten the liver is green as grass, and tastes like strong, hot curry. Knud had two such livers, and he apportioned them around by the spoonful when the party was at its gayest. It made the gourmet catch his breath and brought tears to his eyes, but the success of the whole gathering was assured by this delicacy.

The day before we intended to leave I was called to a conference. Uvdluriark had been looking at the map, along with a number of the other natives who had been with Peary, and he thought it would be a waste of time to follow the coast around to the east.

"Why can't we go straight across?" he asked. "It looks as if it would be a short cut."

I tried to explain to him that such a course would lead us directly over the icecap—that we would encounter no land, and no game!

"The icecap is only a road without rough ice," he persisted.

We all talked it over and argued the possibilities. Then Knud joined the discussion, and asked me if it would not be possible.

Thus did we plan our inland ice voyage in the year 1912.

There was nothing to prevent our trying it, except that we had insufficient provisions, no goggles to prevent snowblindness, and we knew we would find no wild game until we came down on the other side.

"If you can navigate us across," Knud said, "we'll look out for the food!"

And so it was decided.

I went to my igloo to check my figures once more, and could find nothing amiss. I had my theodolite, and my two watches would be of no more aid one route than another. I determined to try to drive straight across the icecap and descend on the east coast at the head of Denmark Inlet. At any rate, all I had to do was guide the party up to the right latitude and then continue eastward. We would in time be bound to strike land and could later ascertain what land it was.

Next day we started out—thirty-four sledges and three hundred sixty dogs. The natives would return to Neqé as we made room on our four sledges for the extra meat they hauled. Wise men of the tribe told us to ascend the icecap via Clemens Markham's Glacier—named for the old English admiral whose splendid explorations had been made near Neqé.

The first day we did not go far. The glacier was steep, and the humidity and heat were exhausting. The thirty-four sledges stretched back from us in a long, ragged column. The teams were eager to overhaul each other, even our own dogs who did not realize they had so far to go. We had used an old trick to advantage here—harnessing the bitches in heat among the forward teams; then the team of dogs where they really belonged could haul any load in order to catch up with them. It was springtime, and we had plenty of she-dogs to encourage their teammates to superdog efforts.

A hodometer was attached to my sledge—a wheel that runs between the uprights and indicates the distance covered. It was scaled in kilometers, but it is impossible to travel in a straight line with dogs, and we could not figure the distance exactly. Nevertheless, it was better than nothing.

The glacier was surfaced better than any I had ever seen. It was slightly uneven in places, with a few bowlders of ice caused by running water the preceding summer, but there were almost no crevasses, and none large enough to swallow a man.

We did not feed our dogs the first night, so we had the whole crew with us another day. The four who were going farthest had tea and sugar. Next morning soon after starting out we reached a spot where the going was terrible. All the snow had blown off the ice, leaving no foothold for the dogs—and we were constantly ascending. We had to unload, drive on with half our loads, and return for the rest. Late in the afternoon we reached snow again and kept on until our dogs were exhausted. The third day there were only twenty-seven teams, and we sent more home each day as our dogs consumed the walrus meat. After three more days we reached the interior dome of the icecap, and bade good-bye to all our helpers.

We were at last at the spot where the success or failure of the expedition would depend upon our speed. And our speed de-

Top. BREAKING CAMP ON THE ICECAP. HOLES HAVE BEEN CUT IN THE IGLOOS AS AN EXIT.

Bottom. THE START OF THE FIRST THULE EXPEDITION. ASCENDING CLEMENS MARKHAM'S GLACIER.

pended upon native methods, which no expedition of whites had ever used before.

The icecap is especially difficult to traverse because of the soft dry snow through which the runners cut easily. We had brought along from Neqé walrus hide sliced into long strips as broad as the palms of our hands. These we fastened beneath the runners of the sledges. Then we melted snow with our primus stoves and poured the water over the long strips, letting it freeze. It took us twenty-four hours to prepare the runners, but when we finished the sledges were almost as easy to shove as a baby carriage. With such runners much greater loads can be hauled over loose snow, and we had the advantage over sea-ice travelers that we could spread out our load without danger of its catching against ice hummocks.

At three o'clock on the morning of April 14, 1912, I took the hour angle, and we set out. Our course lay east-northeast, and it was no task to hold the direction so long as we could see the sun. Later on we shifted to northeast, so that we had the sun directly in front of us every morning when we set out.

Inside the icecap the snow drifts constantly. Even when one is unaware of the wind, dry snow sifts through the air covering everything, like flour in a mill. In no time the sledges were white, and the loads saturated with the stuff. We looked like ghosts driving ghost dogs. When we put our hands in our pockets we even encountered the snow dust there, and it was not very pleasant.

My special job, of course, was taking observations. Knud had never learned much about astronomy as mathematics had always been difficult for him and he had had a schoolteacher who always tried to humiliate him before his classmates. As a result he hated everything about figures, and a table of logarithms was enough to make him vomit.

So far as I was concerned I did not mind this task—at first. My talent made me especially valuable to the expedition, and in the evenings when the others were cooking I could figure out my observations. But in the mornings it took me a long time to get the hour angle, take the temperature and pack my instruments, and do all those tedious little things which are annoying for others to watch. They always drove on without me. I had a number of bad frights when the drifts had covered their tracks before I was ready to follow, and once, when they had gone far out of the prescribed course, it was only by chance that I caught sight of them through the valley between two drifts. Of course, we all had enough common sense to realize that in case we were separated, the only thing to do was to lie down and wait for calm weather before we tried to find each other.

I felt an especial responsibility, since, if I were lost, the others would be unable to return home and might wander for days, or until they died of starvation, on the icecap.

At night we tied the dogs with walrus hides, although they were usually too tired to try to break away and only amused themselves by gnawing at the blubber on the inside of the hide. At the time we saw no reason why they should not do this—it even lessened the load—but later we became so ravenous for fat that we wanted nothing else, and by then there was no fat left.

Every morning Knud woke us with his Danish songs, and his voice was so wonderful that it gave us energy to get started. Knud had once planned to become an opera singer, but had met with discouragement from the impresarios. Now he declared that his voice was too good for opera. Be that as it may, his lively humor carried us through many a bad day.

We were determined never to give up—that was our motto. We were both poor—terribly poor—but we assured each other that even if we were overtaken by our creditors—which seemed unlikely in the middle of Greenland's icecap—our sense of humor would never be squelched.

We made up to ninety-five kilometers a day, though our dogs were not in the best condition. They had been ready to shed their winter coats, and now we had driven them into the coldest section of the world where it was impossible for them to find any shelter at night.

All of us soon looked terrible. We were at an altitude of six thousand feet, and the sun's rays were white-hot metal in our eyes. Everywhere we looked the landscape glittered, and at the same time it was so cold that our faces froze and our skin burned under the ultra-violet rays. It commenced to peel off. The skin on Knud's and Uvdluriark's cheeks hung in ragged splotches, and my nose was raw and bleeding.

We could not have endured water, even if we had had any, and soon we had no fat to apply to our affected parts. Our craving for fat became an obsession. Each man carried his own food, and I remember that one night all four of us sorted out clear blubber and cooked it. The soup was nothing but liquid fat, and we drank it like sweet milk. To swallow lean meat was as difficult as eating dry flour. The dogs were similarly affected. They refused to eat meat and, if they tried, it stuck in their throats. Whenever possible we thawed out pieces of walrus hides and cut chunks for them. There was much fat on it, and it satisfied them. But soon there was no more blubber for our lamps—we had eaten it all.

Until we reached the center of the icecap the wind was in our faces, but when we came to a large area in the very center there was no wind at all—apparently there never is any wind there; the snow remained so soft that we could not cut it into blocks for igloos, and had to resort to our tent. It was constructed of fabric not much thicker than bed sheets, but it lasted the whole time, and it served as a home for us during the summer. We anchored it in the snow and, even if it was cold, we were so fagged out by night that we never again made igloos during the whole trip.

The dogs began to be unmanageable, and we had to resort to our whips. We realized that they had to be fed more than planned on, and we saw our supplies running out faster than we had thought they would. If we could only get down to land before we had to eat any of the dogs, we could find something for them—and us—to eat. But they grew lean, and so did we. We had overestimated our endurance, but there was nothing for it now but to go on to the end.

The worst calamity of all—for all of us—was that I was slowly falling a victim to snowblindness. Unless a person has experienced it, he cannot appreciate the torture. Your eyelids feel as if they are made of sandpaper. Knud Rasmussen, who had much dark pigment in his eyelids, was not troubled, but I am rather light. Added to this, I had to take all the observations. Each time I shot the sun a hot poker seemed to be plunged into my right eye—a rather unpleasant feeling. I tried to shift over to my left eye, but it was soon as irritated as the right. The lids were so inflamed that I could scarcely open my eyes at all.

But my observations must continue. Now that we were nearer land, it was all the more important that we know our approximate position. Each night I painfully made my calculations. And how I blessed a howling gale which kept us inside the tent for a day or two! I would pray that the storm would continue, but since we had decided that unless we traveled we did not eat, I was torn between the gnawings of my stomach and the scratching of my eyelids.

We traveled whenever humanly possible, and I continued to

make my observations as accurately as ever. Finally a day came when I announced that tomorrow we would sight land. I was none too certain of it myself, but my figures told me we should. I had allowed two kilometers on my hodometer to count for one mile (taking into account the tortuous route pursued by dog teams)—one minute of a degree. Then I had only to obtain the latitude, which I could do at noon and at midnight.

The icecap was now definitely dipping toward the sea, and the going was easy except for the snowdrifts. We were hardened against everything, cold and wind and pain, and there was in us only a concerted drive to reach land again—and fresh food. Suddenly I heard a shout and pried my eyelids open. There before us, between the drifts, were mountains! We were as happy as if we had found an unexpected cache of provisions. We even discussed eating our fourteen pounds of oatmeal, the last resort.

Now that we had hard ice to drive on we had no more use for our walrus-skin runners, so we took them off, chopped some up and fed it to the dogs.

Descending from the icecap is always more precarious than climbing onto it, for one cannot be certain what he will find at the foot. When we were close enough to the edge Uvdluriark went ahead to explore. We waited for him, I with my eyes closed and my coat over my head. He was gone for hours, but when he finally came back he said he thought he had discovered a route down.

Once again we started the dogs, and this time the ice was so smooth and the slope so steep that the sledges ran up onto the dogs' traces. Knud's sledge ran over the neck of his left wing dog and killed it on the spot, but we could not even stop to pick it up and save it for food. There was no controlling the sledges, and I had to open my eyes regardless of the pain. The sledges chose separate routes down—there was nothing we could do to guide them—and I wondered whether we could stop them in time to avoid their crashing off the final drop onto the hard ice of a lake at the foot.

The wind was strong at our backs, and occasionally I caught a glimpse of my three mates whizzing along amidst a scramble of tumbling, snarling, yapping dogs. Then suddenly our paths converged in a kind of glacier river bed, and we all drew to a stop and unscrambled our dogs.

We looked about us, and found that we had stopped just in

MY TEAM FORDING A STREAM ON THE ICECAP

THE PERPENDICULAR WALL OF ICE IN DESCENDING WHICH I HARPOONED MYSELF time. The glacier dropped in a perpendicular wall fifty feet to solid ice below—and there was no mattress to land on!

We tied our three harpoon lines together—it was impractical to detach the points from the lines as they were fastened on with leather stitches—and figured that they would reach the bottom. It was hard to get a foothold on the smooth ice at the top. We chopped holes to make it rough, and dug a couple of deeper holes for leverage. We also had to have a double line so that the last man to descend could, by a hazardous process, bring himself and the lines down together.

Glacier ice is brittle in comparison with salt-water ice, and I was to go down first, since I was the heaviest. If the lines would hold me, the rest could descend safely. The idea was not particularly gratifying to me, but there was nothing else to be done.

A sealskin line is slippery and hard to grip, so I had to wind it once around my thigh. I lowered myself carefully over the edge, and started down as slowly as possible. Everything seemed to be going well until I happened to glance down. Within two inches of my thigh was the point of the second harpoon. I tried to grasp the line tighter with my mittens and hold myself up. I screamed, but they could not hear me above; even if they had heard me they could have done nothing. I had to make my way over the point somehow.

My hands continued to slip, and I felt the point penetrate my pants, and then my flesh. I kicked and finally got the loop free of my leg. But the harpoon point was already well into my thigh, and in coming out it tore a long, deep gash. It was over in a moment—I was rushing down now holding the line only by my hands—but I had time to realize that it must be rather unpleasant to be a seal. My swift descent was stopped when I struck the first knot below the point. I fastened the line round my leg once more and continued slowly to the bottom.

4

My entrance into the new country was not auspicious. I tried desperately to stop the blood with the use of snow and my inner mittens. It was cold, especially with my pants torn and soaked with blood, and now added to the pain in my eyes was the sharp throbbing of my leg.

I could do nothing but wait for the others. They lowered the sledges and dogs, three at a time, but some of the dogs at the top grew panicky and jumped—beautiful flying arcs that ended in death. The boys were the last to descend.

We cut up more of the walrus-hide runners and cooked them for ourselves; then brewed some tea. We tied the dogs; the three that were dead we chopped up for their teammates. The dogs did not eat them at once, but next morning there were no signs of the carcasses.

Unfortunately I was now in such a state that I could do nothing. My eyelids were as thick as my lips, and I could only pry them open with my fingers. I could not walk without reopening the wound in my leg, and so there was nothing for me to do but lie quiet for a few days while the others explored the country and procured something to eat. They left one dog behind with me to warn me of bears or wolves.

All I wanted to do was to crawl head first into my sleeping bag and get away from the everlasting glare. I wanted no food but fat, and there was none. I wound my watches, but I did not look at them— I felt the need of complete relaxation for my eyes after nineteen days of observations on the icecap. We had actually traveled for only eleven days, but sometimes for more than twenty-four hours at a stretch; the rest of the time we had been laid up on account of storms.

Now the last thing I wanted to do was *observe* anything, and I kept no account of the passage of time. It was foggy, too, and Knud and his companions would have been unable to observe the movement of the sun, had they thought of it. At any rate, they did not think of it; they were after food and food only.

After two or three days their dogs would go no farther, and they were compelled to butcher the poorest ones and throw them to their fellows. Yet among dogs are found characters almost as various as among men. Some dogs do not give a damn what they eat; some will eat their own mothers, as I have often witnessed, and others will starve to death before touching the bodies of their teammates. Again some refuse to eat the meat while it is still warm, but perhaps after it is cold they will forget what it is and devour it greedily.

Knud and his companions explored widely and, after crossing a range of mountains, found nothing but two musk-ox cows and their calves. Yet we still had forty dogs with us, and we could easily consume two musk oxen daily. The look of the land did not encourage them to waste their time, so they returned to me with what meat was left.

I felt sure that five days had passed since their departure, and they did not know. When a fellow is alone, has nothing to eat, and can't see, time passes slowly. And the others were tired enough to believe they had been traveling five days, so we took it for granted. Later we suffered for our error. In reality they had been gone only four days.

We had our first regular meal and the odor of soup in our tent was glorious. After we had eaten and drunk tea I felt almost as strong as ever.

Next day we went on toward the sea. We came to a waterfall which I marked on the map, but that mark will never betray the difficulty we had in torturously lowering our sledges over its frozen cascades. In order to place it correctly I had to wait until noon to take the latitude, and the others went on ahead. They warned me that conditions were bad—the ice free of snow and in places splotched with blown sand—on down the river, but there was nothing I could do about it, and I watched them drive off. They had also told me that they had cached some musk-ox meat down the river, and they would leave a piece for me in case I should not catch up with them before I slept.

I observed the sun again—and felt the snowblindness returning. Toward evening my eyes grew even worse. The river, which I had thought was easy after the glacier and the waterfall we had negotiated, turned out to be a devil. The crystal-clear ice was beautiful to look at, but the dogs could hardly stand upright. The sandy splotches made it all the worse; the dogs would make eagerly for them and then pass on diffidently to the clear ice, leaving the sledge moored on the sand and their claws scraping uselessly on the ice. I had to push and yell and swear, and occasionally unload before the dogs could move the sledge.

I have never been nearer giving up and rushing hysterically after my fellows with an empty sledge. I was weary and sick, and each time I unloaded I swore that this would be the last. Finally the blood pounded in me until my whole body ached, and I lay down on my back. Perhaps, I thought, I was not meant for adventure. Adventure demands strong men.

But when it was time to take observations again I was up, though I believed it might be the end of my eyes. And when I finished I felt a little better mentally. At least I knew that I would never be lower than I had just been.

And then at last there was snow and I could see the tracks ahead of me. I could even sit on the sledge and rest. I sat there with my eyes closed and let the dogs worry along in the tracks of my companions. Suddenly they spurted forward only to stop and snarl at each other. I opened my eyes and discovered that they were eating something!

It must be the musk-ox meat left for me! I leapt from my sledge and hurled myself headlong into the mass of snarling dogs, fighting like a wild animal myself for my share. I grabbed a bone—there was still some meat on it—and ran back to my sledge. I sat there a while gnawing it as if it had been an apple. It must be, I thought, the hind leg of a musk-ox calf, so delicious and tender it was. I could smell the odor of raw beef, and with my eyes closed I ate and ate, until I reached a spot on the leg which felt peculiar. I opened my eyes, and discovered that the nails of a dog's foot were all but scratching my face.

It was a dog's leg I had grabbed—one of the dogs which Knud had had to butcher! When I finally reached the place where the boys had pitched the tent and told them what had happened they roared with laughter. Later on this episode was related by the Eskimos as the funniest thing they had ever heard. The story even reached South Greenland ahead of me.

The following day was cloudy, and my eyes were grateful. We drove a short distance and then decided that we would cut the expedition down to three teams, using the fourth sledge for fuel. We butchered the four scrawniest dogs, and fed them to their teammates and ourselves. Dog meat is not too bad when the dog is young and fat, but ours were half starved and worn out with fatigue. Still, the meat was filling. The soup, however, was so strong that we had to drink tea afterward to get the taste out of our mouths.

Next day we went out in scouting parties—Knud and Uvdluriark to the east, Inukitsork and I to the west. We shot a rabbit and ate it raw, saving the skin for a handkerchief, but on the second day we returned to camp, realizing that this was no place to stay—no musk-ox tracks, no sign of big wild game anywhere.

Knud returned after four days with news that he had seen the sea. (He also brought three rabbits and six ptarmigans—he had eaten three of the latter already.) We looked at the map, and Knud was positive that what he had seen was Independence Bay, and the land across it, Peary Land.

If that were the case, then my calculations were haywire. If we were only as far as Independence Bay, we had a long way yet to travel before we reached Denmark Inlet, and the country looked anything but promising.

I determined to have a look at the sea for myself. I took my theodolite and my gun and set out, but not far from camp I saw something that erased all thought of my destination from my mind—three musk oxen. They were walking slowly, two of them together, the third a short distance behind. I saw that they had been fighting—their horns were broken—and I fancied that they were a pair and an intruder. As I followed them I tried to reconstruct their lives in this wilderness, living off only a little moss and twigs. And even for this they had to dig.

It is no great sport to shoot musk oxen, because the beasts will turn and await the bullets with the stoic stupidity of Russian soldiers. Their best weapon is their color; when they stand still it is difficult to distinguish them from the stony background. I killed them all with six shots, and found them to be three bulls, an old one and two younger ones. I cut out the stomachs, so that the carcasses would not ferment, then extracted the tongues and hearts and, caching my instruments at the carcasses, walked back to camp.

I tried to approach my companions as if nothing had happened, but my face betrayed the fact that I had a prize. I tossed the tongues and hearts to the ground as if this were an ordinary, everyday occurrence, but they let out such a whoop as I have seldom had the pleasure of hearing.

After we had eaten I turned in and slept while the others went ahead to the spot where I had left the cache. Next day when I joined them I found the dogs lying about stuffed with meat, and before the tent a big fire made with Cassiope Tetragonalis.

Unfortunately Inukitsork had a touch of snowblindness, and we could not go on until he was better. The poor fellow lay with his head beneath the musk-ox skins and suffered intensely. We made tea and applied the steeped tea leaves to his eyes. Peary had discovered that tea leaves are soothing for sore eyes, and much better than cocaine. If cocaine is used, one must bandage the eyes immediately, as the drug completely desensitizes the area, and caribou hair, or some other irritant, may lodge in the eyes and cause permanent injury.

While we waited for Inukitsork to recover I made sufficient observations to prove that we had reached Denmark Inlet, not Independence Bay. Our journey down to it, via what we named Zigzag Valley, had cost us more days and dogs than the whole journey over the icecap. This was, evidently, the place where our old friend Mylius-Erichsen had spent the summer prior to his death. The knowledge was anything but reassuring to us, and we lost no time in moving on as soon as Inukitsork was fit to travel.

The feel of the tough salt-water ice under us once more was good. It was late spring now and the scenery through the fjord was gorgeous. The dainty red saxifrage smiled at us from the rocks, and occasionally yellow poppies bloomed in the more fertile spots. Our dogs were filled with food again and we were happier than we had been for a long time.

Soon we sighted signs of habitation on shore, and when we drove closer we discovered that it was actually the summer camp of our three unfortunate friends, Mylius-Erichsen, Hagen the soldier, and Joergen Broenlund, the brave Eskimo who had succeeded in bringing back the records of their explorations at the cost of his life. Their camp had been made in a most desolate spot. There was no game for miles around, and during the summer no possibility of getting away. Nothing to do but settle down to a lingering, horrible death.

Near-by they had burned a sledge—the ashes were still here. One of the iron runners was stuck in the ground to attract any travelers who might pass later. The dung of the dogs contained innumerable pieces of cloth, wood and rope, which indicated that they had consumed anything and everything. There were also bits of clothing which I recognized as belonging to the Danmark Expedition.

The men had built a cairn, but there was no written message in it or any indication of where they had gone. Later on we learned that Ejnar Mikkelsen (the man we were looking for) had been here before us and had taken the script in the cairn without leaving any word of himself.

However, we assumed he had never been here and wondered whether we should go northwest in search of him at Independence Bay and the Peary Channel, or turn south along the east coast. Our equipment was equally inadequate for either venture, but I knew that if we were compelled to stay over next winter we could live to the south—I had spent months alone there a few years before. So we decided first to head north, and rounded the northeast corner of Greenland—Cape Rigsdagen—named for the Danish parliament.

It is not a very conspicuous mountain, but I determined to climb it, as it offered the only vantage point in the vicinity.

To the south was the promontory which cut off the view of the east coast. That promontory had been the goal of any number of explorers before us. They had either died or been forced to give up. That we had reached this spot was not due to our ability, but to the fact that we had Eskimo friends and had adopted their technique of travel.

I let my gaze wander out across the ice-jammed sea. The atmosphere was exceptionally clear. Far out to the northeast where the maps say there is nothing but open water, I believed, and I still do believe, that I saw mountains and the outlines of land. It may have been "water sky"—the steam rising from an open stretch of water. This phenomenon has deceived far more learned men. Remember that Robert Peary thought he saw "Crocker Land" from Grant's Land at the northern tip of Ellesmere Island. I am still not convinced, however, that I did not see land from Cape Rigsdagen, and that section of the sea has been insufficiently explored to prove me wrong.

The coast looked none too inviting, so we crossed over to Peary Land. We had heard of this locality from the leader of the only expedition that had been there, I. P. Koch, and we expected much of it. We were not disappointed.

From the sea we glimpsed a herd of grazing musk oxen—it is always a good omen for hunting when you sight game before touching shore. We pitched our tent again, and cooked a fine meal. Then we slept and three of us went out hunting while Knud stayed with the dogs and patched his underwear. He hated sewing for himself, but there was nothing else for him to do, and I made fun of the picture he made sitting there with needle and torn garments slung over his knee. He took his revenge on me by using for patches the great blue handkerchiefs my mother had sent me.

We shot the oxen and had to make a number of trips to carry all the meat to camp. The country was a delight to the eye after the bleakness of Zigzag Valley and the glacier. The warm colors were like welcoming smiles. I heard the hum of a bumblebee, a sound unfamiliar to me since my departure from the green pasturelands of Denmark, and saw the green leaves of the little willows which dared not lift their branches in the air but crept furtively among the stones along the ground, pretending that this was the way to greet the summer and bask for a few weeks in the Arctic sun.

We crossed over to explore the Greenland side, but the steep cliffs of Hagen's Fjord were forbidding, and we returned to Peary Land. It is as if all God's favors were distributed on the Peary Land side of Independence Bay, and as long as we remained we were rewarded with an abundance of seal meat and musk oxen.

Our plan was to follow the coast down to the Peary Channel and then, if we did not find Mikkelsen, take it for granted that he had retraced his trail down the east coast. Later we learned that this was, indeed, what he had done.

At one point of the entrance to Broenlund Fjord we camped beside two ancient stone rings which indicated that ages ago tents had been pitched here by Eskimos. The most amazing thing, however, was the fact that straight across each of the rings were left two long wooden tent poles. Looking at the rings gave me a peculiar feeling. We measured and photographed them, but the natives with us were interested in locating the winter houses of these former inhabitants. The dark period, here north of 81 degrees, would be long and rigorous, and it would have necessitated so much meat to carry them through that it seemed almost impossible to kill and store a sufficient quantity.

The obvious thing, of course, was that they merely camped here during the summer and then went on south. One theory had been advanced suggesting that the Eskimos on the east coast of Greenland had arrived there via Cape Farewell, but this cannot be true. We had apparently found proof of the actual route of immigration.

We sat and speculated about the strange people who had once passed this spot. We wondered what they looked like, what hardships they had endured. Inukitsork talked about the women, and said he wished he had brought his wife along. If other women had been here, Tukumeq could have stood what they did and, he said, "We could easily have lived on the food I am eating now. Besides, she is fat and can go a long time on little food.

"It is too bad," he added, "that now one sighs and longs for one's wife, and then as soon as he returns home he will have to beat her terribly. That is the drawback of being married. As long as one was single and hastened from one girl to the next such troubles were not at hand."

With the aid of the field glasses, Uvdluriark sighted a herd of musk oxen in the hills back of us. Though we did not need the meat at present, the ice ahead looked treacherous, and we might have to return to this spot, so we decided to kill them and cache the meat. There were a few calves in the herd, and it was necessary to kill them too. We lay down and sucked the fresh milk from the udders of the cows. The taste was heavenly, at least to me, and the milk gave us badly needed vitamins. I did not know at the time what vitamins were—I confess I don't know any more today, but it is such a handy word to use—and each of us had a cow to empty.

The cows also had some fat on them. Curiously enough, the cows with calf are never so lean as the bulls—nature seems to take care of them. The tallow was mostly on their backs; later in the summer it would be thicker. The marrow was nourishing too. When musk oxen are lean, the marrow in their bones is like water, and tasteless. We took the largest bones, crushed them, and ate the raw marrow, and had a fine dinner afterward of boiled tongues —two for each of us—and boiled hearts. Then we lay down to a long, uninterrupted sleep.

5

As we progressed up the bay the ice changed from bad to worse. I made short observation trips into the hills at the side, and one day I came back to the party with some information which no one would believe: there was no such thing as a Peary Channel between Greenland and Peary Land. I had discovered that a glacier came down to the head of the inlet, and there would be no chance of our going much farther on sea ice.

Knud and our Eskimo friends would not believe me. Knud thought me an incurable pessimist anyhow, and besides, what Peary had said was good enough for him.

We went on up the bay slowly. It was now the middle of June and the brooks were swollen with water. We walked in wet kamiks, and there was no breeze to cool us off; the sun beat down ceaselessly, night and day. Our feet were sore from being saturated for months, and the ice under us was a path of needles which bit through our soles. It was too warm at night to sleep in our bags, and we merely took off our footgear to try to get them dried. And they never dried.

The farther we progressed the more evident it became that there was no Peary Channel—nothing but a high glacier awaited us at the head of the fjord.

Academy Glacier, which Perry has indicated on his map, slopes down from the south in a broad stream of ice, breaking up into small chunks with no more than two meters visible above the surface ice. It was evident that the ice in the fjord did not break up every year. Occasionally it did, however, sweeping the small icebergs into the open sea and leaving broad expanses of open water between the two shores. Now we could see the little icebergs frozen in a long row horizontal with the mainland shore of the inlet.

Along the north, or Peary Land, shore were the two glaciers, Marie Louise and Josephine, so named by Mylius-Erichsen on Hagen's map which Broenlund had brought back to us. I doubt very much whether they had been able to see, judging from the cairn that marked their farthest west passage, whether the Josephine Glacier reached down to the sea. Actually, it does not.

Since 1912 the Danish explorer, Lauge Koch, has been up there and has changed some of the names. I have been interviewed about it, but it makes no difference to me what names are applied. My enjoyment was in being there, not in having been there, and if they place more worthy names on points of interest I shall not turn a pin to prevent it.

The year was advancing fast, and in one more day we would be at the glacier which Peary had believed to be the passage. And then what to do?

If we went back down the east coast it would mean that we could not return home until next year. Our dogs were in wretched condition, their paws cut by the sharp needles that form at the bottom of all the shallow ponds. We had to make kamiks for them, adjust them every morning and take them off every night— if they are left on, gangrene is apt to set in because the tightness of the strings prevents adequate circulation.

The only thing to do was to try to hurry home via the glacier. We had eaten freely of our supply of meat, and the last few days had caught no seals. There were a number on the ice, but they were wild, and when we went after them we often had to swim across pools of open water.

There were twenty-five dogs and three sledges left. If absolute necessity faced us we could kill some of the dogs, eat them, and feed them to their teammates. We could last about a month in that fashion. If we got only one musk ox we thought our journey would be possible.

Our immediate problem was to find an approach to the glacier which we named for our friend Nyboe, one of the two men who had made our venture possible. Uvdluriark was to climb it and find a route back of it; Knud and Inukitsork were to hunt seals; I was to cross the inlet, shoot the sun from a cairn Mylius had left, and collect any notes that might be there.

Laden with my usual outfit, the theodolite, which I carried in a little box in my hand, and one of the ancient tent poles, I set out, leaving to Knud the pleasure of swimming about in the ice water for seals. It was remarkable how strong the pole still was. It must have been several hundred years old, yet the core of the wood was fresh and sturdy; being much longer than my harpoon, I thought it might come in handy in case of bad ice.

The distance was a good deal longer than it had seemed, and I came to many open leads of water which I either had to walk around or jump. I was wet and soon grew tired. When one lives on nothing but meat he eats much more than he ordinarily would to fill himself up, and as a result feels logy.

I had been out more than twenty-four hours when I discovered that the low promontory which was my destination was cut off by a current of fresh water running down from the hills. I had come too far to give up, however, so I determined to try ferrying across on a block of ice. The only piece I could find was fairly small, but I tried it and it seemed safe. With my old tent pole in my hands I stepped on it.

Perhaps a curse of the old Eskimo who had once owned the pole was upon me. At any rate, the ferry did not work. I had to push, and I presume my efforts were too strenuous. Suddenly the ice cracked beneath me and dashed me into the water.

My one thought was for the theodolite, and I had the extreme pleasure of seeing it slide slowly down the cake of ice and disappear in the water. The chill I felt was not exclusively a result of the ice water, since without the instrument it would be impossible to recross the icecap. I could not navigate without it, and we would have to stay here for the winter. And *then* how to get home?

I swam to the edge of the ice and clambered up. Peering down through the water I saw the sparkle of the brass handle on the box. It was in fairly shallow water, but the bottom sloped off to dark depths near-by, and each moment I feared it would slide farther down. I tried to reach it with my pole, but could not, so I threw off my coat and lowered myself into the water. It was terribly cold to my naked chest. Hanging onto the ice ledge with my hands, I tried to reach the instrument with my feet. That was a mistake; I only succeeded in dislodging it and shoving it farther down the embankment. Now I could barely see it. I remembered all the swimming prizes I had won as a student, and thought, "What the hell good are they if not for this emergency?" I dived, and at last felt the box between my fingers.

But I was moving, moving under water. Suddenly I realized that the current was sweeping me under the shadow of the ice. I had forgotten that skin pants are not the best diving suits. Using my last ounce of strength I shot upward, and when my head broke through open water, I was so relieved that I could have cried.

There was no point in my going on now. I was wet and cold, and there were clouds over the sun. Even had I been able to see it, my theodolite was wet and clogged with salt. And so I returned to camp after two days, emptyhanded. I related my adventures to the hunters, who had got two seals, and they told me I was a fool. An Eskimo looks upon a man who can swim as a minor idiot. They listened to my story of having dived head first, and they said nothing in the world could have persuaded them to do such a stupid thing—they could have got home anyway.

And so, instead of being considered a hero, I was greeted with hoots of laughter and rewarded with the terrible job of cleaning the salt out of my theodolite.

It was now the middle of summer, June 23rd, and I should have had the opportunity to correct my date. Remember, we were running a day ahead of the calendar, but here I could see both Navy Cliff and the cairn indicated on Mylius-Erichsen's map. The sun, however, was so high and its angle of declination so minute at this time of year that I failed to discover my error.

Before we ascended the glacier I tried to teach Knud how to secure the hour angle in case I should go snowblind again. But he was a strange man. Possessed of a marvelous brain, he still had made up his stubborn mind that he could never learn how to do it. I tried to teach him, but we both got sore and gave it up amidst hearty laughter at our own sensitiveness. Then Knud celebrated the occasion with tea and pudding. Astronomy had always been a nightmare to him, and now he decided to give up its study once and for all. This, for Knud, was sufficient occasion to celebrate.

I remember the five days it took us to ascend Nyboe Glacier as the worst in my life. Climbing three thousand feet with heavy sledges which the dogs were now too weak to pull, was a task that nearly finished us all. Then crossing it, living on an occasional rabbit or ptarmigan, following the crests which were a labyrinthine confusion, balancing our sledges to prevent their

Top. TWO OF OUR DOGS HOLDING A MUSK OX AT BAY.

Bottom. MUSK OXEN IN FIGHTING FORMATION.

slipping into the crevasses, weaving in and out and doubling on our tracks, we were taken much farther west than we had intended to go, so that finally we looked down into a deep valley. With our glasses we could see that it was covered with flowers and grass, and the glacier sloped smoothly into it.

Under these circumstances we decided to descend and see what we could find there. Knud wanted to look for traces of ancient Eskimos, I desired to mark it on my map, and the Eskimos with us thought they might find musk oxen.

It was a real Arctic oasis. Poppies bloomed abundantly—we named it Poppy Valley—and we were met with a reception committee of twelve musk oxen. Like soldiers they were organized in a square, their horns pointing outward. Musk oxen have learned thus to organize against the wolves, but it would have been better for them to run from our guns. In that way they would learn what cruel animals human beings are. But pursuing the tactics they do, the hunter must kill the whole group. I have tried at different times to kill only one of a group, or as many as I needed, but it is impossible to do this—the others always remain to protect the fallen. No matter how long one waits to approach the carcass, the live animals will never stray far and will return instantly to surround and defend their dead companion.

We were badly in need of fresh meat. We had eaten nothing but rabbits and ptarmigans and some horrible pudding powders which Knud had brought along, so we let our dogs loose. The movements of the musk oxen are lightning fast. They always stand quiet until the dog comes close, then one of the big bulls jumps forward more quickly than the dog can move and often hurls him high in the air. Musk-ox hunting is more dangerous for dogs than a bearfight. I have seen them thrown twelve feet.

The bulls take turns charging, and as soon as one is out of the square, the hole in the ranks is filled by a calf. When the bull retreats from his charge, he is given just space enough to enter.

It is an impressive sight to see one of these huge animals storming forward. The earth resounds with the pounding of his hoofs, stone and gravel sprays to both sides, and the air is electric with his ferocity. I remember that once I wanted to photograph a charging bull, and I stood at what I considered a safe distance. Suddenly through my finder I saw one of the beasts almost on top of me. I fell backward, but in my fear pressed the button, and later developed one of the best pictures I have ever taken. Fortunately my movement frightened the bull, and he retired.

We lived in the valley for several days, making observations and trying to get our dogs fat. Their coats were thin—it was summer where we had been—and they had to face the rigors of the icecap again. The best protection would be to put some fat on them. It was pleasant in the valley. Occasionally it rained, but it did not freeze afterward, and the feel of soft grass and vegetation under our feet was a welcome relief after months of ice.

Before leaving we erected a cairn and named it for Adam Bierring, who, with Nyboe, had financed our whole Arctic venture, and then set out on the ice once more.

We crossed two ice-choked rivers (or rather, crossed one twice) and it was too cold afterward to take off our clothes to dry them. We were so pleased, however, at having crossed the stream safely that I must have been a little careless. At any rate, I remember that I was walking ahead when suddenly I heard screams from the rear, and turning around, saw one of the sledges with only a few dogs in sight, and the other dogs rushing toward it. I hurried back, to discover that five dogs had broken through a crevasse and swung there in their traces. Below them was nothing but cavernous darkness.

We all struggled to pull them up, but before we had succeeded two of the animals had slipped from their traces. I heard them squealing in terror as they fell; fainter and fainter was the noise, and then silence.

I had crossed this very spot without being aware of the crevasse, as well as three other crevasses which we discovered now that we were on the lookout. I realized that, as Knud Rasmussen said, success does not always depend upon intelligence, but at least half the time on luck.

For two days we climbed, and we realized that we must now be at the very spot from which Peary had looked down upon the Nyboe Glacier. It, and the presence of Poppy Valley and various other formations, had seemed to him sufficient reason for believing that there was a channel. Nevertheless, he did not state positively that there was a channel—he only said there seemed to be one. He had actually *seen* Independence Bay; he *knew* there was a similar inlet to the west; and he had every reason to believe that the two inlets met to produce a single, continuous passage. From here we could see the mountains on both sides, and anyone, I believe, would have proclaimed it to be a sound. It is rather interesting to read the Peary and Astrup accounts. Peary *thinks* there is a sound. Astrup states that there *is* one. The younger and more impetuous man was not so cautious as his master.

Our disappointment in finding no channel was somewhat mitigated by the continued laughter of the two Eskimos with us. The fact that the great Peary could have made an error was so humorous that they could not confine themselves to just one laugh.

We had lost a great deal of our supply of food in the river, and knew that we must find another source of meat before we came to grips with the icecap. From our height on the glacier we could see what appeared to be several fertile valleys ahead of us, and so again we descended into one of them, camped beneath a great overhanging rock and remained for three weeks.

There was plenty of fuel in dried willow twigs, and the first thing I did was to remove my clothes to dry them, and lie in the sun. While I slept Knud and the two natives scouted for game and returned with a load of twenty musk-ox tongues and the remark:

"Well, that saves us from staying here all winter!"

They had killed twenty oxen and seen many more. We had found a country richer than our wildest dreams. The land was green, the lakes free of ice and specked with salmon. We repaired our shoes—the soles were nearly worn out from walking over the rocks—with the raw hides while it rained and the weather was too bad for hunting, and piled the meat onto our sledges.

We then cut it up into large chunks and used the hides to bind it. We packed it all on our backs by a strap around our foreheads. In this manner of carrying, if the packer stumbles he can with a deft twist of his neck drop the burden, perhaps saving himself a painful sprain.

We stuffed our dogs with food, and kept them close to the tent so that they would not frighten the oxen away from what we called our "field," in which the vegetation was heavy. We had, in all truth, found a true paradise in the Arctic. The animals had worn paths through the grass, and alongside the vegetation was knee-high.

One day I walked with Knud Rasmussen. We had been out after musk oxen (I could not in truth call it "hunting," it was more like "butchering") and we had used up all but seven rounds of ammunition. We were walking slowly, loaded down with as much meat as we could pack homeward, when we saw before us seven musk oxen. The path was narrow, and the animals blocked the way.

In spite of the fact that musk oxen quietly await the hunter's bullets, they are devils to kill. Their long, shaggy coats make it difficult to estimate the position of the heart, and their great, bony skulls deflect the average lead. We knew it would be a test of our ability to kill seven animals with seven cartridges—and it was a test that showed us up badly. After our ammunition was gone three cows still blocked the way, and two of those brought down were not yet dead.

Knud grabbed my long knife and determined to become, for the nonce, a bullfighter, asking me to be the picador. I was to attract their attention, and approach them with a stone in my hand. At the psychological moment, I was to throw the stone, and Knud was to creep up stealthily from behind and plunge the knife between their shoulders.

The scheme worked on one of the cows, but then they became much more interested in the matador than the picador. Our guns were useless, so we had to stab them between the ribs—which is no decent way to kill a musk ox. We finally saw them all dead before us (we had both been stabbed by their horns), and I decided that this was the last time I would hunt musk oxen without ammunition. Later the Eskimos told us that in former times, before they had guns, musk oxen were not much favored as meat since, like the polar bears, "they did not like to have harpoons in them."

We now thought we had sufficient meat for our trip back across the icecap. We would use only two sledges—which would give us a chance to burn the third and what was left of mine. One more dog was dead, leaving us with only twenty, but enough to haul two sledges.

It rained steadily for eight days and while we waited we had to sit about on the wet stones. I remember that Knud said to me once during this interval:

"If you were home and could choose anything you wanted to eat, what would it be?"

I thought for a long time—we had a long time to think anything over—and finally said: "A piece of musk-ox meat would be as good as anything else!"

He roared, for the same thing had been in his mind. And wasn't it a blessing, as musk-ox meat was all we had to eat for two months?

One morning Knud complained of a pain in his left leg.

He limped slightly during the day, and when we packed meat I noticed that he carried less than the rest of us. That was not like him. In the evening he said he thought the pain had come from sitting on cold, damp stones, and he remembered that our mutual friend, Count Harald Moltke, had been ill all his life from sitting on cold stones as he sketched.

During the night he woke me up and said there must be a rock under his sleeping bag. I knew then that something was wrong; no man would wake a friend on such a slight pretext. He could not sleep, and he said that the worst thing that could happen to us was for someone to be taken sick. Somehow we had never taken this possibility into consideration.

6

Next morning Knud could not walk. He looked bad, and evidently ran a high temperature. There was no doubt that he had sciatica in a violent degree—caused by his having been wet the whole summer.

He grew worse instead of better, but it was not his intention to let us neglect the purposes of our expedition to care for him and he insisted that I go to the cairn left by Admiral Peary, which we expected to find at Navy Cliff. Inukitsork and I left for the spot, leaving Uvdluriark to guard Knud.

With the aid of the theodolite we had little difficulty in discovering the cairn which had been left by the first man to view the sea northeast of Greenland. The cairn itself was not high, perhaps because of the dearth of building material. Peary's cairns are all small; he may have built them so purposely, since they have withstood the weather better than the larger ones left by other explorers.

I stood on the spot exactly twenty years and twenty days after the cairn was built, yet we could still see where Peary had picked up the stones to make it. Round the cairn the sand was trampled and the footprints were plain. The stones were both large and small, and a few had been left beside it after the cairn was finished.

Some matches on the ground indicated that the men had been smokers, and in the cairn itself we found two objects: a brass pipe—in which there was a statement to the effect that this cairn was erected by Robert Peary and Eyvin Astrup, and that the following year Peary had visited it again with Matew Henson and Lee; and a white whiskey bottle. It was corked, and contained

KNUD RASMUSSEN (*right*) AND MYSELF DRESSED FOR THE ICECAP

several newspaper clippings concerning Peary's expedition, as well as a delicious alcoholic aroma. I copied Peary's record for my own information; then I added to the original document the fact that I had visited the cairn twenty years later, and such information of our expedition as might be of interest in case we should be lost.

Navy Cliff is inadequately described by Peary himself. He was a most matter-of-fact author, and never wrote more than was absolutely necessary. Astrup, on the other hand, indulges in a lyric, and sometimes inaccurate, description. Navy Cliff, for instance, does not rise high above Academy Glacier as he says. In fact, one cannot see Academy Glacier from Navy Cliff. A tall mountain intervenes, and between the mountain and Navy Cliff there is a deep valley. But the slope from Navy Cliff is steep, and negotiable only with difficulty, as Astrup's drawings indicate. All his drawings are good, but he should have placed the mountain farther inland.

I duplicated all Peary's observations and bearings, and could not help admiring his eyes for having spotted this excellent observation post. It is true that he was wrong about the channel, but he made a fine survey, and anyone would have believed as he did. Every geographical formation viewed from Navy Cliff points toward the existence of a channel, as it does also from the icecap.

If it had not been for Peary's work and experience we should never have been able to do what we did. I felt vastly inferior, and grateful to him for the souvenirs he had left us. The few matches that lay exposed for twenty years, the footprints of the man himself, the stones he had touched and built with became dearer to me than the countless stories I had heard of him and the many books written by and about him.

I stood for a few hours on that historic spot. The stones in the cairn had, in its erection, been turned bottom side up in many cases, and again I was presented with proof of the sluggish pace of the Arctic. The black lichens which fasten to the tops of stones and rocks as the result of a partnership between bacteria and fungus require perhaps hundreds of years to reach the size of a quarter. It is impossible for them to exist on the bottoms of rocks, yet those now on the bottoms of the topsy-turvy stones had not, after twenty years, begun to wither. Twenty years is, of course, nothing compared with the length of time these stones had lain in their original positions before the American explorer arrived to disturb them.

When we returned to camp Knud was no better. He was too ill even to enjoy the tobacco I had brought from Thule for him, knowing that sooner or later he would run out of his own supply. It was now the middle of August and growing colder daily. We did not know what to do.

We could remain the whole winter and return home next spring, of course. So long as it was light we could travel to the ice for seals, and we had enough musk-ox meat cached to last us. But, after thinking it over for a night, Knud decided that one of the men had better stay with him, while the other man and I returned to Thule and saw to it that reports of our expedition reached South Greenland by the first ice. Then next year very early I could come up with some natives and fetch him home.

It was a good plan, but I refused to leave him. If he had to stay, then I would stay. Next morning Knud said that he would feel no worse traveling than staying here, and that he would go home with us. On the last day I shot two fine cows and drained them of a large cup of milk which I allowed to freeze. We would save this lump of milk ice for the celebration at the center of the icecap.

And so we left this beautiful land that had given us shelter and food and joy and sickness, and so much beauty that I shall never forget it. "The Camp Under the Big Stone" always bore a special significance for Knud and me.

We made only ten kilometers the first day. I packed Knud on my back over the little glacier to the sledges, and then laid him on Uvdluriark's sledge, his legs hanging over the upstanders. His face was white as the snow, and his lips were pressed tight together on the pain.

Our dogs numbered only sixteen now, as four of them had been killed fighting musk oxen, and we had to select our route with care. When we crossed river beds it was especially bad for Knud, and I regretted my deficiencies as a pilot. We asked him a couple of times if he could endure the jolting of the sledge. He only lay with his eyes closed and muttered:

"Shut up, and go ahead."

Oddly enough, in the evening Knud felt like eating a little supper, and he brought out a lump of sugar which he had saved and dropped it into his tea. We all felt better because his color was improving and once more he seemed to take a little interest in what was going on.

Every day he grew stronger. It was as if his old occupation, sitting on a sledge, was doing him good. A bad snowstorm kept us in our tent for three days, and this, too, helped him. We had agreed, as usual, not to eat when we were laid up, but the third day we felt weak, and our dogs looked worse than they had, obviously suffering from the increasing cold. We decided then to eat a little more before we lost our strength.

Uvdluriark told us not to worry. People, he said, are tougher than dogs. He remembered the days before the immigrants from Canada had introduced the kayak to the Greenland Eskimos. Often during the winter they had run out of meat. Then they merely lay on their sledges and slept until the sun came up, since there was nothing to be gained from hunting in the darkness. Many died of starvation, but their dogs died long before them.

Thus consoled, we fed the dogs double rations, even throwing them meat which we had counted upon for ourselves. Then each of us brought forth what remained of our emergency rations: I had two musk-ox bladders stuffed with melted tallow and marrow. Inukitsork had a bagful of the contents of a musk-ox stomach, which tastes like a sour salad, and dried meat. Uvdluriark had saved the used tea leaves, and a few lumps of crystal sugar to sweeten his warmed-over tea. But Knud had the most. All his boots were stuffed with the finest dried ribs covered with tallow. All this spare food we tossed into one bag—and we ate it long before we reached home.

From then on the dogs began to give out alarmingly. After six days the first one dropped, and the next day a second went down. When it snowed, of course, we could give them a rest and ourselves a fast.

During these periods of enforced idleness we thought only of food. I remember the gorgeous visions of steaming food that crowded my mind, and Knud and I could exchange only a few words like, "Scrambled eggs!" "Right you are! Or pancakes!"

We had a few books with us, and as the dogs died and it became necessary further to lighten our sledges we left them behind. One day we built a cairn in our own honor—nobody else would—and I left my old copy of *Homer* as a memento. Anyone interested in the contents of that cairn might be somewhat surprised to find in it a year's file of a housekeeping magazine. Knud insisted he had brought them along merely for the value of the paper, but each night on the trip he had read me a complete menu for a week, and we had discussed it weightily for hours.

He continued to improve daily, and after we had tied two

pairs of skis to the runners it was easier for the dogs to haul him. But as a result, two of us had to ride because it was impossible to walk far without skis.

The hodometer was a great help to our morale. We set a minimum of twenty-five kilometers for each day—and that is a long distance when every inch of it must be beaten out of the dogs. It was cruel, but our lives depended upon the dogs and there was no other way.

A little bitch of mine whelped during the journey. We could not stop for her or take her on the sledge. When I took her out of the traces she lay down to rest; as she would not have caught up with us after the puppies were born, we had to harness her again. One pup after another dropped from her during the afternoon. It must have been uncomfortable, of course, and it was especially sickening to me as the other dogs watched her delivering and snatched up the newborn pups as fast as they were born. The mother tried to prevent her teammates from this cannibalism, but her final victory was gruesome. When pup number nine was born she whirled about and devoured it herself. After that she resumed her march as if nothing had happened.

We talked, as I have said, of almost nothing but food. Uvdluriark could not contain his laughter because he had many caches, some of them three years old, scattered along the west coast—and they were doing no one any good. Inukitsork possessed hundreds of pounds of seal meat and blubber, and Knud and I even had delicacies to sell. All this only proved to the natives how full of humor the world was.

My kamiks began to wear out, and for several days I had been having trouble with my left leg. Now both feet commenced to pain me. In the evening when I unfastened my skis, it was almost impossible for me to walk, and whenever I had to stop for observations it took me half an hour or more to get back into my stride. The creaking and stretching of the stiff tendons above my heels was racking.

When I tried to remove my kamiks at night the pain was so excruciating that I slept in them. This was not a wise thing to do, I was well aware, and finally one evening we had to cut my kamiks off. My feet and legs were puffed up, because the ski-bindings were meant to be worn over stiff Norwegian boots and not soft sealskin kamiks.

And yet I had to forge ahead to direct the party through the fog which began to drift in.

We were down to the last piece of musk-ox meat and a few drops of kerosene when, late one evening, we saw land ahead. I had felt certain, from my calculations, that we ought to be close to land, but when one is dealing with such rudimentary instruments he can never be too sure.

It was now rather dark at night, but we could definitely see three black spots on the horizon. Uvdluriark said that the land to the south was Cape York, directly ahead of us was our own Thule, and to the north, Nunatarssuaq.

I could not definitely promise that we could reach home next day, but we ate our last meat and used the last kerosene to cook it.

Next morning we were up early. I walked ahead on my skis, but had great difficulty in moving my legs. They were twice their normal size, and my feet were stiff as wooden blocks. But the sight of the land ahead was like a magic lubricant to them, and I rapidly put space between me and the sledges worrying along after the sick dogs.

I mounted the crest of a snow wave, and there before me was the land stretched out like a relief map. The sun was bright, and the mountains rising against the sky were an invitation to hurry. I turned about to look for the sledges, my skis twisting ninety degrees with me, and at that moment I felt the snow giving way beneath me. The next thing I knew I was clutching at the icy shoulders of a crevasse.

I had been standing on top of the crevasse when I stopped, and in turning my skis had broken through. Instinctively one flings his arms wide in falling, and that act saved me.

My skis were still on, and I swung my legs to feel the walls of the crevasse. Even with my skis I could touch nothing solid! There was nothing I could do but hang on and wait for my fellow travelers. It seemed hours before I heard them shouting at the dogs, their curses ringing out over the icecap. But when you are suspended over a crevasse it is an age from the moment you first hear voices until they are close enough to be of any assistance.

They had no trouble in extricating me, but when we examined the hole I had fallen into we discovered it to be the worst type of crevasse—narrow at the top and widening out immediately as it descends, because of the unevenness of the terrain below. We had run into a bad stretch indeed, and the only thing to do was to backtrack, and cut around to the north. This took us many hours and precluded the possibility of our reaching home that day.

And so there was another night without food, but we did not mind it very much. Tomorrow we would be at home. Surely we would be at home tomorrow.

One dog died during the night, and the next morning those that were left refused to be hurried. The edge of the icecap is always more difficult than the center, and its surface was slashed with steep gorges. But finally we ascended a hill to find that we had reached the land. It was a land we did not recognize!

The letdown was sickening. Knud asked me to check observations again, and the natives were sure the cursed theodolite was responsible for our confusion. I had to confess that I did not know where we were—a deplorable admission for a navigator—and I felt, quite rightly, that my value to the expedition had suffered a severe reversal.

Only two things were certain: we had nothing to eat but eleven lean and hungry dogs, and the dogs had nothing to eat.

Whether to go north or south was our ultimate problem, but meanwhile we knew we should try to find a settlement and secure food. Then suddenly the fog about us lifted, and a cry escaped the lips of Uvdluriark. Directly ahead was the sea, and innumerable icebergs lazed about. He recognized Herbert and Cumberland islands, where we had hunted many times. But . . .

We were north of Inglefield Gulf, and we would have to ascend the glacier once more and cover a considerable stretch of it before we could reach home. Now that I knew where we were I could take my bearings. The trouble, I discovered, was that we had thought it to be the 15th of September, and in reality it was the 14th. At this time of year the angle of the sun changes more rapidly, almost half a degree a day, and we were just that far off our course. We had struck the coast at least thirty miles too far north, because months ago I had been snowblind for four days while my companions had been immersed in fog and we had thought the four days to be five. When we had reached Independence Bay the sun had been at its zenith and the angle of declination changing imperceptibly from day to day. With my crude instruments I had not been in a position to correct the error, especially working from the rather uncertain maps at our disposal.

There was a slim chance that we would find caribou at Qaqujarssuaq, which was not far from us, and we camped there. My legs were in terrible shape, however, and next morning I was unable to take part in the hunting. The natives scouted far afield, but Knud could not walk very well as yet, and he returned to camp after getting a rabbit. We heard shots in the distance, and figured that the boys had got something, so we two finished the rabbit, though I could scarcely eat anything for the blinding pain in my legs.

The boys returned in the afternoon with several rabbits—they, too, had eaten one—and we boiled the meat over our burning skis. The ten dogs shared five rabbits, and we had one left over for the trek home.

I now thought it was time to celebrate by handing out the tobacco I had held in reserve. The boys howled with delight, but decided they would save a little of it so that they could be smoking as they walked toward their houses, and the first couple of men who greeted them could be casually invited to fill their pipes.

Next morning when we were ready to go, we had only eight dogs left, so we cached one of our sledges, my instruments and the tent—we would return for these when we were stronger—and set out. I had to ride for, they informed me, I had been out of my head during the night. Yet the trip over the ice seemed to give me strength, and as familiar landmarks passed in slow procession I jumped off the sledge and ran alongside.

We pushed the sledge at times and did everything we could to save the last dogs. Still, one dropped out the next day. We slept when we had to, but we rested only long enough to give us strength to move. We were growing weaker by the moment and could not travel far without stopping.

And then finally we were back on our own glacier, and far below lay our own fjord and the dots that were Thule and home —the spot we had been longing for during the endless, tedious months.

We called a halt and waited for Uvdluriark to explore the crevasses between us and home, and while I sat there Knud walked over to me and gave me his hand.

"Many times during the summer," he said, "I didn't believe we could go on. But now that we have completed such an expedition together, we ought never to be apart again. Wherever we go in the whole world, we must always stick together."

I have heard many speeches in my life, most of them stupid libels on friendship and loyalty at banquets or meetings. But there on the glacier Knud dared put into a simple declaration exactly what he felt. I replied in kind. It is seldom men have the courage to do what they want to do, and say what they really

THE ICE FOOT AT THE
BASE OF THE MOUN-
TAINS. AT CERTAIN
TIMES OF THE YEAR
THIS IS THE ONLY ROAD
FOR ONE TO TRAVEL
NORTH OR SOUTH

SLIDING DOWN THE
GLACIER, THE DOGS ACT-
ING AS BRAKES

think, especially to other men. But Knud said these things, and I never forgot those words while he lived, and I shall never forget them so long as I live.

A short, solemn moment between two friends can do much toward cementing or breaking a friendship. There we were in the open. We had faced death and the prime essentials of living together. There could be no false embarrassment between us now, and no clouded motives or misunderstandings in the future.

We did not go down to the settlement until next day, since the night was too dark to permit our scouting the crevasses. But early next morning we made the final dash. In spite of the pain in my legs I ran with the rest of them, and it made us laugh, because we kept well ahead of our teams. But when we left the icecap and crossed the last ten miles of stone and gravel to the grass plains behind the houses Inukitsork and I were left far to the rear. He also had a sore foot, and we walked slowly. It made us happy to realize that Knud was so well now that he could outrun us all. Five weeks before I had not believed that he would live.

Yet when we came near the houses Knud and Uvdluriark waited for us—they thought we should all enter the settlement together so that no one person would have the pleasure and glory of coming in alone.

In our excitement we had not observed four girls who had been fishing for salmon in the little lakes near-by. They had seen us approaching, but thought us foreigners or ghosts from off the icecap, and had concealed themselves. Now that they knew who we were they hurried forward to meet us. They told us all the news of the place and that no ship had been here. Natives at Cape York had gone south and learned that a whaling vessel had tried to come north, but had been unable to get through Melville Bay.

We had seven dogs left, and we tried to make them howl to herald our arrival. But we could not bear to whip them, so we let them loose and gave them the old bear signal. The bedraggled animals, who had not been loose for months, lifted their tails and rushed forward. Some of them even jumped in the air. It was my triumph to have three of my own dogs left, and they all ran direct to my house.

All our neighbors either saw the dogs or heard their yelps and the sound of our gun, and stampeded toward us. Our Eskimo friend, Harrigan, was the first to reach us. He dashed forward as if shot from a cannon, but when he reached us he simply stood and laughed, unable to speak for joy and embarrassment. Two others were directly behind him.

"Have a smoke?" said Inukitsork.

"They have got tobacco!" cried the three men in astonishment. And their joy was turned to momentary resentment, as they had long since run out of tobacco.

Soon all the neighbors were gathered round us, and we were escorted triumphantly to the house of the minister. His wife, Ane Sofie, had coffee and bread for us, and it tasted like all our dreams come true.

But our wives were not present. All of us had the good taste not to inquire after them, but soon we excused ourselves and went to our homes. On the way Uvdluriark met his little son, Inuiteq. He stopped and bent down to look at the boy. "Anau!" he said. The boy did not know him and began to cry, and Uvdluriark went on.

When I went into my house I saw everyone but Navarana. "Where is Navarana?" I asked.

"She is upstairs working," Arnanguaq answered.

I yelled: "Navarana! Navarana! I am home!"

"What of it?" I heard her voice saying from above. "Somebody is cleaning a few skins!"

After a few minutes she came down, hurried across the room and out of the door. Not until everybody had gone would she consent to come back and greet me. Then she explained that she had been afraid she might embarrass me, and also she had no way of showing how happy she really was.

She was no less relieved that I was home—she was merely conforming to the ways of her people. Inukitsork found no one at his house. Tukumeq, his wife, had just left to walk round the point and "see if there was much ice to be seen." It was very important to her just then. Inukitsork followed and found her.

In fact, the natives resent public displays of emotion, and stifle all evidences of it except humor. A man and woman never say good-bye when taking leave of each other, and it would never have occurred to our wives to mention our names during the many months we were away. To do so would have been an enormous breach of good taste, and a certain indication that their minds were upon us rather than their work. Every man and woman is, theoretically, self-sufficient in his emotional, as well as actual, needs, and to express worry or concern over an absent mate is shocking.

7

I believe that neither Knud nor I realized exactly what we had accomplished in crossing the icecap. We had begun our expedition with the casual and humanitarian motive of rescuing a countryman, Ejnar Mikkelsen. We had not found him or any sign of him, but in our search we had made many important discoveries and observations, proved the nonexistence of Peary Channel, and accomplished the feat of traversing the North Greenland icecap, something no man had ever done before.

When we first reached home our minds were too much occupied with the task of regaining our strength to dwell particularly upon our plans for informing the world of what we had done.

It took my feet a long time to heal. The ankle tendons were exposed, and the skin stubbornly refused to grow there. I wrote, compiled maps and drew conclusions from our observations, and occasionally drove out with Navarana. The trading occupied only a fraction of our time, because we had practically nothing left with which to trade.

Our house was more crowded than ever. There had been a split between the two native missionaries in Thule, and one of them, Sechmann, had moved into our house—which had been more than crowded before he arrived with his wife and four children.

In his youth he had been a companion of Knud's. He had gone to the Eskimo high school in South Greenland and become a missionary. But the poor, simple fellow did not have the equipment for it. When he reached Commandment Six all of them became a jumble in his brain, and he could never absorb the rest. Which ruined him as a preacher, and he was permitted to leave the service.

And so we took him in as an assistant. What else could we do? His family was thankful for the shelter, but the confusion added nothing to the repose necessary for scientific work.

Still it was something to be in a warm place, and to listen to the whine and roar of the wind without having to brave it day after day.

As soon as I regained my strength Knud and I planned on taking our foxskins to South Greenland and bringing back fresh goods for the natives. They thought this a fine idea, but some of them offered to make the trip themselves.

PHOTOGRAPH OF MYSELF THE DAY WE RETURNED FROM OUR EXPEDITION ACROSS
THE ICECAP, SHOWING THE EFFECTS OF PROLONGED HUNGER AND EXPOSURE

"Such great men as you," they said, "are too dignified to fool around with such humble things as foxskins!"

We told them we were only too glad to "fool around with them."

I had the misfortune to break my left arm in a clumsy fall one day when we were hauling some meat—and this, when my legs were nearly well! It was very uncomfortable. I had heard that the latest stunt of the natives was to leave broken members alone and permit them to heal as they would. But Knud was of the old school and he set it while Navarana sewed a bandage of wet barbed sealskin. When this dried it was tight and rigid.

The natives have a unique method of determining when the time is ripe for the removal of the bandage. They place lice under it. So long as the healing bone hurts so much that the patient disregards the lice the bandage must remain. Later, when the parasites grow irksome, the support may be removed. The scheme was successful in my case.

But for a long while afterward I was unfit for travel and spent my time at writing.

Just before Christmas Navarana and I left for the north to get foxskins from the natives and to ask some of them to follow us to the south. They were willing to go, but we had to make them promise not to give their belongings to the southern beggars. Navarana and I stayed with friends at Herbert Island, where she was now regarded as the first lady of the tribe. We had a fine time, and reluctantly departed in order to visit Neqé before we returned to Thule. It was but a short distance, and we took only a little frozen meat for a lunch.

The day was dark—it was now winter—but we were not worried. We sat on our sledge and thought how fine life was for us both. We were young and healthy, we loved each other, and had everything we wanted on earth. But all this content and happiness made us neglectful of the lowering sky which had blanketed the stars, and suddenly we felt the lash of the wind and the sting of drifting snow in our faces.

We were in the midst of one of the worst gales that ever struck that part of the country. The dogs were whisked off their feet and tangled in a pile together, yet we had to reach some shelter. It was impossible to go back into the teeth of the gale— I could not even crack my whip in that direction. The only thing to do was to try to reach Neqé. Navarana pulled a blanket over her head, and I worried along with the dogs, keeping the wind to our backs, and at last we reached a sheltered inlet which Navarana recognized as Igdluluarssuit, where she had once lived. We found two empty houses, and took possession of one of them. We had nothing with us but our sleeping bags and a few candles, so we crawled into the bags and went to sleep, hoping that the weather would improve by the next day.

It did not. We slept as long as possible but whenever we wakened the whining gale was strong in our ears. The blow was not constant; one moment the air would be almost calm, and the next the wind screamed like a siren. There could be no thought of trying to reach Neqé in this weather, but we were growing more hungry by the minute. The candles, too, would not last long. In order to save them for an emergency we huddled together most of the time in utter darkness.

Next day we lit a candle, and I told Navarana that I would go out and try to find a rabbit; I knew they were plentiful here. She did not protest. I walked and walked, as long as there was any light at all, but I saw no rabbit. When I returned to the house Navarana, who had been standing outside peering into the darkness, ran to meet me.

Navarana was like all good, sensitive Eskimo wives. Never would she ask her husband if he had found any food—that would only embarrass us both if I had not. I returned emptyhanded in this case, and she pretended that my bringing back any game was furthest from her thoughts. She had been longing for me because she was alone and cold, she said, and wanted to carry my gun since I had been walking with it the whole day and must be tired.

She had swept the floor of the house and arranged our skins on the ledge.

"Oh, what a bad wife you have," she exclaimed, "I have no supper for you! Men who go out to work for their families ought to have their meals ready for them when they return. A poor wife does not remember to bring along anything from whence one came."

The next day was no better. The short jabs of the wind were as bad as a boxer's blow. Navarana told me I had better stay inside and not expose myself. She probably said this just to encourage me, so I went out. Between blows I walked upright; when the wind came I clawed the earth as best I could. Perhaps on such days rabbits remain buried under the snow. At any rate I saw none, and my gun became clogged with snow. It was almost impossible to breath because of the ice in the wind.

When I returned Navarana was trying to fry something in a little tin held over five candles. She told me that in tearing down the old stone rack used formerly to keep the meat away from the dogs she had found two seal flippers. "Here is one for you," she said.

I was ravenous and wolfed it at once. Flippers contain a great deal of fat, and taste not unlike pigs' feet. It was not fresh, but it was food, and I felt much better. Then I looked at Navarana, and noticed that she gazed greedily at the bones I had left.

"Where is the other flipper?" I asked.

"I ate mine, because I could cook only one at a time in the cup."

I realized she was lying, and I demanded that she tell me the truth.

"Well," she said, "when one sits doing nothing one deserves not so much as the big man who wanders around to bring something home!"

I told her I detested liars. To prove it, I laced on my kamiks again, grabbed my gun and went out. She looked after me, but said nothing. Eskimo wives never say anything.

I immediately felt humiliated and ashamed of my conduct. Women have ways of proving their superiority over men, ways which leave men feeling inferior forever after. In my egotism I had given her no thought until I had finished my own meal, that rotten seal flipper. Yet I could easily have shared it with Navarana.

I decided not to return until I could bring some meat with me. It was moonlight now, and I could see fairly well, but every time the wind struck up the snow floated about me like a London fog and I had to seek shelter. While I waited my mind seethed with self-recriminations. A mere native girl could instruct me in the common decencies and at the same time prove her love superior to mine. I had had enough experience in hunger to realize what it must mean to prepare and offer one's food to another while the donor remains famished.

Then in the moonlight I saw two rabbits. The gale broke over me again, but I knew where I had seen them and waited. As soon as the wind let up a bit I raised my head. I was completely covered with snow, but I had kept my hand over the gun and the barrel was open. I approached the spot quietly and waited. I could not see the rabbits, but I knew they must be near-by. Suddenly the snow moved close to me, and a little nose poked up through it. Then the other. I waited until they had crawled out of their holes, then fired. The shot killed them both, and I had two fine animals weighing almost eight pounds apiece to take back to Navarana.

The dogs announced my arrival, and she came out. The moon was bright; she saw me and ran pell-mell. When she discovered the two rabbits she screamed her joy as if she had never known such fine game existed. She took them out of my hands and assured me she had never expected anything like this. She was sorry she had offended me by doubting my ability to procure food, and especially humble now that she witnessed such magnificent proof of my marksmanship.

Our meal lasted for hours. We lit the candles, and first ate the raw viscera. Then, our appetites sharpened on these hors d'œuvres, we boiled the meat in the cup hanging over the candles.

Next day the weather calmed down and we drove on to Neqé and arranged for a number of the younger men to go south with us. My arm still hurt a bit after we returned to Thule, but I thought I could manage the trip, and Knud and I left for Tassiussak shortly after Christmas. The going was splendid, and it took us only five days. We remained a short time with the Nielsens, visited two other trading stations farther south, and returned to Thule with ten sledges groaning under trading goods.

8

Knud and I had come to believe that we had done something rather splendid in twice crossing the Greenland icecap by dog sledge. The feat had been accomplished only once before—by Nansen, in 1888—at a point much easier to traverse. And yet, far up north in Greenland, who was there to appreciate what we had done? Our trip had been unheralded prior to its advent, and unsung since its accomplishment. No radios broadcast our progress from day to day, no newspaper headlines screamed our achievement. No organizations offered us prizes, no cigarette companies sought us out to endorse their products.

We were both young and avid for recognition, and eager to bask in the spotlight after years of virtual isolation. We would go home to Denmark and let the world acclaim us!

We planned upon being gone for only a few months. Navarana did not wish to stay in our house, as she did not want to share it with the missionary's wife. They were good friends, but both wanted to be boss, like women the world over. I left Sechmann, the ex-missionary, to guard our property and, rather than have Navarana return to her mother's house, I proposed that she go with us to Tassiussak and live there with the Nielsens until we returned.

She had only two days in which to get her clothes in order, so she invited all the women of the place in to do the sewing. They sat up all night, and Navarana entertained them with stories of what she was going to see in the south. They brought their own meat, and told me afterward that they had had a fine time.

We set out with three sledges, Knud's, mine, and one belonging to a young Eskimo boy, Ajago. Ajago was virtually Knud's adopted son, and devoted to us both.

Between Thule and Cape York I made an amazing discovery. We took shelter in a cave at Pakitsork during a storm and while we lay over there Navarana showed us how well she had learned to read and write while we had been on our trip across the icecap. She had picked up the accomplishments herself from listening to the children in the missionary's school, and in a few months she had advanced farther than many children do in as many years. She had not told me before, she said, as she had been afraid I would not like it—it was considered unnecessary for women in that tribe to possess such knowledge.

We had no kerosene to cook with, and each night kindled a big fire with blubber. This always left a greasy layer of soot in our pots, and we all became black as pigs—except Navarana. She seemed to know instinctively how to keep herself clean. She refused to drink soup out of the pot—which always leaves two broad stripes across the cheeks—and dipped the fluid up with her own cup instead. A woman as dignified as she could at no time be seen drinking out of a meat pot!

At Cape Seddon we encountered the usual hospitality. Itukusunguaq and Mitseq, the two brothers who had accompanied me on my first trip across Melville Bay, lived there, and were both uncles of Navarana. As a result, she could take anything she wanted in their houses, but we remained only long enough for our dogs to eat as much as they could. Mitseq's wife, Eqariussaq, was a remarkable woman. As a young girl she had been in America with Peary. The Americans had called her "Miss Bill." After she returned to Greenland she refused to reveal anything about her

Top. NORTH STAR BAY (THULEFJORD) IN THE SUMMER, WITH OUR STATION AT THE RIGHT.

Bottom. MOUNTAINS BETWEEN THULE AND THE ICECAP.

trip. When asked, she either said that she could not remember or was not inclined to tell. After we left Cape Seddon, Navarana told me that she had been walking with Eqariussaq down on the ice, and suddenly the woman had turned to her and said:

"When you go down to the white man's country, be careful not to absorb too much of their spirit. If you do, it will cause you many tears, for you can never rid yourself of it."

Poor woman! I understood then that it was a desperate, hopeless longing that stilled her voice.

The passage immediately north of Tassiussak is always bad. We had to take to the land in a number of places, and it was difficult with our heavy loads. Navarana worked like a man, and wielded the whip with an expertness I could never achieve. The natives who followed along after us were much impressed, as no woman in that part of the country could drive dogs. Navarana and Ajago made one bad error because they had never heard of "wages." When they saw so many empty sledges around us, all the drivers silently watching us in our difficulties, they suggested that the empty sledges take on part of our load. The natives were quick to accept this suggestion, but each of them selected only a light bag of kamiks or a small bundle of skins, threw it on his sledge, and drove off. Knud had been left a short distance behind to drink coffee, and when he caught up with us he said we would have to pay the natives by the mile for their aid. He was right. When we reached Tassiussak next day they all presented their claims and collected one kroner per Danish mile (four English miles) for transporting only about thirty pounds each.

The night before arriving in Tassiussak we stopped with Abel, the great hunter. As usual, his house was spotless, his daughters in white underwear, and Navarana was much impressed. She told me that she thought the household so pretentious that she ought to mention it to the women in criticism. When I asked her to explain, she said anyone ought to know that men bought fine white linen only to make sails for seal hunting. Perhaps the white men would be disgusted and cease manufacturing the linen if they learned that ignorant women used the fabric to make themselves beautiful beneath their outside garments. I assured her that the white men would be only too delighted to weave more, and that she herself would be dressed in similar luxury as soon as we reached Tassiussak. She smiled, as people do when they doubt and hope simultaneously.

The Nielsens were delighted at the idea of having Navarana

for six months—or until I returned. I asked her if she wanted to accompany me to Denmark, but she said she realized the trip would be a hard one, and living here with the Nielsens would be enough excitement for her now. She could also learn much about housekeeping from Dorte Nielsen. The minister in Tassiussak suggested that he instruct Navarana in religion so that she would be ready for baptism when I returned. He might even be so kind as to take her into his own house after a while. Navarana was interested—she had often talked about religion—and I told her that, in any case, she might take some lessons from the minister, and then she could judge for herself whether or not she wanted to be baptized.

We could waste no time as we had to reach Holstensborg by the 15th of April when a ship made the port to pick up passengers for Denmark. After three days Knud, Ajago and myself drove off. Navarana stood with the Nielsens and waved to us. This in itself was a concession to new ways.

Our journey down the coast was uneventful except for the familiarity it gave me with all the inhabitants of the west coast of Greenland, and if this were a book covering only my physical adventures I should tell nothing of it. To me, however, these contacts with the natives and with the white men who had lived for many years among them, are much more interesting to recall than my hand-to-hand combats with wilderness, inclement weather and wild beasts.

In Qaersserssuaq, the first stop, lived a teacher whose salary was one kroner per month—none too munificent a sum. He was also the local preacher. The poor fellow had a terrible life, and I pleaded his cause before the bishop when I met him later. The good cleric said he doubted very much that the fellow earned even one kroner a month, but at my request his salary was doubled. Even at that he got only about forty cents per month, but he was satisfied as he had received an hundred per cent raise.

We met a famous murderer at Aipik. From the looks of them both, he and his wife were violently insane. They had been accused of killing their three children and throwing their bodies to the dogs, yet every year when the inspector arrived the couple disappeared into the mountains and no punishment could be meted out. Some time later the husband took his wife out on bad ice and she was drowned—perhaps accidentally, perhaps not. At any rate, before anything could be done to the husband, he himself was found dead—and thus evaded his earthly sentence.

At Aupiglartok lived a native trader. He was well educated—
having been a member of several Danish expeditions in his youth
—and talked Danish fluently. Unfortunately the books he studied
were such ancient tomes that his speech was characteristic of the
Middle Ages. When he was addressed concerning an everyday
subject, he replied as a Shakespearean king might have spoken
to an honored guest. The trader had the good fortune to be sire to
an unknown number of daughters, and all of them were wives of
hunters in the community. He was the father-in-law of almost
everyone—which gave him complete power of attorney.

Only a few single men lived there, including the teacher.
This resulted in a bitter struggle between church and affluence
which was not settled until the old man died several years later.
It was then discovered that his children, and his children's children, all of them kept out of public school and taught by himself,
were far better educated than the others, and were even better
informed than children of the same age in Denmark.

At Aupiglartok I also met a woman of considerable renown,
the "Virgin Mary." She was now old and unattractive, and she
approached me to intervene in her behalf, for the celestial powers
had deserted her. She had been married, after her short and
glorious career as the mother of Jesus, but her husband was now
dead, leaving her a pension of fifty kroner—ten dollars—a year.
She received a monthly remittance, but it bewildered her. One
month she got 4.16 kroner, and the next 4.17. Now everyone
knows that February has less days than any other month, yet she
received 4.17 that month, and only 4.16 for some of the months
having thirty-one days. This idiosyncrasy ought to be ironed out,
she thought, because the extra ore she received some months could
buy a piece of chewing tobacco. In order to get rid of her I gave
her wages for two months, and she seemed contented but still a
little puzzled.

The poor woman had created a sensation many years ago at
Tassiussak. In the middle of the winter she had given birth to
a baby boy outside of wedlock and without, she insisted, the co-
operation of any man. The baby had been born out on the rocks
and died almost immediately. But while it lived it spoke, according to the mother, and pronounced itself Jesus reborn, come to
aid the mother and the dignified inhabitants of Tassiussak.

The mother was held in great esteem for the honor she had
brought to the community, and she spoke many wise and mysterious words. The teacher at the village believed in her and was

appointed her secretary and publicity agent, as she herself could not write.

By the teacher she sent word to the minister at Upernivik: the child had proclaimed that she was to be paid a hundred kroner; if not, the child would see to it that the seed withered in the white men's country and no ship would visit the Eskimos during the following summer. This, of course, was serious, but the minister's money could not be tossed to the winds without some investigation, so he sent back a message for her to come down to the colony and talk things over. Perhaps they could compromise.

But the child visited his mother in her dreams the very next night and told her by no means to go—let everyone bring her all he possessed of fat meat, and a certain rich man buy her no less than two pounds of coffee and serve it to the villagers immediately. The teacher was sent for to entertain her with hymns, the women instructed to sew boots for her, and everyone commanded to visit her and kiss her several times each day. Encouraged by this success she began to issue orders to neighboring communities, and the poor teacher did not know what to do. The minister had written him not to give in to the woman's whims, but everyone else in Tassiussak thought her a saint. He was reprimanded severely by the elders for his dubious position, and finally took his sledge and drove to Upernivik for advice.

The worthy minister, a native himself, knew it was his duty to cut short this Virgin Mary's career. But it was also his duty to look out for his own personal security, and he dared not approach the woman's home, where she was alleged to possess her greatest powers. He took his problem to the post manager and received the authority to bring her, willing or not, to Upernivik.

Thus ended the dictatorship of the "Virgin Mary." Her last days had been especially difficult as the child had instructed her one night that nothing but the white man's language was to be spoken by the Eskimos. This limited conversation considerably since they knew only two English words, "boots"—they had heard it from the whalers who always wanted to buy kamiks—and "Hurray." Those two words constituted the entire vocabulary of the community, and if the inhabitants could not pronounce them they could not receive the blessing of the Virgin.

Even when she was taken to the sledge which was to transport her to Upernivik she insisted that everyone come down and see her off, receive her blessing, and talk with her in the white man's language.

At Upernivik the minister tried to persuade her to renounce her blasphemy. When she insisted that her doctrine was not blasphemy but the true word of God, he tried to persuade her further by a few smart slaps on her cheek. Nothing would bring her to her senses. She was then tried and sentenced: her hair was cut off and she received twenty-seven lashes of the whip beneath the hoisted flag—this to impress her with the gravity of her offense. The flag is used for many marvelous purposes the world over.

Several of the Danes followed us from Upernivik to Proeven, the next stop. Among them was a young but generously proportioned lady, the teacher of the post manager's children. She was very sweet, if heavy, and Knud cleverly arranged for her to ride on my sledge. We had to pass over the Qasorssuaq, a beautiful pile of rocks but a bad climb for the dogs. She sat stolidly on the sledge, as if it were a Pullman, while I walked. Somehow it never occurred to her that all the other sledges were passing us because of her bulk.

In Proeven we met our friend, Jensen, the cooper. It is impossible for me to do this man justice—he deserves a book by himself. He was a widower, and lived with a raft of children in his house, some of them his, some his children's playmates. There were so many of them that he did not always know which ones were his, and when he got tired of the confusion he would often chase his own out with the rest.

Little Jonas, barely five feet tall, was the most important man in Proeven. He was one of the best friends we made in Greenland, and a great hunter. His whole house was as clean as a tablecloth, and his wife, Agathe, though no great beauty, was a faultless hostess. She was never caught unprepared, always had plenty of cookies when we arrived, never permitted us to take our skin clothes to anyone else for mending and accepted no pay for her work. Their home was decorated with pictures and photographs of all the people they had known for years.

Agathe had just one fault—she was terribly jealous of Little Jonas, and if he so much as looked at a girl, she would grab him and take him home. While we were in Proeven Jensen decided to give a ball in our honor, and Knud furnished the drinks. Jensen's housekeeper, Fat Sofie, was a wonderful cook, and his house was large enough for us to swing the girls. In the middle of the night Agathe came for her husband. He protested and looked pleadingly at us. I dared not go to his aid, but Knud jumped up and tried to intervene, talking to Agathe and offering her a drink. He was rewarded with such a slap in the face that he sat down hard and only recovered as he saw Agathe stalking out with Little Jonas trudging meekly after her.

The Danes in Proeven joined those from Upernivik and followed us to South Upernivik where we were the guests of Mr. Dahl. Each night we were given banquets and celebrations, and as guests of the Dahls we were especially well treated. We expected a farewell dance on the second night but Knud spoiled everything. He sat at the table beside the hefty young schoolteacher and, trying to make conversation, said to her:

"It's too bad we didn't think of it before, but if you had some more clothes with you, you could have gone with us to Umanak Colony and returned with Little Jonas." (Little Jonas took it for granted that he was to guide us. He wanted no pay for the task but, of course, such free helpers are always more expensive in the end than those who work for a salary.) "Peter would be only too pleased to take you on his sledge!"

The girl jumped at the bait: "Oh, I can be ready in a hurry. Just give me a night here and I will have my kamiks made over. I would love to go, and can do some errands for Mr. Harries, the post manager of Upernivik."

All of which resulted in our having to forgo the celebration and set out that night in order to shake the girl. We were more than a mile on the journey before Knud dared smile and call his soul his own.

9

Between Igdlorssuit and Umanak Colony there is a long stretch of perhaps eighty miles broken only by a small colony of which a cousin of Knud's was post manager. The Danish state also operated a coal mine there. The manager was a Swede, an intelligent, forceful man with a certain reputation in his homeland. He had been a worker in one of Sweden's big mines, and had become president of the miners' union. As such he had organized the strike won by the workers in 1906, and one in 1910 which they lost. After the defeat of the workers he had been discharged.

The Danish government at that time decided to develop the mine at Umanak Fjord, until this time worked inefficiently and hazardously by the natives. The Danes asked Sweden for a man to head the project, and the broad-minded management of the Swedish mine recommended their old enemy who was, they admitted, strong-minded, clever and honest. Mr. Lundberg had proved himself the man for the job. He had instituted system and routine, and developed a remarkable spirit of initiative among the native workers, most of whom were victims of one of the strangest nervous complaints in the world—kayak disease.

In Greenland as everywhere else nervousness manifests itself in one form or another. When the hunters row out in their kayaks on still water they are often becalmed with the sun's bright glare reflected in their eyes as from a mirror. Suddenly as they wait patiently for seals to rise to the surface they are gripped with a paralysis which prevents their moving a muscle. They sit as if petrified, and they say they have a feeling that the water is rising over them but they cannot lift a hand. Then, if a slight wind curls the surface of the sea, they are freed of the spell and come out of it. Or if a companion happens to see them and paddles close, rests his hand on their kayak or touches it with his oar they are enabled to move again.

The poor victims often become so frightened that after one experience they never dare venture out to sea alone again. And as a result they are left without means of support for themselves or their families. Such men, otherwise fine and industrious workers, had been drafted for the coal mine. The working conditions were pleasant, they received good wages, lived in sanitary houses, and had enough free time to do a little hunting during the winter. The experiment of turning a community of primitive hunters into modern industrial workers under the guidance of a sympathetic, understanding individual was certainly a success.

The trader of this community was, as I have said, a cousin of Knud's and possessed an unusual talent for singing the old Eskimo ballads. Unfortunately the ministers disapproved of these songs being sung. They desired to suppress the remains of the original Eskimo culture and replace it with their formal hymns. It resulted, of course, in the old bards singing their ballads well hidden from the Lord's agents, and this secrecy instituted a definite opposition to the church which, in wiser hands, would have nourished the natural love of a race for its native land.

We tarried so long with Knud's cousin that we barely had time to stop at Umanak Colony, for we knew our longest layover would be at Ikerasak, the home of Knud's Uncle Jens.

Uncle Jens was the brother of Knud Rasmussen's mother. He had been born in Greenland. After a short trip to Denmark, ostensibly for educational purposes, he had returned to Greenland and been in government service for almost fifty years. He should have been pensioned long before this, but he was too industrious to quit his trading post. Unfortunately, he managed it very badly, although very gaily.

All the natives knew and respected him for his abilities. He had once been the foremost dog driver, the most daring hunter and the best kayak rower in the land. He knew every Eskimo in North Greenland at sight, and followed the career of each one of them with unflagging interest. He greeted us with Greek and Latin quotations, and had an amazing knowledge of history, zoology and the natural sciences. He had been of great service during his long life to various of the expeditions to the North, and a title of nobility, I. P. C. von Fleischer, had been conferred upon him. Not a blasphemous or unkind word could be uttered in his house, and he treated all women, from the frowsiest old hag to the beautiful Danish girls who occasionally visited him, with most elegant courtesy. Besides his own government dwelling, he owned another house composed of sleeping rooms for his guests and for parties arranged by his close friends at such times as his own house might be occupied with more important gatherings.

The love between Knud and Uncle Jens was a beautiful thing, and the old man's admiration for his nephew was great enough to include all Knud's friends.

Uncle Jens had even organized a choral union with only one duty—to sing songs when Knud visited the place. The club was sent for at three o'clock in the morning. Soon all its members were gathered at Uncle Jens' house, and hard at work. And how they worked! I had been traveling the whole day and thought myself entitled to a few hours' sleep, but Knud instructed them to come into my room and serenade me. There being no opportunity for sleep, I got up and joined the celebration. Uncle Jens then decided that upon such an occasion no one should sleep, so he rushed about the village with strong coffee rousing everybody out of bed. Soon the house was filled with dancing couples, singing, and wrestling bouts.

In the middle of the feast Uncle Jens, overcome with love and generosity, threw open his store and gave the natives whatever he thought they needed. (I must explain that next day all the natives came trudging back with these supplies and surrendered them gladly. They realized that the old man was moved to such an act by the presence of his well-loved nephew.)

Next day came the inevitable shooting match. Uncle Jens and his brother, Carl, from Disko Bay, could never hold a real festival without the ritual of the pipes on the fence post and the matchbox in the snow. The old gentleman was delighted to win first place, with Knud a close second.

It was only natural that the whole settlement should be fed and offered free coffee during our stay; as the generous host was unable to pay for it himself, the burden fell on Knud. Knud, being completely charming and generous, felt that the party was well worth the price.

From there we drove across the hazardous "Majoren," the high pass between Umanak Fjord and Disko Bay.

Disko Bay is famous all over Greenland. The inhabitants there consider themselves just a little better than any other people in the world. They never say "Disko Bay." "The Bay" is sufficient. Five colonies are situated rather close together and, as there is sufficient ice for intercommunication in the winter, they visit back and forth constantly, maintaining a certain social life. The hospitality is as fine as that found anywhere in Greenland. We visited Uncle Carl there (we had spent several days with him on our way to Thule in 1910), but he was displeased because our whole supply of liquor had been drained by Uncle Jens' celebration, and we moved on south.

The farther south we drove, the more trouble we had with government officials over bringing our dogs into Danish Greenland. Dogs in the Arctic are afflicted with two diseases. The first and most important, rabies, must, of course, be spread from dog to dog by their teeth. It is sometimes completely wiped out; then a dog will attack an infected fox, or a fox will attack a dog team. Then, after a time, the dog will go mad and run amuck through the villages. Oddly enough, I have never seen humans infected with it. Perhaps it is because the mad dog would have to bite through thick leather boots before penetrating the skin of a man or woman, and by then his teeth are free of the infectious saliva. This is only my own surmise, and probably has no basis in fact.

The second disease is of epidemic proportions, and once a dog is sick will spread through his teammates within an hour. The surface effect is much like a bad cold, and leaves the animals weak for many weeks after they have seemingly recovered. They seldom die from this complaint, however.

At Ritenbenk, where we slept in the clean beds of the manager, we were awakened one morning by a stranger poking his head into our room. He was a young assistant post manager on his way from Godhavn at Disko Island to Egedesminde, where he was being transferred because of the former manager's death.

We knew immediately—we would have known anyhow without his telling us six times during the first half-hour—that here was an important young man indeed. He had heard, he said, that we were traveling south, and wouldn't it be much safer for all of us if we teamed up and went together? We assured him that it certainly would, and he seemed very pleased. As he was a government employee the natives would all obey him, he said, and we agreed this would take a great burden off our shoulders.

The young assistant was a rank newcomer to Greenland, and had with him as pilot a half-breed, Karl Tygesen, son of a former manager and educated in Copenhagen. Karl, because of his ever-ready humor, had never gone far up the social and official ladder. He was, however, eager for any joke, and assured us that the trip with the young man would be better than a circus.

As we drove on next day the royal assistant thought we ought to settle one thing now: Who would be the leader? We elected him unanimously.

After we had conquered the first hill he turned to us and asked if we had ever climbed such a hill before. Of course, we had not. Karl Tygesen then announced that he could not tackle the next hill without a stimulant. He was, he said, on the verge of exhaustion.

Our leader produced a bottle from a case on his sledge. The weather was cold, the liquor was so strong that it had not frozen, and the glass was filled twice and passed around. To drink on the trail, our commander said, was not his practice, but if we ate something with it he could permit this letting down of the bars. He brought forth cookies which his mother had sent along with him, and served them with jam. Then before we started on he graciously offered us much good advice about how to get the best out of our dogs.

After another stop, and another drink, we climbed the third and last hill. The bottle was empty now. Fortunately I never drink myself so I was able to drive ahead and take care of our leader, who was sound asleep when his sledge drew into the next settlement.

It was Asa, and there we met my old pal, Tobias Gabrielsen,

the Eskimo who had been with the Danmark Expedition. We were overjoyed to meet him, and he told us immediately that he now belonged to a religious sect but that, since he was far from home, he would not be held in disgrace by his group if he talked with people who carried bottles on their sledges.

We had none, of course, but we were sure as rain of the fact that if our royal leader had been awake he would gladly have furnished refreshment for a party in honor of our colleague, the Arctic explorer. We let him sleep and helped ourselves to two bottles. Tobias' eyes glittered. He prefaced his conviviality with a little speech:

"As a whole I am not a friend of liquor. I am a religious man and due to be elected a member of the board of trustees. So I deny and protest in advance the foolish things I may be saying after a while. Whatever I tell you, or promise you, from now on until we wake up, does not count. . . . And now let us pull the corks!"

When our worthy assistant manager came to he looked at his bottles, but evidently thought he had handed out three yesterday instead of one. We thought it best to leave him innocent of what had actually occurred.

The next day the bad ice forced us inside the usual route along the fjords, and it meant crossing more mountains with the help of the bottles and the cookie jar. We did not get very far, and had to stop over at the house of a hunter in Qilerssiut.

The hunter's dwelling boasted two rooms, and we were assigned to the inner one. The hunter himself was an old friend of Knud's—he had been married in Knud's father's church—and was delighted to have some fresh seal meat to offer us. This, of course, was especially welcome to us as we had been eating nothing but delicious delicacies in the Danish houses.

Our leader and protector turned slightly green at sight of the meat, and asked us whether we had ever tasted seal meat. (It is not eaten by the better-class Danes in Greenland.) We said that a few years ago we had sampled it, and so far as we could remember, the stuff was edible. Karl assured him that it really was a sort of food, but could by no means be eaten unless accompanied by a glass of gin.

The young man hurried to fetch his bottle, and Knud, always the cook, proceeded with the preparation of the seal. He gave the assistant a generous portion, and we all fell to. All but the assistant. After a few moments he timorously asked us if we minded his getting a tin of sausages and boiling them himself. He was sorry but he had only enough for himself and could not offer us any.

Knud took the tin to warm it, but unfortunately emptied the contents into the seal soup and boiled it in that fashion. The young man ate nothing but hardtack and coffee. Nevertheless, he was soon as gay as ever, and told us more about the land and the natives than we could ever hope to know.

For instance, one of his friends had seen—he could not guarantee this, but his friend swore it to be true—an Eskimo eat the warm liver of a seal without cooking it. The poor friend had almost vomited. We all said this must be a lie, and under no circumstances would we believe it. But Knud secured the liver from the seal we were eating, and began to eat it before our eyes. The young man bolted.

We passed Jakobshavn, the greatest source of icebergs in the world and, our leader trailing us, reached Nordre Huse, a community without a trader, under the supervision of the teacher. Our leader was impatient with us, as we wanted to stay a while and talk with the natives, so he said he would drive on to Claushavn and there arrange for our accommodations with a Danish host.

The natives at Nordre Huse specialize in fishing, and are most adept at hooking comparatively small fish in deep waters with simple paraphernalia. They can detect the smallest fish on their hooks, and bring them to the surface. On the other hand, they have lost all spirit for big game hunting. One of the men told us that only the previous spring he had seen a bear while he was out on the ice. But "fortunately," he said, his dogs did not see it, and he was lucky enough to drive home without any harm coming to him. This indicates the difference between the "wild" Eskimos far north and these natives in the middle. In the southern part of Greenland the people are once more great hunters.

At Claushavn our young friend had secured a separate room for himself and an adjoining one for the three of us. He had, however, planned without being aware of Knud's rule never to permit anyone to sleep when he wanted to dance. The house was an old log structure once used as a whaling station and fortification, and there was plenty of room to dance.

Several girls and boys were invited, and Knud arranged a little bar in our room for the delectation of his special friends. Unfortunately we had no refreshments to offer, and once more we had to resort to the young assistant's case of liquor. Not to make the donor too angry with us, Karl Tygesen refilled three bottles with water and restored them to the box. Later it occurred to the boy to do his share in the evening's festivities, and he went out to bring in a bottle. The three bottles were frozen and broken open. We assured him that the dealer must have furnished him with inferior liquor. Knud tried to cheer him up by telling him that the boys at Egedesminde would undoubtedly have taken the liquor away from him anyway. The lad soon became somewhat enamored of one of the native belles, so the evening was a great success.

The trader of the place was an energetic musician. Though a son of Danish parents, he had never been in Denmark and his greatest pride was his accordion. He and Knud were the only two people in the Eskimo world who could play "The Germans' Entry into Paris," and it served as a great bond between them. The tune had found its way to Greenland via a German who had been in the War of 1870. He had deserted, and everyone believed that he had either killed an officer or, finding him dead, had stolen his papers. At any rate, he had come to Greenland and stayed there for the rest of his life. The trader loved the tune and played it until he drove everyone nearly mad. More strength than musicianship was demanded to play it, and Knud could only do so when no one was watching him. It was a fine tune, but it would have sounded much better in the open air.

The poor trader, like so many men of his time (and ours), was sure that the world was going to the dogs. Young people especially were, in his estimation, a frivolous lot. Each year he went down to the colony to meet the ship and learn some new tunes for his accordion, but the old sailing vessels were being replaced by steamers, and the old brand of sailor was dying out. Last year he had gone to Kristianshaab at ship time and found not a single accordion on board. That was a tragedy.

Our prominent young man, though on the verge of falling asleep, was kept awake by the growing fascination of the girl. When the dance was finished he followed her like a dog to her home. What happened on the walk I never did learn, but when he returned he came up to me.

"Peter," he said, "you are married to an Eskimo, aren't you?"

"Sure thing. What about it?"

"Then you must know! Are all the girls up here just liars and cheats? Tell me the truth!"

"They are!" I assured him. "Every one of them."

"I thought so," he said, and was very low indeed. He told Knud that he was as unhappy as any man could be. Life held no attractions for him. What was a man to do at such a time?

Knud and Karl were experts at giving advice; they both said they knew nothing better for such a condition than a fresh new bottle.

"To hell with all that stuff!" he cried. "Pour it out. Take all you want. Keep that poison away from me—it can never make me happy."

In defense of my two medicine-men companions, I must say that each took only one bottle and returned the balance to him in the morning.

It was only a short distance from Claushavn to Kristianshaab, the large colony. Binzer, the manager of the post, had four small sons who stood about the piano in the evening singing Danish songs to their mother's accompaniment. This sight and the ring of the familiar airs brought tears to my eyes and a nostalgia for old scenes which I had seldom felt since leaving Denmark. The family were most charming, and lived in an old log house built by the first explorers in that part of the country. Binzer's wife was a cousin of Knud's—he had relatives all over Greenland—and she made us each a fine new anorak, the national shirt with hood attached, to be worn at parties farther south. From Kristianshaab south it was the custom, when Danes visited one another, to wear white anoraks and blue cloth trousers rather than skin pants. It is exciting to come down out of the north, for the farther one goes the more civilized are the people.

At Kristianshaab also lived old Iversen, a cooper, who had arrived in Greenland aboard the same ship as our friend Nielsen, Nabaja of Tassiussak. There had been a certain amount of ill feeling between the two men since the day they left Copenhagen. The director of all the posts had shaken hands with Iversen but neglected to do so with Nielsen. Since their arrival in Greenland they were stationed in neighboring colonies, yet they never visited each other. They believed all the malicious stories they heard about each other, and multiplied their significance, each refusing to credit the other with a single honorable act or motive.

Iversen had been married three times, and his present wife was in the final stages of tuberculosis. Though she was in bed, her husband celebrated our arrival with a furious ball in her room so that she might be amused. Supported by cushions, she reclined in a white blouse and watched us swinging the girls and yelling and screaming. She would not have had our good time dampened by the mere fact that she was dying.

Iversen himself had been in Copenhagen a few years earlier, and had brought back a police uniform and helmet, the trophy of an adventure he never tired of relating. He donned this costume on all such occasions as the present one. He boasted of two parrots and three tiny spruce trees which were doing their poor best to grow in three separate pails, and he was going to write home for a couple of canaries and a monkey. He wanted me to report this affluence to Nielsen the next time I saw him. He also showed me a list of his children, which he wanted Nielsen to see. They were numerous and each was named for a Danish war hero. He asked me to read the names to Nielsen and tell him that he, Iversen, was intelligent enough to give his children names other than "Hans" or "Jens" or some other everyday cognomen.

At Egedesminde we stopped at the "hotel." It was not much like the regulation hotel, but it was at least a frame house with the essential equipment and was presided over by a native housekeeper who accommodated the guests at a minimum rate. It had been found necessary to have a public house in the community: many tourists traveled this far north, and the natives and the few Danes who lived here had tired of putting them up.

Mr. Binzer had accompanied us from Kristianshaab to Egedesminde in order to aid the widow of Mr. Evinsen, former post manager, in handing over the colony to our young friend. The new assistant was now for the first time manager of a colony and, after he had been sworn in, decided to honor the occasion with a large party.

In those days a fixed quantity of gin was requisitioned by each manager every year—it was then believed that gin was necessary for white persons living in cold countries, and few of the managers took the trouble to enlighten the authorities. And the majority of them had long since ceased pouring out liquor to their workers. Mr. Evinsen, indeed, had hoarded a considerable quantity through the years. After his death the inventory revealed a certain number of inches of liquor in the barrels—the barrels lay on their sides and the measuring rod was inserted through the bung hole.

Now that Mr. Evinsen was dead, the workers, who for a long time had felt themselves cheated of the precious fluid, set the barrels on end and syphoned it into their bottles until the liquid in the bottom of the barrels approximated the same number of inches it formerly had. Thereby the government inventory and the men's appetites were both satisfied, and the new manager's party was a howling success.

In Egedesminde we also found my old pal from the Danmark Expedition, Peter Hansen. He was now skipper of a schooner, but he was not always so contented as he should have been. He had married a native girl, and from that moment on had found himself ostracized from Danish society in the town. Of course, Danish society there did not amount to much, but it was all there was, and Hansen was disgruntled.

A great many of the Danes, not unlike white men of other nationalities who dwell among a preponderance of primitive persons, struck up sexual relationships with the native girls which often resulted in half-breed children. Later on many of the men married Danish women, and then denied their own progeny. Such cases are pitiful, but apparently irremediable. It was rather humorous to me, however, to see the Danes' obvious distaste for native women, and then to learn from the Eskimos exactly what their conduct had been toward the women before, and often after, their marriage to white women. None the less, I can still boast that the Danes have dealt the natives in their colonies a better hand than has any other power, not excluding the English.

But Peter Hansen saw that men of his class married to Danish women were invited with their wives to official parties at least once or twice a year. He was not. He admitted he should not feel badly about this, because the parties were deadly dull, but he could not overcome his annoyance.

I tried to cheer him up. Being married to a native girl myself, I enumerated our advantages over men married to white women who dominated them and complained constantly. I explained to him the pleasure it gave one to be married to one's children's mother instead of having them running around ragged. I also said it was a joy to teach them and watch them grow. He seemed to feel a little better after that.

There was an epidemic of whooping cough in Egedesminde, which had killed all the babies under a year old. Because of that there was some difficulty about our going on to Holstensborg, where we were to get the boat for Denmark, but it was decided that if Peter Hansen went with us we might proceed. Why four of us would not carry the germ and three of us would, I was unable to discover. At any rate, he was to go with us and stop us before we reached any houses while he went ahead and talked the situation over with the doctor.

Our young friend, the new manager, assured us of his everlasting friendship and future protection as, he said, "such a trip as we have made together, with its dangers and privations, brings people close together and should produce lifelong friendships." He was really a good boy, and later in life he came to understand what a conceited young pup he had been and often laughed with us over his harmless stupidities.

The stretch between Egedesminde and Holstensborg was easy to traverse. It is mostly a broad plain, intersected by occasional fjords. I remember passing one community ruled over by an ancient trader, Iginiarfik, his wife and ten daughters. He was convinced that Greenland was on its last legs, and that his next pay check would be worthless. This philosophy, which had supported him for many years, I gathered, encouraged him to spend his money as soon as he got his hands on it. His wife did all in her power to prevent it, but she could never stem the tide of his thirst. When his ship arrived, his order of old wine was delivered at once; then he retired to his room and stayed there until the year's supply was exhausted. It usually required about ten days, and during this interval no one dared approach him. He could be heard bellowing Danish songs, talking and arguing with himself, laughing and shouting commands to imaginary inferiors. When the wine keg was empty he came out of his room looking very green. Then he meekly surrendered himself and his rights to his industrious wife, and remained obedient to her until the ship arrived next year.

We were now actually in South Greenland, a lovely country. The time was April, but the nights were still dark here, and the northern lights even more spectacular than at Thule. Vegetation had sprung up where the snow had melted, and one's footsteps were muffled by a resilient carpet of delicate spring shoots.

Grass and small trees flourish on the northern slopes of the hills. The sun's rays are so direct on the southern slopes that the snow melts fast and the soil dries out. But the northern slopes always retain some snow and moisture to feed the bushes and flowers.

The day before we reached Holstensborg we met a group of natives who told us that the whooping cough epidemic had already invaded that city. When we finally saw the community, Peter Hansen warned us to keep well behind him, as he must be the first man to enter the place. He was self-conscious in his best clothes, and instructed us as to the order of our entry. We agreed to obey him—then cracked our whips and gave the dogs the bear signal. They had not heard this sound for months, but like old cavalry horses at the blare of a bugle, they leapt forward. Soon Peter Hansen and his boys were well to the rear.

We stopped with Mr. Thron, the manager in Holstensborg, who had lived for many years in Greenland and made a detailed study of the natives and the history of the country. He had read many rare old books and manuscripts, and was a living encyclopedia of the saga of Greenland and its colonization. The minister, Mr. Frederiksen, was a student of the Eskimo language, and had noted its similarities to various American Indian tongues.

Our time together was all too short. Within a few days the shout "Umiarssuit! Umiarssuit!" rang over the village.

The ship from Denmark was here!

Nowadays when radio flashes us the news hour by hour, it is almost impossible to comprehend our emotions at the sight of a ship approaching us there in the wilderness, bringing with it news, good and bad, of our homeland. Before this one had anchored the sailors shouted to us that our old king was dead; that our people in Denmark were worried about us; that Ejnar Mikkelsen had been rescued by a Norwegian seal hunter; and that it was known we did not possess the provisions to attempt the venture which we had, indeed, already accomplished. Prominent explorers had informed the public that it would be impossible for us to cross the icecap.

We hired two trustworthy boys to look out for our dogs and feed them twice a week while we were away. The dear people of Holstensborg, both Danes and natives, had been most kind to us. We had danced many, many miles during the evenings in the open, wearing out a pair of soles each night.

When we sailed we discovered that a sweet but feather-brained Danish girl had given up her job as teacher to follow us to Denmark. She had heard from the captain and others that we would doubtless be feted and wined and dined because of our accomplishment. This, to her, was a thrill she could not afford to miss. Neither Knud nor I was responsible for her going, but each of us suspected the other of an intrigue. As a matter of fact, both of us were innocent—this time.

10

It was fine to be on the ocean again, and we nearly went crazy at the sight of the first ship riding the horizon. Ajago's opinion of ships was somewhat jaundiced, however—he could not endure the drinking water from the tanks. He said, and I must agree with him, that it tasted of oil. When he sighted another ship he hurried onto the bridge and told the captain that now was his chance to borrow clean water. The captain sympathized, but assured him that the water on all ships was alike, and Ajago returned, crestfallen, to his cabin. The trip was distressing to our fair admirer too, for she was confined almost the whole way to her bunk with mal de mer.

Our ship, the *Hans Egede,* on which I had once been a stoker, put in at the Faroe Islands, and we decided to telegraph messages of our safe return from the icecap to all our friends. These evergreen islands emerge like ghosts out of a gray mist. The Faroes endure three hundred fifty-four days of rain each year—yet they depend for a livelihood upon selling dried codfish to the Catholics of Southern Europe.

Here we decided to send messages to all our friends, telling of our safe return from the icecap. We walked straight to the telegraph station and secured a sheaf of blanks, the manager eyeing us apprehensively and asking whether we had the money to pay for them. When he saw that our first message was to the King, he sprang to attention like the loyal subject he was. We dispatched telegrams to the Geographical Society, the papers, officials all over the world, our families—and sent them all collect with no further objections.

Ajago had his first glimpse of civilization, but he scarcely took the time to explore it. He ran straight through the town to the mountains, where he lay down beside a brook and drank copiously. He then filled as many bottles as he could carry, and lugged them back to the ship. Only then would he take an interest in his surroundings.

Faroe is the one place in the world where the tradition of the old Vikings still lives. The ancient dances, as executed by the knights and their ladies, have come down through the centuries unchanged. The same old songs, the endless ballads, are still sung as accompaniment to the dances; the same verses are chanted over and over, the same long rows weave in and out of the complicated figures. They are fascinating to watch—for a while.

The lovely girls, with their long, yellow tresses, their fresh complexions and beautiful, open smiles, are incomparable. Life is dangerous on the sea and in the mountains where they must go for birds and eggs. Only a strong, virile people would be able to endure the climate, let alone wrest a living from the scant resources of the islands, half-hidden dots on the surface of the sea. Yet the girls who toil endlessly in the daytime at grueling physical labor are utterly feminine in the evenings, sweet and guileless, devoted to their traditional songs and dances, and the very epitome of courtesy and grace.

A furious gale blew us away from the islands and sped us on our journey.

The lighthouse at Skagen is our "Statue of Liberty," and we esteem it highly. From there it is only twenty hours to Copenhagen.

11

Before the port is the world-famed Castle Kronborg, where Hamlet is alleged to have grown somewhat melancholy. His "grave," a hoax which preserves nothing more romantic than the skeleton of a cat, is pointed out to tourists, who bare their heads for long moments in quiet reverence and contemplation. The castle, nevertheless, is perhaps our finest relic of the Nordic renaissance, and we always feel ourselves at home once Kronborg is passed—it is only two hours more to the harbor. Boatloads of journalists met us there, and brought along plenty of welcoming spirits, my share of which Knud consumed.

The boat was boarded many times during the trip down to Copenhagen, and we were lionized by the publicity purveyors. At the harbor we were greeted by relatives and government representatives. Long and windy speeches were made, eloquent things were said of us, and tall glasses emptied. We replied as eloquently and evidenced our joy at being home—and then the prominent men went away.

On shore the girl from Holstensborg was my special burden, in spite of having a clear conscience about the whole thing. Knud, of course, had rushed to his home as he had a three-year-old daughter whom he had never seen. My dear mother looked at my human baggage as any mother would, but the girl had to be disposed of somewhere, so I put her up at my hotel.

It was delightful to be with my family, and I did not miss the acclaim we had anticipated until, after some hours, Knud telephoned and asked me if I happened to be busy that night. When I replied that I had no definite plans, he said:

"Well, it wouldn't be you and me if we didn't do something. It doesn't look as if anybody is going to do anything for us, so we'd better do it for them."

We scurried about and sent invitations to all the prominent men, and many others, for a big party in our own honor at the best hotel in Copenhagen. Always a little more cautious and prosaic than Knud, I asked who was to pay for it.

"You and I," he said. "If we crossed Greenland and came back alive, it would be too bad if we couldn't tackle this!"

Such a party! A few of the prominent citizens actually turned up, but Knud stole their thunder. Dressed in kamiks and the costume of our icecap expedition, he bewildered the guests by leaping onto the table and delivering a speech of welcome to the guests whom we had longed to see for three years. Then he organized dances between the different courses, and the maître de hôtel hurriedly snatched away the more expensive china.

The party was later referred to as the greatest event that had ever struck Copenhagen, and our little schoolteacher was wide-eyed with wonder. As the evening progressed Knud ran down to the restaurant and invited more guests from among the late diners. We had returned home expecting to be feted; if no one would fete us, we would make up for their thoughtlessness.

But next day we were abandoned again, and I remember Knud and myself walking the streets in the evening and comparing our reception with those other receptions tendered the much publicized expeditions which had gone out with government support. Even Arctic explorers need publicity.

We dropped into a circus and watched it with Ajago who saw thirty tame polar bears. He became so excited that he began to shout, and attracted a large crowd. He said that the next time he went out to the edge of the ice he would toss his gun into the water in honor of the white man who had tamed the bears. The circus made the most of this, and proposed hiring Ajago as one of its feature attractions, but we put our foot down on that suggestion.

Eventually we were sent for by the new King. From him we learned that we had committed a great faux pas in naming the land we had discovered for a Danish king without first receiving his permission. Such a thing, it seemed, was just not done.

Knud assured him that we meant it as a compliment, but the King was not certain that the land was large enough or worthy of the dignity of his name. Knud said it was, indeed, and I confirmed his assertion.

His Majesty then declared that he must have some one of authority look the land over before he could accept the compliment. Angered by now, Knud exclaimed:

"I know it is not permitted me to contradict a king. But I say it is worthy of you because I know the land better than you do."

Which, of course, was no way for a commoner to speak to a king, especially in those days.

But we were not much in vogue at that time. We saw in the papers that various Geographical Societies throughout the world had interested themselves in what we had done, so we applied to the "Carlsberg Fond," a famous scientific institution in Denmark, for $700 to cover the cost of our expedition across the icecap. The sum was, after all, trifling, and the members of the dignified institution felt a bit embarrassed at giving us the money which, after a great deal of haggling, they finally did. However, they advised us to apply for more next time as most people would think that nothing of any great importance could be accomplished with only $700.

I had been so long out of contact with civilization, facing nothing but elemental problems, that I felt like a stranger when I encountered my old friends—during the three years of my absence many of them had become learned men and women. I was proud of my strength, and of my ability to live for long stretches without food, but these things meant nothing to them. The things I had done were by no means so important as I, in my isolation from the world, had believed them to be. It is dangerous for a man to isolate himself from daily criticism and changing values.

One friend in Denmark did not disappoint me. On a former lecture tour I had met a fine girl, Magdalene, and I had been especially fond of her ever since. The day after I arrived I went to see her and was met by a nurse who told me that Magdalene was ill. At that time no mere nurse could keep me from seeing anyone I wanted to visit, so I pushed her aside and went into the sickroom. My dear friend was in bed suffering from a nervous breakdown. I told her to get up, but she could not. I said, "Forget

everything. Let's go out and get some fresh air." It came to me
with something of a shock that there were other things in the
world to fight, besides ice and dogs. After having disturbed her
rest considerably, I departed and was warned by the nurse that,
if I really wanted to help her patient, I would stay away from her.

Yet the day before I left I meant to say good-bye to my dear
Magdalene, nurse or no nurse. The nurse, I thought, could always
cure her after I was gone. I was just about to start for Magdalene's
home when a taxi brought her to me. She had seen in the papers
that I was leaving next day, and had got out of bed to bid me
farewell. I felt immediately inferior to a woman whose weakness
was unimpressed with my strength or any of the things I was able
to do. My place, I felt anew, was not here with people who could
see through me, but up there in the North. I would go back, I
thought, and never come again to Denmark.

While I sat with Magdalene I was aware of little except that
she had embarrassed me by asking why, if I liked the Arctic so
much, I had come home at all. I could only admit that I did not
know. In reality, of course, Knud and I felt that we had accomplished something extraordinary and that the world would desire
to pay us tribute. We had arrived home at a bad time, however.
The day we visited the Prime Minister he handed in his resigna-
tion. My trip to Denmark had been, as a whole, disappointing,
though I did not dare admit it to Magdalene, and I felt that all
the publicity, the parties we had attended were only so much
hot air. I longed to go back to Navarana and the cold North.

I remained at home for five weeks, and sailed for Greenland
once more through the kind offices and faith of Mr. Nyboe. He
was the brains and the working force of our committee. When
no one else believed in us, he stuck fast; without Nyboe, North
Greenland would never have been secured for Denmark. When
I reached Thule, it would be as governor of the province.

12

Now that our trading post was established, Nyboe bought us
a little ship, the *Cape York,* and secured for it the best captain
in those waters, Peder Pedersen, who has since made innumerable
voyages to Greenland under the most adverse conditions and year
after year has added to his reputation as Denmark's foremost ice
navigator.

The plan was for Ajago and me to sail on a commercial vessel

Top. THE "DANMARK" AT ANCHOR IN DANMARKSHAVN, 1906. THIS SAME BOAT
LATER MADE A TRIP TO OUR STATION AT THULE.

Bottom. OUR BOAT, THE "CAPE YORK," AT THULE.

as far as the cryolite mine at Ivigtut in South Greenland and there await the *Cape York*. Cryolite is a source of aluminum and is used for enameling china and making glass. The only cryolite mine in the world is at Ivigtut, and the output is shipped only to Denmark and the United States. When, many years later, I met Herbert Hoover he told me that as a young engineer he had experimented with the stuff, and had once intended to visit the mine in Greenland.

Our voyage was long and unexciting. Toward the end of it Ajago recovered from his mal de mer, but peace came to him only when the cliffs of Greenland grew out of the blue of the sea.

Only two women were permitted at Ivigtut, the state inspector's wife and the chief engineer's wife, who kept house for the officers. The scenery was dull and drab and, though the hospitality was excellent, the general tone of the place did not appeal to me. The working conditions were not to be complained of, and the company did what it could to provide entertainment. That was no easy matter during the long winter months. Half the crew returned to Denmark each fall, and it was the custom among the rest to let their whiskers grow until the first ship arrived in the spring. My face had been so badly frostbitten during the journey across the icecap that I have never since been able to shave, and I was not especially popular at the mining camp. The men gave me the name, "Peter Summerwhiskers," and to this day I am called that at Ivigtut.

Near-by was a copper mine owned by our friend Nyboe. I knew both the manager, Lindaas, a champion Norwegian ski-jumper, and Hoegh, a former classmate of mine who was a mining engineer. I felt much more at home with them, and, as they were always delighted to see strangers, I decided to stay there until our boat sailed in.

Perhaps I should say they were delighted to see any strangers except ministers of the gospel. Whenever the minister arrived to conduct service it meant a day off, with pay, for the miners, and a consequent loss to a company employing several hundred men. Nyboe had assured the minister at Julianehaab, in whose district the mine was located, that he was always welcome, but also promised him a fine big jug of spirits and several slabs of bacon each fall if he had conducted no services during the preceding summer. The arrangement proved satisfactory to everyone concerned.

At Ivigtut it had been the tradition to give the minister so much to drink on the day he arrived that next day he would be in no condition to conduct his meeting. Year after year the poor theologians swore to refrain from the fiery fluid, but they were never able to do so. When the day of service arrived, the minister was, without exception, sick in bed.

Finally, a new circuit minister arrived in Julianehaab. He was a Goliath of a man, weighing over four hundred pounds and tall in proportion. When he went anywhere in his skin boat, he always sat deep aft; his rowing girls, far forward, were still unable to balance him, and perched high in the air threshing at the water below them.

In due course he reached Ivigtut and announced his intention of holding service next day. He was received with the utmost courtesy and at dinner that night was liberally plied with wine. After the meal the more potent liquors were served, and the minister signified his approval.

At length the manager went to bed, but warned the engineers of their duty: perhaps they had best take turns sitting up and drinking until God's man was under the table. The engineers smiled and assured the manager that even the runts of the polytechnic class had always been able to outdrink any theologian.

Next morning at six the manager rose to get the work started. He was startled to find the minister walking back and forth outside memorizing his sermon. But he was even more startled to see his engineers hanging on the fence around the mine. The minister had picked them up as they had fallen and carried them to the open air where he had fastened them on the posts by their collars so that they would be sure to hear his preaching. The service was above reproach, and the honor of the Divinity restored once and for all.

The *Cape York* did not arrive, and I had no idea what could have happened to it. Mr. Nyboe came to Greenland to inspect his mine and he and I talked over the situation. It was already so late in the year that there was extreme doubt of our boat's breaking through to Thule even if it did arrive, so we decided that I should try to get there in a motorboat. These craft were extremely rare in Greenland, but through Nyboe's intervention I secured one to carry me as far north as Godthaab, where I hoped to get another. It was likely that someone would give me a boat rather than have me on his hands for the winter.

Henrik Olsen, my old Eskimo friend from the Danmark Expedition, was at the copper mine and, as he had been trained in the operation of a motorboat, I took him along and promised him a job as assistant at Thule once we arrived.

Our voyage to Godthaab was easy, the land along the coast dotted with settlements. In Godthaab the inspector gave me letters of credit to secure motorboats along the way north. From Sukkertoppen we were permitted to ride with the doctor. My greatest trouble was with Henrik. Here he was a very prominent man, as he had been decorated by the King. He had made a number of contacts with young women in the small villages en route, and there he now renewed on the overnight stops. Each morning I had to rouse him and get him under way.

The trip along the coast was an unforgettable experience. The late summer sun struck cold fire from the mountaintops. So long as it shone each day its twilight glimmer was lush as an autumn sunset.

We encountered our first real difficulty at Holstensborg. I had been promised a motorboat belonging to the fishing master, but he had not been consulted. He told me that if he heeded every man who came along with a note from the inspector he would be unable to do any fishing with the natives. Each morning he towed a string of native boats far out to sea, and there they fished with their long lines for the giant halibut so plentiful in those waters. In the evening he brought them back to shore. He was within his rights to refuse me, as his work was independent of the district manager, but it made my situation a serious one. After days of delay and argument I was promised a boat owned by the fishing department and stationed some distance away.

Before it arrived, however, I was in hot water with Ajago; he had had the misfortune to fall in love. Ajago was a fine fellow and an expert hunter, and badly in need of a wife. The object of his affections was an excellent, unattached girl. Her mother had recently died, and she was desperately in love with my boy. I could see no objection to the match, so I told them to get along and be ready to leave with me next morning at five o'clock. The impatient bridegroom found boxes in which to pack the girl's possessions, and borrowed money from me to buy many items he had never before thought of owning.

Suddenly he was a man of means and responsibility, and I was like a happy father-in-law—until I met the minister of the community outside his church.

"What is this I hear?" he asked. "I am told that your man is going to take along one of my ewe lambs."

"That's right," I smiled. "They're getting married."

"What do you mean, 'married'? He is a pagan, and I will not permit one of my flock to marry as they do in his country."

I tried to make him understand what a fine fellow Ajago was, and how much better off the girl would be with him in our community where there was enough of everything for everyone. Here the natives were all dreadfully poor. "Besides," I ended lamely, "she is in love with the boy."

"What difference does that make?" he countered. "What does it matter if she becomes a wealthy woman if she loses her soul by cohabiting with a pagan?"

I was doing my best to persuade him when Ajago arrived and demanded to know what the trouble was. The minister explained that the girl could not go along with us without being married.

"I have heard that," Ajago admitted somewhat contemptuously. "All right, here is the church and here are you. Let's go in and get it over with. I'm in a hurry to pack the stuff."

The minister then warned him that no man could marry unless he was a Christian and understood the meaning of "original sin" and its place in the scheme of human happiness.

"Up in our country," Ajago explained, "we consider it wedding enough when one gets the pants off the girl, and one has done that long ago. One sees nothing more to talk about. One happens to feel embarrassed, as if a woman occupies the whole mind of a man."

God's man considered this blasphemy. He could not understand how clean and unspoiled and uninhibited this young Eskimo was. I thought it time to intervene, so I stated that I had already given Ajago permission to take the girl along and I never went back on my word. We were all leaving together in the morning.

"I shall be down at the dock with a number of my men and prevent your going," the minister said.

"I have several rifles on the boat," I warned, "and anyone who tries to come on board without permission will be shot down."

"You shall be reported to the inspector," said the minister, who was employed by the state, "and due punishment will be meted out."

"I shall be only too happy," I bluffed, and turned on my heel. Before the inspector arrived in Holstensborg, I would be in Thule where no judgment could touch me.

But during the night the minister summoned the girl's relatives, and they warned her not to go; also the crew of the boat refused to transport us if the girl accompanied us. They wanted to help me out, but they said that after I was gone they would still have to face the authorities and might be punished for complicity.

I had to give up the struggle. The girl told me that she had never loved anyone but Ajago, and that a certain blacksmith was showering her with unwelcome attentions and she did not know how long she could hold out against him. I urged her to wait until next year when we could come down with our own boat and pick her up. She gave me a letter stating that if she was married to the blacksmith by the time I returned she would have been forced into the bargain by the minister and the groom.

Nevertheless, when I came back next year she was married to him and had a son whom she named Peter. Whenever I am in Holstensborg I have to fit the boy out with a full suit of clothes. Which is all I got out of a rather unpleasant incident.

When we reached Egedesminde once more I found my old friend Peter Hansen in a bad mood. He was immensely proud of his little schooner, and kept it as spotless as any navy craft. During the summer a navy vessel had visited Greenland on a tour of inspection and Peter had raised his flags to salute the boat, and had lowered his Danish flag to the correct angle. The government boat had sailed straight past him without the slightest indication of having seen him. The slight had humiliated him and left him morose. I told him that it made no difference, surely, whether a petty navy officer saluted him or not. But he was far from satisfied, and said that he intended to make a complaint to the admiral.

There were no motorboats at Egedesminde, and the only course seemed to be for us to row across the bay to Godhavn on Disko Island and try to borrow the boat belonging to Dr. Porsild, manager of the scientific station there. I rounded up a crew of rowers for the skin boat, but at the last moment we discovered that it leaked like a sieve, so that venture was out of the question. After searching about frantically for another boat, I learned that Peter Hansen was planning a trip north within a few days in his schooner, and that he would take me as far as Umanak Colony. From there I could get dogs and travel north over an arm of the icecap—a bad trip, but the only way of reaching Thule before Christmas.

The night before we were scheduled to leave I was awakened by a number of girls squealing inside my room. Half asleep, I chased them out, but one, whose voice was louder than the others, shrieked that Knud was outside.

"What Knud?" I asked. I knew that my Knud was far off in Denmark with his wife. But at the same moment I realized that if he had been here he would have found some way of reaching Tassiussak.

"It is Knud! Your Knud!" they shouted, and, suddenly awake, I rushed down to the pier. The nights were already dark, but in the harbor I saw a motorboat and in it Knud Rasmussen!

The man could accomplish anything and could scent trouble no matter how far away he might be. He had heard in Denmark that I was marooned at Ivigtut waiting for our ship to arrive, and he had worried lest it arrive too late. He had jumped on a steamer bound for Ivigtut, expecting to find me there and plan with me some course of action. At any rate, he had wanted to be with me if I was in difficulties. He had reached Ivigtut at the very moment that my old friend, Colonel I. P. Koch, had arrived there in his motorboat to embark for Denmark.

Playing in luck, as always, Knud had purchased the motorboat and followed after me. Just outside Ivigtut he had encountered our ship, its motor disabled beyond repair, and had taken Captain Pedersen into the harbor at Ivigtut to purchase sails for him; then back to the ship and collected Pedersen's engineer, who would be of no further service on a motorless vessel. Knud then towed Pedersen's boat outside the fjord, and the *Cape York* promised to proceed at once with its cargo to Tassiussak.

Knud's motorboat was a beauty, designed along the newest lines. At last we had our own craft, and nobody could tell us where we might or might not go. We proceeded at once to Godhavn, and sailed on north with gasoline purchased from Dr. Porsild. On the way we sighted the *Cape York* and headed for it. The ship was becalmed, its sails hanging limp and lifeless, so we took it in tow and progressed slowly for several knots until a gale struck us, the sails billowed, and we had to cast loose in a hurry or be run down.

Finally, we reached Tassiussak. Navarana could scarcely conceal her joy at seeing me, and later confided that she had been very apprehensive of my safety. The Nielsens had told her that she would never see me again, that I would desert her and probably never come back to Greenland, and a number of other things not especially heartening for a young wife to hear when she is alone and far from home.

I asked her about the minister and her preparation for baptism. She told me that he had begun her religious education by kissing her and had attempted further liberties, but she had merely kicked him and walked out. After that experience she said she had no use for baptism, as one does not have to be baptized to be insulted. She took the incident very seriously: it seemed to her that persons who desire to teach others ought first to learn to control themselves. The minister was later given a year's vacation to contemplate his transgressions, but when the year was up he became once more the revered and sacred agent of the Divinity in Greenland.

It was all very puzzling to Navarana. She had seen one missionary at Thule unable to curb his emotions toward women of the tribe; she had heard of many ministers in South Greenland discharged from office for the same offense. Why, she wondered, were rules made which were obviously contrary to men's impulses, and women's too? Why persist in making laws which could not be kept?

I could not answer her. I only knew that I would not care to have been a missionary.

13

Already the nights were dark and bitter cold, and Melville Bay a labyrinth of ice. It was impossible for the *Cape York* to be sent any farther north, yet the ship held a cargo of trading goods which somehow had to be stored or transported to Thule.

Fortunately for us, Nielsen had built himself a new house. He would soon be at the retirement age and could settle down to enjoy his pension. Nevertheless, he sold the house to us—we paid him twice what it had cost—and the next year he built himself another home twice as large as the original. We filled the house with our materials, but there was still more for which there was no room.

In our need we visited the missionary and persuaded him to permit us to utilize the attic of the church. He was not at all sure this was lawful. We explained that it was the church's duty to aid the poor pagans in any manner possible—we had brought these goods north for them, and if the stuff was left outside it would be ruined and the pagans, who might later be converted to the true faith, would suffer. This argument was sound, especially when accompanied by a small gift. Only one thing worried him: perhaps he had sold out too cheaply.

Nielsen had built the church too, and he was not the best carpenter in the world. Before all our goods were safely stowed away the ceiling of the edifice began to sag. The minister was in a lather of fright lest his holy house come tumbling down beneath the burden of supplies meant for pagans.

Again Knud proved himself equal to the emergency. Churches, he said, were constructed in many different ways. There were the Gothic and the Roman architectures, and this church could easily be transformed into the finest temple in Greenland if a few columns were added. The columns were added forthwith, and the preacher was given money to paint them next year when the weather was warmer. Everyone was satisfied.

It was a question whether the *Cape York* could even return to Denmark without a propeller, but Pedersen swore he would not spend the winter in Greenland. I towed him out of the harbor and waved good-bye to him in the dark. When I left him the snow was already sifting down, but he hoisted his flag in salute, and sailed for home. They had a hell of a trip, we learned many months later, and only reached Denmark late in January, 1914.

Knud remained with me. He was in hot water because he had promised his wife he would return to Denmark with the ship, and she came up to Julianehaab in South Greenland in order to travel home with him. When she arrived, the poor girl could find no one who knew anything about Knud. Someone told her he thought Knud had traveled north, but no one remembered how or when or why.

Like most women, she was not particularly pleased at being marooned without a word from her husband. She was then, and still is, a grand sport, but she did not quite recover her sense of humor until the next year when she learned that the native bearing letters to her from Knud had used the epistles to build a fire after having fallen into the sea.

There was still a little open water around Tassiussak, so we transported some of our goods to our "hotel," Bjoerneborg, where we felt we could pick it up with sledges and transport it to Thule.

Henrik and I made two trips with the motorboat well loaded and towing a skin boat; on the second the ice was forming so fast that we knew we could make only one more effort before it closed in entirely. On the third cruise Knud and Ajago accompanied us with their dogs and sledges, which had been sent up from Holstensborg.

That trip was bad. We were weighted down with goods, dogs, sledges and five men—a young native named Polo had come along as a helper in case we needed him. We fought ice all the way—not only new ice but countless icebergs, as the fjord had recently disgorged a flock of hummocks and bergs. It was too dark to travel at night, and we had to lie up rather early each evening.

One night we tried to put in at Sarfak, but one of the bergs looked too dangerous to us, and we dropped anchor around the opposite side of the point. During the night a number of the local celebrities visited us, including the big Solo and several natives named Gaba, who were delighted to be in our cabin and listen to our stories about the unknown land to the south. As we sat talking a rending crash electrified us. We thought first that we had been struck by an iceberg, but the sea was calm and nothing had hit our boat. Then faint cries of terror reached us from the nearby village, and someone called "Solo."

We all hurried from the boat to the houses; we were close to the scene of the disaster before we learned what had happened. Solo's house was completely demolished by an iceberg, a huge monster that had pitched over onto the shore.

Four persons were buried and mashed beyond recognition. One poor woman, Benina, had lost her husband and two children. All of them had gone visiting Solo's wife because her husband was away. It was said later that they had made coffee, which he would not permit when he was at home. And this sin was mentioned from the pulpit as being the cause of the catastrophe. The fourth casualty was also a man, and the amazing fact was pointed out that none of the persons killed was named "Gaba."

The superstitious popularity of the name grew even more widespread and, as it is an abbreviation of the Angel Gabriel's name, the Divine Messenger was paid greater tribute than any other deity.

The pitiable natives were terrorized. We asked some of them to come out and spend the night in our boat, but they dared not. In their panic they ran out into the cold night and cried and howled like wolves; the sound was not a pretty one.

But even this tragedy was not without a bitter humor. By the middle of the night we had the village fairly well calmed down. We had brought food from the boat and lighted our primus stove to prepare it. When it was ready I went outside the house we had appropriated and found a few mourners wailing and running blindly about. I got them inside, but one young girl began to cry again and dashed out. I went after her. She told me that she had lived in the house which had been destroyed, and had lost everything she owned. I suggested that she come out and sleep on the motorboat for the night. At which she turned upon me and exclaimed: "Oh, no. I could not do anything of the kind tonight. You will have to wait at least until tomorrow—then I will be in normal condition again."

I had intended no attack on her virtue, but this was no time to attempt an explanation.

Perhaps the most surprising thing of all was that later Solo rebuilt his house on exactly the same spot. And the next winter I saw another iceberg frozen in the ice in the same relative position as the one which had crushed his dwelling.

When we finally reached Bjoerneborg the wind was whipping up such a gale that we had to wait in a shelter behind the island for two days before we could unload. The first things off were the dogs, which had not been released from the skin boat since we had left Tassiussak. They were mad for water and exercise.

We said good-bye to Knud and Ajago and cast off. Those two had enough to live on, but they intended to do some bear hunting before the ice could support them across Melville Bay to Cape York and Thule.

The swells were heavy, and we had to go now or never. I shortened up the sails as much as possible, but still the wind harried us. It was stronger than we had thought from the looks of the water, since the floating ice helped to calm the sea. Our idea was merely to round the peninsula that separated the fjords, but the wind continued to rise, and soon it was impossible for us to use the sails at all. I gave the rudder to Polo and helped Henrik save the sails, and while we tussled with them Polo had no means of controlling the movements of the boat, which veered off before the wind.

I dashed back to the rudder and Henrik went down to the engine. It started, but we were tossed about like a cork. I used all the tricks I knew to keep on a course, but each time we finally got the craft under control an ice hummock blew down upon us and we had to veer sharply to avoid smashing into it.

Then we tried to get hold of a large hummock and tie the boat to it. We made several unsuccessful attempts, and finally I jumped onto one myself but could not get the ice anchor into it.

I was lucky to climb aboard again after having been in the water up to my waist.

Apparently we could do nothing to help ourselves. To run the engine and waste our oil was foolish, yet we dared not stop it as a lull might come and we would need to take advantage of it. The engine was a kerosene motor that seldom failed, but it took half an hour to start it, after it had been thoroughly warmed up by a lamp. We had but one desire—to get hold of an iceberg and hold onto it so that we would not drift too fast.

We were blown along with the wind, which took us farther and farther away from our dear Greenland. The waves, bombarding us with big cakes of ice, were dangerous but sporty, and Henrik was at a loss what to do. Polo cried. He had been married only a short while, and had gone on the trip merely to earn enough money to settle down in a place of his own. He was Abel's younger brother, and both he and his young wife had to slave to earn enough for their board with his brother. Now he gave up the idea of ever seeing his wife again.

To be lost in the Arctic Ocean with two helpless men, and realize that you yourself are the only person who can save the outfit is a tempering experience. In a sense, I grew up there. The wind howled and the spray whitened my face with salt and pulled the skin taut. The waves were not especially heavy, as the wind was so strong that it flattened the water and caught up the ice-charged crests into the air.

We could see but a few yards, and it was impossible to look eastward toward the land without being blinded. Finally, directly ahead of us loomed a great iceberg. I yelled to Henrik to give the engine everything he had, and I ran the boat in as close to the ice as I dared. In the shelter of the mass, the rudder grabbed the water. Slowly the boat turned. I leapt to the hatchway and roared at Polo, who dashed up thinking we were home again. I ordered him to steer for the iceberg and not talk back, and yelled at Henrik to help me. Then I went out on the foregear and, at the moment we struck the berg, jumped down on the ice foot with the ice anchor. I shouted at them to keep the boat hard against the ice and hand me a rope. With this I scrambled upward and round a peak that acted as a small tower on the side of the berg. There we moored to the giant, a giant that might at any moment object to our presence and flop over on us.

Henrik was a great help. He almost fell into the water in

order to grab hold of me again, but I got my hand on the gun-wale and at that time I was in such excellent physical condition that this was the same as being safe on board again. After I was back on the boat I could never understand how I had climbed up the steep, smooth ice to tether us to the tower.

The lee of an iceberg is calm compared with the outer side. We remained there for three days, floating about Baffin Bay entirely ignorant of our whereabouts. We watched the ice hummocks march past in bobbing procession and disappear to the rear. Most of the time we slept below. Whenever we woke and opened the hatch the whole fury of the Arctic rushed down upon us, so we decided to take it easy until the storm was over. That was dangerous, of course, but we were worn out from the exposure and the toil and strain.

And when at last the wind abated we could tell it by an almost imperceptible change in the movement of the boat. This time when we went above the sun was shining, and the cakes of ice bobbing aimlessly up and down with the swells. No longer were they driving past us as they had for days. The evening sunlight was refracted in multifarious colors from the ice hummocks, transforming the sea into a vast field of sparkling gems.

It was late, and we dared not cast off for Greenland until morning. By then the swells no longer rocked us, and a thin sheet of surface ice bound the hummocks together. But before we could get away a new gale blew up. Though our compass was not much good, we could tell by the stars that this wind came from another direction. The first storm had blown out of the south and east, and this one came from southwest. The southwest winds are the bad ones in that section of the globe. The sky was soon threatening, and after a short while snow began to fall and blotted everything from sight.

We had the same thing all over again, except that there was apparently an inexhaustible supply of ice to the south which drifted up and hemmed us in. For two more days we dared not show our heads abovedeck. Polo was certain that we were headed for a starvation party, and thought perhaps we ought to put an end to it immediately. But no wind lasts forever, and when it was over we found ourselves in the middle of an ice pack, lashed to an iceberg, we knew not where.

Only Henrik was game. He had had the time of his life on the Mylius-Erichsen expedition to the east of Greenland, and now he thought he had taken a similar task on his shoulders.

He would not complain—you had to take times like this along with the good ones.

Then a snug north wind whipped up, an Arctic trade wind which we felt we could depend upon. Next day we were tossed back against our iceberg by the wind. We could see by the water that it was turning ponderously, so we waited patiently for it to lead us back to land, Polo sobbing like a little child. We climbed to the top of the iceberg and looked about us. There was nothing but ice, though far to the west we thought we could see land. The sky was overcast and we could not be certain, but if it was land at all it must have been Baffin Land.

Once more we climbed back into our boat and went to sleep. We had enough food to last us some time, but how to get home?

That was our darkest moment, and, like the proverb, it proved to be just before the dawn. Next morning we saw the mountain, Qasorssuaq, which lies directly south of Upernivik. The ice about us had spread and we could afford to accept our iceberg's protection no longer. It was growing colder, and sheet ice once more forming on the surface. We cast loose. By now we had lost all fear of the iceberg, and I shall remember its shape and its shelter all my life.

In two days we were back in Saitoq. We had left there just nine days before.

Polo had been given up as dead and his belongings divided among various relatives who now refused to return them. Even his wife had moved in with another man, but as this was a Christian country and no real marriage could be performed until the minister came along, she returned to her Enoch Arden. She returned to him, however, without clothes or any worldly goods. As a result we had to take them along with us and set them up at housekeeping again.

My return was a happy one too, but Navarana had not for one second believed me lost. She said that time after time the local ladies had advised her to cry over my demise, but she had told them that such an act would bespeak a lack of confidence in her husband and disgrace him, a thing no woman from her country would do. As for herself, she had been out in the fog with Jacobine fishing. They had seen a little piece of ice with a bear sitting on it. They rushed to shore with the news, and all the men had jumped into their kayaks and rowed madly to the spot, only to see the bear sprout wings, turn into a gull and fly

Top. A WEDDING PARTY AT THULE, THE GROOM SMOKING, THE BRIDE BLUSHING.
Bottom. POLAR ESKIMOS SUMMERING AT THULE.

away. Thus can the fog deceive one. She told this as the most embarrassing thing that had ever happened to her.

We waited until the ice formed, and then set out on our sledges, Henrik with one and Navarana and I with the other. When, after six days, we reached Bjoerneborg, Knud and Ajago had already been gone for two weeks.

At Savigssuit we found that Qidlugtok boasted a new gun which Knud had given him in payment for discovering the meteorite which we had sought so long. I was glad to learn this, because the search had been Knud's hobby for years. He insisted that all Eskimo stories and traditions were based on fact, and if there was said to be a meteorite in this part of the world, there must be one.

We also learned that we were no longer the only white men in the district—a big American expedition had come up the previous summer and settled down at Etah with their ship. It had been reported that they had many dogs and had built a house, but little else was known as there had been no direct communication with them.

At Cape York a letter from Knud was awaiting me, assuring me everything was well with him; he would be anxious to receive us at Thule.

It was touching to witness the genuine pleasure of the natives in seeing me once more as we neared home. Navarana, too, had grown in poise and gained the respect and favor of her people without in any manner being impolite or assuming false dignity. She was proud of her ability to read and could barely wait to reach home so that she could put into practice many of the things she had learned from Mrs. Nielsen.

Two days later we arrived at Thule, and Knud received us like the king he was. He had installed himself comfortably in his room, and now he had to share it with us and Henrik, but there were never so many people about that Knud felt crowded.

PART IV

1

WE had to face the situation of having other white men in the Thule district. (The expedition later proved to be MacMillan's.) In the first place, they would keep many natives busy and away from their normal pursuit—fox hunting. Second, the American market for fox pelts was excellent, and these men could easily compete with us since their expedition was financed at no cost to the men themselves. Their supplies might also prove to be more desirable to the natives than ours. At least, they would inevitably be different, and that would make them desirable for a time.

Food was our immediate problem, since we had arrived in Thule in the middle of winter. The meat caches of the natives were already quite low, and hunting in the polar night was a thing almost out of the question. The need of our dogs was greater than our own, though even our household stores were ill-stocked, as the boys we had left had spent the spring at games and love-making and had stored away only a fraction of the amount they would have gathered had we been at home.

The night after our arrival Dr. Elmer Ekblaw of the Crocker Land Expedition called upon us. He was a tall, husky man. He had been born of Swedish parents, and we consequently found it easy to converse with him. He was on his way down to Savigssuit to take possession of the meteorite for the expedition. MacMillan planned to take it back with him and place it in the American Museum of Natural History, where Peary's two meteorites were already on display.

Unfortunately we had had nothing to eat that day. Ajago, however, had just been to Saunders Island to recover an old walrus flipper he had left there, and we had planned to help him eat it.

I was housekeeper and master of the empty store, and much concerned over our shabby treatment of such an important guest. I proposed to Knud that we confess to him that we had nothing to eat, and suggest that he bring in his own food and cook it in our house. Knud, however, assured me he had a better idea. He would never expose his poverty—that would only multiply it in the visitor's eyes.

Greeting Ekblaw enthusiastically, he said:

"We are delighted to see you, and are especially pleased to be able to serve you a very rare dish! Have you ever tasted real Eskimo rotten food?"

"I haven't tried it yet," Ekblaw answered, "and I'm not sure that I would like it."

"Marvelous! I am so happy!" Knud cried. "We can give you an especially light walrus flipper, without too much or too little flavor. How wonderful that we have saved this for the occasion."

Ekblaw looked slightly dubious, but Knud brought the flipper in, chopped off a chunk with an ax and handed it to our visitor with a flourish. Knud talked incessantly, never permitting Ekblaw to get a word in:

"How lovely! Yes, it is exactly as I said—good, very good! No one could help liking it, and I can see that you appreciate good food—rotten meat with the Eskimos, fruit in the tropics, and pâté de fois gras in Paris." Knud set an example by eating a piece of the meat himself, and there was no way out for Ekblaw. Knud's enthusiasm was so magnificent that the courteous Ekblaw could not find it in his heart to express his real opinion; he said that it was good and had been quite a treat for him.

That was a mistake, for Knud immediately handed him a more generous portion. The blubber was green with maturity—almost the same color as Ekblaw's face by now.

"Take it, take it!" Knud urged. "No modesty here. I knew you would like it, and you have not disappointed me. Take it and eat it; it may be a long time before you eat such a meal again!"

Ekblaw silently thanked heaven for that, but there was no resisting Knud. Somehow he managed to swallow it without vomiting. Knud, however, had not finished with his efforts to uphold our honor:

"We Danes always used to take coffee after our meals. But you will admit it would be a pity to drink coffee after such a meal as this. It would not only run counter to custom, but would also kill the taste we still have in our mouths." I was frightened when he first mentioned coffee; there was none within five hundred miles.

We had a fine evening, and it was easy for Knud to talk

Ekblaw out of the meteorite. The meteorite was already claimed for the Danish Museum, Knud said, and he had no right to present it to America. He offered, however, to take Ekblaw to the spot and show the stone, and later to have a piece of it shipped to the museum in New York.

Next morning we had a welcome surprise. Ekblaw asked our permission to bring in his own food and let us sample his cooking. We were very pleased.

Knud and Ekblaw went south together to look at the meteorite, and Knud did not reveal the fact that he had not yet seen it himself. Ekblaw could have claimed it quite as honestly as Knud, but Knud was the superior diplomat.

Later we both went to visit MacMillan at Etah. MacMillan was already known to the natives, as he had been with Peary on the North Pole expedition. The Eskimos remembered him especially for his amazing skill at acrobatics. Now they both liked and disliked him, the latter for no other reason than that they wanted no one but Peary to lead any expedition.

MacMillan's hospitality was above reproach. Knud could not help comparing him with Dr. Cook, who insisted that Knud eat with the crew before the mast. In MacMillan's house everyone, scientists and sailors, ate together—their outfit was lavishly supplied. Their victrola and many books, combined with their companionship, made it pleasant for me to have them in the district for the next four years.

We still had at least forty loads of goods to bring up from the south, and the only way to get it was to convince the natives that the hauling was little more than a pleasure trip for them. Knud was the man to arrange this.

Those who had foxskins to sell were asked to deliver them to us and then go south and pick up their goods at Tassiussak. They could easily bring back a few boxes, and Knud told them that they had such fine dogs that he was eager to see how much they could haul. They would also be able to feed their dogs from his meat at Bjoerneborg, so that the journey would in the end be a saving.

We traveled back and forth, back and forth. No longer were we hunters or adventurers, but freighters and haulers, and this took away much of the excitement of crossing Melville Bay. The anxiety of driving tired dogs through the darkness, the snowstorms, the everlasting cold, was disheartening. Melville Bay was

a highway that winter, and the natives grew as weary of it as
we did.

But Knud Rasmussen blossomed under the grueling routine.
I can still see him standing in the middle of Melville Bay, the
going bad through deep snow or rough ice, the dogs balking, the
Eskimos disgruntled, no dog food, no fuel or provisions, and
home far, far away. Then he was gayest and most at ease. He
loved to manage people, to praise some, scold others. He knew
them all, and knew how to keep them going.

Not until March was nearly over, and we had secured everything but a few boxes of rifles left on shore at Melville Bay, did
Knud leave us to join his wife. Once more he was off for Holstensborg. How he could get there at this time of year none of
us knew, but he made it in better time than any man ever had
before. I was left alone to maintain my position as governor of
the province and ruler of a handful of Eskimos. But I was proud
of the responsibility, and determined to show our backers in
Denmark that I could make the post a paying proposition.

I wanted to go north again and map the remainder of the
land on the north coast. All our plans were made, all the provisions secured and clothing prepared. Indeed we set out, Henrik
Olsen and I and a few natives, leaving Sechmann, the ex-missionary, to take charge of the post. But on the second morning, little
Iggianguaq and his sledge disappeared in a crevasse. We rescued
the man, but my theodolite, which had been on his sledge, was
gone beyond recovery. Two days later we were at home again, and
I was very, very depressed.

Once more the crevasses had defeated me. They have tried
to lure me into them time after time. This time we had camped
directly on top of one—but they hadn't got me yet!

In the spring Mr. Allen of the Crocker Land Expedition
came down and attempted to set up his wireless telegraph. The
foolish boy had the idea that he might be able to communicate
with the outside world through the nearest station in Canada.
MacMillan also was a firm believer in the future of wireless, but
sober people who knew it would never be of any more importance
than a toy thought him a fantastic optimist. Nevertheless, he had
brought up an expensive outfit. This was set up in a specially
constructed shack outside the harbor. There sat poor Jerome
Allen, working and freezing. At that time he was one of the
Navy's electrical experts—today he is an officer of high rank—but

all he got for his toil were a few dots and dashes impossible to decipher.

In 1925 when Admiral Byrd was in Greenland the first message was received by him from New Zealand!

In 1914 we were all very much impressed by the mere thought of wireless communication, and MacMillan said that he had been laughed at and ridiculed by the experts for having brought the set along with him.

The spring was beautiful. Navarana sewed a large tent for us, and took charge of the collection of eggs for our household. We stored away nearly ten thousand for the winter, and they were hidden so that no whalers could find them—but the whalers did not get up to Thule that year. The ice clogged Melville Bay, and only a few walrus could get through.

I had time now to indulge some of my hobbies and was perfectly happy. I began to make notes concerning the lives of the natives, to jot down Eskimo recipes, and to itemize their games and folk plays.

Navarana showed me the spot on Saunders Island where, as a little girl, she had found six candles left by white men. The discovery had been a sensation, and they had been snatched from her by the great conjurer, Sorqaq, who considered them dangerous in the hands of anyone but himself.

Poor old Sorqaq was now in a bad state. Both his arms were almost useless, and his shoulders ached constantly. He walked with great effort, and carried a hunter's chair between his teeth so that when he grew exhausted he could sit down and rest. The women all laughed at him—his wife leading the chorus of jeers and exposing his impotence before all her friends. The old stoic must sit and listen to it in silence, because the women were beneath his contempt. When he could endure it no longer he occasionally addressed the men:

"It happens that somebody thinks! There were days when one traveled about, now to the north, now to the south, making love to the women. And then one traveled not in vain. The time has gone when the girls hid themselves when one happened to come to their village. It makes a veteran think!"

When we brought in a walrus he stumbled down to the beach and threw small stones at the dead animal so that he would be entitled to his share of meat. His dogs were tied up constantly, but he fed them whenever he had meat of his own.

The natives took delight in teasing him and leaving the

Top. OUR NEW MOTORBOAT AT LAST IN THULEFJORD.

Bottom. DOGS AFLOAT ON A SMALL ICE PAN WAITING TO BE RESCUED.

walrus just far enough out on the ice so that he could not come down to collect his share. I asked them what they would do if they were old and weak.

"We would die rather than expose ourselves in this way!"

Mequsaq, Navarana's grandfather, was his worst tormentor. He had, all his life, been a rival of Sorqaq's, and now he was on top of the world, being a member of the household of the only white trader in the country.

Tatarat, Sorqaq's son, had now reached the final indignity also. He could no longer chew. His mouth had to be pried open with a stick at mealtime, and the process was a painful one. His family came to me for help. I examined the unfortunate man and found it impossible to wedge a pair of pliers into his mouth, so I knocked the four front teeth out with a hammer as we had done with the dogs. This gave him an opening into his mouth and he was happy. His mother and others chewed his food, put it between his teeth, and he enjoyed perfect digestion.

Knud had promised him that he should have tobacco so long as there was any to be had. That delighted him. Each morning he was carried out and laid on a sledge, where he smoked the whole day. When he dropped his pipe he would shout:

"A pipe happened to drop. Somebody is required to put it back where it belongs."

Tatarat could neither pick it up nor light it, and old Sorqaq refused to help him. "One happened to be full grown when fire was used only to cook and not for food!" he would say.

Many of the younger people who came to help him light the pipe smoked it themselves, while the helpless Tatarat screamed at them to put it in his mouth.

During the summer we hunted narwhales in the fjord. White whales (Belugas) appeared too, those almost mystic monsters which suddenly emerge without warning and crowd a fjord like pack ice. But if a hunter attempts to harpoon one or even to hurl his spear, the whole school disappears in a flash. No one knows how the animals communicate the warning to each other, but they obviously do in some fashion.

It was at this time that I experienced the trance, or "kayak disease," or whatever it is. I sat in my kayak day after day waiting for seals. The water was, as the natives say, "merely oil." The air was calm as an empty room and the sun like liquid fire on the glass of the sea. The hunter must not move, for the slightest shift of his body will disturb the small craft and frighten the seals away.

It is then that the mind begins to wander crazily. I dreamt without sleeping, resurrected forgotten episodes from my childhood. Suddenly great mysteries became for the moment plain to me. I realized I was in an abnormal, or supernormal, state and reveled in it. I cannot explain the feeling exactly, but it seemed that my soul, or spirit, or what you will, was released from my body, my life and obligations, and it soared impersonally, viewing everything as a whole. I was at home in Denmark and saw all my people once more. I asked myself whether I had grown tired of the life I had elected to live, and answered no, for I was not. Still, I realized that I was not such an enthusiastic hunter and adventurer as I had believed.

I remember that I told myself I must stop this dreaming, but I remember also that I did not tell myself this until it was no more a temptation to do so. I have often wondered if this was a touch of brain fever, or "kayak disease"—or merely a state which everyone experiences at one time or another. I have never known, and no one seems willing to talk about it. But I do know that on sunny days, sitting in a kayak on the surface of a still sea, I approached a comprehension of mysteries otherwise denied me.

Henrik went to Tassiussak to meet the *Cape York,* and brought back our motorboat with it. We had the usual parties when the ship arrived, and every night a dance was held. Our natives did not dance very well, but Navarana had learned in the south and her friends liked to try any of her accomplishments. Navarana believed herself the hub around which all Greenland society revolved.

On the *Cape York* this summer was one sailor who enchanted her as he did all of the other girls. He wore white flannel trousers and brown canvas shoes and, wonder of wonders! he had red hair. The natives had never seen its like. Navarana told me that he took all the girls for a walk in the hills and gave them cigarettes, economically breaking them in two so that each girl could have half a cigarette at a time. He was an inveterate dancer, also, and danced with a lighted cigarette in his mouth, which the girls recognized as true elegance. His worldly manners were discussed for months after his departure.

He was, in fact, not a bad boy, and always a good sport.

He was a college lad, who had seized the occasion to see a little of the world during his summer vacation.

When the ship departed it was fine to be left alone to read the papers. I made it a rule to read one newspaper a day, a paper just one year old, which worked out beautifully. If you receive mail only once a year, it is silly to read everything at once—you will forget most of it immediately, and when you reread it the news will be stale.

On the other hand, it is no fun to sit about in the winter, the storm howling outside, and read about bathing and summer sports. So I watched the dates, read a paper a day, and never (well, hardly ever) cheated. When you stop to consider, it is amazing how little one year matters.

Only once did I break my rule. Madame Caillaux, wife of the French minister of finance, had shot Calmette, editor of *Figaro*. She was consequently tried for the murder, and I could not resist running through the papers lying on the shelf to learn whether or not she was acquitted.

She was.

2

Darkness came with the winter, bringing natives from near and far to trade. Of course, those up north went to Etah with their fox pelts and sold them to MacMillan, but we had many friends who would trade with no one but ourselves. They knew our method of trading—quite unlike any other trader's, perhaps, but it was one we found most successful with our peculiar brand of customers. They were all received as guests and, since they traded only once a year, it was natural for them to look forward to it as the event of the season.

The whole family would arrive on a sledge. They came no matter what time of day or night it was. When it was dark they had no means of telling the time. Besides, the natives have no special period reserved for sleep. They sleep when they are tired.

In our house someone was always awake to receive them. Often they had traveled long distances, and there were invariably certain formalities to be observed in greeting them. Some would begin by refusing to come in, saying they were only out for a little trip or on their way to another settlement.

But eventually they came in, the wife and children first and the man after he had cared for his dogs. I always observed their luggage, watched them hang their meat on the racks and carry

READING MY NEWSPAPER, JUST ONE YEAR AFTER IT WAS PUBLISHED

AT MY DESK DURING THE LONG ARCTIC NIGHT

the rest inside the house. Usually there was a bag or two which looked suspiciously unlike meat, yet this they hung on the rack and kept under constant surveillance.

They were always delighted to see us, anxious to hear whatever we had to tell them, and to relate the events of their own lives—anything to break the monotony of existence. We had a bathtub now which was a special marvel. Anyone could bathe in it, but first he must chop ice, melt it and warm the water on the stove. The tub was so well liked that I have seen men lying in it for hours at a time. When the water grew too cold their wives warmed it with hot water from the stove, and the hygienic effects of such a bath once a year soon became evident. Some of the natives, however, did not allow themselves to be contaminated with new ways, and would not stoop to the insanity of a bath.

We talked of many things—the games and the dogs and the children. What else is there to be mentioned in men's company?

And when the visit had lasted for three days, which, after Danish custom, should be the end of tolerance for a fish or a guest, I would ask—just to be saying something—whether the visitor had any foxskins. He would be astounded, as if it were the silliest question in the world:

"Foxes? Who, me? Oh, no! It happens that a very poor hunter is present. There are no foxskins in my house. It takes a skilled hunter to catch a fox. It never falls into my lap to be able to do that."

"I am so sorry," I would answer. "I am in great need of really fine foxskins, and I knew that if I was to have the very best ones, I would have to go to you."

"Oh, at last I have something amazing to tell at home! Peterssuaq has made a mistake, which was not believed possible. It happens that a poor man has been bold enough to enter your house and has teased you. I am no fox hunter at all. Oh, no. I am unhappy! Where are my poor wife and my miserable children? We have to go away and leave at once, because the great white man will be angry with us. He thought we had foxskins, and we have none."

"But I am desolate. Here I have been waiting for you to complete my supply. What is it that you have in your bags out there?"

"Nothing to be spoken of in this splendid house."

"I thought they were foxskins. I hoped they were."

"Well, this is my chance to laugh. He thought they were

foxes! They are nothing but some old scraps we have brought along to wipe our hands and our rectums with. We have used them at home to swab up the grease from the floor."

"Suppose you let me see them. I am not accustomed to seeing really fine fur, and I'd like to have a look at them."

"Positively not!" he would answer. "They should have been thrown away before we reached this settlement. We should never have brought them to a place where such mighty people live. We only did so because we are ignorant and clumsy. We could never bring them inside this house."

After endless haranguing I would persuade the man to fetch his bags inside tomorrow and let me see their contents. He would sigh and groan as if he had appendicitis. (Remember, he had come to sell his skins to me.) Yet he would only consent to rest the night or visit his friends in neighboring houses after he had assured me that he would not sleep a wink because of his embarrassment and shame.

Next day I would remind him of the promise. First he would look bewildered, then, like a man being led to the electric chair, go to fetch his skins. He and his wife would return with their burden, both wailing and regretting that they had ever visited the village.

At last both man and wife would be induced to empty their skins over the floor. Most of the natives would, of course, be present to witness their triumph.

I remember one customer, not unlike most of the others, who dumped fifty or more skins on the floor. They were beautifully tanned and mended. The wife had chewed every ounce of fat from them, and the fur was rich and lustrous. At this point it was my turn to talk.

I sat down and rubbed my eyes, as if I could not believe it possible that I beheld such excellent skins. When the customer protested at his boldness in allowing me to see them, I showered him and his kin with praise in trapping such superlative specimens. And finally, after this palaver had wasted several hours, I asked him to stuff them in his bags again! I wanted to buy them, I said, but I was unable to—I had nothing with which to pay for such incomparable pelts.

"You wouldn't fool me and pretend that I would dare take anything for such a filthy heap! Oh, no! I wish you would be gracious enough to accept them as a gift, but perhaps there is no possibility of that—you would feel offended at a fool's offer."

"But I want to have them. I would at last have something fine to send to Knud in Denmark."

"Oh, no!" the man protested. "Not to Knud! He knows good skins when he sees them. Don't tell him they were mine—though he might realize it at once. When he sees an abomination he knows it has come from us."

And then at last came the actual bargaining. I said:

"I am overjoyed to own these skins, and I would like to give you some of the stuff we brought up with us this summer. But it is so worthless, all of it such junk, that I hesitate to offer it."

The tone changed slightly:

"We would be so happy to have anything you gave us. But we dare not ask for anything, for whatever you give us will be too much."

"Here," I said, "you take the key and go out and look over the worthless truck we own. I am ashamed to go with you and witness your disappointment."

This was the high point of the bargaining. The customer and his wife took the key and disappeared into the store. Some of the local Eskimos who were familiar with the stock went with them and explained the value of different items. I knew that everything in the store would be minutely examined and felt of. If there were fifty guns of one make I knew they would all be taken down. Every kettle would be peered into. On many occasions I noticed that if we had a pot that was slightly damaged, a piece of enamel chipped off, that particular pot would remain until all the others were chosen. The natives knew what they wanted and looked out for themselves. Sometimes they remained in the store for more than half a day. If mealtime intervened, we called them in; afterward they returned to their microscopic inspection. It mattered little how long they stayed—I had already appraised the fur and knew what I could afford to pay for it.

At long last the couple had seen everything in the store. Now came the real test between trader and customer. The natives felt that the more modest they were in the beginning, the better the deal they would make. I asked the native what he would like to have. He said that, after seeing what a magnificent collection of goods we owned, he would not humble anything by taking it to his house. But . . . if I cared to give him something, he might be bold enough to ask for a few nails.

It was up to me to do the talking. Would he like a gun?

He would, indeed! Ammunition? Oh, yes, naturally! What good was a gun without ammunition? What about a knife? He needed a knife very badly. An ax? An ax was the one thing he had come for.

A pot? If he owned a pot he would be everlastingly happy. Tobacco? If I could spare him some tobacco he would smoke it during the winter and think of me all the while. And so on.

Once in a while his wife put in a word: "Oh, are my ears full of human excrement! What horrors do I hear? Must I listen to my husband insulting a white man and disgracing himself by robbing the white man while he displays the most unbelievable impudence? The ice will break and the mountains fall, for the world will be embarrassed because her people have forgotten how to behave."

Her idea, of course, was to call everyone's attention to the amazing ability of her husband to drive a fine bargain. He told her to shut up, and roared with laughter because women had the courage, in this house, to interrupt while men were talking.

But finally the husband completed his bargaining. Then I turned to his wife:

"Aren't you going to trade too?"

"Who, me? Does one hear a white man address a woman? Oh, let not that embarrassment come to her on top of everything else!"

"But don't you want something?"

"Oh, someone speaks to me! I do not know how to answer. I have never been talked to before."

This last statement, of course, was an obvious untruth, and I continued my campaign. Husband and wife always pretended their dealings had nothing to do with each other—they felt they would receive more in this fashion. The wife wanted needles and thread, undershirts and scissors and mirrors and needleboxes and kettles and tobacco and soap, and whatever else we possessed.

"Wait a little, wait a little!" the husband cried. "Let me come and drag that woman out by the hair. Now everyone knows that I never wallop her enough to teach her modesty. Let me get hold of her and beat her up!"

But even this had to come to an end. Finally husband and wife departed with Henrik or Sechmann to secure the goods which they had already chosen. But now came the most acute moment of all—they had forgotten a great many things they needed. Both of them came running to me:

"Oh, I am dreadfully sorry, but I want a file. I only came for a file and if I go home without it I will know my luck has deserted me."

"You may have a file." The man ran to get his file.

The wife cried: "I want to give you back the thread. Instead, I would rather have a cup I have seen."

"You may have a cup too!"

Of course, the dear people did not realize that I had expected this last minute bargaining and had left at least two fox pelts unpaid for until this moment. Teaching a primitive people how to trade is not so simple as most persons would think. The Eskimos had been accustomed to trading with the whalers, giving what they had to give and receiving whatever the whalers chose to hand out. Which, in most cases, was decidedly unfair to the natives.

Next year we introduced money to the tribe so that the natives might compute the values themselves. As we had little money ourselves, we manufactured the coins. It cost me only a hundred and twenty kroner to manufacture thirty thousand kroner out of aluminum. Perhaps there is the germ of an idea in that for a number of hard-pressed governments today.

3

The winter of 1914-15 proceeded without incident. I made my customary trip to Tassiussak for the mail—letters from home and one from my devoted friend, Magdalene, who believed me exposed to never-ending perils and deplored the terrible conditions in which I lived. She could never realize that I was far happier than she had ever been herself.

I also went on as far south as Upernivik and found there an old university friend, Dr. Bryder, who was the first physician to be stationed in this northern colony. Upernivik was a metropolis now with a manager, an assistant, a doctor and a minister. It was a treat to me to sit with these men and have my mind jarred out of the lethargy into which it had settled. Of course, I had my usual fight with the minister.

Some of the native boys went with me to pay our respects to the dignified old man. Among his treasures was a picture of the Christ, which he reverently showed to the boys. They stood and looked at it for a long while. The minister, hoping to sow the seed of faith in the untilled field before him, asked:

Top. A TYPICAL HOUSE IN UPERNIVIK.

Bottom. LIVELY TRADING AT A POST IN SOUTH GREENLAND.

"Do you know this man? Who is he?"

The natives conferred and consulted their memories. Finally two of them admitted they did not know him, but the third, Ajago, smiled and said he did. Beaming, the minister asked who he was.

"Well," said Ajago, "I don't know his name, but he came up to our place on the ship with the missionary."

The minister's smile broadened. What a poetic way of expressing it! he thought. "Yes, that is true. But did His missionary never tell you His name?"

"Oh, no," exclaimed Ajago; "the man was bosun on the ship, and that was all we ever called him. But we had a lot of fun with him, because he tried to sleep with all the girls and they disliked him and only teased him along and made fun of him."

The worthy man was furious. Here he stood among pagans, enemies of Christ, and listened with his own ears to rank blasphemy! He must, of course, throw the boy and his friends out of the house at once. I tried to explain that Ajago in his innocence had really mistaken the son of God for a certain boatswain, because both possessed whiskers. As a result I, too, was ordered out.

I was at home again for New Year's, 1915, and spent it in quiet, peaceful celebration. I had brought back another theodolite to replace the one I had lost in the crevasse, and had determined this year to go north and map the land at any cost. MacMillan, who was always friendly and felt no sense of competition, offered me enough pemmican to last the journey, and promised to help in any way possible. Dr. Harrison Hunt of the Crocker Land Expedition also proposed to go along with me, and I was more than pleased to have him. Thus the Americans would send a member of their staff along, and I would have the advantage of their superior equipment.

Dr. Hunt was a fine person. A strong, well-educated man, he was also a great soul and a fine sportsman. He had lived much of his life roughing it in the Maine woods, hunting and fishing. Having him along opened up vast new vistas of thought to me—he was so different from the Scandinavians I had known. And the companionship also gave me the opportunity to learn English.

But I was never to map North Greenland. Never!

Once more we were at Neqé ready to set out. Meat was lashed to the sledges, pemmican had been transported from Etah, everything was in order. I waited only for Henrik's return from Tassiussak so that I could turn the trading post over to him.

And then he came! I remember that it was the 5th of April, 1915, and he came like an arrow from the south. Exhausted and thin, he none the less had obeyed orders and rushed home to reach there before I left. With him was a letter from Knud Rasmussen, mailed October 1, 1914.

There was war in Europe!

It was extraordinary that the letter should have got to me so soon. It had reached South Greenland the middle of October, and then had come north by kayak and sledge with such incredible speed that it had arrived April 5th!

War, Knud wrote, had broken out in August. It was surprising that it was still bitterly contested, and some of the more pessimistic prophesied that it might last for another three months. Of course, Knud did not believe that himself—three months more would exhaust all the powers involved.

According to the papers there had been a German victory at sea. Three English cruisers had been sunk. On the other hand, the Germans had been defeated at the Marne, the Russians were sending troops via the White Sea to Scotland whence they were to embark for Belgium to help drive the Germans back. The big drive would be launched along the western front the day after the mail had been posted.

Knud warned me that, even though the war was sure to be over before winter (no one, he added, could wage war in the winter in our time), there was certain to be a depression after it, and we would have to be extremely niggardly with what money we had, especially as our last shipment of furs had not yet been sold. I was to hold a firm hand on our supplies as Knud was not certain he could send the ship up to the post in 1915.

Thus ended this expedition to the north.

I hurried to Etah with the news. MacMillan was away on a long voyage with Lieutenant Green to search for Crocker Land. As this left me idle for some time, I decided to accompany Dr. Hunt to Ellesmere Land with a cache for MacMillan and his party when they should return.

We went across to Peary's old house at Pim's Island. The natives had treated it badly, torn out what they could of the partition, then the floor and finally the wall at one end. We repaired it as best we could and spent several days there during a snowstorm.

I was much impressed with Hunt's character. He was a

Top. HEADQUARTERS ON DANISH ISLAND, HUDSON BAY, FOR THE FIFTH THULE EXPEDITION, 1922. KNUD RASMUSSEN AND DR. BIRKET-SMITH IN FOREGROUND.

Bottom. PEARY'S EXPEDITION HOUSE AT PIM'S ISLAND, ELLESMERE LAND, AFTER DR. HUNT AND I HAD REPAIRED IT.

great lover of life and nature, and had thought once of going out to China as a missionary. He had fortunately discovered before his departure that his wife and small daughter were more important to him than his own missionary zeal and, being unable to devote his whole soul to the task, he had given it up entirely.

The doctor and I also visited "Starvation Camp," the famous district where Greely and his party suffered. This regrettable episode has been discussed endlessly. When Admiral Peary returned to America from his final conquering of the Pole, he remarked that he had turned his back on the spot when he sailed by. He calls it the dark chapter in the American history of the Arctic.

We must remember that most of Greely's unwise decisions were a result of his ignorance in practical matters. He was young and ambitious and undoubtedly of the school which believes that an officer's judgment is invariably superior to the advice of his men. His bullheadedness caused many deaths, but it is hard to pass judgment upon deeds committed in desperation.

The one thing I blame Greely for is his exposure to publicity of men who died because of his own bad judgment. It is a well-known fact that a man who dies of starvation will often pass away with a small store of food saved against a final emergency which he is too weak to meet. Yet Greely tells in his book that a number of sealskin lines were later found under the pillows of the dead men. I can never understand, nor forgive, a leader who will mention such facts to a misunderstanding, half-informed audience.

The natives on the Greenland coast told me they had known there were white men starving across the water—but the white men had been inconsiderate of them, and therefore they made no effort to help them. Whether or not this is true I do not know. It is not like the Eskimos to refuse aid where it is needed.

After the cache was secured we spent some time in visiting the scene of the winter camp of the Norwegian Expedition under Captain Otto Sverdrup with the *Fram* in 1900.

A large cross on the crest of a hill marks the spot where Dr. Svendsen of the expedition committed suicide. The poor man had not been equal to the rigors of the Arctic. He may not have been a drug addict before he shipped on the expedition, but it is certain that he was a slave to morphine on the ship. After the supply ran out, he could not endure the privation and drowned himself.

It is surprising that so many men go to the Arctic with no

consideration of the fact that it requires will power and endurance to live there. You have only yourself to depend upon, and there are always around you a number of fools in a worse state than your own. The Arctic is merciless, sorts out the weaklings and disposes of them in its own harsh manner.

When we returned to Etah we found the two scientists, Ekblaw, the botanist, and Dr. Tanqueray, the zoologist, occupying themselves as best they could with their studies. They could accomplish little in the winter as the ground was buried deep under snow and ice, and they were in many ways disappointed with the fruits of their labors. The wind is constant and rigorous at Etah, and cuts through one's clothes like a whip. Because of this there are fewer plants and animals there than elsewhere in North Greenland.

I told them about the vastly superior conditions in the spring at Thule, warned them that we had no European provisions, but also that a number of the *tringa canutus* eggs, never seen before, would hatch near our station. Ekblaw, a devoted ornithologist, jumped into the air and shouted. Such precious specimens were worth any inconvenience to him, and both men decided to accompany us. They could return during the summer in their motorboat.

We left Etah on the 15th of May and a few days later reached Thule. I installed the two Americans as best I could. They were satisfied in the beginning, but after a time they began to long for their own food—and I could not blame them. At any rate, the rewards of their visit were abundant. The Museum of Natural History in New York now boasts a number of the precious eggs, and Ekblaw also found a hundred and two varieties of flowers in the neighborhood.

It is a surprise to many people to learn that wherever there are soil and firm earth flowers will grow. As I have told, in the northernmost corner of Greenland I have seen yellow poppies and exotic red flowers. These prepare for the short summer season by developing into buds the previous fall. Then they hibernate in the protection of their own foliage and, at the first hint of sunshine and warmth, burst into full bloom.

Ekblaw became snowblind, suffering intensely, and ran a high temperature. He whined like a baby. However, I had my own business to attend to, and I also had to go for the guns we had left almost two years ago at Melville Bay. Later I heard that Ekblaw criticized me for leaving him while he was ill. Naturally,

I had to make the trip at the only time it could be negotiated. On the way back I stopped to hunt seals, and told all the natives that we could not expect the ship this year as there was a war at home. They all advised me to advance my prices.

Our tobacco supply ran out, and that did much to keep down the consumption of matches. I realized now that I had traded too liberally, under the circumstances. A post like ours should have been outfitted to last at least two years, but we never had enough money to purchase such a stock at one time.

In the emergency I invented a system of which I was very proud. I had everyone in the district in my books, so I gave each citizen a ticket which entitled him to a limited supply of the scarcer articles. When I finally returned to Europe I found that this ration system had been in effect there during the whole war. Nevertheless, I was co-inventor of it.

As the American expedition was none too well equipped with warm clothes I arranged to trade them sweaters and underwear, which I had in my store, for foxskins which they had bought from the natives. When MacMillan returned from his expedition he was not pleased. Neither did he approve of his two scientists, Ekblaw and Tanqueray, deserting the station in his absence. I could see his point of view. The expedition was, after all, his responsibility, and he expected his men to remain where he had left them.

MacMillan had had his own difficulties on the voyage. One of the Eskimos was killed, and this made a bad impression on the natives, especially as none of us accepted the weak explanation. Many of them came to ask me what tactics to pursue, and I was unable to advise them. The country was not officially in the possession of any power at that time. Knud and I had settled there without protection and, as a result, the upper hand ruled.

The only satisfactory solution would have been to arrange a pension for the widow for as long as the children were in her care. But this was difficult for MacMillan to manage under the circumstances.

As soon as the water opened he came down with his power-boat to fetch the two men back to the base at Etah. MacMillan himself had found many ornithological specimens in the territory he covered and, combined with those gathered by Ekblaw and Tanqueray, they had a grand collection.

I watched MacMillan's boat disappear to the north with a great sense of loss. It had been a rare treat for me to live with the two Americans and learn about America from them. Ekblaw was very much interested in college life, especially the intramural activities. He had been editor of his college paper and still received copies of it. I tried to read them, but found that, even when I could read English, I could not understand what was meant. At any rate, I corrected my earlier impression of Americans as rather wild men whose favorite pastime was training horses and shooting off revolvers in saloons.

But I had no time to be lonely. Once more I was absorbed in hunting and in supervising all the activities of the little community. Something, however, was missing. Something in me had departed with the white men.

Meanwhile there was a murder in the next village to occupy us. Quanguaq, a strong-limbed but weak-minded widower, lived near Sekrusuna and his wife at Granville Bay. Sekrusuna had been a great one to tease poor Quanguaq; he would taunt him by suggesting, when they were hunting together, that they go home to their "wife" now, sometimes adding references to their intimate relations which were almost more than the young and wifeless Quanguaq could endure. Sekrusuna also tantalized the poor man by promising him that he might sleep with his wife when they returned, but whenever Quanguaq attempted to take advantage of this favor he found the woman's lawful husband at her side. The husband thought this a great joke. Such actions can infuriate even more decent men than Quanguaq.

Besides all this, Sekrusuna beat his wife in order to demonstrate to Quanguaq the many advantages of being happily married. He beat her only when the widower was present.

One day in the spring the two men stood out upon the edge of the ice. Quanguaq drove his harpoon not into a seal but straight through the body of his friend, Sekrusuna, who dropped into the water and was carried off by the current. Quanguaq came home with both sledges and teams. He drove straight to the dead man's wife and told her that he was going to stay with her and here were a few birds he would like her to prepare for his supper. The widow meekly accepted her altered status, and cooked for him. After the meal it was decided that Quanguaq and his mother should move into the dead man's house, and it was also arranged that they continue to talk of him, for a few days, as if he were still out hunting and expected home soon. (The weather was fine, and if Sekrusuna were officially dead it would be necessary to mourn for five days, which would be inconvenient now as the seals were thick on the ice.) Kullabak, Quanguaq's mother, was experienced in such sophistries and recommended the plan as being a highly practical one.

During this period I met Quanguaq while we were all hunting, and he did not say a word about the murder. Later on, when we did learn of the tragedy, I was very much distressed, as Sekrusuna had been a good boy and a fine hunter.

When at last Quanguaq came with some of his friends to the store, I took it upon myself to speak to him and let him know how I felt toward murderers. He brought Navarana a large bundle of rabbits, and they recalled at length how they had sat in the little hut starving together and the old grandfather, Mequsaq, had been their only provider. Mequsaq loved to hear this story over and over again.

I had to break into the recollections. My speech was prepared, and everyone in the village was present.

"Quanguaq," I said in a stern voice, "I hear that you are a murderer."

"Let others tell of it," he answered. "One never likes to brag."

"To murder is the basest crime in the world. If you had been down in my country, you would have been killed as punishment."

"Peterssuaq, you are mistaken. White men would not disgrace themselves even to look at me!"

"Yes, they would. You have ruined the reputation of the whole tribe. You are not worthy to eat with us."

"Peterssuaq, stop talking to me. I am so low that it is not worthy of you to talk to me."

He persisted in that vein. His sorrow over what he had done seemed real enough, but the more I blamed him the more he debased himself. "You don't know how bad I am. I have also committed many other crimes."

"Well," I said, "why don't you behave? You could have found other wives."

"No, no. No other women are so low that they could get along with me."

"But that doesn't give you the right to kill."

"I never do the right thing. I am awful."

If I said "terrible," he said "horrible." If I charged him with one crime he admitted it and accused himself of a worse one. It is difficult to scold a man who admits everything and thinks up added degradations. Against my will I found myself consoling him. But to end on a note of logic, I said that it would have been better if he had been murdered and Sekrusuna left alive, because Sekrusuna was a good provider and hunter and delivered many fox pelts to the store each year.

At this point the miserable widow had had all she could stand. I had pitied her for having to live with the murderer of her husband, so she stepped forward and assured me that it had been she, not Sekrusuna, who had caught most of the foxes, and that Quanguaq could satisfy me equally as well as her late husband on that score.

This silenced me for a moment. I tried to think of some argument which would shame them both and make decent persons avoid them. It seemed to me the right thing to have some object lessons to point to in the tribe. But while I thought it over the murderer brought forward eggs dried in sealskin guts, and a bag of rotten eider ducks. The crowd, led by Navarana, hailed the delicacies and shouted their appreciation. The meal was already being prepared before I decided what to say next, and my audience deserted me. I accepted a piece of the meat which Navarana handed me, and I must confess that I forgot the speech and never did deliver it.

Oddly enough it was I who received the only censure in connection with the murder. A short while later the minister told me that the natives had said Peterssuaq had explained it was a rotten thing to kill good customers, but that bad ones could expect no protection. I tried to explain myself, but felt that I made little impression; the missionary had been the guest of the criminal couple and did not seem much disturbed.

4

Our settlement now boasted a considerable population, and more and more were moving there yearly. Much meat was required to feed our guests and customers in the winter and care for their dogs. As a result we had to kill a number of walrus to carry us through the dark season, and our motorboat made it much more convenient for us to haul in our supply.

One lovely fall day we were riding a calm sea with water smooth as glass. Far on the horizon we saw an object which strikes happiness to every Eskimo's heart—a ship. We could see from its tall, slender masts that it was a schooner of considerable proportions. The sails hung useless. We immediately forgot our hunting and made straight for the ship.

It proved to be the *George B. Cluett,* a vessel of which I had never heard. We went in close and boarded it after having saluted the officers. As soon as I told them my name an elderly gentleman ran forward, grasped my hands and told me how pleased he was to see me in person. Now that I was aboard, he said, all his worries were over.

I have seldom been the object of such enthusiasm, but I rather liked it. The man was Dr. Hovey of the American Museum of Natural History, on his way to find and bring back the Crocker Land Expedition. I offered to pilot him to Etah. The motor of the *George B. Cluett,* however, was bucking and refused to burn kerosene, which it was meant to consume, and would only run on gasoline, their supply of which was almost nil. If I would let them have some gasoline they would reward me handsomely and bless me as well. Unfortunately I had no gasoline.

Captain George Comer had come along as ice pilot with the ship rented from the Labrador Grenfell Mission by the museum. Comer was a man with years of experience behind him and one of the finest gentlemen I have ever met. He was not only the last whaling captain to ship out of Boston, but also a scientist and a collector of museum specimens.

I offered to take Hovey to Etah in my motorboat if he would furnish the kerosene. The expedition at Etah, I was sure, had plenty of gasoline. Dr. Hovey accepted the offer. He was anxious to contact his outfit and dreaded the possibility of having to spend a winter in North Greenland.

I left most of my crew on the schooner to be put ashore when the wind came up, and Dr. Hovey, Captain Comer, Henrik, Ajago and I set out for Etah in the motorboat with its tanks filled with Hovey's kerosene and the larder stocked from Captain Comer's provisions. We struck ice between Cape Parry and Herbert Island and had to put in to repair the boat. While we walked on shore to stretch our legs the tide went out leaving the boat high and dry. There was nothing to do but wait for the tide to flow back.

Dr. Hovey was furious. He could not seem to realize what he was up against. He was a mild little man at home, I understand, and had taken this trip more or less as a vacation—it was no vacation to run into such dullards as I and my kind. It took a long while to calm him.

He was an economist and betrayed his petty economies with his very first actions in the Arctic. He showed me the gifts and trinkets he had brought along to please the natives and to pay them for their favors—empty rifle shells of two different makes, one a little larger than the other so that they would fit together.

"These can be polished and used for needle cases," he said. "Eskimos like to sit about during the winter and polish things to make them shine. They will be delighted with these."

He also explained that he had many other little pretties in his suitcase, and when I assured him that the natives had all they could use of ammunition and shells he felt momentarily let down.

While we waited for the tide he decided to have coffee. As a matter of course, some of the natives followed us into the cabin and Henrik, who was the cook, poured coffee for them. Dr. Hovey's face fell open:

"Do you allow him to give coffee to the Eskimos?"

"Certainly. Why not? They serve us meat when we visit them."

"But that's different. Your cook has no right to serve the ship's provisions to the natives. The museum has to pay for everything, and I have to see that expenses are kept to a minimum."

Captain Comer and I laughed and explained to him that he was in the Arctic now, not at an accountant's desk. He did not seem to relish the mild rebuke.

When the water returned we set out once more, but before we reached Etah a terrific storm blew up and we had to put up for the night near Cape Alexander—much to the good doctor's dissatisfaction. During the trip I had the pleasure of really getting to know Captain Comer. I had heard his name mentioned in admiration many times. He was well acquainted with the Hudson Bay Eskimos, and had lived at Southampton Island for many years making collections of great value. He told me confidentially about the trip north and the politics he had had to use in an effort to get around Dr. Hovey. It was not an easy task, especially for a man who had for many years been captain and sole commander of his own boat, but Comer was a very strong character.

Dr. Hovey had come north, he said, to untangle certain difficulties that had arisen. The expedition was much more expensive than had been anticipated. Evidently he had believed, and still did believe that the natives were anxious to be permitted to give everything away to white men. A needle, he said, was

more precious to an Eskimo than a dog. They need only be told
what to do, not paid for it.

When we reached Etah we found that MacMillan was not
there. All the expedition's supplies and findings had been packed
awaiting the arrival of Hovey's boat; when it had not come, Mac-
Millan and his friend, the handy man, Jot Small, had gone south
to Neqé—which we had passed on our way up. Dr. Hovey took
command and supervised the loading of the gasoline and supplies
into the motorboat and a second boat which we were to tow. The
members of the expedition could bring along only their notebooks; everything else would have to be left until sent for at some
future date.

We reached Neqé early in the morning. MacMillan was
roused from sleep and came out to our motorboat in his kayak.
He could not, he insisted, go home yet. He had not accomplished
half the work he had set out to do, and the journey he was going
to attempt next year was made possible only because he had bred
his own dogs, had become accustomed to the native mode of
travel and could now rely on past experience to guide him through
future difficulties.

Hovey finally consented to permit MacMillan and Jot to
remain. It would have reflected a certain amount of discredit upon
the museum for the leader to leave behind him the major portion
of his collections.

So we said good-bye and set out for Thule once more. In the
Arctic a man may always expect a few unforeseen disasters, and
one came our way. The boat we had in tow shipped so much
water that it sank. Allen, the young American, volunteered to
jump into the water and rescue all the gasoline cans. Much to my
annoyance he did—I thought we were already carrying as heavy
a load as possible.

We reached the *George B. Cluett* safely, however, and everything was put on board. The captain of the ship was anxious to
get away, since new ice had already begun to blanket the sea.
Mr. Green, of the expedition, who as a naval officer was supposed
to understand something of motors, was asked by Dr. Hovey to
go below and examine the engine. Green looked it over carefully,
and discovered, much to his amazement, a tank full of gasoline.

"By God!" he shouted, "what do you mean sending to Etah
for a boatload of gas when you have plenty?"

"Shhh," the captain hissed. "I know that, but don't say anything about it. I can't make the damn thing run anyway!"

Dr. Hovey was pleased and grateful for our help. Just to make me realize that a man of his intelligence was missing nothing, he asked me what crime I had committed that had banished me to the Arctic. I was, he said, a fine fellow, and ought to be able to find a decent job somewhere in the outside world, even if I were guilty of a misdemeanor; such things are always forgotten sooner or later. He would be delighted to recommend me.

I was touched by his kindness. He gave each of my crew one of his patent needle cases to pay for the work. The natives thought the cartridges must be badges of a secret society but, as nothing accompanied these gifts, they simply threw them overboard and forgot all about them. I felt very sorry for the fine old gentleman who had troubled to carry them so far.

We returned home and prepared for the winter. Our supplies were none too plentiful, but we could manage. Because of the war each man was permitted five small boxes of matches (sufficient, as there was no tobacco) and fifty rounds of ammunition. We had enough raw food, and I was certain we could get along somehow.

And then one day shortly before the ice had frozen solid for the season I saw the tall figure of a man on the crest of the mountain. I could not imagine who it could be—no native would choose such a perilous route. I hastened out to greet the stranger, who proved to be Fitzhugh Green of the Crocker Land Expedition. I had thought him safe at home in Missouri by now.

He related the sad tale of their adventure. The *George B. Cluett* had sailed away only to be left stranded in the ice when the wind died, and jammed against the cliffs where it lay helpless for a day. Then once more the ice grasped it and took it for a round-about journey, finally spitting it into the snug little harbor of Parker Snow Bay, not fifty miles south of Thule. Green had come across the icecap and the mountains with a letter from Dr. Hovey asking me for help "in the name of humanity."

Green remained at Thule—he preferred life in my house to that on the crowded boat—and I hurried down to the ship. The old doctor was in a bad frame of mind. He had never even considered remaining through the winter in the Arctic, and, in truth, such a prospect was none too promising for a man of his years and physical condition. Now he asked me to furnish him and his men with clothes and other necessities, and to help him get in touch with MacMillan.

The captain of the *George B. Cluett* had contracted to bring along sufficient emergency supplies to last for the winter. But he was a sailor and had taken a long chance in not fulfilling the letter of this agreement, and had lost. He had sold all but three months' provisions, and it would be difficult for him to stretch these to last nine more months, especially as he now had a number of new passengers.

Still Dr. Hovey liked to torture him and daily reminded him of the contract. And Hovey would remain on board and eat his fill, in spite of knowing that what he ate now would be subtracted from the crew's mess during the winter to come.

There was only one native family at Parker Snow Bay, and poor Manitsok, half blind, could secure only a limited amount of meat for the ship's party. His wife was a fine sewer, but she had to work without pay, as they had nothing to give her and dared not send her food in return for her sewing.

I helped them as best I could, and the sailors were grateful, but I had quite a job making both ends meet now. I must care for the sailors on the ship, look out for my own natives, and at the same time secure as many foxskins as possible. We were planning another big expedition to map the north coast of Greenland as soon as we could get the money, and it would take many pelts to pay for that.

MacMillan came down shortly after he had been informed of the plight of the *George B. Cluett,* and took Dr. Hovey back to Etah with him. Hovey insisted, however, that no food be sent to the ship from Etah. Did not the captain have a contract for supplying all rations? I pointed out that he was forcing the sailors to suffer for the captain's imprudence, but he refused to listen. Fortunately MacMillan was not so relentless, and sent a great deal of food to the boat though he must have had to fight Hovey every inch of the way.

I also explained to Dr. Hovey that he could not trade with the natives if I helped him out of his difficulty. If he would trade, of course, no one could stop him, but this would put him into direct competition with me and would alter our present circumstances considerably. He whined and expostulated over the poverty of the museum and the drain of this expensive expedition on it. He was most certainly devoted to his museum. On the other hand, I had often heard it said that the museum never sent out trading expeditions, and that it did not permit its representatives to indulge in anything but the most dignified and scientific pursuits.

Green and I had a grand time together. The naval officer

was gentle and understanding, and fit comfortably into the household. He was extremely considerate of Navarana, and kind to all the natives. He told me at great length about his training as a cadet, about his father in Missouri and his mother who had sent him, by the *George B. Cluett,* the richest fruitcake I ever tasted. We saved it and ate it at Christmastime. It was unnecessary to entertain him as he occupied himself for long periods in reading.

At the ship all was not so smooth. The crew, most of them from Newfoundland, were game and took the hardships standing up. They realized as well as anyone that the captain had gambled and lost, but they believed that he would get his reward when he lost his job. Meanwhile they did not believe in grumbling, and they trapped foxes and played ball as long as they could see. But there came a day when a row, almost a mutiny, was imminent. The captain had no more tobacco. He sent a messenger to my store, but we had had no tobacco for many months. Dr. Hovey had some left, but he would not share it with the boys. He should have gone down to the boat and seen them chewing on old cigar boxes and pipes.

There was nothing for me to do but drive down to Upernivik and try to get it. Tanqueray and MacMillan went along, the latter only part way, and we came back with a large box, which made the sailors shout with delight. I bought thirty-two tons of coal from the captain and the crew packed it ashore for that one box of tobacco. We all felt amply repaid for our parts in the transaction.

The winter dragged along toward its close. It would soon be light once more, and it was decided that several members of the expedition should go home via sledge and South Greenland. Dr. Hovey returned to the *George B. Cluett.* The crew restrained its enthusiasm, but he must, of course, organize the trip south as he was to be one of those to depart, along with Green, Allen and Tanqueray. I promised to take them as far as I could.

Dr. Hovey was to ride on my sledge, and I secured a number of reliable boys and a complete outfit to accompany us. The old doctor irritated us all, especially me, by fussing over everything, inquiring about the cost and complaining because it could not be done for less. He wanted me to assure him that he and his men could stop as guests with the Danes on the trip down the coast— surely the Danes would all be delighted to have such important and interesting guests. I could not promise him that, of course, and I would not have wanted to bother my countrymen and friends with four visitors who represented the richest museum in the world, especially as Dr. Hovey was such a tactless, impolite person. He preferred not to comprehend my point of view, and asked favor after favor—for none of which I was to be paid.

The captain of the boat asked me to buy, if possible, more tobacco for his men. It was wartime and he was well aware that no fresh supplies could be shipped in from Denmark, but if it was at all possible he wanted me to do it. Dr. Hovey cantankerously objected. He had paid the boys for their trip, he said, and he controlled their return voyage. If the captain desired supplies he could send sledges south himself. Since I was hired by Dr. Hovey, I was to do no favors for the captain.

That was too much! It was many years since I had had cause or opportunity to cut loose, but I did so then and felt much better for it. I told the quaking old man exactly what I thought of him and his forebears, and made it quite clear that only his age protected him from physical violence.

The crew stood by and silently approved. When it was all over they came to me individually and assured me that the man had had this coming to him for a long while. The captain had often rowed with the doctor, but he was inarticulate and invariably came off a poor second. To get the spleen out of his system he would climb down on the ice, set up some empty tin cans and empty his revolver into them. He had been in Alaska in '98 and was, I understand, quite a good shot.

Dr. Hovey had a flock of suitcases, most of them heavy as lead, and it was up to my dogs to haul them. The weather was favorable but the ice between Parker Snow Bay and Cape York was rough. Occasionally we all had to jump off our sledges and run alongside to ease the dogs over a difficult stretch. My passenger, however, sat rooted to the sledge. "You said," he would remind me, "that I could ride the whole distance."

After passing Cape York the passage became so bad that Green, the only experienced traveler among the Americans, saw clearly that we would have to turn back to Cape York, reduce our loads and await colder weather. Hovey grumbled at the delay, but there was nothing else to be done.

As we were walking from our sledges to the houses Hovey fell in a dead faint. Startled, we picked him up, carried him into a house, undressed him and sent to the *George B. Cluett* for Dr. Hunt.

Hovey told us that the trip had really been a great strain upon him. For the first time I realized it was not laziness that had kept him on my sledge when everyone else walked—he really was unable to do anything else. We knew then that it would be impossible for him to endure the rigors of the journey. Dr. Hovey was heartbroken. He pleaded with me to take him along. He loathed the Arctic, and realized that he was very much disliked here, but the poor man assured me that he had only done his duty.

When Dr. Hunt arrived he confirmed our decision to leave Dr. Hovey behind—his heart, Hunt said, could not stand the hardships of a long outdoor trip at this time of year. Dr. Hovey cried when he saw us go off without him. To return to the ship was not a pleasant prospect for him.

The trip south was fairly unexciting in itself, though it was a great pleasure to me to be associated with the three Americans. The natives did not care for them especially as they were accustomed to being allowed to use their own discretion about details of traveling, and the Americans were great ones for discipline and routine.

At Tassiussak we conquered the Nielsen home as usual. Green had toothache and was running a temperature, however, and could not enjoy himself as much as he would have liked. We took him on to Dr. Bryder in Upernivik, and he was cured within a few days. The Americans were charming, and delighted all the Danes. Dr. Tanqueray's beautiful baritone voice was a joy to them, and the colonists only regretted that they could not stay longer.

As there was a not unusual epidemic among the dogs in the Upernivik district we had to leave ours at Igdlorssuit, and exchange them for the time being for local dogs and sledges to carry us on to Umanak Colony. We prepared to say good-bye to the Americans at Ikerasak. They could secure safe passage with natives to Egedesminde, whence they could drive south with the mail carriers and catch the first steamer to Denmark. Uncle Jens, however, was in his best form, and would not let his guests leave until he had given them a sample of his unique brand of hospitality. He was an amazing man, and never lost his dignity in whatever predicament he might find himself. I remember his exhibiting a number of curios he had collected. If the guests expressed approval of any of them, he simply gave his keepsakes away and would not be refused.

One night he had wined and dined so well that he had great

difficulty in speaking clearly. He passed around a number of photographs of members of the Greely Expedition—he had been postmaster at Godhavn when the expedition passed on its way north. One of the Americans was amused at the appearance of one of the men in the photographs. Uncle Jens immediately took exception to the remark.

"Sir," he said ponderously, "this man you are joking about has been my guest. He is dead now; and by his death he saved a number of his fellows who received his rations. My name is I. P. C. von Fleischer. I am a nobleman—even if I am drunk—and a man who has been a guest in my house must not be insulted. Now you are also my guest, and I cannot argue or fight with you. Sir, I must go."

The going was a little precarious, but he made it to the door, and the young American had to follow him out and apologize.

I have only the fondest memories of the Americans' stay in my district. They were fine fellows, and I shall never forget them.

The trip back was much more difficult and longer. Meanwhile my dogs were at Igdlorssuit and being cared for at my expense. When we finally reached there, after having been forced to mount the glacier for a part of the distance, we found that the natives who had been paid to care for the animals had used them daily and thrown our food to their own dogs. Besides this, the harnesses were in a deplorable state, and the dogs all but worn out.

Nothing can anger an Arctic man like the abuse of his dogs. I saw red and went to the native president of the village and complained. His name was Balakasik, and he was a very wise man, even for a judge.

"I can do nothing about it," he said.

"But aren't you the judge in such cases? Don't you know that the boys have used my dogs? The dogs were in quarantine, yet they have been taken into the village. The boys were paid to remain out with the dogs, and instead they have used them for hunting."

"You are right, of course," the judge replied. "But I can do nothing about it."

"Why can't you, if you are the ruler of the community?"

"Because my son-in-law is one of the guilty men. He lives in my house and will make life miserable for me if I punish him. So will my daughter and my wife. You are right, of course, and can take your happiness from that. But you are leaving here. The guilty men are staying, and I must live with them."

I bought what I could get of supplies in South Upernivik. The colonies were always well supplied from Denmark, and even during the war, when nothing could be shipped to us at Thule, I was able to buy a few necessities. This was not lawful, of course, as the traders were supposed to supply only their own districts, but they were all my friends and did not take the law too seriously. As a result I brought home considerable trading material. During the hard times it was my policy to buy foxskins from the natives with my money, which they could take south and spend—through a mutual understanding with southern traders—as they wished. Thus I had a number of pelts when our ship, the *Cape York,* finally arrived.

Melville Bay is never to be trifled with, and the going was, as usual, extremely difficult. This was the time of year when bears forage deep into the bay to dig the newborn seals from the holes. A baby seal, of course, cannot swim. The cows dig a cave in the snow on the ice, usually in drifts near icebergs, and deposit their calves there. The bears can smell them out and dig for them. The cow being no match for the bear flops into the water through a near-by blowhole and the cub is killed. Often the bear does not eat the little seal, merely kills it and takes a few bites of skin and blubber. He never eats meat unless he is very hungry.

We killed several bears and had all the seals we wanted, and when we reached Cape York the little auks were already there to furnish us a change in diet. The sailors at Parker Snow Bay were busy catching them for provisions on their way home.

They were a fine bunch of boys and were grateful for the tobacco I had brought them in spite of Dr. Hovey. They were almost ready to leave, and said they would all join the army. They had a peculiar notion that Kaiser Wilhelm was to be exiled at St. Helena, and the ship to carry him there was to be manned by a crew made up exclusively of Newfoundland men. Where, or how, they had got this idea I never learned, but they were positive it was true. I bade them all good-bye, and never saw any of them again. The captain made the mistake of taking Minik, the native who had once before been to America, back with him. We were glad to be rid of him, but the poor man, born to misery, died soon after he reached America a second time.

5

And now began a new phase of my existence; when I reached home I was greeted with the news that there was soon to be a third member of my family.

My whole life was changed, given impulse and purpose. Before the arrival of children a man is seldom aware of the need for them. Afterward, he can scarcely credit life as holding any interest without them.

Navarana herself was not at home. She had had news from the north that her mother was dead, and she had gone there to look after her small brothers. But she returned soon, and already there was on her face that expression of almost mystic dignity which pregnant women acquire. She was much more of a personality, and I thought her a different girl.

We went to Saunders Island as usual, the weather being favorable this year. We killed many walrus, and for the first time I mastered the art of spearing them from the kayak. One night Navarana warned me to be careful as it was dangerous work. That was the only time I ever heard her indicate her realization of our coming responsibility.

We hunted eggs when the time came, and there were plenty of them. Navarana saw to it that they were buried in the rocks. We were sure of saving our supply this year as all the whalers were engaged in the war.

Then one night when the weather was so fine that we could sleep at the island, we heard shots. The boys, we thought, must have sighted a bear, because ammunition was scarce and they would not be wasting it. We considered it for a moment and then went to asleep again. But not for long. Again we were awakened by gunfire, and I decided to go home and find out what it was about. We could expect no ship—I had heard that in South Greenland—and all this powder was apparently being wasted.

It was not a ship, but a familiar, heart-warming figure—Knud Rasmussen! He stood there on the beach waving his arms at me in greeting—Knud Rasmussen, the most amazing, the most wonderful friend a man ever had. Not even a war could keep us apart for long.

He had come up to Greenland on the first boat permitted through the North Sea, had bought a sledge and worried his way as far north as Egedesminde where he had met the three Ameri-

MY SUMMER TENT MADE OF SKINS

cans I had piloted south. They were stuck there, and considered it impossible to go any farther. Dr. Tanqueray had lost two of his toes through frost.

Knud hurried on north, bringing with him a young geologist, Lauge Koch, who has since become one of the foremost Arctic explorers. They had come to Thule by sledge and boat, had been soaked through most of the time, yet kept persistently on the move.

Europe, Knud told me, was still in the grip of war. Denmark was one of the few neutral countries. For Knud, reading of the other nations at war, the strain of enforced idleness was too deadly, so he and Koch had determined to come north and try to accomplish the mapping expedition up the north coast which I had had to abandon because of the war. Knud had to postpone that until fall, however, as the dogs were in too poor shape to drag the sledges across snowless stretches of land from Thule to the glacier.

Knud brought word that the Museum of Natural History was going to try to force another boat through to pick up its expedition and Dr. Hovey's first rescuing outfit. We notified MacMillan by the last ice, and Knud hurried down to Parker Snow Bay to carry the news to Dr. Hovey. The poor old gentleman was overjoyed. He had been in a quandary over whether he should order the *George B. Cluett* to proceed to Etah for the supplies and findings, and then sail back to the States, or whether they should go south at once. His meditation had been effectively ended by the captain, who stated that his boat had been thrown up against the cliffs just once too often, and if it went anywhere it would go home.

Knud also brought letters from the museum—one for me from President Osborn, thanking me heartily for my assistance. He did not yet know that I had been fighting bitterly with his old curator.

Knud invited Hovey, Captain Comer, Dr. Hunt and Ekblaw to come to Thule and stay with us until the new ship arrived. He moved out of his quarters into a tent placed beside our house. As always, he gave daily parties. He had brought a little coffee with him, raw as usual in Greenland, but it had already been brewed at least twice during his trip. He dried it out again and warmed over some of it each afternoon, using his familiar mesmerism to silence criticism. Each day there were more peas and fewer coffee beans in the brew, and finally there were no beans at all. Nevertheless, his little circle seemed grateful.

Captain Comer, an old hand at scientific investigation and excavation, occupied himself by digging into the kitchen midden, exploring for the first time the now famous "Comers Kitchen Midden" at Thule. When we saw what he had struck, Lauge Koch and I set to work on the opposite end of the refuse pile. It was difficult work, since the ground was frozen solid an inch from the surface, and it required many days for us to reach any depth, digging a few inches and then waiting for more earth to thaw out.

Our discoveries proved that the spot had been inhabited by three successive groups of people; each midden was well covered by a thick layer of vegetation and soil, and completely hidden · from the inhabitants who settled there hundreds of years apart.

Those were the first indications of the now well-known "Thule culture." Indications of the same Arctic culture were later discovered in many localities in northern Canada.

Life settled again into a routine of habits. There were many of us in the settlement now and Lauge Koch, who slept in our attic, was youthfully excited at being with us. He told me he was happy during the first day, but that night he slept in his bag between two murderers. Later he admitted that he had never known murderers could be such fine fellows.

It was at about this time that Navarana's grandfather admitted he was ill, and gave up trying to care for himself. His life had been an exciting one. He had traveled far from his birthplace at Admiralty Bay in Canada; he had fought cannibals in his youth, had immigrated to Greenland and taught the natives here to use the bow and arrow, to construct kayaks and to eat certain meat such as caribou and ptarmigan which they had never dared sample before. He had been a great man among his people.

His last years, he said, had been made happy by Navarana and me, and he thanked us for them. He could have done nothing more to please us. Finally, with the greatest dignity, he told us that he was tired.

"It is not impossible that someone is going to sleep and keep on sleeping," he said. And shortly afterward he died.

We placed him on his sledge and hauled his body to the crude stone mausoleum which we built for him. His sledge still stands there and his harpoons and tools lie beside his bones. We shot four of his dogs to do him honor, and one of mine. That is, I traded one of my old animals which had served its time for five of his good ones, which seemed to me better than permitting five good dogs to rot away beside their old hero. He had given me so much in his life that I was sure he would have been glad to grant me this last gift.

And life once more stood still for five days. There was no hunting in kayaks, no sounds of dogs on the scent of a bear.

Then he was gone and would never more be mentioned. He had been born, he had lived, and now he was dead.

Mequsaq, the grand old man of the North!

We could do almost no hunting that summer because we had to stay at home awaiting the *Cape York*. The summer days at Thule are incomparable. The sun is bright, the sea is calm, and there are no mosquitoes. I occupied myself by writing a great deal.

One night I fell asleep after having written for a number of hours. Navarana had gone down to the tents to eat mattak, as two narwhales had been caught that day. I had been invited, too, but for some reason or another I had not gone.

In the middle of the night she came home complaining of a stomach-ache. We thought it nothing more important than eating too much mattak, and she went into the other room and to sleep.

A few hours later Arnanguaq, who still lived in our house, came to me with the news that Navarana's time had come—she was going to give birth to her child.

I was frightened half out of my wits. I had realized, of course, that this moment would arrive sooner or later, but we had not known when the baby was due. I cried to Arnanguaq to look out for Navarana, and I bolted out to call Knud. He came running out of his tent, and was as bewildered as I.

"But anyway," he said—he had two children and was therefore an authority, "I know that when Hanne was born we made coffee and had plenty of it. Let's go for water. They will need hot water too."

We went for the water, as I knew it would be a long while before the actual birth took place. Each of us carrying a pail we walked to the brook, doing the one thing we knew would be of help. When we returned the boy was already born!

I had to let everyone know at once, and ran shouting from tent to tent. Everyone was interested—everyone is interested in anything in the Arctic—but not very excited, I thought. So I ran to the house where Dr. Hovey and the other white men slept.

Top. MISSIONARIES AT THULE—GUSTAV OLSEN, OSAKRA, SECHMANN AND THEIR WIVES.

Bottom. KNUD RASMUSSEN WITH A GROUP OF NATIVES, MUCH ENTERTAINED BY HIS STORIES, IN MY ROOM OF OUR HOUSE AT THULE. *First row, left,* IS MEQUSAQ, THE GRAND OLD MAN OF THE NORTH.

They made it plain to me that this news could well have waited until morning. Captain Comer alone got up and dressed, and sat over coffee with Knud and me. Navarana was sleepy, she said, after having drunk a cup of coffee too, and there was nothing more for us to do.

As a matter of fact, a father at the delivery of his son is not the most necessary person in the world. It is true that he does not suffer much physically, but his pride in his importance is dealt a severe blow. And so, after a while, we went to sleep again.

The boy had been born at 3 A.M., June 16, 1916. At eight o'clock that morning Navarana got up again, straightened her house and walked out with the boy on her back. At five o'clock that night she led the ball with Knud and danced with abandon. She went to bed, however, before all the guests had departed, complaining of being tired.

The boy himself was a healthy specimen. One of his eyes had a slight cast—in fact, he is still just slightly cross-eyed—but everyone knew that this misfortune was only to assure us that he was really old Mequsaq—his one-eyed great-grandfather—reborn. He also possessed the blue Mongolian spot at the base of his spine, as does every Eskimo child. This would fade by the time he was three or four years old. But in addition, there was another birthmark farther up on his back, near his kidney. This would seem to indicate that he was also to be named "Avatak." A boy of that name who had lived up north had just been shot by his uncle in a fit of hysteria. The bullet had entered the body at the same spot as the mark on our son. Thus the boy entered the world with names already provided.

Navarana did her work as if nothing had happened. On the fifth day her dress with the trundle hood was ready. She placed little Mequsaq in it and climbed to the top of the mountain, Umanak, and pointed out to him his hunting grounds and bade him be a big killer of game and provider of meat.

6

Still the boat to rescue Hovey and his reluctant companions had not arrived. Lauge Koch and I drove down across the glacier to Parker Snow Bay only to discover that the *George B. Cluett* had sailed away at last. We brought home with us a load of the coal I had bought from the boat, and then Navarana and the boy and I rode down to the cliffs where the little auks nested.

There were just the three of us and we were as happy as it is possible for humans to be. The boy lay in the sun each day and grew strong and healthy, and we regretted having to return home after we had secured a load of the birds. They were delicious at this time, the meat tender and juicy, the bones so soft that they could be swallowed without danger.

We returned to find the Americans more upset than ever. Dr. Hovey regretted that he had ever left the *Cluett*—it must be almost home by now—and blamed Knud for bringing him to Thule. From the look of the ice in Melville Bay it seemed fairly certain that no ship would be able to reach us this year either. But just as we gave it up, we sighted a boat coming round Cape Athol. Dr. Hovey went almost mad with joy and yelled and shouted like a boy.

But the ship brought wild tales of dangerous ice. It had been forty-five days crossing Melville Bay, and if the captain was to get back at all, he must leave at once.

The boat was the *Danmark,* the old tub which so long ago had carried us to Greenland's east coast. Mr. Nyboe had bought it for service to and from his copper mine, and had sent it up with a load of graphite (which took very little space) to pick up the findings at Etah. On board were a number of passengers, among them a Swedish friend of ours, Dr. Torild Wulff, naturalist and student of maritime life. He wanted to collect specimens of vegetation while the ship was anchored at Thule.

They told us more about the war, and informed us that mail and supplies had been sent to us, but the steamer transporting it had been sunk by German submarines. Later we learned that the boat had been granted permission to make the journey, but an over-zealous submarine commander had thought a boat was a boat, even a Scandinavian merchant vessel.

Once more we bade good-bye to the Americans, and for three days we watched the *Danmark* laboring to get away from us. Then it turned about and came back. It could not get through the ice and would have to lie over for the winter.

Our consolation was that we would have company for another long season and that the sailors were well enough supplied with their own food.

We sent Dr. Hovey, along with Captain Comer, to join MacMillan at Etah. MacMillan and his inseparable companion, Jot, were great sports and took things as they came. Knud and Lauge Koch went south to spend the winter away from us, taking with them Ekblaw and Dr. Hunt, so there were comparatively few left at Thule aside from the sailors who made their home on the boat.

They were Danes, and not such a high class of men as the crew of the *George B. Cluett.* They grumbled constantly of conditions, and especially of the watch I had to keep over them: some of the men had syphilis and could not be permitted to contaminate the village.

Dr. Wulff did not get along well with the sailors, so he asked if he might move in with us. Naturally I consented, especially as he brought along his own food. He was not, however, fit to consort with the Eskimos. He had recently been in China and he loved to tell how he had once kicked his cook until he dislocated his own toes. He believed that was the way to treat our natives. A man of superior education and mentality, yet he did not realize that the Eskimos are independent and nothing can be accomplished with them by such direct methods.

He wanted to photograph the natives, and I agreed to help him. One picture was to be of a mother with her child slung in her hood. The woman smilingly agreed to pose, but Dr. Wulff was dissatisfied with the appearance of her child and said: "Tell her that she's all right, but her baby is ugly as sin. Let her trade for the time being with that other woman there."

No mother in the world likes to hear it said that her child is not pretty enough to be photographed, so she refused to comply.

"Then I'll make her do it," he said, and tried to pull the squirming baby away from her. The woman bit and kicked, and all of her friends came to her aid. Dr. Wulff got no picture at all. He was so furious that I had to hold him to prevent his striking the girls—which could easily have started a riot.

With the coming of darkness the idle sailors aboard the *Danmark* grew lazy and began to complain of their food. The captain himself was intimidated by his crew and could not force them to move about and exercise. Some of them even refused to get out of their bunks at all—which is dangerous, especially in the Arctic. As a result, two came down with scurvy, a dreadful sickness. It can be cured quickly by eating fresh meat, especially mattak of narwhales, which is an excellent antiscorbutic, but no one could persuade them to eat it. They were certainly a sad lot compared with the crew of the *George B. Cluett.*

The dark season was rather dull, but in my house we were happier than ever. The boy developed nicely. His mother had plenty of milk for him and enough left over to suckle a little child whose mother was not so well supplied. I had Dr. Wulff to entertain me with his stories of China and Japan, India and Bali. It is amazing how much one man may learn from another when the two are cooped up together for a winter.

Knud returned shortly before the sun, and Dr. Wulff and I planned to go south, visit Tassiussak together and bring back Lauge Koch.

There had been a mild spell of weather which opened the water outside a number of the capes, so we decided to make the journey via the icecap. I remember that it was on the big glacier that we saw the sun for the first time, about February 22nd. The Eskimos with us all removed their mittens and hoods, and asked us to do likewise. I complied, but Wulff laughed and said he had no intention of humoring the natives in such a stupid fashion, and kept on. Old Ulugatok from Cape York stopped him long enough to say:

"We are only poor, silly people. We have few ways of protecting ourselves for the sake of our children, so we only do as our forefathers have taught us to do. If you need not do the same thing, it is convenient for you, but you should not laugh at us merely because you are the stronger. We think that if we do this we shall not die at least until the sun returns next year. Even if it does no good, we enjoy life so much that we do anything to keep it."

We spent the night on the glacier and Dr. Wulff shivered all night. Next morning when we were ready to break camp he desired to sleep a couple of hours longer. We thought it a strange mode of traveling, but waited for him. I intended going straight along the glacier to Cape York, as I had done before, but the natives were disgusted with the man and told me they were going to descend near Parker Snow Bay. I let them go, and Wulff and I drove on alone.

As usual, I was wary of the glacier. I made a long detour to avoid the crevasses I knew were there, and as a result we struck deep snow in which both of us had to walk. The going was tough, but I knew that sooner or later we would be through it and on smooth ice.

Soon I heard Wulff calling from behind me that he could go no farther and would have to make camp for the night. I laughed. We had been driving only four hours and that could scarcely be called a day's journey. But he said his heart was bad and, what was more, *he* was the man to decide how far we traveled each day.

I explained that this trip was merely to get him in condition for the trip he had decided to make with Knud later on to the north, and Knud certainly would make him finish a day's travel. However, we camped—I made an igloo as we had no tent—and slept a long time. Certainly he had enough rest—we camped at two o'clock in the afternoon.

When we started again we ran into terrible crevasses. At this point we should have turned down onto the ice along the shore, but I was sure we would soon be past the most dangerous of them and we kept on. It was the worst route I had ever traveled. We passed crevasses more than thirty feet broad, and the snow bridges across the tops were frighteningly insecure.

Suddenly we heard one of the bridges crash behind us. The glacier was on the move, and we were on top of it! I was panic-stricken, but dared not admit it to Wulff. Our only hope was to keep going. On all sides of us now were fresh, yawning crevasses. There was no turning back, but perhaps we could reach the edge of the glacier and find a route to descend. I remember that I looked forward to the sea ice as I would to paradise itself.

At that moment Dr. Wulff chose to lie down! No more for him today, he declared. His heart was troubling him and we would have to camp.

There was no material to build a snowhouse, so I scooped out a hole in the snow and ice, dumped our sleeping bags into it and pulled the sledges over the top. The wind made it difficult to cook, but we made some tea and ate some frozen meat and felt better.

The snow came on the wind, drifting over us and filling up our hole. Dr. Wulff stirred and complained of the cold. It was like lying in a grave, he said. Yet there was nothing I could do. "Well," he grumbled, "I can't stay here. You'll have to get me out of this!"

That was impossible. He was furious and started up—which would have been dangerous as we could not see two feet before our hands and he would surely have stumbled into a crevasse. I had to resort to force to keep him quiet, and he told me bitterly that I was a tyrant. But what of that?

We lay there for two days. When we finally climbed out the snow had obliterated all our tracks, and most of the crevasses were hidden beneath a thin white layer. After a while we could detect the crevasses by the depressions—an interesting phenomenon, but little help in our situation. We cooked some meat, and then set off in a fog so dense that we could not even see the mountains. I may have taken the wrong direction.

Dr. Wulff following me, we crept along. At one spot we had to cross a snow bridge which sagged six feet below the surface and hung across a gaping crevasse nearly forty feet wide. The bridge seemed thick, but I was timid as a rabbit and walked tremblingly out on it to test its strength. If I had fallen I dread to think what would have happened to Dr. Wulff, but there was nothing else to do. I held my breath and crossed, and then watched him come after me. Crevasse after crevasse we negotiated in that manner, all new. I had been over this route in the spring and at that time the icecap was solid.

Again and again we detoured. Again and again we took our lives in our hands, and the way only seemed to grow worse ahead of us. The fog lifted and descended and once we discovered that we had been traveling in a circle.

And then the doctor gave up. He was sullen, and said it was up to me to bring him out.

We camped again. This was the one trip of my whole experience that I believed it would be impossible to complete. And as we lay sleeping we were wakened time after time by the roar of the glacier as it cracked and groaned and thundered its Gargantuan body toward the sea. When Colonel I. P. Koch crossed the icecap he encountered the same experience—the glacier suddenly commenced moving for no ostensible reason. Round and under us the ice shook. I had never felt anything like it before, and only once since—a California earthquake.

After two more days of terror we reached the edge of the glacier only to find it impossible to descend. The ice was jagged, cut in long, sheer slices like a crazily frosted wedding cake. A few miles off we could see the smooth ice of the sea. And no way of reaching it!

We had to go back. I was horrified at the idea of retracing our steps. Wulff was hysterical and screamed that he would not do it. I made him obey.

I was perhaps as frightened as he, but he could complain that it was I who had got him into the mess. We passed spots where the snow bridges had caved in since our crossing; we even watched one huge mass of snow disappear and heard the thunder of it as it struck the earth hundreds of feet below. If it had not fallen we would have used it for a passage across the crevasse.

It grew dark again and we had to stop. We were exhausted, our nerves raw, our sleeping bags wet. Our supply of kerosene was low too, as Wulff had required warm tea in the middle of the day.

At last the moon rose, and I declared that we must keep going as it looked as if bad weather were coming. We should remain here no longer than was necessary.

Wulff stubbornly said that he would travel no farther than he wanted to, and he was going to stay here. Poor man, he was actually ill from fear and discomfort, but I went on and he had to follow me. He kept yelling that he was tired, but I answered that I was as tired as he, and yet we must keep going if we were to save ourselves.

At last he dropped and began to unlash his load.

"You got me into this—now get me out!" he said angrily. "I decide how fast we travel, and you can't leave me here alone."

I protested once more, but he refused to move. "It is up to you to guide me out when I'm ready to go. I'm tired now." Over and over he repeated this. The poor fellow was ill; I was even growing anxious for his sanity.

And so at last in desperation I took my whip and cracked it in the air. I am a fairly good man with a whip; I have driven dogs for many years. He looked at me in bewilderment, and cried out that I could not whip him. I said: "I not only can, but it is my pleasure to do so, and I intend to do it immediately unless you get a move on."

"I'm not going to move until I have had some sleep," he shrieked.

I swung my whip in the white moonlight. To the right and to the left the lash crashed into the snow beside him. Closer and closer I let it crack, until he could feel it whiz past his ears. And then he jumped. He was thoroughly frightened. I realized that he was afraid of physical punishment and this gave me the upper hand. Never once did he try to defend himself, and a wave of sickness swept over me.

I have never told this story before, and I am by no means proud of my part in it. Yet I had no choice. Our dogs were growing weaker as they had eaten nothing for several days, and I knew that I could not endure much more myself. Poor Wulff was physically unfit even for the cold, as his last explorations had been in the tropics.

We came the rest of the way in silence. I knew that Wulff

was suffering, but only his eyes pleaded with me to let him rest. Once in a great while he cursed under his breath. That was what I wanted him to do—it was a slight indication of spirit. When we finally got out of the crevasses I built a windbreak, and we lay down to rest. Next morning the atmosphere was changed. Wulff obeyed blindly without the customary cursing and pleading for more sleep, even volunteering to help harness the dogs.

"It proved," he said, "that I could do more than I had believed myself capable of doing and I thank you for forcing me to do it."

That gave him the victory over me—he was frank with his understanding and appreciation. And I had believed him my enemy!

"But," he went on, "I can't go to Cape York now. I really must go home and rest. This has been too much for me."

I agreed with him, and we returned to Thule after an absence of twenty days. We learned that the natives at Cape York had given us up, as the icecap had begun to move during that time and had dropped many huge bergs into the sea. Old Ulugatok had told of Wulff's refusal to bare his hands and head to the sun on the glacier: he was certain that the icecap had been embarrassed and tried to swallow us.

"Well," he said, upon learning that we were safe, "the year is not yet gone." He was right.

7

Knud was to leave shortly on his expedition to the north, and we decided that I had better stay at the post, especially because of the crew of rather unruly sailors. I drove to Upernivik for a few supplies and to pick up Lauge Koch at the Nielsens'. I met him on the way—perhaps the Nielsens' daughter Jacobine had become too much of a problem for him.

When I returned from the south to Melville Bay I met Dr. Hovey, who had finally made up his mind not to wait for any ship. He was in better condition now and had found a good man to drive him down. Dr. Hovey was bundled up as I have never seen another human being. He was, of his type, a brave enough old man. We both agreed, now, that perhaps this country was a bit unsafe for him. He thanked me for my help, but hinted for the last time that, while he did not want them for himself, he would be pleased if he could secure the foxskins—which he had traded me—for his museum. I laughed and told him they were now "on the books," and could not very easily be taken off, so we said good-bye once more, and finally. There in the shadow of the great mountain, Devil's Thumb, yearning toward the sky he warned us to be good boys. He had undoubtedly fought for his conception of the right, and you could not help respecting him— especially after you had finished fighting with him.

I returned to Thule in time to see the mapping expedition off to the north. Time after time while they were gone I thought of them fighting their way up there, and I wished I could have been with them, I was so familiar with all the details of travel. Yet what I was doing here was just as important and difficult.

There were a number of good fellows on board the ship, but there were more who were not so good. To eliminate the danger of syphilis I evacuated the entire village, taking everyone to Saunders Island. Our business was unimportant now, as we had nothing to sell.

If the Arctic is at all appealing to a person, it exercises a spell over him. I had my son, and I was happy. He began to take his first steps, I made him crude toys, and my whole life was filled with him, my dreams of nothing but his future which, somehow, meant so much more to me than my own.

When the ice in the fjord began to break up we returned to Thule and watched the preparations for the sailing of the *Danmark*. I thought how different that boat was to me now from what it had been when I had been alone at Pustervig on the east coast. Now it was merely a nest of quarrels and dissatisfaction. The sailors were all impatient, and the captain betrayed his weakness day after day by climbing the mountain and looking for open water, then calling a conference and listening to everyone's advice and desires regarding departure, though few of the men were worthy of an opinion. The stoker, who had lain in his bunk all winter with scurvy, was loudest of all with his proclamations.

They departed long before they should have, and were stuck in the ice for days. Still, the old ship was strong and could withstand the pressure. They went north and we saw them for the last time lying at Cape Parry. Perhaps the captain had asked the stoker which way to proceed.

We hunted in the fjords. Our kayaks were covered with new skins, and our tents pitched on the crest of the land so that we could overlook both fjord and open sea. There I sat one day looking out over the ocean expecting to see nothing at all. But suddenly I saw that rare, yet by now familiar, sight—the masts of a ship and a puff of smoke on the horizon.

We all rushed to the beach and our boat. We had no idea who might be coming, but we could tell that the ship was having a hard fight against the ice. Eventually the steamer found a patch of clear water and headed full speed toward the point where we idled in our boat.

"Hallo, Peter!" cried a voice that no one in all Greenland could ever mistake—a tender voice belonging to a great personality—Bob Bartlett, the greatest ice navigator in the world. He had come with the third boat sent up for the same purpose—to fetch home the Crocker Land Expedition.

The first question I asked, of course, concerned the war. It was worse than ever. "The world is crazy," declared Bob. He asked about the *Danmark,* and I assured him that he could undoubtedly still find it somewhere near Cape Parry. Bartlett had been instructed, he said, to order the *Danmark* to leave the MacMillan expedition alone. I advised him not to remain here long as the wind had already begun to blow and the ice was on its way in.

I asked him if he had any provisions for me. Now Captain Bob is an Arctic expert in every way and he was in a hurry.

"Have you received any message," he asked, "telling you that I was to bring in supplies?"

"How could I have got such a letter?" I countered.

He then assured me that he had brought nothing. But, if he could assist me in any manner in a hurry, he would be glad to do so. He had to depart instantly. So he gave me six oranges—and for those I shall never forget him—and ten pounds of plug tobacco, which I hid from the natives, said good-bye and good luck, and steamed off.

Later on I heard from home that twelve tons of provisions had been sent along by him. I did not receive them, nor was I told that they were on board. He promised to stop in again on his way south. And that was the last I ever saw of him until we met many years later in New York. He is, nevertheless, a wonderful man.

Never, as I have said before, did we use the last bit of anything in the house. We still had about a third of a plug of tobacco, kept in a drawer of my writing desk. Once in a while Navarana would cut off a thin slice for her pipe. I hid the ten pieces Bartlett had given me in another drawer with my papers.

Next day a native woman brought some meat to us, and

all of us chatted merrily and enjoyed ourselves. When she was about to leave I asked her if she would like a piece of tobacco. She looked as does a longing soul when the minister promises heaven.

"Where would you get it?" she asked.

I opened the drawer and took the piece—scarcely three pipe-fuls—from it and gave it to her. Navarana's eyes were like saucers but, being an Eskimo woman, she could not protest against anything her husband did. As soon as the woman had gone Navarana hurried to the desk, flung open the drawer in very evident anger—and there found a whole new plug of tobacco. Her expression was indescribable. She acted as if she had seen a ghost, and I could not resist laughing. She laughed too and begged to know where the tobacco had come from. I merely told her to have a smoke. She cut off a slice and placed the remainder where she had found it. Next day there was another uncut piece there, and she never learned where I kept the apparently inexhaustible supply. That tobacco contributed greatly to our happiness. We could distribute it to our choicest visitors occasionally, and Navarana could be the donor.

Summer passed and fall arrived. It had been a bad year. The weather had prevented our hunting in kayaks, and ammunition was low. There was not enough to waste it shooting birds, and, although we did not suffer, we had to resort to the ancient methods of hunting. This takes endless time and patience. To bring down a bird with a gun is much easier than waiting for it at the nest or beside a piece of meat laid out advantageously to lure it to earth.

The natives were unable to comprehend the situation. Why should they be deprived of what they wanted? They did not fight each other or kill. And why did I tell them that it was against the law to kill one another when armies of white men shot each other? Logic should follow the wise white man like his dog—but it often strays.

Winter was at hand and the ice in—and still no word from Knud and his mapping expedition. I planned to go north and cache meat along the route for them, after I had secured the meat. I tried to persuade some boys to follow me north, but they excused themselves. It was the time when they had to remain beside the seals' blowholes to secure their own food. We could not yet cross the fjords, but we went after seals and managed to kill just enough to keep ourselves and our dogs alive.

NAVARANA AND MYSELF AT THULE

Then suddenly they ceased to show themselves. We hunted for blowholes, and found them all frozen over. There were no seals out in the open water, nor were there any walrus to be found.

Little Mequsaq was growing so lean that I was frightened. He still lived on his mother's milk, but she, too, was under-nourished. Had Bob Bartlett given me the provisions he was sup-posed to have had on his ship, they would certainly have come in handy. Those were the conditions in the fall of 1917.

In those times of stress I could not help admiring the tact of the native housewives. Each night when I returned from hunt-ing Navarana was at the beach waiting for me. Yet never did she ask if I had brought home any meat—she had merely come to help me with the dogs, or to take my coat and put it in the store so that it would not thaw out by being worn into the house. But whenever I had a seal on the sledge she saw it immediately and shouted in surprise. She called all the girls and anyone else who happened to be in the house to come and admire her clever hus-band and his catch.

An important event in the development of little Mequsaq occurred that fall. The widow Aloqisaq lived in a small house in front of our own. It was she who tanned our skins, thawed out the dog food and so forth. Once the boy had been taken to visit her, and, while he was there, one of those sudden Arctic hurri-canes had blown up. It was a devil of a wind and no one could stand upright in it; the atmosphere was charged with needles of snow, and even small pebbles bombarded the houses. Fortunately our windows were covered with a thick layer of ice and did not break.

Navarana ran to me as I sat writing, and called out that Mequsaq had been caught by the gale and could not return home. I had seldom seen her so pleased. Now, she said, she was a mother who could sit at home and await the return of her son, as he had to remain away until good weather returned.

I offered to go for him, but this would spoil her enjoyment of his "bravery." That he was completely innocent of either bravery or cowardice, being only a year and a half old, had nothing to do with the situation—this was the first time he had been hindered in his movements by the weather. And because of that we would have to give a party when the storm was over and offer to the community most of the eggs stored out at the islands.

I went for them as soon as the wind was favorable, and the

party was a great success. We were all filled to the gullet with eggs, and belched our contentment all over the house.

We talked of Knud and his party—we hoped they would be back soon. Old Inaluk, the most gifted conjurer in the community, suddenly left the house. A few moments later we heard her singing outside. We all ran out and saw her standing in the moonlight, her coat off, her long hair loosened and switching as her body swayed from side to side:

> "Those who have been on the Eastside are back.
> Those who have been on the Eastside are back.
> Satok and his wife will visit us too.
> His wife is preparing by taking off her pants."

That was her song and, after her first seizure had passed, she went on to say that Knud and his party were now coming home, "but two of them are missing." I asked her who was missing. As she could only answer "Yes," or "No," I rephrased my question.

"Is Knud missing?"

She ceased her conjuring long enough to scoff: "Who suggests that the icecap and lack of food could bother Kunuk? Perhaps someone finds difficulties himself on the high-lying ice."

After the guests had gone home we went to bed. I lay reading. I could not get the woman's peculiar portent out of my mind, nor help feeling that there was evil in the air. Should I go up and look for the boys? I wondered. But where?

And then the head of my friend, Knud, poked through the door. I leaped up with a shout to grasp his hand. I shall never forget that moment, and his assurance that he had missed me during the whole summer "every, every day." The look of the icecap was upon him, months of starvation and hardship written on his face. It was several minutes before I inquired after the rest of the party.

"It has been a terrible summer," he said, "with such starvation and hardship as I have never known!"

"Are all of you here?" I asked.

"No. Two are missing," Knud answered.

He went into the kitchen to look for something to eat. Navarana and I scarcely dared ask who might have fallen. When Knud returned he said: "Henrik was eaten by the wolves, and Wulff fell by starvation. It is too horrible to think of."

We sat up all night, and Knud told me of his adventures. He laid out the whole trip before my eyes, and then wanted to know if I thought him in any way to blame for the misfortune. I told him then that I did not, and I still think so.

He was tired but he said that he would have to go south as soon as possible. All the men required some variation in food, and Lauge Koch especially needed bread and cereal badly. Lauge Koch was still in Etah, and I went for him the next day. I found him comfortably installed as a guest of the natives at the house of the American expedition.

Dr. Wulff was dead. He had been a hindrance throughout the trip. Unfit for such a journey, he had neither the spirit of adventure to urge him onward nor the co-operation of the natives, who all disliked him. It must have been a terrible experience for him—a man who is disliked always feels uncomfortable. The constant lack of food and the unexpected scarcity of game made him morose, and he had no eye for the stark beauty of the Arctic.

On the return home across the ice they had no food but the dogs which died occasionally, and Wulff was sick and could not eat. When they had to wade across the paralyzingly cold rivers on the icecap he refused to follow, lying down and protesting that he would not take another step. Twice Knud had to recross the torrents to persuade him to come, and when at last they reached the land back of Etah he was completely exhausted.

Knud and Ajago had walked on ahead to Etah so that Knud could find natives to return for the party and bring them out. Knud had given orders to Wulff and Koch and the two natives to remain at the spot where he had left them or, if they did go on, to follow a certain route. The two natives were anxious to get home to their families and, as they had nothing to eat, they walked slowly on. Each time they climbed a hill they had to wait for Wulff who was weak and could not keep up with them. Once when they killed a rabbit he refused to eat any of the meat except the liver; he must have been very ill, mentally as well as physically. Then the cold began to affect him—none of them had sleeping bags.

Poor Wulff was in the hands of a young man, Lauge Koch, and two Eskimos. Koch, as he has since proved, is an extraordinary person, but in many ways he was impatient, and he rebelled against Wulff's constantly delaying their progress to warmth and better hunting grounds.

On several occasions Wulff told Lauge Koch that he preferred going to his grave there on the icecap—he would not be sorry to be left behind as he had nothing to live for and there were few things in life he had not experienced. (He had made the same remark to me on our trip.) Still he lagged along, and insisted that he would only travel as fast as he chose.

Perhaps Knud might have encouraged him to greater speed and effort—but Knud Rasmussen could not be blamed for his efforts to rescue the whole party. He could never believe that anyone would lie down and die rather than make a last effort.

But Wulff did just that.

I believe Lauge Koch's reckless honesty was the final blow to Wulff's ebbing vitality.

"How far do you estimate that we have gone today?" Wulff asked.

"About two and a half kilometers," Koch answered.

"How much farther must we go?"

"About seventy!"

That is not the best way to encourage a weary companion, but Koch believed this would frighten him and urge him to renewed efforts.

The natives killed two more rabbits, and these he also refused in spite of their liberal offers to give him any portions he preferred. Then he reiterated that he would go no farther. Each time they stopped to rest it took hours to get him started again. Many times he told them to go on without him, but when they disappeared over a rise of ground he would call to them to wait, and this irked the natives. Lauge Koch stuck to Wulff, but it was difficult for him to placate the Eskimos.

Then finally, after a long rest, Wulff said:

"This is the end. I will not go any farther."

They heated a little water for him. He wrote one or two letters and lay down on the grass the natives had collected for him. And they left him behind.

Such an event makes interesting conversation later for groups sitting about in easy chairs, but they can never quite comprehend the true significance of leaving a man to die.

The natives told me later that they did not really believe Wulff was serious. He had been such a trial during the whole trip that they thought him only lazy now. Lauge Koch had exhausted his powers of persuasion and he, also, did not quite believe Wulff would fail to make another effort. He had done all it was humanly possible to do, and is in no way to blame. Yet, as the Eskimos told me, the mere fact that Wulff did not shoot himself led them to believe he still hoped for rescue.

The natives had their own lives to consider; Lauge Koch was young and strong, and it would have been useless, and dangerous, for him to wait for Wulff to die. He had refused point-blank to go on and Koch's waiting would only have resulted in his own death as well as the weaker man's.

Believe me, it would have been much easier for Lauge Koch to lie down and sleep. I know from experience that it is far more courageous to move those tired legs again and again than it is to lie down and court oblivion. Anyone can do that—the man with character and will power never gives up because his body is weary.

We went back to look for the outfit they had brought back across the icecap. It was at the spot where they had left it at the foot of the glacier, and the courageous story of six exhausted men was written in that cache. It had been stripped clean of everything that could be eaten or thrown away, the sledges and boxes ribbed to mere skeletons and utilized for fuel.

We also looked for Dr. Wulff. He could not possibly have been alive, but I thought we might locate his body. We found the spot where the two Eskimos said they had left him, and discovered traces of the grass they had plucked for his mattress. I thought he might have crawled down to the near-by brook for a drink, but he was not there.

I am positive that he regretted his decision to remain behind and tried to follow his companions, and lost his way. If he had not we would have found him.

And Henrik was dead, my devoted friend from the east coast expedition. Born a poor boy, he had become a caretaker of dogs at Egedesminde. There Joergen Broenlund had found him and hired him for the Danmark Expedition, and he had risen to great prominence among his people. He was ever helpful, never lazy, and his love of life had been inspiring. His pride in our motorboat had touched me—he had kept it spotless and petted it like a baby.

Now he was gone. He had fallen asleep far from the others, while he was out after rabbits, and never returned. His companions looked for him only to discover three huge wolves instead, one of them smeared with blood. The poor little fellow will always remain in my memory as the kindest and dearest of men.

Top. LAUGE KOCH.

Bottom. DR. TORILD WULFF IN A KAYAK NOT MANY MONTHS BEFORE HE WAS LEFT TO DIE ON THE ICECAP.

8

Lauge Koch's recovery was miraculous. When I arrived at Etah he was very weak, but after four sleeps he was well enough to travel, and after eight sleeps he felt that a little exercise would be good for him. We drove to Thule as the expedition was due to go south as soon as sufficient dog food had been collected. Knud was the man to get that. Was that man superhuman? I do not know.

We had had almost no meat during the whole summer and fall, and no walrus. Now the moon was bright in December, and Knud asked us all to go out with him to look for walrus at the islands. We knew there could be none, but since Knud wanted to look we decided to humor him. When we reached the islands we found that the ice had cracked up and the water, during the preceding night, had been covered with a new film of ice just strong enough to carry us and weak enough to permit the walrus to break through it to breathe.

We got four big ones, and the provisions for the crossing of Melville Bay were in our possession.

Knud and I believed that whenever a death, accidental or otherwise, occurred, there should be an official examination. We felt that it would be very embarrassing if such an examination should involve us in the Danish courts—there would always be a few persons who would censure Lauge Koch for deserting his companion.

Both of us knew the truth: there was nothing against him and, as he could not carry Wulff, it was his duty to save himself—and we thought it might be better to see the action through in Greenland. There was a judge here, and it would be much simpler to hand his decision to journalists in Copenhagen than to drag the mess through the courts there.

We started for South Greenland, taking with us the three Eskimos, one of whom was Inukitsork. He was an experienced man. We learned later that he had been responsible for the death of Peary's fellow professor, Marvin, who had been shot in 1909. Inukitsork had been exhausted on an expedition and Marvin had given orders to leave the Eskimo behind as he thought it useless to try to bring him back to camp alive. As a result, Inukitsork's cousin had shot Marvin.

Inukitsork, though a native, was very intelligent concerning this latest event, and his statement of great importance.

We decided to travel in separate divisions as it would be difficult to secure food for all of us if we went in one party. I drove with Lauge Koch and, of course, Navarana and Mequsaq, who was to emerge into the great world for the first time.

We set out on a dark winter day, but made little speed because of the rough ice. The snow drifted badly and Navarana had to cover her hood entirely to protect the boy, who slept there cozy and warm with no idea of how hard his mother fought to get him through the wind that slashed at our faces like knives. Eventually, however, we reached a cave, built a fire and cooked some meat. The sheath of ice that lined the cavern flamed with a gem-like iridescence more brilliant than any man-made palace walls.

There was a sort of ledge which had been cut by industrious travelers in the past, and we had with us our large sleeping bag into which we crept with the boy between us. The secret of keeping warm in a bag during the winter is to sleep naked, but getting in and out of it is somewhat unpleasant.

Every household has its own problems. Ours was Mequsaq's habit of crawling up and playing instead of sleeping. To prevent this he was told that a great, ferocious bear walked up and down beside us during the night and looked for small boys who were not asleep. If the boys did not sleep they were likely to have their heads bitten off.

As we slept in the cave for some time while the gale continued to blow outside, the boy grew restless and crawled up to take a peek outside the bag. Imagine his consternation when he actually saw a bear standing close to him with a very ominous look in his eye. The child hurried back into his place with such alacrity that his mother awakened. After she had seen that he was comfortable once more she too looked about, and saw the bear standing beside us.

"Peter," she whispered hoarsely, "there is a big bear right in the cave with us."

There was no doubt about it—there *was* a bear. And he was between me and my gun. I yelled and jumped out of the bag. Now a naked man is not much of a fighter in a temperature of forty below, so I grabbed my pants from under the sleeping bag and stepped into them while I rose to my feet. In my nervousness I put both feet into one leg. At the same moment I noticed that Itukusunguaq was up and had his gun ready, but he could not shoot without endangering us, so I began to run. That is inconvenient with both one's feet in one leg of his trousers, and I toppled forward and rolled down the slope to the feet of the bear. He was as frightened as I was, and leapt away from the thunderbolt that was after him. The dogs had been attracted by the noise, and a number of them tore loose from their traces and attacked the intruder. Itukusunguaq was now free to shoot and did so, but killed his best dog before he succeeded in getting the bear.

Mequsaq was thrilled by the performance and laughed loudly when he saw his father lying between the paws of the bear. Navarana brought him down to toss his little spear against the dead bear so that he might get his share. He had been the first to sight the animal, and she was as proud of him as if he had made the catch singlehanded.

We ran into one snowstorm before we reached Cape York, where we remained only one night. The natives had little meat of their own, so they could give us nothing—and we had to be careful not to give any of our own away.

Our trip was the worst I have ever made. The weather vied with the ice to see which would get us. One day while the moon was obscured by the clouds the rough ice broke my runners. It took so long to repair them that I wasted two days finding the party again. Fortunately there was enough snow to build igloos, but there was little meat to cook. Navarana had to walk with the boy in her hood most of the way, and we whipped the dogs after her.

Finally our food supply came to an end. There was nothing for the dogs either, but we hoped each day to reach Cape Seddon where we had friends. Lauge Koch now began to feel his weakness; his appetite was enormous, and his face looked haggard. We had nothing to give him except dog meat—one was killed each night. The gales toyed with us and made it almost impossible to keep going. I do not remember how many days we were out in the open, but it was so long that Navarana started to lose her milk. We fed the boy soup brewed from dog meat, but it did not agree with him—starving animals do not make very good soup—and we gave him a bone to chew on. Still he grew weaker and weaker, and I was afraid he would die. One evening he was too weak to nurse at all, and his poor mother sat as though petrified. There was nothing she could do for him. We took him between us in the sleeping bag, but we could scarcely keep warm ourselves. Lauge Koch's hunger burned from his eyes. His poor tortured

MEQUSAQ DRESSED FOR TRAVEL

KNUD RASMUSSEN WITH MY SON, MEQUSAQ

body craved food, and he hammered the skulls of the starved, butchered dogs, to secure the brains. He even picked up the bones we had thrown away and gnawed them once more. It disgusted me to watch him—I do not recall why—and I asked him not to do it.

We finally reached Cape Seddon where two of Navarana's uncles lived. They had meat and gave it to us willingly. Within a day all our travail was forgotten. The boy began to cry again—he had lain deathly quiet out on the ice—and once more there was milk and delicious food for him, and he could crawl about on the ledge.

The rest of the trip to Tassiussak was easy, and we waited there for a few days to permit Knud to catch up with us. When he arrived he tried to persuade me to go on farther south with the party. I said I would rather return home at once.

"But," he said, "it would be nice for Navarana to have her baby down here and get it over before going home."

That was how I first learned of the advent of another child. In the evening I asked Navarana if this was true, and she admitted it was. "Why did you tell Knud before you told me?"

"Because he is going to Denmark and won't hear about it there. But you have enough to worry about now with no ship and no meat, so I thought I should wait."

That night she danced and enjoyed herself for many hours, as she did for several nights following.

We traveled south in small divisions. At Proeven Little Jonas had to dig down in his caches to provide food for us. He did not actually object, but he could not resist hinting of times to come when provisions might not be so plentiful. Perhaps Kaiser Wilhelm would send up his submarines; Little Jonas' place at Proeven was, he said, an especially strategic point. If the Germans captured it they could control the whole catch of white whales and get all the mattak they wanted. He had prepared to go inland in such an emergency, and had transported big caches there. Knud made him go for the meat. Little Jonas sighed—but who could resist Knud?

It was at Proeven, of all places, that I first ran up against race prejudice. I visited the manager, a young chap whose chief object seemed to be in proving that he was a sort of superman in the community.

"Please come and eat," he said. "Your wife will be served in the kitchen."

I told him that I would rather eat with Little Jonas who was so well bred that he made no distinction between us and persons who happened to be born in the wrong countries.

The inspector in the south was willing to hold the court we sought. But now Lauge Koch refused to submit to such a trial. He had visited the scientific station at Disko and the Danes there had advised him against it. What arguments they used on him I never knew; whatever they said I am sure they meant to be for his best interests.

But it was the beginning of a lifelong misunderstanding between those two big contemporary Arctic explorers—Knud Rasmussen and Lauge Koch. Many persons later tried in vain to bring them together again. After Knud Rasmussen's death it was most unfortunate that Lauge Koch published an article in the leading Danish paper denouncing his first companion and helper. It made Knud Rasmussen no smaller nor did it make Lauge Koch greater.

There was no object in our going farther. Navarana went to visit some friends at Uvkusigssat, and the rest of us went to Ritenbenk where Mr. Andersen, the best host in Greenland, lived. He is a great admirer of Dickens and cites him upon any and all occasions. He was not at home—in fact, he was on a trip to Umanak Colony with the lady who is now his wife to invite guests for Easter. His maid, Old Sofie, a famous cook and the devoted caretaker of his property, was none too pleased to see us. "We" were fairly numerous at that moment, as Knud had invited everyone along the road to accompany us.

On the wall outside the house hung an entire caribou and two hindquarters—the reason for the invitations Andersen was issuing. First we took down the hindquarters and forced poor Old Sofie to cook steaks. She was a fine cook even when made to perform against her will. When that was done she refused to remain in the house, and walked out in protest. As a result we also took down the whole caribou and finished that as well. Knud then went down into the cellar.

"He has wine," Knud shouted, "wine in wartime!" I must admit that he had no wine when we left.

We took the road to Jakobshavn, and there was the culmination of the trip—the parties are still remembered in Greenland. First a coffee party was given for all the natives. Then a dance, and another, and so on until no one but Knud was able to dance. Then the Danes gave parties, cleaning out their stocks of provisions before Knud left once more for Denmark.

When I returned north I heard that the Andersens at Ritenbenk had spent their Easter eating hardtack and barley soup. Sofie had complained of violence, but the host thought it was a wonderful joke and regretted that he himself had never done likewise. That is the type of humor prevalent in Greenland.

I found Navarana ill. I was unable to diagnose the trouble, but I could see that she was in a critical condition, burning with fever. The doctor from Umanak Colony said it was pneumonia—and the baby might be born at any moment.

That same afternoon a little girl was born.

Childbirth is an amazingly natural phenomenon with healthy native women. Navarana wanted to get up next day and travel, but the doctor advised against it as the ice was bad and the going difficult. We decided she should not go north until next summer, and then that she should stay a while with the Nielsens.

The little girl, Pipaluk, was very tiny, and her older brother sat the whole day long looking at her. We gave coffee to the natives in celebration, and I felt that I was leaving an important part of my life behind when I had to go.

9

My way took me to Igdlorssuit, as I was to take a girl back north to work. She was fat and had been well trained in housework by the Danish ladies at Umanak. Her only fault, I was told, was that she was inclined to tire of her job and run away, but this did not frighten me.

We met the other natives from the north at South Upernivik, and I bought almost the whole supply of Klintrup's shop. We had almost nothing to sell to the natives at Thule. Powder and lead were unobtainable anywhere.

Spring was already on its way by the time we reached Melville Bay, the girl, Karen, exhibiting unmistakable signs of homesickness. She yelled like a stuck pig when we drove after a bear. When she saw this had no effect on us she tumbled off the sledge and was left behind. After the bear was killed I went back only to find her half dead from fear. She had seen another bear, and, of course, was unarmed. She was through with the job, she said, and wanted to be taken home.

Next day the last of the bread was eaten. Karen, the southern girl, said that now surely we had to turn back. She honestly did not think that people could live without bread and coffee.

Poor girl, she had a hard time. At Cape York she was laughed at by the natives because she wanted to shake hands with the men. Everyone thought her a very forward girl with no subtleties of behavior.

I decided to stay at Cape York for a while—there was little reason to go on home; no family, no food. Until time for the birds at Saunders Island it mattered little where I was.

We pitched a tent on the beach and I settled down with Karen to keep house. She was not, truth to say, much of a housekeeper and understood nothing about mending kamiks, so I gave mine to another native woman. When I returned to the tent that night this woman came and begged me to forgive her—she had given birth to a baby that day and, she assured me, "No man can really realize that childbirth takes time and a little attention as well."

Karen was furious and wanted to go home at once. Where she came from women had been educated in the ways of midwives and sickness at childbirth. Nothing, she said, could make her marry a man in this crude, barbarous country. The natives laughed at her and said that such a matter was not for her, but for the men, to decide. And perhaps no one would like her anyhow, the women said. She had not yet exhibited any aptitude for working.

Later she fell madly in love with several of the boys and, finally, got herself a husband, a fine man, son of a missionary and a good hunter. She knew from experience in the south that a missionary is inclined to marry if told that he is the father of a child well on the way.

The summer passed without the arrival of a ship. Hunting can be monotonous as hell, and it was now. There was no kerosene for our powerboat, and no ammunition for our guns, so we had to resort to harpoons. But the sun did not go below the horizon for four months, so we could not complain.

I dreamt of Navarana and the two youngsters, but I had to stay where there was game, and during the whole summer there was no way of my seeing them. One can endure solitude somehow if he has books to read, but I had only one. The others had been lost in transit across Melville Bay, and even this one had been soaked.

It was a most erudite volume titled, *The Relationship Between the Popes in Avignon and Denmark*. The subject was not my special hobby, but it was something to read and, as it was the only book I possessed for a whole year, I read it over and over again. Until I die I shall remember everything there is to know about the Popes in Avignon and Denmark. I fancied them my companions and I grew so weary of them that I was tempted to burn the book. But I could not do that, of course.

The author was a learned, in fact, a great, man. Long afterward when I returned to Denmark the government gave a banquet in my honor, and the Danish Secretary of Foreign Affairs was the author of that book, the one man in the world I hated above all others. He sat next to me—Dr. Moltesen was his name—and smiled and talked in a friendly fashion. I told him he would have to excuse me. Later on I gave him the oil- and water-soaked and often dried book, and had it bound in fine leather. He appreciated my thought and seemed to be very fond of the book. He could not have liked it half so much as I hated it.

In the fall I went south for my family. Melville Bay! How many times have I traversed it! But how much easier it seemed when I knew I would find my wife and children at the other end of it.

At Tassiussak I encountered a surprise. An assistant had been sent up from Denmark to help me out, since it looked as if once more we could turn to legitimate trading. A ship would in all probability be able to get through to Thule whether the war was over or not.

The assistant's name was Nygaard, and of all the human specimens I ever met he was the strangest. He had come to Tassiussak on a ship which the Allies had permitted to make the voyage. A number of years before he had spent a few months in Greenland, but he had been unable to learn one sentence in Eskimo. To call him an original would be understatement.

Navarana, Mequsaq and Pipaluk were in the full bloom of health. The little girl was infinitely tender and looked much more like a white child than did her husky brother. He had learned to talk a little, and was full of the devil. He liked me immediately, and accompanied me wherever I went, sitting in an improvised bag slung over my shoulder.

My arrival and reunion with my family was the occasion of a coffee bust for the natives. A few days later it was discovered that

Mequsaq had worn out his first pair of soles—another coffee party. And still there must be a third before we left.

The Nielsens were, as usual, marvelous to us. They had had Navarana and the children on their hands for a long time, but that was no inconvenience whatever compared with Nygaard's presence. He had a reform complex. Nielsen assured me the man would help break the monotony of the long Arctic winters if I didn't kill him.

Nygaard said the sledges would have to transport two large barrels of butter for his bread. When I told him that we had not even owned any flour for several years he looked crestfallen; but then, to show us that he was nothing if not a sport, he agreed to "go native" with the rest of us. He would bring along only the absolute necessities!

We were somewhat amazed then to see an enormous, heavy trunk piled on the sledge. This did not look like "absolute necessities."

Nygaard had never seen an igloo and, as I made one the first night of our journey home, he told me that I went about it in a very slipshod manner. He had no improvements to suggest just yet, but even he could see my method was bad and he would think up something later.

We took the trip slowly as the children had to become accustomed to native foods after the fine bread and delicacies they had eaten at the Nielsens'.

At Cape Seddon, Nygaard informed us that he had brought along a number of albums with glazed prints which the natives might like to look at. I asked him why in hell he had carted along such junk, but I was in for more surprises. He also had in his trunk a complete library on agricultural subjects, and several years' output of a magazine devoted to bee culture. As well as pictures of dozens of friends in many lands—the man had evidently traveled widely—and old newspapers he had not yet had time to read.

By this time I was almost speechless, but the worst was yet to come: he had brought along a fifty pound chunk of soapstone from which he intended to fashion an iron to press his clothes! As we already had three mountains of soapstone at Thule this was carrying coals to Newcastle with a vengeance, and I assured him we would not haul the damned stuff any farther across rough ice and glaciers. But the man was utterly guileless and innocent of ill intentions.

When we reached Thule, life was as near to normal again as it ever could be with Nygaard present. His first suggestion was that we rebuild the store so that the snow would not drift so badly. We began work. The weather was cold, and he worked from early morning until late at night at a breakneck pace. After three days I told him I would have to go down to Parker Snow Bay for more coal. The trip was a two days' vacation for me. I knew the trade of dog-driving well, but Nygaard's brand of carpentry was wearing. Once he went along with me for coal, but he grew so exhausted that he had to go to bed for two days after we returned.

If it had not been for the kindness of the natives, we should have been unable to exist. I had been traveling and surveying and neglecting the meat supply, but the natives always brought us portions of their catches.

Navarana had grown up now in every way. The mother of two children, a woman of experience and travel, she could not be looked down upon by anyone, and she had many ways of maintaining her superior position.

A certain native was in the habit of sending us small portions of meat whenever he made a catch, and Navarana decided she would teach him a lesson. I told her that in reality we had no right to any share, but Navarana assured me that if Ivik desired to remain in society it was up to his wife to bring us decent meat. I promised to speak to Ivik about it. She laughed:

"In the first place, he is only a silly man, and who can blame him for what his wife docs? It is the wife who looks out for the meat in the house; the man only has the fun of bringing it home from the hunt. Second, men never know how to scold so that it hurts. Perhaps someone else better do it!"

I stood by and watched, and that same evening Ivik's wife came past with a tiny piece of meat, as usual.

"Oh, how grand of you to remember us!" exclaimed Navarana. "One sits at home regretting that one's poor husband cannot go hunting, and then arrives more meat than we can possibly eat in many days. Oh, at last our poor dogs can have more than they can swallow. But I suppose you must divide this up amongst the other houses too, mustn't you? Let me help you. It cannot be your intention that we shall have it all!"

The bewildered woman assured her that it was all meant for us.

"But, as it is," Navarana went on, "let me give you a few

NAVARANA WITH OUR TWO CHILDREN, PIPALUK (RIDING IN HER HOOD) AND
MEQUSAQ

of my poor, silly things—not as pay, because it never can be paid for, but just to show my foolish little thanks."

Navarana gathered together our most precious items and piled them into the woman's arms: half of our sugar—little enough but all we possessed, cereal, two handkerchiefs and a fine case of needles. The poor woman refused to take them, but she had no choice, and Navarana piled more and more on her. There was a sizable audience to witness her humiliation, and Navarana kept on without pity. Several things which had been presented to Navarana in the south she now gave to the woman. When she finally commenced to cry, Navarana exclaimed:

"We are happy you enjoyed your visit so much—and here is a little something you may like to have as a souvenir." It was the little piece of meat, and Navarana slapped it down on top of the gifts and pushed the woman out the door.

Ivik himself soon arrived and wanted to know what was the trouble. Navarana, innocent as a fawn, knew of no trouble whatever—she had only enjoyed a visit from her dear friend. The natives, however, informed Ivik, and soon we heard him beating his wife, her screams piercing the air. Next morning I found three seals in my meat rack, as well as Navarana's gifts. Ivik and his family left the community altogether—they had lost caste and moved to other hunting grounds.

Unfortunately wolves suddenly appeared in Thule. Formerly there had been almost none, but when the men went to Ellesmere Land to hunt, the wolves followed them back in the sledge tracks. I had hated the animals ever since my experience on the east coast, and it was terrible to see them prowling on the hills looking down at the children playing about our houses.

I had caught two bear cubs for the kids—we had shot a bear not realizing she had the cubs with her—and they made fine pets, for a while.

When the children awoke in the morning the house began to fill up. Two little playmates stood outside and waited until sounds of life within assured them that Mequsaq and Pipaluk were awake, then they stalked in silently. Next came my old king dog, Ersulik. He was old and worn out, reduced to little more than a plaything. Then there were always at least two pups and, finally, the two bears. The old dog was tortured unmercifully. The children played hunting games, and Ersulik was always the prey. They attached chairs and boxes to his tail and made him haul them about the floor. One day I heard him yip and ran to discover the trouble. Mequsaq had run a fork into his left eye. The poor dog was blind in that eye forever after, but his love for the boy never faltered.

The bears were good wrestlers, but eventually they grew too big and strong. The children cried once, and said that the bears had beaten them in their games. I chained them outside, but the children still continued to play with them. One day I stood at the window watching the fun and, as soon as the children turned their backs, the bears biffed them on the backs of their heads. I had to put them in a cage after that.

The spring came and I was happy. Navarana was a bit huskier and looking her best in anticipation of the great event of her life—a trip to Denmark to see the white people in their own country and learn many things from them. This she had been anticipating for years, and now that the voyage was imminent she spent all her time making elegant clothes for herself and the children.

We had talked it over and come to the conclusion that this was the best time to make the trip. Nygaard could remain at the post for only a year—he was needed, it seemed, in Canada by someone who wanted him to construct a bridge which could not be built without his advice—and we might as well take advantage of his presence in Thule for our trip. We would go down to Tassiussak by sledge on the last ice and catch a boat there. We might never get through to Denmark as we had no recent news of the war, but the latest gossip we had heard seemed to indicate that Germany was about to give up.

Navarana had to look her best. She would pass through many settlements on the way south and half the fun would be in her triumph at saying good-bye to her friends.

We had already moved out of the houses into tents, and I went across the peninsula to fetch some dog food for the trip. We would not need much as the seals were abundant on the ice, but it would be well to have something in reserve for the children in case of bad weather.

Mequsaq was only three at the time. He saw me setting out and, joined by a little boy his own age, toddled after me. I did not notice them. When I returned home it was to discover that they were nowhere about so I hurried back up the hill to look for them. There they were, two small dots waddling across the plain, playing as they went and unaware of the lurking danger which tracked them—two gaunt wolves.

I shall never forget how fast I ran, faster than I ever dreamed I could, yet I was too far away to head off the wolves. I knew too that I should not shout; I had been told that when a wolf is disturbed he will sometimes jump on his prey in a last desperate effort to capture it. The wolves were almost abreast of the children when the boys lay down to drink from a brook. This was the opportunity the wolves had been awaiting. In my desperation I called upon luck, aimed my gun and pulled the trigger. Luck was with me; I hit one of the animals in the spine. The other heard the report of the gun and bolted.

The two little boys were not in the least surprised or frightened at what had happened. The sound of the shot was to them the most natural thing in the world. By the time I reached them they were sitting beside the dead animal playing with it.

10

With our sledge full enough to carry us across the bay we left Thule. Two other families accompanied us south to trade. The little auks were already chattering in the cliffs, and the fine ice in Melville Bay permitted us to make haste. When we shot two bears the boy thought it was a game, even remaining on the sledge with me when we went after one of them. We saw it far out to sea, cut the lashing strings, threw the women and the loads off, and made a dash for him. I gripped Mequsaq with one arm and used my whip with the other. I was not the first to reach the bear, but the thrill of having my son with me more than made up for that.

We remained at Tassiussak until the water opened up, and then went to Upernivik by skin boat. There we stayed with our friends the Bryders. Mrs. Bryder's new baby was a little younger than Pipaluk, and Navarana had so much milk that she could easily spare some for him.

Upernivik, a large colony, was exciting for Navarana who had never been in such a big, snowless town. The houses were clean and so numerous that Navarana asked me if there were really as many people in Copenhagen as there were here.

Finally, after weeks of waiting and exhausting our meager fund of gossip concerning the war, a ship steamed into the harbor. For me there were four whole years of newspapers to be read, with a complete, day by day, account of the war. Four years during which we had remained in solitary peace.

I also met a Mr. Daugaard-Jensen, president of the Royal Company which manages all the trading posts in Greenland. He is a most pleasant and agreeable man with a heart big enough to accommodate everyone in Greenland, but naturally he was none too pleased with me. Knud and I were the only two traders in all Greenland outside the supervision of the Royal Company. The organization had not bothered with Thule, thinking that nobody would be fool enough to try to establish a post there.

That was a thorn in Mr. Daugaard-Jensen's side. In addition to it, I had been running my business during the war without any trading goods. I had taken fox pelts from the natives and given them our homemade money, which they had spent in the south. The traders had received orders from home to be careful with their stock, but how much weight does an instruction from an almost mythical supervisor thousands of miles away carry when a friendly countryman from the north comes along during a dark winter with a well-concocted story and new companionship? Also the money saved them weighing the natives' products to determine the value.

Daugaard-Jensen assured me, however (after he had told me how much he regretted my cutting in on his trade), that he wished he had a few men like me in his posts. And that was that.

With him was a young Danish woman, Miss Inger Illum, who gave Navarana some chocolate candy. As a matter of course, Navarana sent a number of fine fox tails to her. The girl knew the value of the fur, and sent more sweets to Navarana who asked me if the girl was angry with her and was trying to heap shame upon her for being too penurious. I assured her that Miss Illum was merely very much impressed with the gift. Navarana could scarcely credit this, but finally said that so long as Miss Illum in her ignorance did not know how to behave, she would surrender and send her nothing more.

We asked for permission to return to Denmark with the steamship, but as this was the first boat to visit Greenland since the war, many others were entitled to passage before we were— space was at a premium. Perhaps, we were told, if we would go farther south, we could catch another boat.

We also learned that at last a ship was coming through to go up to Thule. It would pick up the leader of a new expedition, Commander Godfred Hansen, at Upernivik and carry him north to leave a cache for the Norwegian explorer, Roald Amundsen, at Cape Columbia far north in Grant's land. Godfred Hansen and

Daugaard-Jensen said they would like me to accompany them north in our boat, taking the cache as far as possible so that Hansen would not have so far to haul it with dog teams.

We spent four more weeks in Upernivik awaiting the coming of our ship. Navarana became familiar with the life of the colony, with girls who broke into the store and stole money, with men who tricked her and took money under false pretenses, and with beggars who merely begged because they knew she could not embarrass them by refusing. She said:

"I had always believed that Christian people were honest and truthful. Haven't they been taught that honesty is the principal virtue? Or have they had bad teachers?"

Our boat finally arrived, a little schooner which had been expensive for Knud but was not much good. I accompanied Hansen to Thule, during which trip the boat was almost wrecked, and left him there to the mercies of Nygaard who was, when I departed, already retelling his stories to the unfortunate Godfred Hansen for the fourth time.

I brought two bear cubs back to the children in Upernivik, and they were delighted.

We all sailed down on our boat to Umanak Colony where a bark, the *Thorvaldsen*, one of the last two sailing vessels plying between Greenland and Denmark, was scheduled to call. It had not yet put into port and, as the wind had been against it, chances for its arrival were rather slim. Since our own boat was to call in at the copper mine at Ivigtut and thence go on to America, there was nothing for us to do but wait. If the *Thorvaldsen* did not show up, I could return to Thule by sledge.

Our friends were good to us as usual, and made the stay more than endurable. Mr. Otto Mathiesen and his new wife loved the children, and Mequsaq liked to show them how brave he was in playing with the bear cubs. Navarana also made many friends. The population is of a far superior order to that of Upernivik. No begging is ever seen, nor are there any disorders of any kind.

The *Thorvaldsen* arrived at last—a fine vessel commanded by Captain Hansen, a grand sailor of a type now almost extinct. We had a little trouble persuading him to take the bears along, but I finally told him that they were gifts for the King from the natives, and that made everything all right.

The trip was uneventful but pleasant, for me at least. Navarana thought it was monotonous, especially as our fresh water was limited, and she could not accustom herself to washing her

face in the brine. One day while we were becalmed I got a small whale, and the bears had the time of their young lives.

We encountered a little difficulty when we reached the mine-laden waters of the North Sea. A patrol boat approached us and warned us of danger, but this was only after we were deep within the danger zone, and it would have been quite as dangerous for us to turn back as to proceed. To maneuver a heavily laden sailing vessel through narrow lanes dotted with mines is something of a trick, and Captain Hansen issued orders for the passengers to sleep fully clothed. He set a course and held to it. The old Greenland sailors found mines just one more impediment to take in their stride.

And nothing happened. On the 11th of December, 1918, we sailed into the harbor of Copenhagen and the pell-mell of newspapermen and parents and relatives which one anticipates for so long and so soon wishes to be rid of. By the end of the first evening I was all for turning around and returning to Greenland.

Navarana, like all Eskimos visiting civilization for the first time, was disappointed. White men are apt to exaggerate the commonplaces of their homeland.

"Oh, I thought the houses were bigger—they are not much higher than an iceberg. I believed the horses were much higher than a man." There were few surprises for her—everything she saw was no better than what she had expected.

Only two things impressed her: first, it was winter, still the sun was shining; second, a team of horses eating from their nose bags. The horses could be driven about and still feed. This device Navarana thought a certain proof of white men's intelligence.

Next day we had an audience with the King. The ruler of our country was gracious and asked Navarana the conventional questions: what did she think of Denmark, etc., etc.?

Navarana turned to me: "Is that man really the King we have heard so much about? How can he think for everybody in Denmark if he is stupid enough to suppose I have any opinions about this magnificent land after only one day's stay?"

"What does she say?" asked the mighty man.

I translated freely: "Your Majesty, she thinks it is wonderful and grand!"

"I thought so!" said the King, and was content.

I took her to my father's home where she stayed with the children. I had to be out of town lecturing and could not be with her as much or as often as I wished. She grew tired, I am sure, of sitting about doing nothing, and would have preferred being in a house of her own where she could cook what she wanted and say what she thought. She had everything she needed, she said, but all things came too easily. One had no feeling of living when there were no difficulties to surmount.

An epidemic of Spanish influenza swept over Europe, and I contracted it. I was walking along the streets of Copenhagen when suddenly I felt dizzy. I staggered up to a couple of policemen and asked them to call me a taxi. Unfortunately there was a telephone strike on at the moment, and they could not call for a cab. Also, they thought I was drunk. When I denied this it only convinced them they had been right and they bundled me off to the police station where, fortunately, I was recognized and rushed to a hospital.

I was kept there for four months, and for a long time was so ill that I was isolated in a ward reserved for dying patients. I remember that the room was meant to accommodate six beds, but the epidemic raged so furiously that on one morning eleven patients were brought in alive, and nine bodies carried away before evening. I was one of the lucky two who survived. The other was a champion wrestler and a devil to handle in his delirium as, they told me, I was. It took three porters to hold me down, and I played football with them, tossing them from one side of the bed to the other.

Then Navarana came to visit me, and she was the only one who could keep me quiet. My mother and my sisters also visited me as well as a number of newspapermen. Navarana sat beside me most of the day. She lived, during this harrowing interval, in a hotel and had a long distance to walk each day, but she knew the streetcars by their color and followed the tracks between the hotel and the hospital. She said she preferred walking to riding. If she walked, she said, she could stop in wherever she desired to eat and drink coffee. I asked her how she managed to pay for what she ate:

"That is easy. They all know the price of what they sell. I give them my purse, they take the money out of it and give the purse back to me."

Strangely enough she was never swindled, and I know that she dealt with some notorious crooks. It has been my experience, however, that the worst crook will not trick a person who is absolutely naïve—there is no sport in it for the crook.

I was so weak after being released from the hospital that I

could not walk for a long while. My hair fell out, I was thinner than I had ever been, and tortured with sciatica. It looked as though I would be out of the picture for months, and Knud told me that they had decided to send another man up to Thule to replace me for a while. I protested, but when Mr. Nyboe, supervisor of our post, also agreed with Knud and the doctor, I had to submit to their judgment.

This was my first serious defeat, and it was a great blow to me.

I went to a little island, Slotoe, to rest for a few weeks, and also spent some time with Knud. For the next year he was planning an expedition into Hudson Bay for the purpose of studying the Central Eskimos' customs, and was counting on both me and Navarana to help. He suggested that Navarana return to Thule as soon as possible and supervise the sewing of clothes for the expedition, then come back down to Umanak Colony during the late winter and join us there next summer.

We discussed this with Navarana and she was anxious to do it for, while she had liked Copenhagen when it was new to her, now the life, or rather the lack of it, was beginning to pall. She was tired of being a curiosity. The citizens had been tactless, staring at her as she passed on the streets, offering her money and fingering her garments. She would be glad to get back to Greenland.

We decided to leave Pipaluk with my parents. Both my father and mother were anxious to keep her, and Navarana said she wanted the little girl to have the advantages of Denmark— and the safety.

A number of theological students were scheduled to depart for Greenland and had cast their bait before Navarana, hoping for a conversion before they so much as set foot on the boat. They bored her, and she came to me with her problem. Her experience with the minister and the missionary in Thule had been disquieting.

Yet one night I took her to the Royal Theater to see a ballet, which was at that time the most celebrated in Europe. She was entranced. After we returned home and I went to bed she sat looking out the window. "Tell me the truth," she said. "Were those real angels we saw in that church? If so, there must be some truth in that Jesus stuff."

I was cruel enough to laugh, and it hurt her. I explained that we had not been in a church, but a place of amusement.

The leading lady was certainly a lovely person, but positively no angel, and I promised Navarana I would take her to visit the woman, who was a good friend of mine, the next day.

We lost no time in calling upon Mrs. Elna, the ballerina, who was then one of the foremost dancers in Europe. She chatted with Navarana pleasantly, and gave her a large bottle of expensive perfume to take back to Greenland—it should have lasted at least a year.

Navarana was disappointed with Mrs. Elna's obvious earthly bearing and said later that it would certainly have been nice if Jesus had such a theater where the doubters might go and be given a glimpse of the workings of heaven.

We gave a farewell ball for our many friends and all the Eskimos of South Greenland who now happened to be in Copenhagen. Navarana was a great success. She was so lovely and her happiness shone from her eyes. She wore the finest gown and bright, shiny new pumps. As this was to be her last public appearance in Copenhagen, she danced gaily the whole night. When the Hudson Bay expedition was over she would return and visit her Danish friends again. That was the plan, but it never materialized.

We drove back to the hotel after the ball was over. Her feet hurt her so badly she could scarcely hobble from the car to the lobby, and when she was finally undressed she could not sleep.

I awakened after a few hours and found her sitting with her poor, swollen feet in a basin, into which she had poured all of Mrs. Elna's choice perfume. The perfume was, she said, the only thing she could feel. Water was worse than nothing.

"Whether she was an angel or not," Navarana went on, "I thank her for the bottle. The stuff smells terrible, but it is wonderful for cooling sore feet."

That was the end of Mrs. Elna's gift.

11

A few days later Navarana and Mequsaq left with Captain Pedersen. I was still so weak that I could walk only a short distance without resting, so I returned to my island where the doctor told me that the sciatica would prevent my ever swimming again. This was a hard sentence for a former prize swimmer, so I went in bathing immediately, but could swim only a few feet. I tried to do some physical labor; that, too, was impossible. I was less help to anybody than a baby, and my disposition was worse.

But soon a telegram arrived from Knud which changed everything. Since I had been in Denmark we had built a ship of our own, the *Soekongen*, a sturdy little boat constructed especially for ice navigation and expeditions. Its cost had been almost prohibitive, but we found that, after the war, the prices of our furs skyrocketed and we had much more cash on hand than we had anticipated. Captain Pedersen was commanding our boat, but word had come from him that he had run into a gale, broken his bowsprit, and had had to stop in at Norway to have it repaired. A short time later, between Norway and Scotland, he lost the boom, and had to dock in Scotland and waste more valuable days. Chances were he and Navarana would not reach Tassiussak until fall, and we would have to organize transport from there to Thule by sledge during the winter.

Now Lauge Koch was going north with an expedition of his own and planned to operate in the Thule District. As his ship was small, we had agreed to transport a portion of his supplies, and had sacrificed part of our own load to help him out.

Both Knud Rasmussen and I were needed; there was no doubt of that. A steamer was sailing tomorrow for Upernivik—the last boat of the year. Could I go along?

I did not even stop to say good-bye to my mother—she would have thought it suicidal for me to travel. Within four hours I had purchased a small outfit, and next day Knud and I were once more bound for the Arctic.

When we reached Upernivik we were informed that the ice to the north was worse than usual. A few days later Lauge Koch appeared with his schooner, which had been furnished by the Danish government, and I accompanied him as pilot across Melville Bay. The boat was overloaded, and goods piled high on deck. Koch had brought dog food—dried fish—from South Greenland and piled it on top of everything else. In fact, to reach the deckhouses one had to burrow through holes.

He had more food than was ever seen before with a Danish expedition. Koch had entertained an offer from the government to help him outfit the expedition, and had been crazy enough to accept—hence, the unbelievable amount of food, so much that we had trouble in devouring our daily rations.

I was a very poor helper. My weakness and sciatica made it

painful even to stand at the wheel. Often I was desperate, but since I had got into the mess I refused to complain.

A gale blew up and the ice began to pack around us. I routed all the men out to work, pushing and shoving, anything to save the little ship. During the storm I fell in the water and soaked my clothes. When we had traveled through the worst ice, the snow kept falling steadily and I had to remain in the crow's-nest for twenty-four hours in my wet garments.

When the sun returned and permitted us to relax, my sciatica was cured. Everything the doctor had told me to avoid as a death penalty, I had disregarded. Since that time I have never felt a twinge in the nerves of my leg.

When we reached Thule we found that Nygaard had managed well enough, but his singular notions had got him into considerable trouble. Our good friend Mayak had been denied the privilege of trading because he had two wives. Nygaard believed in monogamy. He refused any single woman admission to his house as he would allow no gossip about him, and he had thrown my poor adopted son, Usugodar, the deaf and dumb boy, out of the house because he had helped himself to food in the kitchen as he had always done when we were at home. Nygaard had also completed the collections which various museums had ordered, as well as the observations for the meteorological institution. Unfortunately he had neglected either to label his collections or date his observations. The institutions had not told him to do so, he said.

Commander Godfred Hansen had accomplished what he had come for, and was healthy and happy, happy especially at our arrival as he now knew all of Nygaard's stories forward and backward.

We were about to set out for Lauge Koch's northern destination when we heard the natives yelling. They were announcing another ship—the fjord was filling up. This ship was our own, the *Soekongen*, with Knud, Navarana and Mequsaq, and Hans Nielsen, the new manager, aboard.

Seldom had I seen Navarana so happy. She leapt into the air and danced with joy to be at home once more—she could not put into words the emotions she felt.

We sailed north next day with Lauge Koch's provisions. It was a whale of a job unloading the stuff, which included two tractors, and we had barely finished the work when a gale broke out. We sailed off, leaving Koch to his own fate. We felt, however, that we need waste no sympathy on him. He was a fine young man, quite capable of accomplishing what he set out to do.

At Thule we said good-bye once more to Navarana and the boy. He was still finicky about his food, and thought he should eat nothing but bread and butter, but we knew that notion would not last. Navarana settled down to the making of the outfit for the expedition next year, and she arranged that the boy should be taken care of by a new missionary when she left for the south. And once more Thule faded away behind us.

Knud and Commander Godfred Hansen boarded a navy ship at Egedesminde and I went on with Captain Pedersen and the *Soekongen* to the southernmost part of Greenland to investigate the old Viking ruins there. I have always had a desire to be a farmer, and it had occurred to me to look over the possibility of raising sheep near Julianehaab.

It was an entirely new and different country to me. The landscape was lush and green with excellent grazing lands surrounding the deep, silent fjords where the ancient Norsemen had settled. Over all was a hush which gave it the quality of a dream.

But the ruins themselves were disappointing. The Vikings had certainly exaggerated when they sang their sagas. I had studied the sagas on the way to Brattahlid, the spot where Eric the Red had lived and established a colony, and I remembered an episode in one of the later sagas: two adopted brothers were attempting to revenge themselves upon each other. One of them was especially furious, and for a practical joke crashed in the skull of a slave of his host during a beer party. The host heard the noise but "because of the distance and the many guests he could not see what had happened."

I measured the largest room—I supposed it to be the dining room—and found that at most eleven people could have been seated at one time. Of course, the sagas have been told many, many times and something added to them at each telling.

The conditions for sheep raising were excellent, and I might well have moved there to farm if something else had not turned up to prevent me.

The Eskimos at Julianehaab are fine people and possess a certain culture. In fact, they are quite as advanced as the inhabitants of Scotland's northern islands, and are sufficiently intelligent to enable them to compete with immigrants when, eventually, the country is thrown open to foreigners. They are most

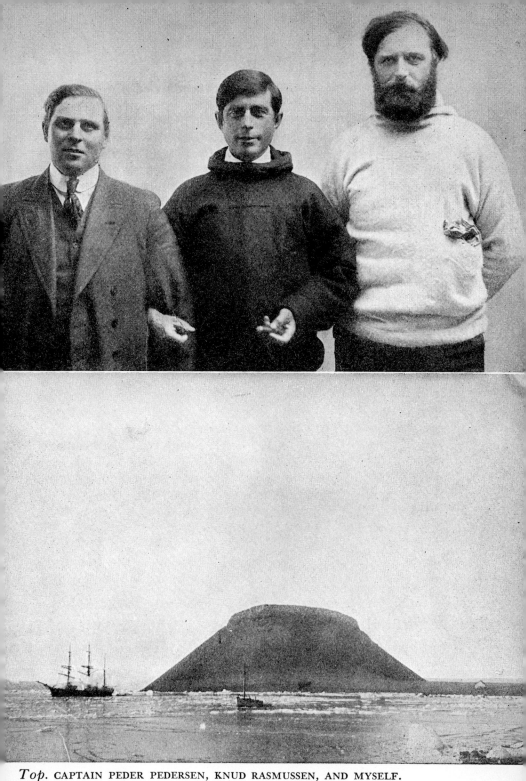

Top. CAPTAIN PEDER PEDERSEN, KNUD RASMUSSEN, AND MYSELF.

Bottom. THE THULE MOUNTAIN, UMANAK, AT THE HEAD OF OUR FJORD, WITH THE BARK, "DANMARK," AND OUR MOTORBOAT AT ANCHOR IN THE HARBOR DURING THE SUMMER.

frugal, and that automatically gives them an edge on the new-comers.

Greenland is still closed territory except to those granted special permits to visit. That condition will not last forever, and eventually I believe it will become an unparalleled tourist mecca.

It was late in the season when I reached Copenhagen again. Christmas was at hand, and I spent it at my old home with my parents, my brothers and sisters and especially little Pipaluk, who had turned into a lovely little white girl, and was accustomed to all the comforts and privileges she had never known before.

Unfortunately I had to go on another lecture tour. These are not pleasant, but they pay fairly well. I have only one real ambition in life, and that is to be independent enough to refuse lecture offers. The fulfillment of that ambition seems far away.

We were also busy preparing for our new expedition, which was to take us to Hudson Bay and the Central Eskimos. Our old friend, Captain Pedersen, was to transport us there, and he was a man always to be trusted. Two young scientists, Dr. Birket-Smith and Dr. Therkel Mathiassen, were to accompany us as ethnologists, and as an assistant we were to have the young writer, Helge Bangsted.

A chance to combine anthropological research with money-making arose in the person of our friend, Schnedler-Sorensen, who offered us the capital to film a travel and adventure motion picture. It was decided that I should leave ahead of the main party, with Schnedler-Sorensen and an actor to film the movie which we had often planned to make.

And so in May, I set out once more for Greenland, this time as a motion picture director, actor or whatnot. We shot a few scenes on the voyage, and more at Ivigtut. From there we sailed to Julianehaab on an oil tanker and I arranged a big dance in which I took part and grouped the entire colony in the background. We photographed everything, including the Eskimo cattle farmers, leaving not the least thing of interest unrecorded, before we returned to Ivigtut.

Ivigtut is a grand little town—a perfect slice of Denmark transplanted to the north. Most of the improvements have been made by the very successful mining company which operated there under the supervision of Niels Jagd, a friend of both Knud and myself.

It was 1921, the two hundredth anniversary of the arrival of Hans Egede, the "Apostle of Greenland," who first brought Chris-

tianity to the pagan Eskimos. A great celebration of the event
was planned, and even the King of Denmark had consented to dig-
nify it by his presence. As it was the first time any king had ever
visited Greenland, everyone was in a state of wild excitement.
The principal celebration was to be held at Godthaab, the capital
of Greenland, and every person who could get there planned to
attend.

Our friend Niels Jagd had not been invited. There was at
the time a ruction between the Royal Company and the mining
company, and as a result a representative of the miners was very
pointedly omitted from the invitation list. Friend Niels, however,
was not a man to be deterred by the mere lack of an invitation
and when the *Soekongen* arrived to take the movie outfit and
myself to the jubilee Niels accompanied us.

Next day, the first Sunday, was to be devoted to prayer and
thanksgiving. The town consequently was crowded with two
bishops and a wholesale assortment of high priests, ministers and
simple teachers of the gospel.

Knud Rasmussen and his wife were there too. She had come
up with Knud on the *Soekongen* to bid us good-bye when we
sailed for Hudson Bay. Knud was in his best humor, a brand
better than anyone else's. A navy vessel represented Denmark,
and Eskimos were collected from remote settlements. Niels Jagd's
arrival was most embarrassing for the high officials. He explained
that unfortunately his invitation had not reached him, but it had
doubtless been sent by a kayakman who had lost or forgotten it.
Nevertheless, he had come, since he knew how vexed the officials
would have been had he not arrived. Everyone agreed, of course,
and I saw the officials huddle together in an effort to find a place
for him at the tables.

At 9:30 Sunday morning I received a message from the Su-
preme Bishop of Denmark informing me that he had mistakenly
failed to invite me to take part in the procession at ten o'clock.
Would I be sure to show up?

I showed up—perhaps more than anyone else. The truth
was that I did not realize the gravity of the occasion, as I had
spent few hours of my life marching in church processions. The
evening before I had worn a scarlet anorak to the party, and it
did not occur to me that the same garb might be incongruous at
the service.

I had had only three hours' sleep, but I leapt out of bed and
made for the line of march. The procession was already under

way, marching slowly and seriously, chanting as they traversed the distance between the high school and the church. I hid behind a house and waited until the first dignitaries had passed by. Then I saw the native editor of the Eskimo paper in the ranks, and I thought that would be about my place, so I joined him. We continued to walk slowly and solemnly, and the song droned out over the smiling colony where Hans Egede, dear soul, had fought with and conquered the devils in the pagans. The sun was shining brightly, the church costumes were colorful, and the naval officers dressed in parade uniform added so much color that I felt perhaps the country should be thankful for the light Hans Egede had first brought to Greenland.

Later I was somewhat shocked to learn that the one and only discordant note in the whole procession was my blouse—the anorak made of scarlet cloth originally intended for a pillow slip. The bishops and high priests apparently could not appreciate the variation of color. I thought it relieved the monotony; they thought it disgraceful.

But at the moment I was innocent of the stir I caused. As reverent as anyone, I walked into the church where, to make space for others who sought peace and consolation, I went near the altar and sat down, pleased with my own piety, and awaited the blessing. After the show was over we all shook hands and I congratulated the church dignitaries on the success of the undertaking. Feeling quite as happy as if I had not been the thorn on the ecclesiastical rose, I remained with the party and proceeded to the high school for coffee and pious conversation.

Niels Jagd had not remained quite so sober last night as I. He, too, had been invited to join the procession, but he slept soundly through it. Only the sound of eleven cannons booming in the harbor to announce the end of the services wakened him.

On the next Saturday the King arrived in the harbor. This event had been anticipated as the high point in the week of festivities. His Majesty disembarked with his whole family and was greeted at the pier by every notable of Greenland. (The authorities had made certain about a uniformity of costume this time, and white anoraks were *de rigueur*. I behaved myself and was a model of servility.)

The Danish King is a tall man, and the Eskimos had constructed a special kayak to present to him. It had been built to my proportions, and I am the only man who ever rowed in it. The King disappointed local sportsmen by refusing to try it out.

I had been chosen to present it to him, and he examined it with interest.

"I see," he said knowingly. "That must be the hunting coat."

"Yes, indeed, Your Majesty," I replied. "It is certainly the bladder for hunting."

"Well, well. So this harpoon is made of narwhale horn."

"Quite right, Your Majesty. It is walrus tusk."

It was a great day for the natives. The King had promised to dispense coffee, which everyone expected to be extraordinary. When the drink turned out to be merely plain coffee, the natives were sullen with disappointment. He could not have known that the bishops had double-crossed him the Sunday previous by feeding the entire population coffee and cookies, figs, dried prunes and cigars.

I accompanied the Queen as guide and interpreter. A little girl ran up with a model house constructed of peat glued to a slab. The child wanted twenty kroner for it, but had so far been unable to sell it. The Queen took a fancy to it and wanted me to inquire the cost. The little girl asked me what she should demand—surely the Queen would be willing to pay a goodly sum for it. I advised her, however, that I thought it would be a nice gesture, and eventually pay her better, to present it as a gift. The Queen was so delighted that she called the King and showed it to him. "This little girl has given me the house as a gift!"

"Then she certainly shall be paid well," said the King, and took from his pocket five kroner and gave it to her. The girl protested—she was to have had much more.

"What does she say?" asked the King.

"Your Majesty," I interpreted, "she is happy, but she is afraid she should not accept your munificent reward."

The King puzzled a moment and then surprisingly agreed: "Yes. Perhaps she is not accustomed to so much money!"

After promising the girl that I would pay her myself, we left her.

Next day there was a big banquet aboard the King's transport. All the prominent Danes and natives were invited to attend, and the royal family graciously mingled with the throng. After a suitable interval the King went below and remained there. His adjutant walked through the crowd with a long paper on which were written numerous names, and spoke to those whose names appeared on the list. One by one they entered the cabin on the starboard side. Shortly each one emerged from the port side knighted or with a medal or order of some sort pinned to his chest. Those of us who had not yet been approached by the officer stood about in nervous groups chatting desperately about the weather, our eyes following the King's adjutant.

Presently the King reappeared on the bridge, and the adjutant ceased his peregrinations. Those faces that did not beam over a cross or a medal were darkly brooding. Their hopes were shattered.

"Peter Freuchen, I want to talk to you!" shouted the King. I jumped toward my sovereign—everyone witnessed my triumph.

"I want to give you something I know you will appreciate," said the King. "Please come below."

I followed him down the stairs. I knew that I was not in line for a medal—I had only recently been decorated while I was in Denmark—but, I said to myself, I shall undoubtedly receive a gold watch or a diamond pin or something of the sort dignified by the King.

The King picked up a large bottle containing a live beech branch, a branch he had cut himself on the day before he left home. (The beech is the national tree of Denmark, and the King's love for it is well advertised.) He explained to me that each day on the journey he had nurtured it with fresh water and cut an inch from the branch, hammering the new end to keep the leaves fresh.

"And now," he said, "I shall give you one of the leaves!"

"How interesting," I replied. "How can it be that the leaf is still fresh?" I stood for a moment holding the beech leaf, and feeling somewhat ridiculous, my visions of a gold watch or diamond pin fading fast. Still, it was something for King Christian to present me with a leaf.

"Perhaps it may interest the other members of the party also," said the King.

"Certainly, Your Majesty. They have seen no beeches for many years."

When he reached the deck with his prize he said: "I gave away three leaves in Iceland, and I will leave three with you people of Greenland." One he presented to Knud Rasmussen. Near-by stood an old lady. She was the mother of a Danish girl who had just been married in Godthaab, and she had only arrived from Denmark eight days ago and was returning by the next boat.

"I know you have spent ages up here out of sight of beech trees," said the King, "and the third leaf I shall give to you!"

The old lady bent almost double in prostration before her king, and he stooped to hand her the leaf, while the ladies who had actually been in Greenland for years burned in silent fury.

Next on the program was the royal buffet which pleased the natives immensely. The King and Queen themselves served the guests. I saw the King pick up a large cake and present it to one of the natives. "Very good," said the dignified Eskimo. "This is the way one expects a king to serve his guests!" He took the whole cake from the King and proceeded to eat it. The party was a great success, and the tables were stripped clean before they were abandoned.

After the banquet was finished we were put ashore. As I approached the landing I saw the inspector in his splendid uniform running up and down with a harried expression on his face.

"Oh, Freuchen," he cried. "You're not easily frightened, can you help us out?"

He had forgotten all the medals and crosses left with him to distribute to the good people in Greenland who had been unable to be present. After he had received them from the royal hand he laid them on the piano—and they were still there! What a scandal if some unworthy person discovered them! What revolutions could be anticipated! Besides, consider the King's disapproval.

I jumped into one of the boats going out for more guests. The King stood on the deck shaking hands and saying good-bye, and was doubtless glad to be rid of the throng, when he saw me approaching rather than departing.

"What do you want here now, Freuchen?" he shouted.

This was no time to engage in conversation, so I evaded him with an "Oh, just a few things," and ran up the gangway past him, making direct for the saloon. There sat the Queen! But I was unprepared for social graces or court etiquette. I spotted the package on the piano, grabbed it and rushed out. The ladies of the court must have thought me a specimen of the barbarousness of Greenland.

Soon afterward the King's ship steamed out of the harbor and the colony slowly settled back into its usual monotonous routine. Still, for years they had something to talk and argue about. And that is a great boon in the North.

12

We left shortly on the *Soekongen*. Mrs. Rasmussen was along, and was the best possible sport in enduring the inconvenience of the little boat and the crowded rooms. We stopped in at Jakobshavn, Knud's birthplace, to secure dog food and other necessities for the Hudson Bay expedition. There we learned the most exciting news that had come to us for a long time in the Arctic.

A large passenger ship, the *Bele,* chartered to carry the many Danish tourists to Greenland for the jubilee, had been wrecked just south of Upernivik. The boat had run upon the rocks during a dense fog. It was equipped with a wireless, however, and the King's vessel had picked up the SOS and proceeded from Jakobshavn to the rescue of the eighty-three passengers and members of the crew of the *Bele.* The King's boat had also been hampered by the fog, and had nosed about trying to avoid the same rocks which the *Bele* had struck. But after three days the fog lifted and the King sighted the wreck.

King Christian himself is a great lover of the sea and a famous boat racer who has proved his prowess upon many occasions, but here was an opportunity seldom granted a sovereign. Without a moment's hesitation he hurried to the wreck in a little motorboat. Most of the survivors were cast up on a desolate island and protected from the elements—which fortunately had been most kind— by tents made of sails and tarpaulin. They had also built themselves a kitchen.

The captain of the *Bele* was naturally in a bad mood, but when he saw his king coming to save him he burst into tears, and cried:

"You are not only a king, but you are also a *man!*"

That simple expression was perhaps the best, and sincerest, compliment ever paid to the present King of Denmark.

We had planned to supply our post at Thule with enough goods to last a year, and most of those provisions had been on the *Bele.* We were at a loss to know what to do, so we sailed into Umanak Colony.

Navarana was already there. She had traveled down on a sledge and had all the skin clothes ready for the expedition, but she was not very well. She had fallen victim to a cold germ that had been carried north by a ship which had stopped at Umanak, and was in such poor health that it was impossible for her to enjoy any of the parties hurriedly organized for us. Instead, she went immediately to the *Soekongen* and to bed.

We sailed on north and, as we approached Svartenhug, we sighted the King's ship coming south from the *Bele* wreck. Mrs. Rasmussen was still with us, and it occurred to us that she might return to Denmark on the naval vessel. Otherwise she would have to remain in Greenland until next year.

Knud was never a man to hesitate or quibble over etiquette. He ran up our signal flags, and the big ship hove to. The King was on the bridge, impatient to get home. He had been the northernmost ruler in the world, but the distinction was beginning to pall upon him. As soon as they were near us they inquired what was our trouble.

"Very serious trouble," Knud Rasmussen shouted back. "We need help."

"Come over and tell us about it!" the King's officer yelled.

"Can't you send a boat over to us? It is easier for you." Knud thought there was never any point in being too modest and subservient.

They lowered a boat and dispatched an officer with it who took Knud back. He walked straight up to the King.

"As Your Majesty is the protector of our expedition," he began, "I am sure it would disappoint you to see the whole project fall through. We must have more supplies to replace those that went down on the *Bele*. Besides, I would like my wife to return home on your ship."

"Is that why you stopped us?"

"Yes, Your Majesty, and I was sure you would be willing to help us out, since you have always shown the greatest interest in Arctic exploration."

In the face of such flattery the King was helpless. Daugaard-Jensen returned with Knud to help us draw up a list of supplies to be sent up from Denmark by a late boat. We would have to await its arrival before we could start out on the expedition.

Mrs. Rasmussen quickly threw her clothes into boxes and suitcases, and, of course, forgot a number of things. As she worked the King impatiently yanked on the whistle. Knud and Daugaard-Jensen were writing hurriedly, and when the whistle first blew Knud raised his hand as if to indicate that he would soon be ready.

"Oh, no," said Daugaard-Jensen, "you can't do that to a king."

Finally everything was in readiness. Mrs. Rasmussen was rowed across to the King's boat, and we saw her climb up the side of the big steamer. We dipped our flag to the King, who shouted "Good luck" and sailed away.

We sailed on to the wreck of the *Bele*. The captain was still there, but he was to leave for Godhavn with the inspector and thence home. The wreck was doomed, and Eskimos from great distances had come to look at it. A certain order was maintained, but the inspector of North Greenland realized that the carcass of the boat might be washed away at any moment, so he permitted us to break up the deck and try to recover as much of our goods as possible.

I had never known the thrill of piracy, but for once I indulged it to the fill. The first mate slept on board to keep a watch over the boat, but he rowed ashore to eat and we stripped the ship of everything from a few chickens (which I had the pleasure of offering to the Swedish captain of the *Bele*) to the bathtub and table from a second-class cabin (which I gave to the manager of Upernivik colony as a birthday present).

Like more famous gentleman robbers, I required nothing for myself. I gave everything away. I wanted only one thing as a souvenir—the ship's bell—which I chopped loose and took aboard the *Soekongen,* where Captain Pedersen mounted it to carry it home. I could reclaim it later. Unfortunately the King also wanted a souvenir, and asked the officials for one. These good men realized that Captain Pedersen might possibly be in possession of a few "souvenirs," so he presented the King with my bell, polished until it must have dazzled even the King. I never got anything out of the whole mess, in spite of the fact that I had stolen more than everyone else.

When we had secured everything possible out of the *Bele,* and I had made a number of dives into the water to hunt out a few necessary scientific instruments, we sailed to Upernivik, where we were joined by Dr. Mathiassen and Dr. Birket-Smith, who had come up to Greenland on the *Bele.*

Navarana was still very ill. It was difficult for her to walk, and we carried her in a boat from the harbor to the assistant's house, where we slept in our clothes—it was summer and one could drop down to sleep wherever it was most convenient.

It was apparent by now that Navarana had Spanish influenza, the same disease to which I had fallen victim the year before. I

PIPALUK AND MYSELF JUST BEFORE I LEFT DENMARK FOR THE HUDSON BAY
EXPEDITION

did not leave her side, and got our good friend, Fat Sofie, to help nurse her. Navarana was thankful that I could be with her, though she was torn with anxiety for her children. She would have liked me to go up to Thule and see that Mequsaq was being cared for properly.

"Now both the babies are away from us," she said, and asked me to tell her about little Pipaluk—how was she? what could she say? did she ever ask about her mother?

The next day Navarana was worse. There was no doctor in Upernivik at the time, and there was nothing more we could do for her. In the evening she asked me what I thought was the matter. Her head was buzzing with thoughts which came unsummoned, she said. It was ghastly to sit helpless and watch her fade away. I told her to try to sleep, but she could not.

After a while she began to talk about her visit to Denmark and the things she had seen there. That had been the high point in her life.

"But tell me the truth," she said. "Was that girl an angel? She danced like one and looked like the pictures the missionary showed us? I never could figure it out or get it right."

I told her again that it had only been a show, that she had not seen real angels.

"Then maybe one never has a chance to see them," she concluded.

I admitted this might very well be true, and she lay still for a long while. Then she took my hand in hers and told me how happy she had been in having a husband who would talk with her as an equal. And finally she said that she was very sleepy.

I went into the kitchen to brew tea for her. As I sat and watched the water it came over me how much I loved her, and how much she had developed since our marriage. I don't know why, but suddenly I regretted that my good friend Magdalene had not been in Denmark when Navarana was there, and that the two girls had never met.

Navarana was so quiet that I tiptoed in to look at her. As I watched, her lip just quivered. Then she was dead.

I would not believe it. I had somehow never thought of the illness as much more than a bad cold, but I called the young assistant, and he could only concur in what I saw before me.

My dear little wife was dead. I sat petrified. For the first time in my life I was in the presence of the death of someone close to me. My past life had been happy and carefree, and suddenly I found myself the father of two motherless children.

I had taken Navarana out of her natural life and surroundings. I hoped that she had been recompensed for what she had lost. But who knows? She was the bravest little girl who ever lived, and never would have complained about anything that came her way.

Fat Sofie took me to her house, and she and a friend made arrangements for the coffin and funeral. I was almost unconscious of anything that happened, and had lost interest in everything. But soon something happened which brought me to life with a vengeance.

The minister in Upernivik, an undersized, native imbecile, came to me with the statement that, since Navarana had died a pagan, she could not be buried in the graveyard. No bell might toll over her funeral and, he was sorry, he could not deliver a sermon.

It was relaxing for me to be so furious. I told him to go to hell with his bells and his sermon, but my wife would sleep in the cemetery and not be thrown to the dogs. Still, he said, he had already warned his congregation of the horrible consequences of dying without baptism, and this was his opportunity to offer them an example.

I am glad that I did not strike him. I had the good grace only to tell him to get out and let me manage the service.

It was the most pitiful funeral I have ever witnessed. The workers of the colony acted as pallbearers, and I was instructed to pay them each a kroner for the task. I remember that I was angry at the blacksmith because he smoked a cigar during the procession, if such a word as "procession" may be used, since there were only four of us—Aage Bistrup, the manager, and his young assistant, both Danes, and myself, and then Fat Sofie, who made the only gesture of gratitude. She had fashioned a sort of bouquet from gaily colored Christmas tree decorations, and it lay upon the coffin with a silly-looking Santa Claus peeping through the ornaments.

Hidden behind rocks and houses were the natives, terrified at the approach of this funeral procession which had not been solemnized by a minister nor sanctioned by the tolling of bells from the church. They dared not follow such a pagan to her final resting place, my little Navarana who had fed and entertained them whenever they visited her or she came to their houses.

Now, a few days before I wrote this, I read the gracious book written by Mrs. Ruth Bryan Owen, American ambassador to Denmark. Mrs. Owen was in Upernivik in 1934, and laid a bouquet of red flowers upon Navarana's grave. It brought tears to my eyes to read of it, and reminded me of my rancor toward the church at that time.

I had a simple, beautiful stone carved to mark the grave, which is atop the cliff.

I realized all too well that there I left a part of my life—a part I shall always be thankful for. And Mrs. Owen, a lady with both heart and intelligence, made me realize once more that women from every locality, from any station in life, have certain common graces, and I bow my head.

Those were the sad tidings I had to relate to Knud when he returned from Thule. He had always adored the happy and helpful little Navarana. She made her own memorial in the clothes she had put together for our expedition. We had always counted upon her for so many things. The two of us climbed up to her grave and said good-bye for the last time, and sailed away to new chapters in our lives.

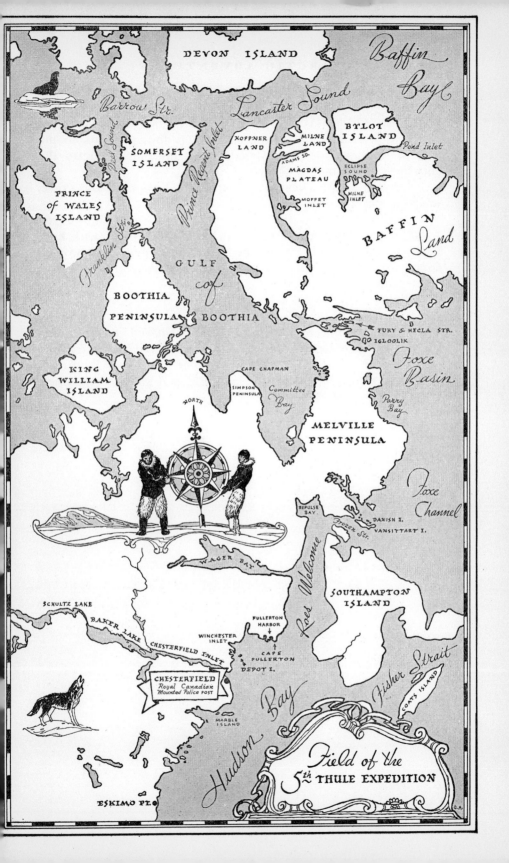

DEVON ISLAND

Baffin

Bay

Barrow Str.

Lancaster Sound

BYLOT ISLAND

Pond Inlet

KOPPNER LAND

MILNE LAND

SOMERSET ISLAND

ADAMS SD.

ECLIPSE SOUND

MAGDAS PLATEAU

PRINCE of WALES ISLAND

MOFFET INLET

MILNE INLET

Prince Regent Inlet

Peel Sound

Franklin Str.

BAFFIN *Land*

GULF *of* BOOTHIA

BOOTHIA PENINSULA

FURY & HECLA STR.

IGLOOLIK

Foxe Basin

KING WILLIAM ISLAND

CAPE CHAPMAN

SIMPSON PENINSULA

Committee Bay

Parry Bay

NORTH

MELVILLE PENINSULA

Foxe Channel

REPULSE BAY

DANISH I.

VANSITTART I.

Frozen Str.

WAGER BAY

Roes Welcome

SOUTHAMPTON ISLAND

SCHULTZ LAKE

BAKER LAKE

CHESTERFIELD INLET

WINCHESTER INLET

FULLERTON HARBOR

CAPE FULLERTON

DEPOT I.

CHESTERFIELD Royal Canadian Mounted Police POST

Fisher Strait

COATS ISLAND

MARBLE ISLAND

Hudson Bay

ESKIMO PT.

Field of the 5TH THULE EXPEDITION

PART V

1

KNUD had brought three families of Eskimos down from Thule to be our helpers on the Hudson Bay expedition. They were all curious about their Canadian cousins, and were fine men and women, but they fell sick, probably infected by the same germs which had slain Navarana, and now were also victimized by the itch. That was a pest which we never had at Thule while we were there, but recently the bugs had infested Lauge Koch's camp, and no one knew where they came from.

Influenza and the itch simultaneously were devilish to combat. Added to this, the ship was overcrowded. Some additional ledges were constructed down in the hold for the married couples, as we had not yet picked up the full load awaiting us in Godthaab.

At any rate, we were already cramped with scientists and natives lying three men to a bunk, which gave each man eight hours' sleep if he held to a fixed schedule. We also had about seventy dogs, and these had to be watched constantly to keep them from fighting. Their presence was no picnic for the sailors either, as the corral was directly over the fo'c'sle, and the odor was ripe, to put it mildly.

Our motion picture cameraman had been to Thule and secured all the pictures he needed for the travel and scenic film, and he left us at Godthaab to return to Denmark. The director and the actor had gone long since, the director unable to endure what he termed "the hardships."

Here the Eskimos were hospitalized. Meanwhile we arranged for carpenters to construct a house for us to take along to replace the one lost on the *Bele,* and I tried to press dried fish into bales for the dogs. Everything was shifted and repacked and reloaded to make additional room.

The poor natives grew worse, and the doctor gave up hope for Iggianguaq. His wife sat beside him and held his hand, crying as she stroked his head. I knew what the poor man suffered, for he had the same symptoms I had had. He found it increasingly difficult to catch his breath, and died one night with all of us standing about unable to help him.

This was the third mortal loss before the expedition started. Yet Knud would not give up, and from then on we were so busy that it was as if none of us had time to be ill. I shot the hour angle of the sun twice a day. I believe ours was the last major surveying expedition which lost itself in the wilds without a wireless telegraph instrument. We had to compute the exact time with our watches in relation to fixed points of longitude.

Knud thought it would be a fine idea to take along a native secretary to help tabulate the traditions and folklore of the Central Eskimos. As the missionaries said that they would be delighted to have one of their number with us to scatter the seeds of religion among the heathen, Knud decided to combine the two offices in one man, Jakob. He was strong and intelligent and willing. He was also an excellent hunter and, even though he did disappoint the church (he had no inclination nor interest in the missionary portion of his labors), we put him to good service on the expedition. He spread considerable seed among the different tribes, but not quite the sort the church officials in Greenland had anticipated.

The natives with us began to recover almost as soon as we sailed out of Godthaab. We tried to make connection with natives in Hudson Strait as we ran up north of Savage Islands, but saw none and had little time to waste looking for them. The season was late, and we knew we would have plenty of ice to fight in the bay as it was. It was also the plan to put in at Cape Dorset and leave Kraviaq and me on shore to drive by sledge north of Hudson Bay and contact the principal party next spring, but the weather was so bad that this plan fell through. We had to anchor in Gordon Bay to await the lifting of heavy fog. While we lay there I saw more seals collected in one place than I have ever seen anywhere else. They popped up around the ship like minnows in a pond; what they fed upon I do not know.

The fog persisted, and we could see almost nothing of the country. A Hudson Bay Company post was supposed to be situated in Gordon Bay, but we had no map to locate it—the map had gone down with the *Bele*.

Finally we sailed out of the western end of Hudson Strait, setting a course to the north of Southampton Island, and thence heading straight for Lyon Inlet where we planned to make our headquarters on Winter Island, the place where old man Parry

MEMBERS OF THE FIFTH THULE EXPEDITION TO HUDSON BAY AND BAFFIN LAND

Top row. Dr. Birket-Smith, Dr. Therkel Mathiassen and Helge Bangsted. *Bottom row.* Captain Peder Pedersen, Knud Rasmussen, myself, and Jacob Olsen.

had stopped a hundred years ago. He had come up from the south and, minus a propeller, had been caught there by the ice. We believed that we would have better luck and could drive north and south with our dogs, seeking out the adjacent natives. No one who knew the Eskimo tongue had ever talked with them before.

But we, too, ran into bad ice—heavy and sluggish. The ice one finds around Greenland, on both east and west coast, is treacherous and never to be relied upon. It grips the traveler, holds him, carries him about and smashes him. It is ever on the move, ever changing. But here in Hudson Bay we encountered for the first time in our lives ice that froze and remained where it froze, some of it gray and rotten and lifeless. Many of the ice pans were brown with dust that had drifted out from the shore. We knew that we were close to some form of land.

We made slight progress. Resorting to all the tricks we knew, we accomplished only a few miles a day through the jungle of ice. It was also difficult to ascertain our direction, for the clouds blanketed the sun and our compasses were entirely useless so close to the Magnetic North Pole.

The wind howled like wild beasts and the days on board became increasingly wretched. It was only Captain Pedersen's fine humor and his way of keeping up the morale of the crew that saved our senses. "To hell with it," he would cry, "we can't stay here all winter, so let's keep going west. There's got to be land there."

And then one day sure enough there was land ahead—a low range of mountains materialized through the fog. I did not know where we were, nor did anyone else, but as we approached it looked like Winter Island as described in Parry's book, and the fjord had the appearance of Lyon Inlet.

There was still no sun and we discovered no harbor in the island (which was more and more like Winter Island), and so we sailed on toward the mainland, where soon we discovered what would serve as a harbor. Explorers who have been at sea for a long while and who realize that the water will freeze shortly and lock the boat in for the winter, are modest in their demands for a harbor. We also discovered a small lake, saw a few rabbits on the hill, and a handy location for setting up the house. We were satisfied.

The motorboat was lowered into the water and the dogs hurried to land. They were so filthy and so lean that they scarcely looked like dogs. They made a bee line for the pond and drank till their bellies bulged. Not until then did they stop to sniff and explore the place on legs stiff from long disuse.

Captain Pedersen had promised to remain, if possible, and help us set up our house. He and I worked on it, and the inspector —who was to go out again with the boat—offered his assistance. He was not much of a carpenter, I knew, but even I was unprepared for his crowning achievement—dropping the big sledge-hammer on my head and knocking me unconscious. If it had not been for his weakness and my solid skull, that would have been my ignominious end.

Finally everything was unloaded and we bade farewell to the *Soekongen.* Captain Pedersen had no provisions for the winter. He was not sure that he could make his way out through the ice, which was now freezing solid, but his face betrayed no anxiety —it never has in his life. We could see the boat fighting valiantly along for five days. On the sixth morning it was gone from sight, and we settled down to our own problems.

We shared the work as usual. Knud took the natives with him and set out to determine the location of the land we occupied and also to secure meat for ourselves and the dogs. He was always lucky and I never was; therefore, I remained at home and finished our house, which still lacked a roof and part of the walls.

To tell the truth, I was a little annoyed because Knud had left me with only two scientists and Bangsted as helpers. They were not much help. They pounded their fingernails instead of the nails, and their backs were too weak to lift a hundred pounds unless they emitted frightful groans. Still they were so kind and interested in the task that during the whole expedition we had no quarrels, and remained until the end the best of friends.

According to the map we were building a house on the open sea. We knew, however, that there was earth under us, and that the map must be wrong.

Knud returned finally with news and provisions. He had discovered that we were situated on a tiny island, and the mainland near us supported herds of caribou. He had shot twelve and a number of seals. There were also many walrus in the sea outside, so we were assured that we would not starve. That was the important thing, and it gave us confidence in the success of our expedition. Two hours after Knud returned a large bear walked straight up to us and was shot not sixty feet from the house.

None of us had seen any native Eskimos, but a few old stone

caches at the point made us certain that we would find them eventually. At any rate, it was nice to be free of them until everything was in order. The worst part of it was that the wind roared, and the snow drifted ceaselessly. The house was warm but terribly crowded. Since our plan was to remain in the field most of the time, however, we did not complain of this.

Eventually we discovered that the island we occupied was a bit of unmapped territory and that the piece of land Knud had thought to be the mainland was in reality Vansittart Island. We were much farther from any habitation than we had thought.

As soon as the ice was hard Knud and I and our adopted boy, "Boatsman," left to discover the native Eskimos—if any lived about. We traveled up the fjord and came to a narrow sound through which ran a swift current. It was, we later learned, Hurd Channel, which never freezes.

Traveling along an unknown coast, not knowing what or whom to expect next, is the most exciting experience in the world. We intended to go as far as Repulse Bay in our search. When we left Europe it was not known whether or not there was any trading post north of Fullerton Harbor, so we followed the ice foot on the west side of Hurd Channel to make our way out to Frozen Strait and on up to Repulse.

We discovered a sledge standing at the point, and not far from it a cache containing half a bearded seal. The sledge was a clumsy affair, badly constructed, and the seal was left in the cache without being cut up. Whoever had left it had merely sliced it in two, and placed no stones beneath it to prevent its freezing fast to the ground. Our Greenland Eskimos would never have left meat in that condition.

As we advanced farther along we began to recognize the coast from Parry's description and, as it was unwise to come upon strange people after dark, we made camp.

It was my job to build the igloo, and I could not make the snow stick together. Knud, who could not help because of an old fracture in his spine, stood by and humorously criticized me. Then just as I cut the hole to get myself out of the structure the whole igloo toppled in on me. I had no idea what caused it—it had never happened before and has never happened since.

Boatsman, with a worried look on his face, suggested that I let him try to make another. I gladly consented, but Knud still stood by with his none too subtle kidding until Boatsman begged him to stop. There was an old superstition, he explained, that if one comes into a new country and his first igloo falls, he had better leave at once. No luck will come to him there.

Later on Boatsman told me that he had been frightened almost to death building that house after I had failed. He had actually made a great sacrifice in remaining with us, as he firmly believed that we would be killed or else meet with some terrible disaster because we had not heeded the warning. The dear boy had tried to transfer the curse from me to himself.

The next day we set out again as soon as it was light and before long we came upon tracks of a sledge. From the tracks we could see that the sledge itself was very narrow, the runners broad. Far in the distance were black dots moving through the snow.

We urged our dogs to their greatest speed in order to arrive among the natives in an impressive manner. The Eskimos stopped when they saw us coming and grabbed their guns. I was a little frightened, and shouted to Knud. He yelled back that he would go ahead and meet them first.

He took off his mittens and raised his bare hands in the air. We followed his example. Instantly the natives dropped their weapons and stuck up their hands. We halted our dogs and stood quiet a few moments to give them time to look us over.

After a little while the chief stepped forward and said:

"We are only plain, common people."

"We also are only plain, common people," said Knud.

They had thought, because of our white clothes and sledges, that we were ghosts, and our whips had frightened them still more. This was the first step toward a friendship of four years' duration between the natives and ourselves. The chief's name was Pappi (The Birdtail) and the three families with him belonged to the Netchilik tribe.

It was no great treat to visit this tribe, for they had no food whatever. We brought in some oatmeal from our supply, and the woman of the house, whose body was tattooed all over, simply dumped it in her pot of old soup. The mixture was terrible to the taste. I noticed that she herself ate nothing, but she later explained to me that she was pregnant, and therefore not permitted to eat from the same pot as the rest of us.

Their dogs were shabby runts and could hardly keep up with ours next day when we left for Repulse Bay together. They told us that a certain man, "Sakoatarnak," lived there. He was, they said, manager of the Hudson Bay Company's post.

Knud was already their dearest friend, and wormed every

secret out of them. He soon knew all about the trader, and had discovered that in this country three different tribes of natives lived near each other, yet kept apart socially. Each tribe considered the other two vastly inferior.

When we arrived at the little post at Repulse Bay we were greeted by a number of natives obviously cleverer and much less frightened than the Netchiliks had been. As soon as they heard us speak in their tongue they were won over. It was a surprise to them and to us how easily we could converse, and we had little difficulty in explaining to them where we had come from.

Captain Cleveland—Sakoatarnak—was quite a person and not without merit. He lived there, the only white man, and his word was law over a district larger than many states in the United States. He ordered the natives to cart our belongings from the sledges to his house and to feed our dogs. Then he asked us if there was anything else he could have done to please us. We said no, very much impressed by his grandeur. The great man then turned to the natives waiting at the door and, speaking in a soft, mild tone, said: "Well, then get the hell out of here!"

The Eskimos understood and scuttled away leaving us alone with Cleveland. Knud attempted to explain our arrival and our mission, producing a letter from an officer of the Hudson Bay Company in London, but Cleveland waved it aside: "I don't care to read it. I know good men by sight. I can trust you!"

These were brave words and we were highly flattered. Later we learned that Cleveland could not have read the letter anyhow.

Cleveland was a great character. When we asked him, during our first meal together, whether he would object to our bringing out a bottle of our famous Danish schnapps, he assured us that we could make ourselves at home in his house as long as we desired. "In fact," he assured us, "liquor is my favorite drink—any kind and any brand."

He was limited to six bottles a year "for medical purposes." But, as he was usually ill the very day after the ship arrived with the year's supply, he almost never had any left over for subsequent illnesses. After he had appropriated our bottle he opened up and confided his troubles to us.

His troubles had to do exclusively with women. "I have," he said, "been too kind to too many." And now he could not get rid of them. They hung about, their husbands were insolent to him, and the women themselves were most expensive to keep. Now if

Top. FATHER DU PLANE, HUDSON BAY MISSIONARY, WITH A NATIVE. THE PRIEST INHERITED A LARGE FORTUNE AND SPENT A PORTION OF IT IN PURCHASING THREE IMMENSE STATUES OF CHRIST.

Bottom. CAPTAIN CLEVELAND AT REPULSE BAY.

we could use a few men on our expedition, he was the man to recommend some very good ones. It would also be a great relief to him to be rid of them.

Cleveland furnished us considerable information about the locality. He had been at Repulse Bay for more than twenty years, first as a whaler (his name Sakoatarnak—The Harpooner—came down from those days). Later he had owned his own ketch with which he had sailed, hunted, traded, and stolen from the natives. After the ketch had been wrecked he became a trader for the Monjo people, fur dealers, until this firm finally was taken over by the Hudson Bay Company, the largest organization of its kind in the world.

Before the party broke up we were all fast friends. We could never grow tired of his tales, but on that first night he drank himself into a stupor, never offering the bottle to anyone but a girl whom he addressed as "Fatty" and held on his lap until she went to sleep and fell off.

Next day we met more of the natives and Knud immediately set to work recording their customs and traditions. In a few hours he had more information about the Eskimos of that district than had ever been written about them before.

2

There was another expedition in the district. This one, said to be under Captain Berthie of the Hudson Bay Company, was to explore Committee Bay and Boothia Felix next spring. The members of it had been caught by the winter, and were lying over at an occasional harbor in Wager Inlet.

I decided to drive down and see the leader. Knud and Boatsman drove back to our camp, and Knud promised me to send a bottle of spirits to Captain Cleveland for Christmas.

Captain Berthie was a fine young Frenchman. He had been in this part of the world for many years, employed by Revillon Frères, the principal competitor of the Hudson Bay Company.

In former times the largest posts of the Hudson Bay Company were along the Mackenzie River. It is still a power there, but since the railroad has opened up that country, a swarm of independent traders has been able to compete with the old organization whose posts operate the year round. These fly-by-nights come north by rail, hire motorboats and go down the river at the time of year best suited to reaping a harvest in furs. As a result, the

Hudson Bay Company was anxious to establish posts in remote districts where only large capital would enable anyone to penetrate, and Captain Berthie was going on a scouting trip to find the best routes to the native settlements at Committee Bay and Boothia Felix.

Berthie received me royally, as did the natives. They were vastly interested in my stories and my clothes and my outfit as a whole. They questioned me endlessly. They wanted to know if all the inhabitants of Greenland had whiskers like mine. They could hardly believe that the sun disappeared during the winter entirely, and they asked whether the Greenlanders were cannibals and did they speak the same language.

Finally one of the men asked whether the natives there con-ceived children in the same fashion as they did, and when I assured them that there was no difference they came to the conclusion that perhaps theirs was not the only civilized country in the world.

In the evening there was a dance, and the girls came dressed in some of the most horrible costumes I have ever seen. They were made of gingham, and apparently designed after a pattern in vogue a century before. The girls were not bad-looking, but their tattooing and the gingham dresses, which they wore over their fur clothes, made them appear monstrous.

They danced the old Hudson Strait which the whalers had introduced a hundred or more years ago. One man sat on the end of a barrel set upon another barrel, and called out. The shouts and laughter produced the same spirit I was accustomed to in Greenland.

"Everybody goes to the west!" We danced in a long file to one side of the room. "And then home to the east!" Back again.

"Girly in a cake and three hands around!" We fought for the prettiest girl and three men lifted her up and whirled her round, their touch not always the most modest. Screams and yells!

"Four in a bunch and snappy as hell!" We divided into groups and the commands fell fast and loud:

"Cocky flies out and girly flies in!"

"North couple to the west and balance forth!"

"Swing her in and out!"

"Everybody in a barrel and step to the devil!"

It took hours to finish one dance. When one caller wore out or ran out of invention another took his place. The captain gave way to the boatswain, and his commands were occasionally indecent, but everyone laughed and exclaimed how marvelous he was.

I heard there for the first time the exchange of off-color stories and remarks with a sexual significance by the Eskimos. The girls raved and whined when they heard anything suggestive, but they could not seem to stop the flow of vulgar witticisms. Captain Berthie told me that he did not think the white men were responsible for this sex consciousness, since these natives were in reality very primitive, but that he had found all the Central Eskimos different, in their attitude towards sex, from their cousins to the east and west. Their jokes were certainly highly colored, and would not bear repeating even in America today.

I left for the north again after a most pleasant visit. During the next year I learned that Captain Berthie, after having sought out the natives on Boothia Felix, returned to Revillon Frères. He had, it seemed, been in their service the whole time, but had pretended to be fed up with them and working for the Hudson Bay Company. Now that he had scouted out the information his employers wanted he was promoted for besting their competitors. The Arctic has its own code of trading ethics!

When I returned to Repulse Bay I found both Dr. Birket-Smith and Dr. Mathiassen there. Knud had thought them in condition by now to make a visit to Captain Cleveland and secure information from him in order to plan our work for next spring.

They were both overcome with joy as I met them. "He is the most amazing man!" they said. "He knows everything! He's worth his weight in gold!" They had their notebooks in hand and jotted down every remark he made.

They were both great scientists, and suspicion was not in their trusting souls. Unfortunately I have never been a saint, but I was saved by experience from believing in the old man, and I told them that he was a damned liar, and nothing else. I recognized the stories he told as the same old ones that were always used in the North to impress greenhorns. Later I learned from the natives that Cleveland had never been north of Lyon Inlet. Nevertheless, he told the good doctors all about Fury and Hecla Strait and his experiences at Igdloolik and of his inland travels. There was nothing Cleveland had not done. He had even eaten human flesh, and had seen one of the "Tunit," the giants which the natives believe once inhabited Canada. This was too much even for my scientists.

Knud Rasmussen had sent two bottles by each of the scientists as Christmas gifts for Captain Cleveland, as well as two for me to give him. He was handed his presents the very first thing in the morning, and he decided to test the comparative strength and flavor of each of his bottles with his girl Fatty.

The day looked rosy. Captain Cleveland boasted of his cooking, and said that he would prepare a Christmas dinner of eight courses, no more and no less. At two o'clock he would start to work, but to gather physical strength and morale for the ordeal he would first have a drink or two. He gulped them down, and we listened to some of his stories. When it was lunch time he asked me to prepare it, as he would need all his strength and enthusiasm for the dinner. He was going to cook us a dinner of five courses, no more, no less, just to show us that one of the best cooks in the world lived at Repulse Bay.

But he needed a little drink to fortify himself. And after some moments he said that he was about to prepare us a dinner, a *real* Christmas dinner, of four courses, no more, no less. But surely a man deserved a drink before he commenced work.

He was almost stiff after that, but the three-course dinner he was about to prepare would be better than anything we had ever tasted—especially as he was to serve us caribou roast. First, of course, it would have to thaw out, and while it thawed he would occupy his time with a little drink. Unfortunately he took the drink first, and the caribou meat remained outside in a temperature of forty below.

By this time the rest of us were ravenous. Captain Berthie, who had come up for Christmas, volunteered to cook the dinner himself, but Cleveland vetoed the idea. No, sir, he would cook us a real, northern Christmas dinner. He knew that we did not believe in many courses, nor did he. There would be just one course, but it would be caribou roast like nothing we had ever tasted.

It was rather difficult for him to stand now, but he asked me to help him, and I got him into the kitchen where we discovered, much to our amazement, that the meat had not come in by itself. It was still outside frozen hard as a rock, but Cleveland said, "To hell with it; we'll put it in the oven and let it thaw out while it roasts."

We did. Then he thought the least he could do was to offer himself, his girl and his guests a little drink. By now Fatty was out cold and, as it was her husband's night to possess her, he came for her and was pitched out of the house. He got the idea from this that he was not wanted, so he went home by himself.

Cleveland proceeded with his incredible yarns, but was interrupted by the odor of something burning. We rushed out and found the kitchen full of smoke. It was, however, only the meat roasting as it thawed.

He and I now proceeded with the meal. Cleveland was actually a fine cook. Quickly he took the meat from the oven and carved away the burnt portions. By now the interior was thawed out and ready to roast. He had brought a bottle with him to see him through the monotony of cooking, and in the other room the poor fellows grew more and more restless.

Finally it was ready, a tender, delicious roast. And now came the time for the great Cleveland specialty—gravy. He poured the juice from the meat into a pot and stirred up a delicious fluid. I know, for I tasted it.

Unfortunately, the labors of the day had left him unsteady, and the pot slipped out of his hands to the floor. The man of action as usual, I grasped the dishcloth and swabbed the gravy into the pot. By some curious process the dishcloth gave the gravy a tang of things long dead. Brother Cleveland, now almost sobered by the accident, produced spices to kill the taste. Pepper and cinnamon and cloves and whatnot we stirred into the mess, let it bubble again, and announced dinner ready at last.

We sat at the festive board and enjoyed ourselves and the meal. I stuck to the meat and let the others eat the gravy which, they said, was excellent, and they all asked for the recipe. Fortunately Cleveland's moment of sobriety had passed, and he was in no condition to answer intelligibly.

It turned out to be anything but a peaceful Christmas. After dinner Cleveland snored so stentoriously that even his girl woke up and went to bed. Finally we all turned in. I slept on the floor in the dining room with the other guests. During the night the big host had to get up a number of times, and on one of his trips upset a box in the kitchen where he kept two live lemmings. In their search for shelter and warmth they discovered what they were looking for in my beard. I woke from a dream of two wolves tearing at my throat, grabbed the innocent little animals and hurled them from me. They hit Dr. Birket-Smith who jumped up and started to swear. I began a hunt for the mice, but Cleveland heard me and ran out to save his pets. He was wearing a long nightshirt and stumbled about the room in a daze. Suddenly he was electrified by the sight of Captain Berthie. Berthie had served in the war and had a glass eye as his reward. He had removed it for the night. Cleveland, sighting the one-eyed man, shrieked and was thrown into a spasm of horrors. He thought he had injured the man himself during his drunkenness.

With one leap he landed in his bed, smack on top of Fatty, who yelled bloody murder. On examination later it was discovered that a number of her ribs were broken.

3

On our island—Danish Island we called it—we prepared for our spring journeys. I was to go north on a mapping tour while some of the others were to drive south and inland in order to visit unknown tribes.

The natives roundabout our camp were frightened of us at first, but soon learned that we were different from some of the other white people in the district; the Eskimos were welcome in our house at all times, and we in theirs. This gave us a great advantage in studying them and their history.

Dr. Mathiassen was to accompany me and assist in the surveying and mapping. We divided the wasteland between us and Fury and Hecla Strait, so that he should go up Admiralty Bay and I through the strait and along the west coast of Cockburn Land.

We traveled with an old couple, Awa and his wife, and their adopted boy, a child who had to be fed crackers and sugar constantly so that he would not yell and annoy us.

We spent an interesting time along the Melville Peninsula as the natives embraced Christianity while we were there. At the first they were very strict in abiding by their ancient pagan rules. This made it difficult as we needed a great deal of help, and the women could not sew caribou skins while the sun was on the decline. When they were pregnant they could not eat out of the same pot as the men, and had so many rules that life was extremely difficult for them.

Then one day a man named Kutlok (The Thumb) returned from the south where he had gone to deliver a letter. The man to whom the letter was addressed had moved, it seemed, and Kutlok had spent more than two years completing his mission. While in the south he had visited a school and received a taste of the Christian code of morals. The day after he returned home his wife gave birth to a child.

So he became a teacher. In a short time he had won over all his people to Christianity. The conversions took place at a meeting, and immediately all the old restrictions fell by the wayside. In fact, it was a great relief to the natives to be able to sew all sorts of skins at any time of day or night, to be permitted to hunt whichever animals they needed, etc.

On the other hand, there were a number of beliefs and rules which it was difficult for them to grasp. It was said that the missionaries did not favor wife-trading, and that would have to be stopped.

However, not to make it too dull for the poor ladies, it was decided that Kutlok and a few of the mightiest men of the tribe should have the privilege of entertaining the girls, as it was considered healthy for the women themselves and also for the children they would bear.

Awa told us that only last summer he had had a remarkable experience, which might have been even more remarkable if it had not been for a little girl who laughed at the wrong time. He was sitting outside his tent carving a walrus tusk when he saw three men approaching the settlement. He did not know who they might be, but suddenly recognized them as the new gods of the Trinity, the Father, the Son and the Holy Ghost. Awa shouted for everyone to come out and receive the dignified guests. And then, when a certain little girl discovered they wore pants of rabbitskin and very tall caps, she had to laugh. This made the Trinity angry, and, while they smiled forgivingly, they altered their course so that they passed by without stopping or even speaking a word in greeting. The natives had been greatly disappointed, but they said the Holy Ghost presented such a laughable aspect from the rear that they all gave way to their mirth. His posteriors curved in instead of out.

The Trinity had never been seen again.

In our group were also Akrioq and his wife, Cape York natives who had come down to Canada with us. We made good progress up the coast. In the beginning we stopped often because of the wind which blew steadily in our faces, but soon we learned that it never ceases in this God-forsaken country and that, if we were to travel at all, we had to face it. In Greenland the wind does not blow when the temperature is extremely low, but along Melville Peninsula it never stops for temperature, storm, sun or anything else.

It was a joy to travel with Dr. Mathiassen. He could not drive dogs, so he walked. His speed was an unvariable three miles per hour. He started off early in the morning and when we caught

Top. KNUD RASMUSSEN AND DR. BIRKET-SMITH.

Bottom. AKRIOQ CHEWING LINES IN OUR CABIN. HE WAS A CAPE YORK NATIVE WHO ACCOMPANIED US TO HUDSON BAY.

up with him he rode for a short distance. Whenever we stopped he walked ahead, and toward evening he dropped behind and caught up with us after we had camped. On a long sledge journey we seldom averaged more than four miles an hour or forty miles a day, so he found it not too difficult to keep up. While walking, nothing evaded his keen eyes. He scrutinized botanical specimens and all forms of animal life, and nothing of geological interest escaped his attention.

In the evenings Awa built our snowhouses, and stories concerning all the points of interest we passed poured from his lips. Here a number of persons had starved to death; at this lake great battles had taken place; at another point a large stone had killed a man while Awa looked on—the blood was still on it and would never disappear because the man had been innocent.

We also met a party of natives on their way south to trade. Akrioq and Arnanguaq, his wife, were interested in talking with them so that they might return to Greenland and recount it later in their igloos. These natives were the same mild and understanding people as those of Greenland.

A number of small boys played outside, sliding down a slope until their clothes were filled with snow and the hair worn off their pants. The old wife of Awa asked them a couple of times to stop: "Don't you think of your old grandfather who has to walk around and hunt and hunt to fetch those skins for you? Or of your old grandmother whose eyes hurt when she has to sew pants for you?"

The children laughed and kept up their destructive play.

"Oh, how pleased one feels watching them play," she said. "It makes one think of the time when they will be older and learn how to think and behave. How wonderful it is that foolish little children turn into intelligent grown-up people who know how to care for their things."

I had heard exactly the same type of reasoning in Greenland. The Eskimos in their optimistic view of life make Pollyanna look like a confirmed cynic.

The natives of northern Canada have developed a fine method of making their sledges easy to haul. In the first place, the sledges are quite different from ours—long and narrow, and heavy. The runners are at least two inches broad with the crossbars fastened on clumsily. The most surprising thing is in the treatment of the runners: they are made of frozen mud!

The material for this is dug in the summer or else chopped

out of the ground after it is frozen, which is, of course, much more difficult. When a sledge is to be fitted out, the mud or peat is thawed out, mixed in a big ball and plastered on the runners. It is applied in a layer about two inches thick and reaching high up on the sides—then it is left to freeze solid. After this it is smoothed with a knife or, if such an implement is at hand, a plane. When the surface is straight water is smeared on it with a piece of bear or dog skin. To prevent its freezing before it is spread lukewarm water must be used. One may hold the water in his mouth, as body temperature is correct. If it is warmer, it may thaw out the mud.

The thin layer of ice may be applied with a common brush, but I was the only person who owned such a thing. The principal thing, however, is that the layer be thin enough to prevent its turning white. If it turns white it will not stick well. Six-tenths of a millimeter is the maximum thickness permitted.

During a day of travel this ice wears out a number of times, and since it is inconvenient to stop and melt snow and warm the water during the journey, it is easier to use the ice formed from urine, which sticks even better than clear water. Everyone must contribute.

If such a sledge hits a stone the frozen mud may crack, but it is marvelous how much punishment a mud runner will take. It can be repaired with a piece of chewed meat plastered on the crack.

When we came to Hudson Bay we knew nothing about this practice, and though we had better dogs our old style iron runners made it impossible for us to compete with the Canadians on the trail. We had no mud, but we found that frozen oatmeal or rye meal would serve just as well. I made a dough of the stuff and plastered it on the runners.

Later on in the spring when the rye meal was of no more use on the runners I made pancakes of it. As I said before, however, we were rather careless of what we smeared on it, and I gladly dispensed with my share of the pancakes.

We reached Igdloolik after a number of exciting hunting adventures along the way. This is the center of population in the northern reaches of Hudson Bay, a small, flat island at the eastern outlet of Fury and Hecla Strait. The Parry expedition explored it when it was still believed possible to find a route north of the American continent to China and India. The land is all flat and almost at sea level, and the waterways almost impossible for a skipper to navigate.

There for the first time we saw houses made of ice slabs. The natives had built them near a lake where they fished for black salmon before the snow was in the right condition for constructing igloos.

We met a number of interesting natives, among them a certain Christian missionary, Umiling, whose son Nuralak was his assistant and truant officer. Nuralak was famous as a murderer, and his masterpiece was the killing of a white man the year before, which elevated him considerably in the estimation of the population. He worked a racket of constituting himself a "customs department," and anyone who came to Igdloolik to trade had to hand over half his goods to Nuralak.

Nuralak and his father were also interested in keeping the sexual morality on a high plane and announced that the trading of wives would be forbidden. They themselves, of course, being superior beings, would be able to borrow anyone's wife they wanted—and their wants were insatiable.

Nuralak was the only Eskimo I ever laid hands on. He had a very pleasant little wife whom he foully mistreated. I knew that if an Eskimo beats his wife no one should interfere—it is equally insulting to the husband and to the woman. But I saw Nuralak swing his wife round by the hair and kick her in the belly—she was pregnant—and I took him between my fingers and roughed him up a bit. He bellowed with rage and yelled that he had killed one white man and could easily kill another. So I had to rough him a bit more and throw him through the wall of the house.

At Igdloolik, Dr. Mathiassen and I parted, he to go straight north across the land to Admiralty Bay, and I to follow the coast along through Fury and Hecla Strait and up the west side of Cockburn Land to the north, a stretch never before seen or mapped by a white man.

I was to take only one boy with me, while Dr. Mathiassen took Akrioq and Arnanguaq and some local natives. Unfortunately I let Awa make the choice for me, and he recommended a certain Kratalik as my companion.

Kratalik was young but said to be very clever and had only recently married. He was the son of the chief at Igdloolik, a man with two wives. Kratalik also had several brothers, and they planned to follow along after us for three days or more to an open hole in the ice where there were so many seals that one had only to stand by and slaughter them.

We reached Ormond Island to the west, the farthest point visited by the Parry expedition. I climbed the mountain on the mainland and discovered the cairn left by Parry a hundred years before. It was not large, but easily discernible, and though I could find no records of the expedition, there was no room for doubt that this was Parry's cairn.

On the cliff were the most curious designs I have ever seen in stone. The gray sandstones were striped with red in perfect spirals. They were not made of fossils and were too large to be snails, yet there was spiral after spiral a foot or more in diameter, perfect enough to have been applied with a brush.

From Ormond Island we were to go on west. Fury and Hecla Strait, named for the two ships belonging to Parry, was filled with ice many years old, and it was plain to see that it could not be navigated.

The older brother, Takrawoaq, dropped his load at Ormond Island and set off for Igdloolik. I was occupied at the time making observations on a small island near-by, but when I returned I found my proud Kratalik weeping furiously and crying through his tears: "Look! Look! There he goes. I am alone with you and afraid to go on."

Then I made a great mistake. I should have realized that he was impossible as a helper and turned back for another man. But I thought I could manage him, and we went on. We had only one sledge and my own dogs, which I drove. I also had to build the snowhouses every evening and cook the meal, besides observing the landscape and caring for the dogs. Kratalik did nothing but weep. He was the worst fellow I ever had to travel with and, added to it all, I went snowblind.

Kratalik then thought he could take command, and ordered me to turn back. He would leave me if I did not. I made a few pointed remarks, but Kratalik grabbed a gun and said that if I did not obey him he would shoot me. At this I had to open my painfully swollen eyelids, take the guns away from him and hide them in my sleeping bag. He only sobbed the louder and stayed with me.

The boy was not willfully malicious, but old Awa, who had sent him with me, admitted later he was so useless that this was the only way for him to earn a gun, and he had been compelled, much against his will, to go along with me.

We managed the strait and reached Cape Hallowell, a high promontory at the western entrance to the sound which proved an excellent location for observations. From it I looked out over Committee Bay, the scene of so many struggles with nature when Arctic exploration was more of a mystery than it is now.

We advanced along the coast and I found a new island which I named for the Danish Crown Prince, Frederick, and also a number of unknown fjords and traces of ancient settlements. But we bagged no game whatever. I sent Kratalik after caribou when I was busy, but he was invariably unlucky. Finally he became more friendly, however, and this was some help. He admitted that my whiskers had frightened him at first.

He was a great fellow for culinary novelties. For instance, he collected the dung of ptarmigans, chewed meat and mixed the two items with seal oil. It made a somewhat peculiar but not bad tasting novelty, not unlike Roquefort cheese.

Our meat supply was running low, but every other day I cached a part of the fast dwindling supply in the igloo which we deserted, so that we would have a means of returning the same way we had come. We finally reached Nyboe Fjord, which I thought was as far north as we could go, but there we found a herd of caribou and managed to kill five, enough to permit us three days' more travel through low, uninteresting land with no game at hand, and on the sea only fields of rough ice which looked forbidding.

When we turned around, Kratalik became snowblind. I bandaged his eyes. Every time he got off the sledge for exercise I had to lead him, and he cried out with the pain, believing he was going to be permanently blind. I applied a compress of tea leaves, and that helped him.

When we reached the first igloo on our way back it had been smashed in by a bear, and our meat, as well as a spare harness, was gone. The kerosene can which we had left there was upset and the contents drained.

I went after the robber, leading the snowblind Kratalik along as he was afraid to be left alone. The bear tracks led us up over the land where numerous rocks jutting up through the snow menaced our mud runners. We finally gave up the chase—and it cost us another day to repair our runners.

The next caches had been visited by wolves—the meat was gone. Then we struck the track of a wolverine, the most annoying animal in the Arctic. These overgrown weasels are persistent

Top. MYSELF ON DANISH ISLAND WEARING A SHIRT WHICH I MADE FROM AN OLD TABLECLOTH.

Bottom. KRATALIK AND MYSELF.

devils, and this one had lived up to his gluttonous reputation. He had consumed the meat in one igloo, then slowly, as is usual, followed the track to the next igloo and finished the cache there.

We had been entirely without food for days, but we could travel a little faster now that Kratalik's eyes were better. The dogs began to drop, though, and three of them were eaten by us and the live dogs. After we came to Fury and Hecla Strait once more we managed to find open water at Ormond Island and shot some seals, so that from there on it was easy going to Igdloolik.

I waited two days at Igdloolik for Dr. Mathiassen to return from Admiralty Bay. He had encountered better luck than I, as he had found plenty of game the whole distance, and had finished the task he had set himself. As a matter of fact, both of us could return to camp with a feeling of satisfaction. Poor Mathiassen, however, had been very ill during the journey. He could not exist on the diet they supplied; he was accustomed to eating bread, and the meat diet did not agree with him. Akrioq told me that they had discussed what to do if Mathiassen died.

We did our best to map the coast on the way back to Danish Island—fortunately we had made a preliminary survey on the way up, and recognized points we had passed. This land, however, can be accurately charted only from an airplane. From a sledge it is impossible. Sometimes we thought we were well out over the sea only to notice grass poking up through the snow. It was difficult to tell which was land and which was water.

My main trouble was in transporting the sick man. He did not complain and he rode a great part of the distance flat on his back. Toward last he grew strong enough to sit up for short periods, and even take a few steps. Boatsman, our boy, met us with his wife at Awa's place. He had brought a little flour with him and his wife was an expert pancake maker. After Dr. Mathiassen had consumed a few of them he felt fine, and we drove on to our camp.

4

The house was completely buried under the snow. By the use of our snow knifes we cut a passage into the store and found spades to dig out the door of the house.

Boatsman scouted about to find the natives we had left to guard the house, and soon ran back to tell us that they were alive, but buried under the snow.

Sure enough, Patloq, a highly esteemed medicine man, was

buried in his igloo. He was, as his wife said, not a great man for talking and working, but he was a terrible man for thinking, and he took his time when he indulged in his specialty. He had plenty of meat in his house, as well as tea and sugar and flour, so he need go outside for nothing. This seemed as good a time as any other for thinking.

A heavy snowstorm had come up and the snow had buried everything including Patloq's house. But Patloq knew that someone was likely to return home soon, and they would find it much easier to dig him out than he himself would, so he decided to wait.

And hadn't we come along and done just what he had told his wife would happen? Once more he was right, and his wife had to admire his judgment.

Our camp attracted neighboring Eskimos, as usual. Among those who settled down near us were a tall man, Akrat, and his wife and little daughter. He was an elderly man and the best igloo builder I ever met, constructing some snowhouses large enough for dancing. Another native, Anaqaq, a man with a past, determined to settle with us too.

Anaqaq was a Netchilik and came from a distant tribe whose ways were foreign. Over at the Magnetic North Pole, the women are scarce, and it is considered a luxury for a man to have a wife to himself. Instead the men club together to support one woman— and the women love the idea. When a girl has two husbands she is the ruler of the house. She sleeps in the middle of the igloo, which is warmest and coziest, and she does very little sewing. The men repair their own boots, dry their clothes, and do all the housework. Meanwhile the wife lies about making fun of the men if they are not clever enough for her.

When the co-husbands go hunting they compete with each other, and each attempts to bring home the choicest prize in order to win her favor. On the trip the men never eat the tongues and hearts and other delicious bits, but save these portions for their wife.

Anaqaq had been happy, but since faithfulness was one of the tenets of married life there, as everywhere, and two-thirds of his household did not observe the rule, he grew angry.

Anaqaq was both medicine man and physician. His specialty was curing indigestion; when the caribou migrated from the north in the fall many of his patients ate too much and his services were required. Which, of course, kept him away from home much of the time.

While he was absent the co-husband rented out the wife and was paid for her services with caribou tongues, marrow, etc. The co-husband and wife kept this breach of trust a secret from Anaqaq, but the neighbors told him—they always do—and he was deeply hurt. There were but two things for him to do to restore his honor—kill the man or go away. Anaqaq was a decent sort of fellow and chose the latter course.

He merely wandered away, becoming an Arctic nomad, strolling from place to place, suffering cold and privation and loneliness. He visited various tribes for a few days at a time, and then walked on again. He could keep alive by spearing salmon in the lakes and rivers, and he caught an occasional ptarmigan, but it was a hard life. Finally he reached Repulse Bay—he had then been walking for two years.

Captain Cleveland was not of a sentimental turn of mind, and sent him packing after two days. His way led him, along with others of his tribesmen, to our camp, where we thought him only another common, dirty onlooker. As usual, we entertained them all for four days, during which we drained them dry of all the information and stories they could give us. On the fourth day we announced that our hospitality was at an end, and they had better travel on.

Anaqaq left with the rest, but as he walked he thought about us. Something of a philosopher himself, it seemed to him that we were just the kind of people he had been praying for all his life, so he left his friends and returned to us after only two days' absence.

Our faces looked so sympathetic that he could not remain away from us. This flattered me just enough to let him remain until Knud Rasmussen returned. Knud found the unspoiled soul of Anaqaq a gold mine of information and determined to retain the Eskimo as a member of our household. Anaqaq was brimming over with the traditions of his tribe. He had wandered alone over the vast Arctic prairies, and his moods conjured up by starvation and loneliness had made him prey to all the fantastic superstitions of his people. What was left of him was an instrument which only one man could play upon—Knud Rasmussen, whose famous book about these people is based entirely upon Anaqaq's stories.

Knud returned from his trip with tales of adventures and hardships. He and his whole party, including Birket-Smith and

Top. ANAQAQ, THE NETCHILIK ESKIMO, WHO OBJECTED BECAUSE THE CO-HUS-
BAND OF HIS WIFE RENTED HER OUT FOR PRIVATE GAIN.

Bottom. INUYAK, MY PERSONAL SERVANT DURING THE HUDSON BAY EXPEDITION.

Bangsted, had been close to death from starvation, but somehow whenever Knud traveled he always escaped the ultimate disaster and the more hardships there were the more Knud enjoyed life. He was loaded with information and tales.

We always had enough to keep an extra man busy, but for a few days I let Anaqaq idle about acting the summer guest. Then when the time was ripe, I gave him little duties. I returned in the evening from a day's hunting, and saw Anaqaq, as usual, walking about and smiling. I asked him why he had not done his work and he answered, in a very friendly manner, that as he was an angakok he was so holy that he was not permitted to work at all.

I had to fight fire with fire. I said that I, too, was an angakok. Recently I had met a number of ghosts who foretold Anaqaq's arrival, and they also said that while ordinarily he would not be permitted to work, they would especially appreciate it if he tried to be as helpful and industrious as possible while we were in the territory.

Anaqaq and I believed each other, and he plunged into the work and was most helpful. In the latter respect he was quite different from my personal servant, Inuyak, who was the most devoted and the most stupid gentleman's gentleman I have ever seen. The man was a miracle of dumbness, but I liked him. He had been a poor native when I arrived, and he would doubtless be poor the day after I left.

He was a master sleeper. No one else in the world could sleep so long or so often as Inuyak—and it was impossible to wake him. I remember that once he had been lying upon the ledge in a dead sleep for seventeen hours when I needed him to accompany me on a short trip.

Knud had boasted that he could wake Inuyak if necessary, so I challenged him to do so now.

At first he resorted to ordinary methods. These had no more perceptible effect than pouring a glass of water in Lake Michigan. Then he yanked a handful of hair out of the fellow's head. Inuyak, being accustomed to some activity in his hair, merely scratched himself a little and slept on.

He lay on his back with his mouth open, so Knud emptied a cup of sugar in his mouth. Inuyak ate the sugar in his sleep.

Then Knud opened the door and, standing not a foot away from the sleeper, fired his rifle out through the opening. The reverberation rocked the tiny room, and only one man was un-

affected by it—Inuyak. After a couple of hours he wakened naturally, assuring us that he had seldom enjoyed a sleep more.

In all fairness I must say that he was also a great worker. If
neither intelligent nor fast, he was at least persevering. I told
him to shovel the snow away from the front of the house. He
made various objections and excuses, but I finally got him started,
and merely told him to keep at it until I stopped him.

Dinner time came and passed, but Inuyak did not appear.
The cook supposed he had gone hunting, and thought nothing of
his absence. After dinner I walked outside to take my observations,
and after working out the results went to bed. I completely forgot
about Inuyak.

Next morning I saw, far out on the plain, someone shoveling
snow like a wild man—Inuyak. He had shoveled a trench extending hundreds of feet from the house.

I hurried out and asked him what in hell he was doing.

"What you told me to do," he answered.

"Why didn't you come in to eat?"

"Because you said I was to keep on until you told me to
stop."

"But can't you see that there's no sense in shoveling snow
out here?"

"Oh, it has been a long time since I have seen any sense in
any of the nonsense you are doing around here."

The mosquitoes arrived with the first warm weather, and
they added to the general discomfort. Still we traveled about in
boats and added to the many collections we were making for Danish museums. Dr. Mathiassen set up his headquarters at Repulse
Bay, and began intensive excavations of old native ruins there.
The ruins disclosed an entirely different type of culture from the
one now prevalent—the houses had been built of whalebone and
stones, whereas at present the natives lived in snow huts during
the winter and skin tents in summer.

The culture we unearthed was similar to that disclosed by
the ruins in Thule. Those ancient Eskimos had also used whalebone for many purposes, including harpoon heads, etc.

Knud walked to Repulse Bay and came back with a large
package of mail sent us by courtesy of the Hudson Bay Company.
We felt that we were thousands of miles from home (as indeed we
were), yet we were in closer contact with the world than we had
been in Greenland.

I was amazed at the number of letters I received. I had never thought of myself as being popular with the ladies before, but there now descended upon me an avalanche of letters from almost unknown young women who wrote to express sympathy over my wife's death. They offered to marry me and make a home for my two small children—they felt sorry for the youngsters and wanted to mother them, adopt them, send them through school or what-not. The letters made me a little ill.

Only one person did not write and offer to make a home for my children—Magdalene, my good friend of many years. I felt that something was missing.

5

We spent the fall of 1922 in traveling among the natives in the district, and in transporting our collections to Repulse Bay where they were to be picked up by a schooner early in 1923. Dr. Mathiassen and Jakob had been cut off at Southampton Island all summer—the ice in Frozen Strait prevented their returning. We tried to reach the men, realizing that Mathiassen might be suffering again from the exclusive meat diet, but the ice is as bad in the summer as in winter. Eventually Mathiassen managed to return by himself with many adventures to recount. He and Jakob had been almost killed by the natives. The Eskimos had thought them responsible for an epidemic which had visited them as well as a sudden scarcity of caribou.

We planned to be out of Canada by 1924, covering as much territory and making our observations as nearly definitive as possible. Dr. Birket-Smith, with Jakob, was to go south to Port Nelson, Manitoba, and out to civilization via the Nelson River in sledge and canoe. Dr. Mathiassen was to go north to Ponds Inlet in northern Baffin Land, and remain there during the next summer making excavations. Knud Rasmussen intended going west by sledge along the north coast of the American continent to Alaska, Bangsted home south from Hudson Bay, and I to try an overland, overseas route with the two Greenland Eskimo families via Baffin Land, North Devon, Ellesmere Land, and across the bay to Etah and home.

But prior to this I planned to make an extensive foray into the field, mapping the north reaches of Hudson Bay east of Igdloolik along the coast of Baffin Land. With me were Helge

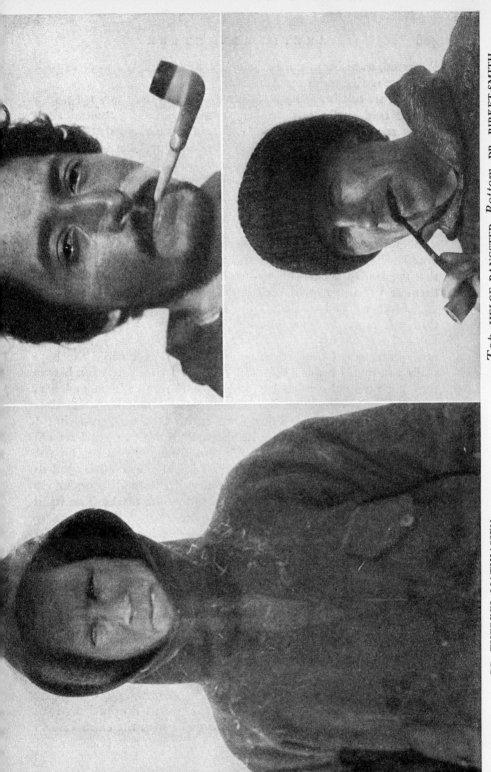

Top. HELGE BANGSTED. *Bottom.* DR. BIRKET-SMITH

DR. THERKEL MATHIASSEN

Bangsted, as assistant, and Akrioq, as headman. We were to pick up more native guides and hunters en route.

We set out immediately after the first of the year, 1923, in a terrific cold spell with the temperature hovering around sixty below zero. Unfortunately we had no concentrated dog food for such a trip, and our sledges were heavy. Our faces had become softened during the Christmas celebrations, and the north wind burned into them. This wind never ceases during the winter months.

We were about a week out of camp when we reached a spot where it became necessary to desert the sea ice for the land. The snow was soft for many miles and we had to whip our dogs cruelly. Both men and dogs did their utmost, but it was clear that the loads were too heavy—we would have to throw off part of them and return for the stuff later.

After we had cached it the snow soon grew hard under a thin soft layer, and we managed to complete a reasonable distance. I was disgusted at the delay our dropping the loads would necessitate, and I decided to return for it myself while the boys made camp and built an igloo. I thought I could be back before they got up in the morning, and thereby reclaim a wasted day.

My dogs were none too pleased at backtracking when they had expected to sleep. They were entitled to their rest, but I was tired too and even more stubborn than the dogs, so I set off.

I made the trip well enough and loaded the boxes on the sledge, but shortly after I had turned about the wind started to blow harder, howling like a fiend. The drifts were alive under my feet, and it was impossible for me to follow the tracks. The wind turned into a storm, the storm into a gale.

I was lost. It was impossible to determine directions, as I could not see the hills. Fortunately it was not a mountainous country, so the danger of falling into ravines was eliminated. Also the direction of the wind was more or less constant, and I could be guided to a certain extent by that.

The storm was blinding, and I stopped several times to examine the snow with the thought of building myself an igloo and holing up until the gale abated, but the snow was packed too solid. Whenever I halted I had great difficulty in getting the tired dogs on their feet again.

Still I kept fighting forward. I was growing more tired by the minute, but the dogs understood me now. I dropped my load again, keeping nothing but my sleeping bag with the extra kamiks and a small square of bearskin. I walked ahead of the dogs and they followed along after me. With no load I ought to be able to get back to camp.

I had to stop now and then to turn my back to the wind and catch my breath. It was so bad that I could scarcely stand upright, and finally had to go back to the sledge and hang on to the up-standers. I could not swing my whip against the gale, and the dogs refused to go ahead.

By this time I could not be far from the others, and I decided that it would be better for me to stop than to run the risk of pass-ing them. I was hungry, too, and when I reached a large rock be-hind which the wind had hollowed out a depression, I stopped. The dogs scuttled into the hole, curled up together and in no time were covered by the snow.

I tried to slice snow blocks with my knife, but the snow was packed almost as solid as ice, and was as hard to penetrate as wood or soil. There was no possibility of making an igloo, so I gave up and sat down. But it was too uncomfortable to sit still for long, and I soon got up. Then I tried the old game of closing my eyes, walking twenty paces forward, turning to the right and walking twenty paces, repeating it twice more and then looking about to discover how far I was from my starting point. I did that for hours, checking on the effect of the wind on my walking, but I soon became too exhausted to stand upright.

Then a craving for sleep gripped me. I felt almost nauseated, and thought that if I could dig a sort of grave under my sledge I might be protected from the gale. I moved the sledge and gouged out a hole where it had been, took the piece of bear-skin and laid it in the hole for a pillow; then I shoved the sledge over the little grave and crawled in at one end, hauling the bag with my kamiks in after me to serve as a door.

The space was just large enough for me to lie flat, and I immediately went to sleep.

It was comforting to be out of the wind and the drifting snow, but I wakened after a time and realized that something was wrong. For a moment I could not tell what it was, but then it came over me that there was no feeling in my left foot.

That is bad. So long as a frozen limb is painful, it is compara-tively harmless, but when there is no sensitivity left, look out!

My first thought was to crawl out and run about to get circu-lation started again. I tried to move the bag at my feet but so much snow had piled up outside that I could not budge it. That frightened me, and I threshed about until I felt a little warmer and more comfortable. Considering my situation a bit more calmly, I decided that nothing could be gained by wasting my strength in this hysterical fashion. In order to get out of my grave I would have to tear down the entire shelter. And I went to sleep again.

When I wakened the second time I was more than ever conscious of the cold. I would have to get out or freeze stiff as a poker. It was still impossible to kick the bag away, and the space was too narrow to permit my bending down and pulling it up. Then I attempted to turn over, lifting the sledge above me, but it was evidently weighted down by a heavy drift. I was buried alive.

Completely up against it, my mind turned to any possible solution. Slowly the desperateness of my situation dawned upon me. The snow was hard and could not be dug away with hands hampered by mittens. I opened one of my watches (I had two in the pockets of my underwear) and felt the time. It was the middle of the day, yet I was in total darkness.

I decided to sacrifice one of my hands, let it freeze and use it as a spade to dig my way out. I pitied myself, as I had plenty of uses for both hands.

But even this was a flop. I satisfied myself that my hands, even if frozen, could not be used for tools. They cannot be kept stiff, and break easily. I had to give up the idea and held the frozen hand against my body to thaw it out.

Then I resorted to using my head. One thought that came to me was to try to move my bowels and form a chisel of the excrement, which would immediately freeze, to dig the hard snow. But first I decided to take the piece of bearskin under my head and scrape with it.

I chewed on the edge of the skin and it froze hard as glass instantly. With this it was possible to dig. I remember that time after time I put it back into my mouth to moisten it and let it freeze again.

I lay there with my eyes closed and scraped away. When a man is in the dark it is some comfort for him to keep his eyes shut —at least then he cannot see even if it is daylight. I made progress, but what slow progress!

My clothes were the same as the natives'—two layers of skin, the inner one with the fur turned in, and the outer with the fur turned out. I wore no belt and the garments hung loose about me so that I would not sweat. The idea is always to remain a little cool, but dry—it not only makes clothes last longer but prevents rheumatism when a man grows older.

Now, however, my movements in the grave pulled the coats up so that the loose snow I scraped away worked its way up against my bare stomach. Still I kept at it, and after a while had a hole leading into the open.

With success in sight I grew impatient. I could not forget that my foot was frozen, and as the hole grew a little larger it looked so tempting that I tried to work my way out through it. I had to bend in a snakelike coil to get my head down to the opening, but I did it and pushed outward. But the hole was still too small, and I stuck fast with only half my face out.

Unfortunately my whiskers were directly beneath the broad frozen mud runner and, as there is always moisture about the mouth, they froze fast to the runner and I could not move either forward or backward. I was so doubled up in my grave that I had no strength to do a thing. Outside I saw the heavens and felt the snow, but I was caught like a fox in a trap, and I felt sure that this was the end.

How long I lay in that cramped position I do not know. Perhaps I fainted. The snow had covered the upper part of my face, filled my eyes and nose so that I could scarcely breathe. The air was a vicious mixture of flying snow and, as I inhaled it, I knew that I could not last for long. My thoughts turned to my home in Denmark, to my mother, and to my good friend Magdalene who had not written to me. I decided that I would have to write her. At the same moment I realized how ridiculous it was to plan anything in my situation.

I was suddenly so angry that I made a last effort and jerked my head back into the hole.

The relief was heavenly. The grave felt cozy again. I wiped my eyes free of snow and rubbed my face which, I could tell, was badly frozen. Then I felt something warm and sticky coursing down my neck. It was blood. I had yanked part of my beard away and the skin with it. I ran my hand along the sledge runner above and felt the hair frozen to it. Then I became aware of the stinging of my face. Since then I have never had quite so much beard around my mouth.

But I had no time to lie idle. I was growing more ravenous by the minute, and once more it was dark outside, so I went back to the job of digging myself out with the frozen bearskin.

Working in spurts of nervous energy I soon had scraped a

hole which I was sure would be large enough to let me through. I was as excited as a young actress making her debut—this was my chance for life and I crammed my head through the opening. The drift filled my eyes immediately, and I was caught once more at the shoulders.

I had heard that a dying man is able to make a last super-human effort to save himself. I exhaled, and jammed myself a little farther into the opening. Then, the craving for air being overwhelming, I sucked my lungs full, expanding my chest to its utmost. It was painful, but I felt the sledge give slightly above me, and I inched forward, repeated the process and this time the sledge moved perceptibly.

Inch by inch I pushed ahead until I found myself with my right arm free. I gave one last lunge and was out!

There standing upright on the sledge, weighted down with snow, was my snow knife. If I had only been wise enough to take it inside with me, none of this would have happened.

I got to my feet, and immediately tumbled over. I thought nothing of it and got up again, only to fall once more. Then I realized that something was seriously wrong with my left foot— there was no feeling in it whatever. I beat it with my knife, and felt nothing. Then I examined it closer and found not only the foot but the leg frozen. It was impossible to bend the joints and impossible to stand upright, so I crawled.

I first looked for the dogs. They were still asleep and buried in the snow, so I did not disturb them. In two hours and a half of crawling I was close to our camp. Suddenly I saw a dog standing just ahead of me. He became frightened, turned about and ran. I followed the dog's tracks and reached the igloo.

My friends cut off my kamik and found that the foot was as bad as I had anticipated. There was but one consolation: it did not hurt so long as it was frozen. I ate enough food to satisfy me, and then went to sleep. When the leg thawed out it would be impossible to rest.

A throbbing pain wakened me before long and we decided to take a look at the foot. Never would I have believed that such a change could occur in so short a time. My foot was puffed up like a football, and Bangsted's false optimism sickened me almost as much as did the injured limb.

Next day it was plain to see that the foot would only handi-cap me in walking, so we resolved to return to our base at once.

All of us were in a bad mood. I cursed my luck, but that did not help us now.

We left most of our outfit—Dr. Mathiassen would pass here later on his trip to Ponds Inlet and pick it up—and with light sledges we set out. I rode on Akrioq's sledge, and made a point of keeping the foot frozen. It did not hurt me then. But it was a bad week.

When we passed Awa's house we discovered a native woman doctor who said she specialized in healing frozen limbs. She volunteered to accompany me to Danish Island, and I accepted her offer.

Thus I returned only to lie flat on my back and watch the others busy as bees completing their three years' researches and investigations.

Gangrene, as it develops in a frozen limb, is not so painful as it is odorous. It stinks to heaven, and one cannot get away from it. The nurse had a special cure. She captured small lemmings, the Arctic mice which multiply faster than guinea pigs, killed them beside me and laid the warm skins on the open wounds, bloody side down. After some hours, during which she caught more, she peeled off the skins, the decayed flesh adhering to them, and replaced them with new ones. She also muttered magic formulas over the foot and sang pain-killing songs.

Nevertheless, the flesh fell away until the bones protruded. I could endure no blankets touching it, and the sight of it sent my nerves jangling. If the room was warm, the stench was unendurable; if it was cold, I froze. I went through a living hell, and each night felt that the old man with the scythe was close after me.

When a man is sick and cold and lonely he gets strange ideas, and one day I told the nurse that I wanted to have those toes off. She thought that might be the best thing to do, and she knew just how to do it—bite them off at the joints and prevent the ghosts from occupying my body—her mouth would close the wounds immediately. I thanked her very much, but took no stock in her method; fitted a nail puller over each toe and banged it off with a hammer.

I cannot attempt to describe the physical pain—but there was a spiritual pain, too, in discarding a portion of my own body, even a part that would never be of any use to me again.

6

It was at this time that we said good-bye to the two scientists. They had completed their investigations and still had a long trip before them. Knud Rasmussen also set off on his big trip along the northern coast of America. He took with him the young Kraviaq and the widow Arnalunguaq. We would not meet again until we reached Denmark.

I was left with two families: Akrioq and his wife Arnanguaq, Boatsman and his young wife. The former couple had been married for many years and now surprised us, and themselves, by having a baby, a little girl. They named her Navarana, for my late wife, which, of course, placed the responsibility for her upkeep squarely upon my shoulders.

Bangsted was to remain at our camp through the winter and go out next year by sledge. Meanwhile it was his responsibility to watch out for all the boxes of valuable collections which were to be sent home next year.

We had been informed that the steamer which visited Chesterfield Inlet every summer carried a doctor, and I decided to go down there to have my foot examined. The wounds refused to heal, and I was in constant discomfort.

I took my pal Inuyak with me. We understood each other, and he had become very helpful to me. We had to hunt on the way, and my foot bothered me, but we finally reached Fullerton Harbor and had company from there on. Captain Cleveland overtook us with a boatload of fur. He was intimately acquainted with the coast along there, and pointed out the spot where Portuguese whalers had burned their ship twenty years ago because of the captain's cruelty, and the location of the grave of a girl whom the whalers had killed. His stories were constantly fascinating.

At Depot Island we met three constables of the Canadian Mounted Police. These fine men were tall and well disciplined, and proved pleasant companions—especially as they had tea and sugar. Still, it was interesting to see them hunting eggs to bring home to the barracks, as one of their duties was to prevent the natives from collecting more eggs than they could eat on the spot.

There, too, I visited a grave which contained the body of an old shipmate of Cleveland's. He had died during a whaling expedition, and been buried. The stones had fallen aside, and the man lay there as if in sleep, his face dry and his gray whiskers curling.

KRAVIAQ

ARNANGUAQ AND HER HUSBAND, AKRIOQ

Cleveland swore that his face was beardless when he died. We covered the body again and went on.

There are houses, a church, police barracks and a number of residents at Chesterfield Inlet. I was invited to be the guest of the Hudson Bay Company post for as long as I cared to stay. Chesterfield Inlet is the main trading post in the district, and the various traders bring their furs there to be sent south by steamer.

George Mitchell, the trader from Eskimo Point, arrived while I was there. He had been lost, like myself, during the winter. His nose was frozen entirely off, as were one kneecap and the toes of one foot. He was still in bad shape.

From the inland near Baker Lake came Mr. MacDonald and others to meet and compare their "take" of skins. The Hudson Bay Company divides the country into districts, and the employees of the most profitable district win a bonus in addition to their salaries each year.

I had ample opportunity to observe the Mounted Police in their barracks. The high standard of this force is world famous, and I found the men to be most superior. I visited them often, and had a grand time with them. Inspector Munday's beautiful wife, who was a writer as well as an interesting personality, was very hospitable.

There was also a Catholic mission at Chesterfield Inlet. The leader, Father Turquetill, was a fine man. The missionaries I had encountered previously had not had much education, and it was a pleasant surprise and a comfort to meet a man of the cloth superior to most in intelligence and learning. Father Turquetill was a delightful person to know.

He was gifted with the ability to attract people to him. Yet it seems to me the danger of such a man as a missionary is that he may win over many natives of minor intelligence merely by the facility of his tongue and his understanding of human nature. And they may actually perceive nothing of the message he brings.

While we waited for the steamer I dug among the ruins sufficiently to convince myself that the ancient culture was closely akin to the "Thule culture" we had encountered in all the other ruins.

I also went out in a whaleboat after walrus at Marble Island. The island holds singular significance for the natives whether they are converts or not, since there is a superstition which forbids their walking upright when going ashore. When a man first steps upon the island he must immediately drop to his hands and knees

Top. THE BOAT IN WHICH INUYAK AND I WENT TO CHESTERFIELD INLET FOR A DOCTOR TO TAKE CARE OF MY FOOT.

Bottom. HUDSON BAY NATIVES CONSTRUCTING A KAYAK.

and crawl to prove his fear of, and respect for, the ghosts. The Eskimos told me about it as we approached the island and asked me to do them the favor of bowing to the superstition even though I was a white man and probably scoffed at it. When the police visited the island they usually refused to crawl and, sure as snow, some tragedy always occurred later. On the other hand, two constables landed on the island one spring and crawled on their hands and knees. Afterward dozens of walrus were killed and a whale was stranded on shore.

One native, I was told, had been converted by Father Turquetill, and after that he landed upright on Marble Island. He fell dead after taking only a few steps. I asked many persons about this unlucky man, and they brought me eye witnesses to the tragedy. I concluded that the man was doubtless so frightened that he had a heart attack. Nevertheless, I crawled and we killed many walrus, and I was thanked for abiding by traditions.

After a number of days the *Nascopie,* a fine modern steamer, arrived with supplies, passengers and, what was most important for me and a number of others, a doctor.

This kindly man certainly had plenty of work ahead of him. George Mitchell was in the worst condition, and his turn came first. The operating theater was the dining room of the Hudson Bay Company house. Mitchell's toes were amputated, but the doctor would not cut off his right leg. He was sure it would have to come off eventually, but he thought Mitchell should wait until he went to England or farther south into Canada.

The former Sergeant Douglas of the Mounted Police arrived with the *Nascopie.* (I wrote of him in my book *Eskimo.*) He was a fine man and a great admirer of the Eskimos and their culture. His actions toward the murderer in the case I described in the novel were actually as I related them. He had now left the service and was employed by the Hudson Bay Company. He held an important position with the company in Winnipeg, but had asked for a minor position at Repulse Bay as there was a rumor that the murderer who had escaped, not from him but from the inspector who had come up to take charge of the case, was now in King William Island. If that was so, Douglas told me, he was going there at his own risk and expense to get his man.

Douglas was assistant surgeon and anesthetized me when I was put on the table. My foot was taken care of, and I was put aside in a corner of the dining room while the doctors worked over the next case. The first thing I remember upon regaining consciousness was hearing one of the young apprentices who had come up on the *Nascopie* being asked to help with the operating. He was unwilling as, he said, he would faint if he looked on at close quarters. There was no one else, and his weak objections were overruled.

He was a youngster who spent most of his time kidding his companions, and he was not too well liked. He usually carried a bag of chocolates about with him, and munched on a piece of candy. Now he was instructed to stand with his hands at the bloodiest point. He begged to be let off, but was ordered to stick to the job. He grew white while the doctor amputated a number of infected fingers and, after a few seconds, fainted and dropped to the floor.

Arctic men are never squeamish. The boy had failed, and in doing so had let himself in for a practical joke. Hurriedly one of the men snatched the bag of chocolates from his pocket, emptied the candy on the table, and dropped one of the fingers of the patient into the bottom of the sack. After which the candy was replaced, and the whole thing stuck back into the boy's pocket. When he came around he was told to go outside and get some fresh air. I never heard what happened to him, because the steamer took him away shortly afterward.

While I was still dizzy from the ether the district manager approached me and inquired whether I knew anything about a certain bank, the Landmandsbanken in Denmark.

"Do I know it? It is our bank, safe as the Bank of England."

Then he went on to say that the bank had failed, the president of it was in prison, and told me a number of other stories to amuse a sick man. I assured him again that it was our bank, that our debts to the Hudson Bay Company were to be paid from our funds in it, etc. He was not especially encouraged by this, but I told him not to worry. If the bank had failed and our expedition was considered shaky, I would guarantee to pay back the money myself.

"Very well," said the district manager, "but who are you? How do we know you are responsible?" The papers stated that every man in Denmark was affected.

I was in a bad situation, but the Hudson Bay people were very considerate and told me that I should continue to regard myself as a guest of the company. The thing could be straightened out somehow. I said that the King of Denmark was the sponsor of the expedition, but this did not seem to impress them. A short time before a Norwegian had received 200 kroner ($40) from the Norwegian King. The fellow thought this sufficient proof that the King of Norway was his sponsor, and had promised to award numerous medals and crosses from his sovereign. They never appeared. Those distant kings had been called upon too often in vain.

I had no reason to complain, however. I realized that the district managers had to be on the lookout for fakers. On the whole, they were extremely kind to me.

The doctor said that he really thought he should cut more off my foot, but gave me the chance first to see if it would cure up as it was. I was not to walk, however, until the wound was entirely healed. In fact, he advised me to go out with the steamer in order to save my leg. I could not do this, however, as I had to take my collections and my natives back home.

The post returned to normal after the *Nascopie* departed. The various traders went back to the outposts, and I embarked on a company schooner to Repulse Bay. Our old friend, Captain Cleveland, had gone out into the world on a vacation; his successor was Jimmy Thom, a vigorous young Scotchman. The task of taking Cleveland's place was not an easy one, because the old man's numerous connections hung about and pestered him, rushing in to help themselves at his table after each meal. Thom soon put an end to that practice.

Douglas, the former sergeant of the Mounted, also went with us to Repulse Bay. Of all the men I met in Hudson Bay I liked him best. We spent a great deal of time together as I had been given strict orders not to walk. My camp was now at Vansittart Island, and Frozen Strait between was clogged with ice. By using a cane, I managed to get about a little and was able to take part in the whaling.

The natives were not bad at it. They had learned the rudiments of whale hunting from the old whalers who in former days had operated in Hudson Bay. The whaling ships never appeared over the horizon any more, since the price of whale oil was low and whalebone was practically useless. Women no longer wear stays, and men have no use for whips since the horse has been succeeded by the automobile. As a result, the whales have considerably more peace.

The Eskimos believe that the whales realize they are better off now, and to express their gratitude they breed more often than formerly. The period of gestation in a whale is seven years, I am told, and it takes considerable time to multiply at that rate. Since the whales are not pursued as they were formerly, however, they are less reluctant about making appearances near the inhabited coasts.

The right, or Greenland, whale, which is present in Hudson Bay, was formerly very valuable. These whales settle into a definite routine and almost never vary from it. They come in to Repulse Bay, feed, and then travel down to Chesterfield Inlet, or a few miles south of it. In fact, more whales were killed inside of Whale Point near Ranken Inlet than in all the rest of Hudson Bay.

Nowadays the Hudson Bay Company furnishes the natives with boats, lines and harpoons for whaling; the H.B.C. is naturally interested in having the Eskimos satisfied.

We went out in the boats. Fortunately Repulse Bay is not deep and two lines are sufficient, though we always had three in our boat.

The whale was first wounded by a hand harpoon which discharged an explosive cartridge. When a whale is struck he dives for the bottom, and can remain submerged two hours or more. The men in the boat must be on the alert, of course—when he starts for the surface he comes with such force that, if the boat is in his path, the crew will be injured. When he appears on the surface he cannot dive immediately, but must take a few moments to fill his lungs with fresh air. This is the moment to let him have the second harpoon. After that, he usually heads straight for the open sea.

Except for human hunters and killer whales, the ordinary whale enjoys as fine a life as can be imagined. He has merely to sink to the depths to find the small winged snails as thick as cereal. Then he opens his mouth, thrusts out his tongue, and moves forward. I have often thought it must be fun to swim about in one's own food. When the whale's mouth is full, he pulls in his tongue, closes his jaws and rises to the surface to spew out the water and swallow the delicious morsels he has picked up. I envy him his narrow throat. Think how long it takes him to get his dinner down—and what can be finer than to dawdle over a good meal!

It takes a great deal of skill and practice to get near a whale, as they are extremely sensitive beasts in spite of their size. When they are submerged there are always thousands of bubbles floating to the surface. These we call the whale's "water," and it is curious but true that if a boat crosses the whale's water the animal senses it and can get away.

There are a number of native superstitions about whale hunting as there are about everything.

From olden times there has been a gentlemen's agreement between men and whales that no woman should be present at the hunting. This resulted from a legend that at one time a woman harpooned a whale and thereby insulted all whalekind and kept them away for many years.

When I was in Hudson Bay an old angakok had revived the tradition, and no woman was even permitted to be outside her tent while the men were hunting whales. I saw them disappear when we set out. Only old ladies past the age of fertility (and therefore regarded as men) could run about from tent to tent relating what was happening out at sea.

The kill is accompanied by the greatest excitement and confusion, but after that comes the dull and tiresome job of towing the carcass home. "Pull and be damned!" the old hands cried. And hour after hour the men hauled on the oars, seeing only the slightest ripple in the water behind the whale to indicate any progress. I pulled on my oars to help drag in the two whales we killed, and my only reward was the thought of the great quantity of meat and blubber we had behind us.

In the days of old—as a matter of fact, it was no longer ago than immediately preceding the war—whaling was profitable in Hudson Bay. Men then killed whales with hand harpoons and open boats, the so-called "romantic" way. The hell it was! Then the whalebone was so valuable that the whalers cut it out and let the carcass float away. This was often the occasion of great celebration by the Eskimos when the meat afterward drifted to shore. Now we were out for the meat and did not even consider the whalebone.

The tides ran so high that it was possible to pull the whale in at high tide, secure it, and have it deposited on the beach at low tide.

When we came in with the first whale the women ran down to greet the fallen enemy and pay their tribute. Each had a white stone tied on her forehead by a piece of sealskin line as a mark of respect for the great animal. They took water in their mouths and spat it out over the whale's mouth. The dead beast was then content and would not take offense at having been killed.

Top. Left: REINDEER ESKIMO WEARING HOMEMADE PROTECTION AGAINST SNOW BLINDNESS. *Right:* REINDEER ESKIMO ON THE POINT OF DEATH FROM STARVATION.

Bottom. Left: NETCHILIK WOMAN. *Right:* NETCHILIK MAN EATING MEAT.

Then the feasting began. The feast is usually the natives' downfall because it lasts at least two days, the minimum for a good meal if an Eskimo can eat as much as he wants.

The mattak of a whale is the most delicious thing in the North. It is the enormously developed epidermis, and tastes similar to, and a little better than, walnuts. It is a dream to chew, and one can eat an almost unbelievable amount. Perhaps this is due to the fact that it is an excellent cure for scurvy and answers a simple craving of the system. At any rate, the natives eat until they can no longer chew.

Then at last they begin cutting up the whale to store the meat and blubber for the winter to come. It is not pleasant stuff to handle when one's stomach is filled almost to bursting. Consequently, the work does not go very fast. After a day or so one remembers that he has skins to cure, another has to go for rabbits, a third must go out and look for caribou to make a new coat. Then they all decide to rest a day or two. Meanwhile the whale is never tied properly; a spring tide or a wind will blow up a storm, and the whale will drift out to sea.

But the natives never care or take it seriously. They think it a good joke. Here they have worked hard and believed the winter's meat supply taken care of, enough for men and dogs and lamps—and now it is gone. The situation is screamingly funny, and it never occurs to them to regret their inefficiency or indolence.

There was little to do at Repulse Bay, and I spent most of the time with Jimmy Thom and Douglas. The natives from Committee Bay came down to trade and, as most of them knew Douglas, he could be of great help to Thom in judging which ones should be given new traps. But since Douglas' interests were now somewhat different from what they had been before, the Eskimos were confused. They could not understand that Thom was now in charge of the post, while Douglas had formerly been the head of the district and had even arrested a few of the natives. Curiously enough, he was invited time after time to visit the men he had previously arrested—they liked him and said they had had the best time in their lives during the period of their incarceration. But from his prisoner who was supposed to be at King William Island he heard not a word, though he inquired of everyone. He learned later that the man had died shortly after he broke away from the inspector.

During the fall the natives turned pagan again. They had been Christian for more than a year and it had done them no good

—the dogs had come down with distemper just the same. The
Eskimos had even gone so far as to hang tiny crosses about the
dogs' necks, but it had not helped. Then a young woman remembered that once as a child she had cured a dog by binding pagan
amulets around its neck. She was a cautious, clever girl, so now
she fastened both a cross and a round piece of wood to several
dogs' necks, and the animals recovered. Then, by a scientific
system of trial and elimination, they set about to determine which
had been responsible for the cure. Half the remaining sick animals were treated with crosses, the rest with the wooden amulets.
The dogs wearing the pagan wood recovered. Whereupon the natives returned to the ways of their forefathers, and doubtless remained satisfied until another problem arose.

I could do nothing but sit around and wait for my foot to
heal. I read and wrote a great deal and listened to Douglas, who
had many tales to tell me of his recent year at home in England.
He had driven about in a little car and looked up all his old
friends. His descriptions sounded so alluring that a great longing
for home came over me. There was an emptiness within me, a
need for something, so I wrote a letter to my dear friend Magdalene and asked her to marry me. It was strange that this had never
occurred to me before. The exciting part of it was that I could not
hear from her for at least a year and a half. I would have something to look forward to.

7

At last Inuyak and I left for Vansittart Island. A whaleboat
belonging to the Hudson Bay Company took us part way, but
turned back when we ran into ice. The Eskimo in charge of the
boat dared not drive it through the ice since the boat had to be
used at the post and he would be held responsible for any dam-
age. I understood this well enough, but I had no inclination to
return to Repulse Bay since I could not make another attempt
to get to the island until the ice was solid. Besides, Bangsted
was alone there with the Greenland natives and did not have
sufficient ammunition to last him through the fall.

I hurt my foot in walking, and soon discovered that it was
impossible for us to go any farther. While speculating on our situation I saw a man walking up the valley toward us. He proved to
be Usugtak, Inuyak's brother, whom I knew well. He was a
friendly but none too industrious man. He said that he had been
stranded here since last spring when he had started for our camp

at Vansittart Island with the intention of attaching himself to the expedition. He was never a fast traveler, and he had remained here so long that he was unable either to cross Hurd Channel or to return whence he had come.

He had something, however, that might be called a boat. It was no prize cutter, but it would float if the passengers bailed constantly.

We announced our willingness to go home with him and remain until he could ferry us across. We were welcome, he said, especially as they had nothing to eat, nor had they had anything for many days.

We remained with his family overnight. He was quite right—they had nothing to eat but seaweed and shrimps, and lived in the most incredible filth I have ever encountered among the natives.

During the night the wind blew the pack ice out of the channel right against the opposite shore. I believed it would be possible to row over the open water and then cross the pack ice on foot to the beach of the island. We would have to traverse the entire island then—it would take us at least three days—but that would be better than staying here where there was no food.

I outlined my idea. The men consented to try to row us across and we walked down to look at the boat. It was a specimen that would have won a prize as a curiosity in any exhibition—certainly it was of a shape never seen before by any boatbuilder. Still, if it would hang together until I was across I was satisfied.

We finally got the boat into the water. All of us had to sit on the gunwale on the port side, because a hole on the opposite side was larger than the tins used for bailing. The boat was constructed exclusively for runs of not more than ten minutes. At the end of that time it was full of water and had to be hauled up onto an ice pan and emptied. It was rather exciting; we had to haul it up twice before we reached pack ice solid enough to walk upon.

Inuyak and I had nothing to carry but Bangsted's mail and some ammunition. We yelled good-bye and jumped. Then I remembered that the doctor had advised me to remain in bed for some time. It was a fine time to think of the advice. The boat had turned back and we were standing on floating ice. The pans were not as large as we had thought, and few of them would support the weight of even one person. This was especially disagreeable to a man whose toes had recently been cut off.

We must run and hop and leap; if we stood still too long the ice began to tip and sink under us. On certain slabs we could not land at all without getting our feet wet. This sort of thing had been my greatest pleasure as a boy, but I lost the taste for it that day and have never done it since unless absolutely forced to do so.

My foot hurt as much as it had before the amputation. The only thing I had actually won by the trip to Chesterfield Inlet was the knowledge that I was broke. But I had no time to consider that now. I kept on jumping, Inuyak close after me. I heard him groan once when his legs slipped into the water but I could not stop to help him. Like Eliza, I leapt from ice pan to ice pan, but my ice cakes were not papier-mâché. Our safety depended upon our speed, and at last we felt the solid shore beneath our feet, both of us hot and breathing heavily. We had been on the ice for only half an hour, but it was a half-hour of grueling exercise.

Then I remembered my foot. Its throbbing almost drove me wild. I sat down and tried to yank off my kamik, but it was too painful. Then the reaction to our labor set in and we began to grow cold. We had to get up and walk, yet I screamed like a madman when I put any weight on my foot.

Inuyak pulled my kamik off—it was full of blood. The stitches had cut through the flesh, and the wound lay open.

This was disconcerting to look at, so I made Inuyak take needles and sinew and sew the ends together. I closed my eyes and set my teeth against the pain I knew was coming—and it did not come. I felt nothing whatever. Inuyak was a splendid surgeon. He said that it is dangerous to get dirt in wounds, and to avoid it he drew the sinew through his mouth, sucking it clean. He also rinsed needles and scissors with his tongue, and the operation did not hurt in the least.

We turned my bloody kamik inside out, then put it back on; but it was impossible for me to walk until the next day.

Inuyak gathered willows and built a little fire to heat some water. We joked about the provisions we had voluntarily left at Repulse Bay, assured each other that we didn't give a damn what happened and lay down to sleep. It was chilly now, so we lay with our backs together and slept until we were so stiff that we had to get up.

From the Eskimos in Greenland I learned to derive a certain pleasure from sleeping while half frozen. It was a perverse pleasure, I know, but it has made it possible for me to endure many cold nights.

We walked on. The sky looked clear, and it would probably

be a good day for traveling if I could stand it. We bagged a few
young gulls—the fools often remain long after the older and
wiser ones have migrated to the South—and boiled them in a pot.
The soup was warm and strengthening. A little later we ran across
two ground squirrels and took them along for lunch.

Still the day did not see us far. I had to sit down whenever
I felt the blood running too fast from my foot.

That night I was awakened by Inuyak screaming out in fear.
He had dreamt he was drowning. In reality we were covered by a
heavy layer of snow. We wore only our summer clothes and were
sure that we were freezing. We thought we might as well walk
on until we came to Bangsted's camp, wherever it was. We only
sat down to rest occasionally, and again found a few gulls and
ptarmigans to eat. There was nothing to worry us especially, except my foot.

Finally, far up the valley we saw a mysterious object moving.
It looked a great deal like an elephant, but since that could not
be, I thought immediately of caribou and brown bear. We approached, and saw four legs moving under something very bulky.
We fired our guns. The burden was tossed off with a cry of alarm,
revealing Bangsted and Akrat, who had been carting caribou
skins from their cache to camp.

Bangsted, poor fellow, had to be told of the death of his
father, a fine man. It is such messages that take the joy out of
life in the Arctic. News from home is an event, and one always
expects only good news.

Bangsted had killed many walrus, caribou and seals; the dogs
were in fine condition, with plenty of meat and blubber for the
coming winter. We decided to move back to Danish Island before
it grew too cold, and take advantage of our house there as long as
any coal was left. The shack was too large to heat with blubber,
and would require too much of the stuff that could better be utilized as dog food. Bangsted guaranteed that there was enough coal
to last until the day after Christmas, and we planned to depart
for good on that day.

All our plans were made with that date in mind. Our provisions for traveling were set aside, the remainder to be divided
between our helpers.

Bangsted had got a good collection of birds. He had played
the ignoramus to advantage, claiming not to know the difference
between game birds and those protected by law. He had "mis-

Top. A SKIN BOAT ROWED ONLY BY WOMEN.

Bottom. Left: TAPARTEE'S WIFE, WHO ASKED US TO LEAVE HER FOR A FEW
MINUTES AS SHE WAS GOING TO HAVE A BABY. *Right:* TAPARTEE.

taken" a number of cranes for ptarmigans, and brought them back home for the museum, where they were very welcome.

We spent the rest of the fall at the house at Danish Island. Practically the only break in the routine was the birth of a child to Tapartee's wife. Tapartee himself was away, and the wife had stayed with us during the summer. We were visiting her tent one day for tea when she told us that perhaps we had better get out— she was giving birth to a baby. It was a girl, which was the more interesting as she had boasted to Arnanguaq that *her* child would be a boy. Arnanguaq's child was the little Navarana.

The woman dug a hole in the ground and stood boxes beside it to support her arms. I asked her if she needed any help, and she said no, she was all right. She got down on her knees between the boxes, and we returned to our house.

Shortly afterward the woman came into the house to tell us what had happened. She had, as predicted, given birth to a boy. However, every child must have its navel attended to before a word is spoken in the room, and the mother was about to perform this rite when the boy's sister had run unexpectedly into the room shouting something about her clothes. This breach of etiquette had so embarrassed the boy that he drew his genitals inside his body and promptly became a girl.

The mother was furious, and the little girl repentant to the point of tears. Arnanguaq was delighted—she had not been bested. I tried to discover whether or not the mother actually believed the story herself. She assured me it was true, and I actually think she believed it was.

As I fully expected, the coal did not last as long as we had figured it would, but we stretched it out as far as possible, and traveled about visiting when the ice grew firm. Also we had to haul our collections to Repulse Bay, and Bangsted made the trip a number of times. We found a short cut which permitted us to complete the journey in three days during good weather.

And so we were all in our little house at Danish Island that last Christmas, 1924—Bangsted and I, the two families from Greenland, and Inuyak, Anaqaq and Akrat.

We were a little sad on those last days. We had resorted to the burning of our furniture to keep warm, and were going to divide the rest among our friends. Four men were to split up the house between them. They were also to share our tools and pots and cups which had not already been given away. Bangsted and I felt rather badly when some distant natives came to visit at the last moment.

Each time we gave them anything we felt the reproachful eyes of the four upon us. They felt that we were giving away their property.

Anaqaq now suffered a change of viewpoint. For many years he had been entirely without possessions of his own, because his position as a cleric permitted him to own nothing. Now he thought perhaps he had done enough for the spirits and the ghosts, and it might be a good idea for him to turn Christian for a while. Also, if he did that there would be nothing to prevent his marrying.

He had heard of a party of his countrymen arriving from the backlands, so he went to them and spent a tiny portion of his wealth in buying himself a wife. He was a powerfully rich man now, so he bought the fattest woman they had—she was, of course, the most expensive, but he could well afford her. She cost him six boards from the inner wall.

A fat wife naturally points to a good provider. Unlike jewels as an indication of a husband's affluence, a woman cannot discard her fat at will.

Inuyak considered following Anaqaq's example, but in the end he did not. He would go back to his brother, Usugtak, to spend a year in idleness, and then doubtless return to his former poverty.

We had prepared for Christmas by saving all our delicacies for one last celebration. Bangsted and I decided to make doughnuts for the audience. I knew nothing about the consistency of the dough required, and I added an equal amount of shortening and flour. The doughnuts consequently exploded when dropped into the boiling fat. I called everyone to take a look, and everyone confirmed what I had seen happen. As soon as the delicious dough struck the boiling oil it disappeared. They all thought it the most amusing stunt they had ever witnessed.

We finally ate the dough without baking it.

Next day was Christmas. The table disappeared into the stove and after it the benches. We sat on our sleeping bags on the floor with the feeling of parting heavy in our hearts. This was the last evening of our years together—tomorrow we would say good-bye forever. Finally I told everyone to go to bed; it was growing colder. Each one went to his room and returned with his bunk. We fed them all to the hungry stove and slept on the floor so that we could be together a little longer.

8

On December 26th, at daybreak, we were up and ready to start.

Bangsted took the least provisions, since he could buy more at Repulse Bay. We had our three sledges loaded, and turned north.

As usual with the Eskimos, there were no farewells. We only shouted at the dogs. But when we came to the point we stopped and turned our heads for one last glimpse of the little house. Bangsted was standing quietly watching after us. He had a long trip before him too.

There were three sledges of us: Boatsman and his wife Akratak on one, Akrioq and Arnanguaq with the little Navarana on the second, and I alone on the third. Anaqaq and his new wife also trailed along for a time as we took with us the last meat from the house—he said that he merely wanted to visit a number of friends along the way. The first night he arrived in camp long after the rest of us, but he bragged that it was simple for the others to make haste with their tiny women; his wife was big and fat and beautiful, and hauling her was a torture to his dogs.

Two days north of Lyon Inlet we came upon the first native settlement, where we stopped over for a while. A terrific gale blew up making it impossible to travel, and the pack ice drifted out far from the always firm ice floe, making conditions favorable for hunting walrus. We wanted to have our sledges loaded with meat and the dogs stuffed with food before we proceeded.

We also met a number of natives whom the Greenland Eskimos loved so much that they invited them to follow us home to Thule and live with us. They were, my natives told me, fine people and not "disgusting" like most of the Central natives.

Aguano was one of these men. He was now en route to Ponds Inlet, and perhaps beyond. Who could tell? He was always traveling, his object being to find his Nuliaqatie—the man with whom he shared wives. The two were especially good friends and owned two women jointly; both women were loved equally well, so they said, by both men. Neither of the women could bear children, and therefore the men had arranged to live with one woman for a year, and then shift. They had done this for several years and all four concerned were pleased with the idea.

Qinoruna, the wife now living with Aguano, was a clever, as

well as a kind, woman. She had recently bought a little baby from another woman, who had inherited it in turn from the mother. Qinoruna had paid one old frying pan for the child, but the day after the exchange loud arguments arose. The baby was sick but, on the other hand, the frying pan was cracked. What to do!

I was called in as judge and settled the whole matter by telling the women that, since both items in the deal were inferior, they should stick by their bargains. The baby was a poor little thing whose face was almost blue, and it was impossible to make it nurse from Arnanguaq's breast. Little Navarana was more than a year and a half old now, and Arnanguaq still had plenty of milk for a second child.

We killed several walrus and, after spending a few more days drying our clothes, moved on north, shooting a number of caribou. They are queer animals with defective eyesight. They watched us approaching across a lake, but apparently believed we were other animals and let us come close to them. They consider nothing dangerous to their safety until they get the scent.

At Pingerqaling I met a remarkable woman, Atakutaluk. I had heard of her before as being the foremost lady of Fury and Hecla Strait—she was important because she had once eaten her husband and three of her children.

It had been a long time ago, before the natives had either guns or wood. Wood was the principal commodity desired and Atakutaluk and her party were driving north across Baffin Land to buy wood for their sledges.

On the way they had to travel with such implements as were at hand. They rolled hides together and soaked them in water, then let them freeze in the shape of sledge runners. As crossbars they used frozen meat or salmon. We saw many similar sledges still in use at Boothia Bay, constructed from musk-ox skin. Theirs had been of caribou skin.

Atakutaluk's party had numbered thirteen persons, and they set out with a load of raw goods for trading. On the way, however, a mild spell of weather descended—this is not unusual even in the Arctic—while they slept in their igloos, and they were awakened by the roofs of their dwellings caving in. The sledges had been left overnight on piles of snow (to keep them away from the dogs) but the sledges, too, had thawed out and been eaten.

It is impossible to travel during the winter without a sledge, and they happened to be in a bad hunting district, so they had to kill their dogs and eat them. Then they devoured their skin clothing, and some of them died of starvation.

Those left resorted to cannibalism.

The next spring by chance our good friend Patloq, the philosopher, passed by with his wife. He saw a half-demolished igloo and drew closer to examine it. On the ledge inside he saw two horrible-looking hags—Atakutaluk and another woman. Neither could walk, and both had great difficulty in speaking.

Patloq inquired about the rest of their party.

"We don't know," the women answered, but indicated with their thumbs a snow pile back of the igloo. There Patloq discovered human bones.

"Inutorpisee? (Did you eat people?)"

"We don't know," they answered.

Patloq could tell by the appearance of the bones that they had been gnawed and split for the marrow which, I am told, is like the marrow of bear bones.

It was difficult to make the women eat anything. When a person is almost starved to death it is painful to eat. They were finally induced to try some meat, and then it was almost impossible to keep them from gorging themselves. Half a day after one has first eaten, a craving for food sets in with such intensity that only a strong-willed person can resist it. The other woman could not do so, and she died three days later in terrible agony. But Atakutaluk resisted her impulses, ate only a little at first, and lived to relate the experience.

Now she was the first wife of Itusarsuk, chief of the community. She was well dressed, merry and full of jokes. She herself told me her story, but she saw that it distressed me.

"Look here, Pita," she said, "don't let your face be narrow for this. I got a new husband, and I got with him three new children. They are all named for the dead ones that only served to keep me alive so they could be reborn."

Her skin was blue around the mouth—which was said to have resulted from eating human flesh—and it was impossible to make the Eskimos admit that she had had the mole previous to the experience. The natives in Hudson Bay do not like to eat bear meat because they think it looks and tastes like human flesh. Which would seem to indicate that many of them know whereof they speak. They also say bear meat produces moles.

Stories about moles are legion. There was said to have been a woman south at Barren Ground whose body was entirely black-

ATAKUTALUK, THE FIRST LADY OF FURY AND HECLA STRAIT—THE WOMAN WHO
ATE HER HUSBAND AND THREE CHILDREN

ened by one because she had slept with a dead man. They had gone to bed together, and she had wakened to find him stiff and cold. She soon turned black all over!

The natives also showed me a pile of stones where it was possible for an angakok to sit and kill people merely by pointing his finger at them. Such tales were numberless, and my two Greenland Eskimos were paupers in native lore in comparison.

We emerged the victors in storytelling, however. The local natives told us an old folk tale about a girl who had refused to marry. Her father then married her to a dog and put them out on an island together. There she gave birth to eight children, whom she placed in a boat made from the sole of her kamik. The children sailed away and eventually became the terrors of the world, namely, the white men and Indians. The island in the incident was said to be Tern Island near Igdloolik.

The local Eskimos were refuted at this point, for we said the event had really happened at Inglefield Gulf where we lived in Greenland. We could weight our argument with the fact that we had seen the grave of the dog—which settled it once and for all. The wise men of the tribe declared us the winners.

I was sorry to leave these people of Pingerqaling, who were as happy as they were remote from neighbors. However, I had to press on.

At Igdloolik I visited my friend Eqiperiang and his two wives, who were sisters. The one in favor at the moment did all the talking and joking, treating the less fortunate sister like a servant. If one happened to pass by a few days later, the former servant might be queen of the day. Eqiperiang then slept on her side of the ledge. It is up one day and down the next for Eskimo women.

We left Igdloolik behind us and set out for Baffin Land. Now we were in an entirely new country, the very seat of all the traditions of the Eskimos. It was, in a sense, sacred ground for a student of these people.

The beginning of the trip was easy, for the country rises gradually from the south. We had trouble, though, with Qinoruna's little baby. It was weak and without proper food. Little Navarana grew fatter by the day and could now stand on her feet and play on the ledge in the evenings. She slept the whole day in her mother's hood, and played at night.

We traversed great plains separated by ravines and lakes. There was an abundance of caribou and ptarmigan for food, and the journey was pleasant for me as there was no rough ice and I could sit most of the days on my sledge and nurse my foot.

One night we were very tired after finally lowering two sledges over a steep waterfall, and decided to turn in and call it a day. I usually slept in the same house as Boatsman—the other two families each had their own igloo. I was soon awakened by Aguano crying outside.

"Pita, Pita! The little baby is dead!" It had been dead when Qinoruna tried to waken it for its feeding. Both the man and the woman cried and said they were sure it must be their fate never to have children. They had had two before—one had been drowned and the other frozen in a snowstorm.

"It is better that he hurry and get rid of me, and try his other wife," Qinoruna wailed.

The little body was sewn inside of two skins, carried out through a hole in the back of the igloo and up to a depression in the cliff where there were many loose stones. Aguano built a grave and placed the baby on it, then covered the dead child with so many stones and in such a helter-skelter manner that no one would suspect it was a grave. He did this, he said, because many Eskimos must pass here between Igdloolik and Ponds Inlet and they might be frightened if they knew this was a grave. He then asked all of us who had helped him with the stones to give him our mittens. We did so, only to see him bury the mittens too. Later on, when it was permitted her to sew again, Qinoruna made us each new ones.

I tried to go on next morning, but we had to remain there for five days. Arnanguaq complained that she was ill; Akratak did not want to drive on, as we had plenty of meat and my foot needed the rest. So we stayed and mourned the customary period, and Aguano was deeply grateful.

When we finally set out Aguano was the last to follow. He and Qinoruna visited the grave once more and stood beside it for a long time. Poor people, they were on their way to their usual divorce, and for some unknown reason would be separated for a year. But there was no doubt that they loved each other. I asked them if they never longed for each other when they were living with their other mates, and they said no. The other ones were just as fine and dear to them.

As we drove on Aguano stopped several times, walked back and swept out the tracks behind our sledges. He did this because the little child who had been so weak in life would, after death, have its full strength and might do violent injury to us if permitted to trail us. It was better to be careful and cover our tracks.

We followed a river with indifferent sledging into Milne Inlet. The inlet itself was hard to traverse, because the snow was deep and soft—the wind apparently never blows at the head of the fjord.

I thought of old Captain Milne, the explorer of the fjord. He was one of the greatest of Scottish whaling captains as well as an explorer. He was also one of the smallest captains I have ever seen on a bridge, being not quite five feet tall. But he knew how to command respect.

It was certainly a long fjord that the old whaler had discovered. It took us two days to reach better ice, and we had to walk along beside the sledges on skis. Aguano owned none, and was handicapped because of it. Finally we came to a seal blowhole and stopped; Akrioq stood beside it, and in less than an hour had killed a seal. We had eaten so much caribou on the journey that we were famished for a change in diet, and sat down to a delicious meal. The dogs ate the skin and blubber, and we cleaned up the whole thing at the one camp.

Next day we reached Toqujan, where many natives were gathered. They were hauling hundreds of narwhale horns on their sledges; many of the beasts had been caught above the ice in Admiralty Bay. According to some of the natives who were able to speak English and to count, they had killed almost a thousand narwhales, and had left a mountain of meat and skin and blubber on the ice. A gale had blown up, broken the ice and swept the meat out into the bay where the natives could see it but not reach it. They saw no less than seven bears eating their cache, until meat and bears and all drifted out of sight.

From Toqujan we could see the big cape at Ponds Inlet on the northeastern shore of Baffin Land—the natives call it Igerssuaq (The Big Pot). We thought we could make it next day, but the Eskimos laughed at us—it was a three days' trip, and the point we could see was a high mountain rather than a little rock.

We drove on toward Ponds Inlet, stopping overnight at a wooden house which had belonged to the unfortunate trader, Janes, who had been killed by Nuralak.

Janes' accommodations had been very scanty. He and his partner were whalers who had decided to establish a trading station on the Patricia River. Janes was left in charge, and his partner failed to put in another appearance. No ship ever arrived to visit him, and he had no material with which to trade. Added to this handicap, Captain Munn established a trading station in the same bay.

Janes got fed up with the situation and decided to go home; but he thought Munn would charge him too much for transportation, so he decided to go out by sledge via Chesterfield Inlet. Before he left, however, he planned to add to his collection of furs. As he had nothing to offer in payment for them, he took them from the natives at the point of a gun. In desperation the natives sent for Nuralak, and Nuralak shot him.

The innocent Eskimos attempted to placate Janes' soul by burying him in a coffin twelve feet long. Some said he was as bad as two ordinary men and therefore needed a coffin twice the usual size. Another man told me that they had constructed the coffin out of boards from his own house, and they dared not cut them lest they injure the dead man more.

Nuralak was given ten years' confinement by a special court which convened in the far north. He was very pleased to be taken south to jail, but he contracted tuberculosis there and died.

The Hudson Bay Company owned the only trading post at Ponds Inlet, having bought out all its competitors. The manager there received me cordially. I also met a native interpreter named Edmonds who had originally come from Fort Chino at Ungava Bay, Quebec Province. He was able to give me much information about the natives and animals around Hudson Strait. As a child he had gone with his father and thirty-six other Eskimos to the World's Fair in Chicago in 1893. All the Eskimos except his father and his own family disappeared there and had never been heard of since.

The natives at Ponds Inlet had "progressed" to the use of wooden houses, but it was certainly no improvement for them. Nothing can be more hygienic than living in temporary igloos and tents, because garbage and filth cannot accumulate. But some of them were living in tiny houses there, and they had no idea how to keep them clean. It was obvious that a great many of them had already contracted tuberculosis. They may have had it before, of course, but their conditions now were far from favorable to a cure. The stench inside the houses was nauseating and the air suffocating. I noticed also that they had bought clothes from the store, and used filthy old rags for bedclothes.

If primitive people are taught to build wooden houses, they should also be taught to keep them clean.

The constable of the Royal Mounted gave us some excellent pemmican (the government kills many buffaloes each year and the Indians turn the meat into pemmican), we renewed our supply of food and ammunition and prepared to set out, stocked sufficiently, we thought, to last us until the spring in case we were lost or held up by the weather.

The manager of the post gave us a large tin box of candy as a last present, and we bade farewell to the friendly people of the community.

9

Ponds Inlet is actually the sound between Bylot Island and Baffin Land. The island's high mountains are stately and impressive. Only the southwestern corner is lowland, a vast plain said to be excellent for pasturage.

Aguano and Qinoruna tagged along with us. They intended now to go as far as Lancaster Sound and hunt, while waiting for their partners to show up. They were supposed to be somewhere along the east coast of Baffin Land.

We had no particular adventures the first few days, caught a couple of seals at their blowholes and encountered beautiful weather. Then as we entered Eclipse Sound a gale struck us and we had to stop for several days in an igloo. The wind was so strong that it tore a side out of the igloo, and the snow drifted until it nearly swamped the shelter. The accident happened because we had made one large igloo to accommodate us all on our last nights together. We scrambled about and got our clothes on—they were filled with snow—and Aguano and I hustled out and repaired the igloo while the other two men stayed inside to protect the girls from the storm.

Next day we heard someone yelling at us far up the coast, and a native staggered toward us begging our help. His people were starving, he said; two of them were dead, and they had no dogs to drive for help. He was the only survivor who could move about, and he looked very ill. I gave him one seal and the food we had counted upon Aguano and his wife using. Then I wrote a note to the police at Ponds Inlet and hurried Aguano back with it.

Thus finally we parted company with the kind young couple, and never saw them again. The three girls cried and expressed their grief at parting in a manner entirely unlike any other Eskimos I had ever met. And at last we were alone and on our final stretch home to Greenland.

Top. ESKIMO WOMEN CARRYING FUEL HOME IN HUDSON BAY.

Bottom. Left: NETCHILIK WOMAN CARRYING HER YOUNGEST CHILD IN HER HOOD. *Right:* TWO HUDSON BAY CHILDREN, FRIGHTENED EITHER BY ME OR THE CAMERA.

Eclipse Sound had less and less snow as we penetrated farther north, and soon the rough ice began to heckle us. We hugged the coast line on the west, and I finally climbed the mountain to discover whether or not it was possible to cross direct to Cape Warrender as the natives of Ponds Inlet do occasionally. It was out of the question now; there was more open water than ice in the middle of the sound. I sighted with my theodolite and discovered that the ice was moving fast; we would have to go farther west.

The weather continued pleasant and the ice fair. Our runners were covered with mud, but as the temperature rose it was difficult to keep the stuff on, so we let it drop as it fell off. Beneath the mud my sledge was shod with whalebone—the sledge is now in the museum in Copenhagen—while the two natives' runners were of iron.

The coast is all mountainous. I climbed to the high eastern cape at the mouth of Admiralty Bay, and the sound was better there, but there was still plenty of open water out to sea. Akrioq thought it possible to cross over, but not a very good idea to try it, so we kept on to the west a few more days.

When we reached a lonely spot called Cape York on the map —the same name as our dear village at home in Greenland—the natives conceived the notion that this might be the place to cross the sound to North Devon. As far as we could see there was a stretch of unbroken ice from coast to coast, and we figured that we could cross in one sleep, reaching the island by the next evening.

We spotted a fine valley on the opposite shore and set out. The going was not bad. In a few places we had to help each other's teams, but this was to be expected. In the middle of the day we saw a bear and wasted two hours hunting it, but in the end he eluded us. When it looked to us as though we were halfway across we stopped for the night and built an igloo.

Not long after we had turned in snow began to fall. This was the worst thing that could have happened. The wind died with the coming of the snow, and, as the compass would not work so close to the Magnetic North Pole, we dared not push on in a blinding storm. Also, the ice had shifted about so much that we could not count upon the old drift marks to show us the way.

After a few hours we heard the wind howling.

We had caught only short naps, but we thought it better to go on now, so we donned our clothes. It was just as well that we did. Before we were ready to leave the house a gale blew up from the southwest, and we could hear the ominous sound of ice breaking up around us.

Loading our sledges in a hurry, we lashed them and hitched the dogs. Then we stood by and waited.

Suddenly Akratak yelled: "Look! There's open water right behind us!"

We turned and saw the open sea at our heels. It looked like a yawning mouth, the jagged edges of ice like teeth grinning at us. We yelled at the dogs and drove on with the wind at our backs.

But soon there was open water ahead of us. The ice pan on which we stood had revolved! We turned and drove the other way, perhaps for two hours, until once more we encountered open water. The ice cracked so suddenly that the dogs almost fell in.

I was frightened now, and we decided to stand by and wait until the gale had blown itself out. The little Navarana needed to get up, so we cut some snowblocks and made a shelter for her mother, Arnanguaq. The two women sat together while we stood and talked about the situation. Suddenly we heard a scream. The ice had parted between the women; Akratak had grabbed up the little child and had run with her. The mother's arms were inside her coat, and she could not get them out in time. Thus the two women were parted by open water, and I ran after Akratak and Navarana. I took the child—she had been lying on her mother's lap with no kamiks on her feet—and stuffed her inside my coat with her feet down inside my pants. She thought this was very funny and laughed hilariously, but her position prevented my jumping back to my friends, and after a few seconds the water was too broad to leap over.

The natives were frightened. We ran up and down the ice searching for a spot where we could cross to each other. Finally Boatsman shouted that he had found a place. I took off my coat, turned it inside out, and poured the child into it. Then I shouted to the father to come and help catch her, and I tossed her like a sack. They caught her, and the mother immediately stuffed her into her hood again. Akratak and I walked farther along the crack until I found a place narrow enough to jump.

Now we came to break after break in the ice. We had stopped thinking about our direction—we only sought to prolong our lives from one moment to the next.

After a while the snow stopped drifting, and the weather turned warmer. The wind still blew, but we could at least see where we were.

We had turned and doubled on our tracks again and again. We saw seals in the water, but none of them came near. A bear was more courageous; he sniffed the air to discover whether we were of any interest to him, but then a wall of ice piled up beside him and he shuffled away.

While we watched the bear our ice pan cracked twice. Boatsman's dogs faced opposite from ours, and he had trouble turning them around in a hurry. He shouted at his wife to jump across to us. He held onto his sledge as long as he could, but it was as if the ice had come alive. An avalanche produced by the milling about of the different pans suddenly grew up around him and overflowed his sledge. He tried to get it free, but the front was entirely buried under ice, and we watched it crack to pieces like a matchbox. Then he tried to save his dogs and cut them loose, but five were unable to dig themselves out as fast as new ice buried them, and they went down.

We shouted at him to try to get to us again—we felt that somehow our safety depended upon all being together—and he abandoned his sledge. On it was everything he owned, and all our spare ammunition, but that could not be considered now. He raced with the sea wall piling up behind him, and won, finally reaching a narrow crack where he could slid over to the rest of us by riding on two small cakes of ice in the open water.

We watched our pan wear smaller and smaller, its edges pulverized by masses of ice that came marching toward us from all sides. Suddenly I saw Boatsman jump up and leap across to the pan where he had left his sledge. It was entirely buried and smashed to bits. I shouted at him to come back, but he did not hear. He sprang on top of the live ice and I saw him scramble to the sledge, grab his harpoon line which had been hung on the upstanders, and dash back again.

It was one of his most valuable possessions and he felt that he could not afford to lose it.

Eventually there seemed to be a lessening of pressure around us, and we thought we could get to a larger pan floating past. Boatsman and I made it across on my sledge, and Akrioq was to follow immediately after. But the pressure began again, his dogs were frightened and pulled his sledge back, so that we were separated after having been but ten feet apart.

We knew that we should wait and not risk our lives in trying to get together until the time was ripe. We were all dreadfully

BOATSMAN

AKRATAK, WIFE OF
BOATSMAN

uncomfortable, our clothes wet from the warmth, and the ice wet too, so that our kamiks were soaked.

But worst of all was having to stand and wait, unable to do anything. We told the women to sleep if they could; they simply lay down on the sledges and were immediately dead to the world. We had been fighting the ice now for thirty hours, and they must have been exhausted.

I also snatched a nap now and then, until Akrioq's ice pan shrunk so small that his family could barely stand on it. His dogs whined in terror, and he knew he would have to try to get across now or never. He started over the ice wall at a spot where it looked fairly quiet, but it began to slip and slide when he was at the very top. The dogs fell and howled in pain. They can stand little ice pressure, because their feet are easily caught and crushed by the heavy, moving ice.

Akrioq yelled at Arnanguaq to get off the sledge and run across, and to us to run out and meet the dogs. We did what we could, but it was not enough. The sledge tipped over and the loose ice overwhelmed it.

"Cut them loose! Cut them loose!" Akrioq shouted. We did so, and he himself slashed the lashings, righted the sledge and hauled it free of the load. Then he pushed it toward us and we hurried after what we could save of the load. It was as if fire were consuming the stuff, but we salvaged some of it. Arnanguaq, who had to look out for the child, leaped like a gazelle onto the boiling ice, which bubbled and frothed under her feet. Her eye was on the bag which held all of the little Navarana's clothes. The child sat with her head out of the hood and found it all vastly exciting to watch.

Akrioq saved his sledge and six dogs, but more than half his load was irretrievably lost. Once more we pulled ourselves onto the middle of an ice pan and took stock of our reduced resources.

I suggested that the rest of them try to sleep and I would keep watch—I had more to worry about than they did.

It seemed to me impossible to make it home to Greenland now. There were only sixteen dogs in place of the thirty-four yesterday. We had no kerosene and no primus stove, and in all only about thirty rounds of ammunition for each of our three guns. Perhaps the worst catastrophe was in losing our sewing materials except for a few needles which Akratak had stuck in her hair for emergencies. Added to that, we had only two harpoons and no tent. It is bad enough to be without a tent in summer, but it is worse in the fall—and in order to sew one we would need more than five needles.

We were, I thought, in about the middle of the sound. With good going we could make it to either side in one sleep: if we returned to Baffin Land we could reach a settlement within a few days; if we went on to North Devon we might be forced to stay over for the summer in an unfamiliar, uninhabited country.

Of course, if I did not reach home expeditions would be sent out to search for me. Knud and I had promised each other that, in case one of us was lost, the other would not send out a search party. But that was one promise each of us knew the other had no intention of keeping.

Thus it meant going back to the land we had just left. I would have liked to try to complete the trip if I had had my own time, but the *Soekongen* would be leaving Thule soon, and we had arranged that, if I was not there when it left, it was to pick me up at Ponds Inlet. I had, by the grace of God, saved my notebooks. It was only my good luck that I had not lost my sledge and load.

Once more we divided everything between us. The two Eskimos drove the two sledges with eight dogs each, and carried the load.

For the first time I met some protests, not from the men but from the two women. They grumbled because I had so many instruments and books along. If it had not been for my foolish theodolite, which, they felt, was of no use at all, I would have been able to haul some of their belongings, and they would not have been lost. Angry women are difficult to propitiate, and their poor husbands dared not take sides. It made them feel a little better, however, to scold me.

We could not build an igloo, and had to camp on the ice by overturning the sledges and lying back of them. Our sleep was interrupted after a few hours by the renewed pressure of the ice and we had to run for our lives.

Now followed two harrowing days. There was no safety for us anywhere. We could neither cook nor dry our clothes and, as it turned cold once more, we were all miserable. Arnanguaq rocked back and forth with her baby on her lap, wrapped in whatever we could provide, and moaned. I contributed my woolen undershirt, but the child fretted constantly. Arnanguaq explained that her distress was the result of the white man's crazy mode of traveling, and, if anything happened, she would hold me responsible for murder.

This made me feel no better, but after a while both child and mother fell asleep. When they woke, little Navarana took up her crying where she had left off. Arnanguaq then found several enormous lice in my shirt, and accused all the white race of breeding lice that bit like wolverines. The situation was anything but merry.

Meanwhile we drifted about aimlessly in Lancaster Sound, and there was nothing to keep the women interested. Akrioq motioned me away from the women and said confidentially that Arnanguaq, after all, was a woman, and "she belongs to those who are angry when adrift on an ice pan if they have small babies." I admitted that one did not encounter the type every day and that if this was her specialty she might as well take advantage of it when she had the opportunity.

Shortly afterward we had to move again. This time Boatsman had discovered a passage that he thought would lead us almost to the shore. We rushed along, and were soon within a short distance of land, separated from it only by a number of loose floating ice pans. We decided that the women and I should jump across them, and the two men try to follow along after with the sledges.

I carried both harpoons in order to push the ice pans about. It was most important that we get the baby to shore in a hurry, and the men would have to worry along somehow with the sledges. Fortunately there were four boxes of matches left, and each of us took one—except Arnanguaq, who had enough on her hands to look out for little Navarana.

It took us many hours to reach shore, jumping across dark, treacherous stretches of water between ice pans, and shoving and pulling the ice together. I could not help admiring the two women who were now in action for the fifth day with no more than four hours of actual sleep. They leapt about like young schoolboys, a little nervous, perhaps, but always courageous. I especially admired Arnanguaq. She was rather small and heavy, but she was as light on her feet as Boatsman's wife.

When we once more stepped on solid ground we were far to the west of the place we had left it, and the two sledges were still far out on the ice. What would become of them I did not know— and the guns were on the sledges. As we watched they drifted westward, farther from us each moment.

Akratak offered to take the harpoons and try to reach the

sledges again while I cared for Arnanguaq and the baby, but I considered this a challenge, gave her my matchbox and started for the sledges. I reached them in less than three hours, but I was so exhausted by then—I had not slept in five days and I have never been able to keep awake longer—that I sank down and passed out.

The Eskimos drove, woke me occasionally to help them, and then let me go to sleep again. We finally landed down in Prince Regent Inlet. All of us slept before we tried to find the women. They were not dying, we knew. Akrioq consoled himself by telling us that a mother can always find food for her child and can protect it when everyone else has failed. We merely said yes and went back to sleep.

When I eventually awoke I was stiff from the cold. Not only my clothes but my limbs were rigid. The temperature had dropped suddenly, and we could see the ice forming solid on the water. If we had only waited a few hours we could easily have reached shore on either side.

We drove east again to locate the women, and finally heard a voice calling to us. Akratak stood at the mouth of a cave in the cliffs. They had discovered a wonderful shelter, and Arnanguaq was still asleep in it but woke when she heard our voices.

"It is thus proved," she said, "that you were going home and leaving us alone here to starve to death." Pleasant greetings, to be sure, but she was cold and tired and hungry. This was the last outburst of her temper, however.

First we needed food—then clothes. If we could hurry and return to Ponds Inlet we would find both, and we decided it was better to pursue that course than to stop here and hunt. Especially did I want to reach there in time to meet Captain Pedersen and the *Soekongen* to be taken back to Denmark.

Boatsman said: "It will be nice when it is all over and we can sit at home and tell of this." I admitted that it might be very pleasant.

So we drove east along the coast. There was no more meat, but the sun shone and we were at least not frightened. It was spring and the seals would soon be on the ice—the wind had kept them below for several days. Before evening Akrioq and Boatsman each killed a seal and we had enough to eat. We scraped the skin of one immediately in order to make kamiks for the dogs, as ice needles were forming on the ice foot along which we drove.

That night Boatsman scouted the shore and found a snowbank in which we could dig a cave—the snow was not strong enough to build an igloo, but the cave was wonderful. We had two lamps, a pot, kettle and two cups. The lamps' flames made it cozy, and occasionally the air became so stuffy that we had to open the snow door to keep the flames burning.

We decided to remain here until our clothes were dry and we were fit to travel again. Arnanguaq grew merry again, and we discussed our adventures on the ice as if they had been arranged for our pleasure. Eskimos are great people.

After a while, however, the reaction set in. It was fine to be on land again, but there was still plenty of trouble ahead. There were now only eighty-nine rounds of ammunition left. We had one big snow knife and two meat knives; the women had their five needles, no stove and few clothes. I was the only one who had saved my whole outfit, and it had to be divided among five grown people.

Besides, my foot started hurting once more. I had completely forgotten about it. Pain is a peculiar thing, a luxury in which one indulges when he can afford it. When something of vital importance must be accomplished, the pain fades away.

Now when I examined the foot it looked like an old newspaper soaked in water, a wonderful but not very pleasant sight. The pain seemed to mount when I lay down, yet I could not bear to put any weight on the foot.

Two days' traveling brought us back to Admiralty Bay where we could see open water cut by the tides at the mouth of the deep inlet. We saw a few seals and shot two, but they sank or were whisked away by the tide. We dared not waste any more ammunition. Lancaster Sound had broken up, and seals never sleep on moving ice. There are too many hideouts in it for bears. A seal insists upon a plain stretch where he can see a long distance.

More could be seen farther south on the smooth ice of Admiralty Bay, so Boatsman and I went south to try to kill some of them in order to have enough provisions to reach Ponds Inlet— we could count on no more hunting until we reached Eclipse Sound. But we had bad luck—the sky was overcast and the air damp, rendering the seals' hearing so acute that we could get nowhere near them. We wasted more ammunition, and it only lured us farther from our party.

We stayed there for three days and had nothing to eat. Boatsman and I then drove up to a bird cliff we discovered at the eastern entrance of the bay and, using our shotgun, wasted all the rounds of ammunition for it in killing a few gulls. Meanwhile the area of open water expanded at the mouth of the bay, and we knew we would have to hurry.

Akrioq, who had been here before with Mathiassen, advised us to travel far down to the head of the fjord. There, he said, was an adjacent fjord leading to the east. He had hunted caribou there and had followed a valley eastward. It was his opinion that the rivers ran eastward to Milne Inlet from there, and he thought it would be safer to take an overland route. In case we could not return to the sea there would be enough caribou to keep us alive while we trekked across to Ponds Inlet.

I thought of my ill-treated foot and hoped to God that we would not have to walk. We argued for a while, and then decided to do as Akrioq had suggested. The seals became more abundant as we traveled up the bay, and the immediate danger of starvation passed.

In fact, Admiralty Bay is not a bad place to live. It was from there that old Mequsaq and his people had emigrated to Greenland. We could not understand why they had left such a fine place, but Boatsman thought it might have been because they had enemies, or perhaps the great spirits advised them to go to Greenland to teach the natives there to eat caribou and build kayaks.

Soon we found the reason why Mequsaq and his people had been tempted to leave.

We traveled slowly, making short jumps overland. The women were occupied in mending our clothes; mine were made smaller for some of the others, and my fine sealskin bag was turned into stockings for us. The women had to be especially careful with their needles. One was broken already, but we ground it sharp again and could use it in an emergency.

10

Akrioq was the first to spot the people.

They looked strange to us, unlike any people we had ever seen before. Their faces were hollow, and their eyes sunk deep in their skulls. They had no real clothes, but were covered with scabrous-looking rags and filth.

They were starving.

Their voices were eerie. I have seen many shocking things in my life, but nothing like this. We thought them ghosts at first, but I talked to them. Thirteen of the tribe had died during the winter, and there was no prospect of anything but death for the rest of them.

They told us that they had been caught by a gale which lasted from one moon to the next. Their chief, the famous Tulimak (The Rib), had died first, and after that no one was able to prevent the weaker members of the tribe from eating the dogs. The starving animals had not been butchered—they had died off faster than the dog meat could be eaten. Eating the diseased and starving dogs had caused a plague among the natives, they told me. It was evident on their faces.

Thirteen had starved to death in a tribe which possessed guns and ammunition in a locality with plenty of game. Where such a thing could happen, one could not blame the old-timers for deserting their native land.

We gave them a seal to eat. Like very poor people, they did not want to take our food and cut off only a small portion and gave the rest back to us. There were twelve of them left, among them a few I had previously met in Igdloolik. After we had built a fire and boiled soup in their pots, they seemed to revive slightly.

They told us that the corpses were left a little farther along the fjord. We could see the spot plainly, but Akrioq, who was more curious than the rest of us, begged me not to look at the bodies. Either the natives, or their dogs, had eaten some of the human flesh. I could find out nothing more definite, as they refused to talk about it to us or each other. They were especially wary of me, because at first they thought I might be connected with the Mounted Police or a mission. They seemed vastly relieved when I assured them I was not.

Our own plan was immediately forgotten in our desire to help these wretched humans. There were four families of them, though I learned that several of the families had been broken up by death. As soon as possible after the deaths they had repaired the missing links in the couples. Akratak learned that one of the girls had had four different men during the winter. She had accepted the men because it was believed that death is always a greater peril to a single person than to a married one.

I suggested that they move farther north, but they said they had no means of doing so. They were too weak to walk. The men admitted that they had a rather good outfit down at the point and, after they had had enough to eat, they might go after it.

It is amazing how fast the human animal recovers. We fed them well—I got two seals the first day and each of my boys got three—and the imminent terror of starvation retreated. The mere fact of outsiders arriving with help restored their desire to live.

I took a special fancy to one of the young men, Mala, who had lost his whole family. He and I stuck together, and he was in good shape again within a week. The men walked to their old camping place and brought up their property. Considerable property it was too, including two loads of narwhale tusks secured at the big killing last fall.

After a while we moved north. First we took two of the local natives with us, and each day when we went hunting we brought more. I gave them my sledge to use, and they hauled up their belongings and settled down. They had plenty of needles and guns with ammunition. But after we got the women started scrubbing and drying skins for tents, there broke out among us an epidemic which covered the victims with so many boils that they could not walk. They insisted that this had been their affliction during the whole winter, and it had come from eating dead dogs.

My Greenland Eskimos put a different interpretation on it. They said it was a sure sign that the people had eaten human flesh. As they, too, began to break out with the same scourge, their talk of cannibalism soon stopped.

Nevertheless, my natives distrusted the others and refused to sleep beside them. They were afraid that if punishment were meted out for the tribe's sins, the spirit might not be able to distinguish between the guilty and the innocent. Therefore they would take care that a tiny brook separated them.

We finally had a tent ready, but our two hunters were beset with the boils. Akrioq's arms were covered, and Boatsman had so many on his seat that he could neither walk nor sit down. Arnanguaq was even worse off. There were boils on both her breasts, and Navarana's nursing was an agony to her.

Mala and I went out hunting alone for several days, driving up the fjords because he would not let me approach the spot where they had spent the winter. The place, he said, would be haunted all summer. Although the dead had been buried, one could hear their ghosts moving about; if we drove near, the ghosts might follow us and kill us.

We fed the starving people and gave them whatever we had. In return they gave us thread to mend our tents and clothing, ammunition and knives. They were not badly off, but the things they possessed could not be eaten. They were just what we needed most.

I still had with me my white anorak from the King's party. This we turned into a seal hunter's hiding-sail. We taught the local natives how to use it. They had always tried to trick the seals by pretending to be one of them, and there are times when the sail is a much more effective device.

Finally we got them all on their feet again. Mala and I discovered tomcods under the ice, and as soon as we had eaten enough of these fish to change the diet the boils and fever abated.

I tried once to walk down to the graves, but it was light and the local Eskimos saw me and came running after me.

"What can be seen," they said, "will not be pleasant. We were there in the winter and we want to go far away from there. Also we believe strangers will harm the dead people."

I promised to keep away in the future, and I did.

Soon afterward we moved farther up the fjord where the men could get out to sea in their kayaks and hunt.

At last I felt that it was time some of us, at least, should go to Ponds Inlet and head off Captain Pedersen. The natives agreed that it would be possible to walk across country, but we could take no sledge with us, and the going would be difficult. I thought about sending some of the Baffin Landers, but we were not sure we could trust them, especially as they were afraid of facing the relatives of their dead companions in Ponds Inlet. I asked Boatsman and Akratak if they would like to go, but she was, after all, a girl and not so strong as we were; it would not look well to send a woman after help.

So I decided to go myself, and my friend Mala volunteered immediately to go along if I would pay him for the trip. He did not know at first what he wanted, but I assured him he could have any and everything he wished if we made the trip safely. This settled the matter and we talked over what we should take with us.

"Are you ready to start now?" I asked.

"Yes. Why not?"

He was right. There was nothing to wait for and every hour we delayed filled the streams with more water. I insisted upon having my gun with eighteen rounds of ammunition to keep us from starving, as well as my harpoon to use as a cane and for emergencies in crossing rivers and ice. It came in handy.

We said good-bye at the top of the hill, and Mala and I set off together. He proved to be without exception the best boy I ever had. He and I endured more hardships together than I ever encountered before or since.

11

The first day was fairly easy. Both of us were well trained, and there was not an ounce of fat on us. It would have been fairly pleasant to walk many hundreds of miles with him if the going had been good, but we had to take what came, and it was invariably bad. The rivers and streams were flooded by the warm weather, and there were long stretches of snow. We had no tent with us, but I had the Danish flag which I had saved as a last resort to patch our clothes. Its weight was negligible, and it was a sort of shelter.

Next day it started to snow, which made the nights less easy to endure. Mala, however, said that it must snow now as the caribou were calving. The calves' feet were tender, and it had to snow so that they could migrate.

There was nothing for us to eat, and we said to each other that soon it would be necessary to look about for game. We did not mention the fact that we were constantly on the lookout. When we went to sleep we remarked that tomorrow we had better shoot a caribou or perhaps a rabbit, because we would not want to carry much.

Then we came upon a plateau of clay softened by the warmth of the sun. We tried to avoid it, but it was impossible to detour and we trotted onward. We could not lie down during the day to rest, as there were no stones to keep us dry. Finally we were so exhausted that we had to drop, and we devised a method of using each other's thighs for pillows; when we felt the moisture from the earth penetrating our clothes we got up and walked on.

The sun was warm during the days and the clay thawed out to a depth of six inches. Our kamiks were jellylike from the constant moisture, and my foot felt as if it were on fire. I considered turning back, but the thought of remaining over at Admiralty Bay until the ice formed in the winter, meanwhile leaving all my friends to worry about me, kept me going.

Mala had thought of something he wanted in pay, he said. "I want a gun and ammunition!"

"You shall have it!" I said, and he slept well until next morning.

Still there was nothing to eat, and our stomachs burned as

if we had drunk hot tar. There was not a living animal in sight, not even a bird.

My foot was growing constantly worse. The clay sucked at the wounds, and we had to stop and take off my kamiks every few minutes.

"I also want a canvas tent!" Mala said when we stopped. His wish was granted, and we walked on again. Then we stopped, for we thought we heard a ptarmigan. It was only the murmuring of the river we were following. We tried to climb hills, but they were of clay as well.

Next day we knew we had to get meat soon, because both of us were tiring and felt the cold. I saw caribou constantly, as did Mala, but they always turned out to be stones.

I asked him questions about the country, and held him responsible for the lack of wild game. He had shot caribou where we were, he said, and could not understand why there were none now unless ghosts had preceded us and frightened the game away. And so another day went by with nothing to eat. We passed the stage of hunger, and were now dizzy, our eyes dull. The thought occurred to Mala that we might eat certain plants, but there were none—only clay, and more clay.

The next day was the worst of all. I shall never forget it. The clay was a slough, and we sank deep into it. We were so completely plastered with the gritty stuff that we lost interest in trying to keep clean. Whenever we stopped it was all I could do to get up. My brain felt doped, my body a dead thing. I walked ahead with the gun, and Mala plodded after with the harpoon. We dared not mention game any longer; it was too tantalizing.

If I could only lie down, I thought. To hell with everything but sleep. Every inch of my body cried out for it, but I knew what would happen if I gave in to my body. I must have slept as I walked, because suddenly I toppled over and fell face down in the disgusting stuff. I could not get my breath, yet I did not have the initiative to raise my head out of it, and only came to when Mala stood over me, shouting and yanking at my hair.

Then I pulled myself together. Perhaps the shock of the boy's sobbing gave me strength. I got to my feet and announced that we would go far today, since we must reach the shore before the ice broke up.

The word "ice" sounded queer in my ears. It was like a ghastly joke. Surely there could be no such thing as ice. There was nothing anywhere, there never had been anything anywhere, but this clay.

Then I thought of Mequsaq and Pipaluk. One step for Pipa-luk—up with the bad leg and forward. One step for Mequsaq—the foot sank and disappeared in the hellish stuff.

One step for my mother, and my father and my sisters and my brothers. I thought of them all, and took a step for each of them. One by one. One by one.

And then I stopped thinking of them. I knew that I might as well confess that I was going through this purgatory to get home to Magdalene. I had never had an answer from her, but I was sure I would have her some day. If it had not been for the thought of her, I could never have gone on with that red-hot piece of iron hanging at the end of my leg.

I would call the whole stretch of clay and hell Magda's Plateau. As soon as the idea came to me, things seemed easier. If it were named for her I could cross it somehow—there must be something good about it.

Poor Mala had to rest. The boy was young and had been through one hell already this winter. He had watched his people die of starvation, and had looked the monster in the face himself. Now he had been tricked into coming along with me only to meet the old terror once more.

I sat down beside him. We were so careless of ourselves now that we flopped into the wet clay as if it were an easy chair. I let it run through my hands as children play with sand at the beach. Mala told me about his father's death.

"Did you think you were going to die, Mala?" I asked.

"Oh, no. One never thought of that. Help was sure to come —just as it is now. We, too, could die, but we are not going to!"

His confidence was a challenge. He was right. We were not going to give up!

We jumped up together. I discovered that the barrel of the gun was full of clay but, worst of all, the sight was gone. It had dropped off and buried itself in the clay. What use was a gun without a sight? I was in such a childish rage that I threw the gun as far as I could. It sank almost out of sight.

"Come, let's go!" I shouted, and set off. I was half mad by now, and my fury possessed me. I walked on, punishing my foot, almost getting a thrill out of the daggers that pierced it.

Mala came along, and I waited for him where some stones poked up through the clay. There was even one large enough to sit on. I turned around, and there was the boy carrying both gun and harpoon, and looking like a dog expecting a whipping.

"You can take this," he said, handing me the harpoon.

He was the wise one; the gun had to be carried. I had not been myself when I tossed it aside.

And then at last we reached a more friendly portion of God's good earth. We saw no living things, but we discovered a few plants, the roots of which we could chew and digest. Besides, here was year-old dung of rabbits. If one has blubber (we did not) it can be eaten easily. We collected the excrement, chewed it, and got it down. It is hard to swallow, but at least gives one a sensation of having something in the stomach. We collected roots and grass and ate as much as we could. The new, juicy grass was not bad to taste, but swallowing it was something else.

We had so little strength that we grasped each other's arms when crossing even small brooks. The force of the water was not dangerous, but the sight of it rushing about our legs made us dizzy. Our brains were as fagged as our bodies. We had eaten nothing for a week but grass and rabbit excrement, and had walked steadily.

We walked for short distances and then slept until we grew cold. Once Mala wakened me by laughing.

"What is so funny?" I asked.

"The idea comes to one's head," he said, "that after having had one tough time before, the same man runs into worse as soon as he has recovered from the first. One likes to be fat and comfortable, but this is a funny way of doing it."

The flag lay over us. It felt better to breathe against something, even if it was sleazy and almost useless.

"I want a knife, a knife of every kind," he said, and I promised them to him before we slept again. Perhaps he dreamed of all his possessions while he slept. I hope he did.

We came to a tributary of the river we followed, and we had to go a distance into the hills before we could wade across. And there at the head of the stream were three caribou, but they got our odor before we spotted them, and we only saw them on the run.

But this tugged at our spirits. We were in a district of game, and sooner or later we would eat.

Mala saw a mouse scuttling into a hole. He threw down his load and dug for it. He assured me that mice taste sweet, but we got none.

And so on we went. My notebooks were growing heavier each day, but if I died, I would die with them. Our weapons were a burden. I was sure I could not last another day. Toward afternoon Mala fell. He had burned up his last ounce of strength. He had been a brave boy, but he was all in. I saw in his eyes the expression I have seen so often in the eyes of dogs worn out and begging to be left behind.

I sat down on a stone and said nothing. What was there to say? I looked at him, how long I don't know, and suddenly he leapt to his feet and screamed: "Don't look at me that way. It won't do you any good!" His language became queer and incoherent, but I understood him. I had never questioned him, but now I knew that the natives of his tribe had turned cannibal back there at Admiralty Bay.

I understood and I was sorry. I could have cried—perhaps I did cry. I don't know now. I lay down and pulled the flag over our heads. This, I honestly thought, was the end. Still it did not matter any more, because nothing in the world was of any interest, not even food.

We slept a long time. I know, because the sun was in the north when we woke.

But we had been wakened by the music of a ptarmigan's wings fluttering on a stone beside us.

Mala forgot that he had given up. His mind was suddenly clear, fully awake. We looked at the bird, and the determination to get it was so great in us that there was no question of its getting away. We could not fail. I took the gun and Mala reached out for a piece of willow twig which he broke into small pieces. One he adjusted to the barrel as I sighted.

There were eighteen cartridges left. I approached so close to the bird that I could almost touch it with the gun. It ignored me entirely. I aimed at the breast, pulled the trigger, and the head and neck flew off!

We could not have been happier had we shot a bear or a walrus. Yet when we held the bird in our hands it felt strange to us.

"Are you hungry?" Mala asked.

"No, not especially. But let's eat it just the same."

"I'm not hungry either," said Mala.

In the back of our minds was the thought of saving this until we had killed another, so that each of us could eat a whole bird. But I remembered the warnings I had heard, and given others, to eat sparingly after a siege of starvation, so we divided it evenly and unhurriedly, toying with the food before us.

It was not true, I discovered, that food does not taste good after long denial. It was wonderful, and when we finished there were few feathers and no bones left over. But we could feel nothing in our stomachs.

We walked on, crossed another tributary of the river, and before the end of the day killed four more ptarmigans. Two of them we killed with stones—they are tame as hens in a coop at this time of year. That night we made a regular camp. We collected grass for a pillow, and ate one fowl each. The other two we saved for the next day, ate them before we set out, and wasted several bullets on rabbits which we did not kill. We did, however, find a nest of mice. I ate one, but did not care for it. The taste was sweet, but I did not relish it.

Now that Mala had had something to eat he returned to his calculations. "Can I have everything? Can I have a wife too?"

I said yes. I had secured several wives for my friends, so why not one more? And I got one for him too.

Next day we came within sight of the sea and Mala shot a rabbit. It helped some, but in order to reach the sea we had to cross a small lake by wading in it up to our bellies. The day was cloudy and we could not dry our clothes. We were both exhausted, and when we got through the lake had no strength to start across the ice. We constructed a rude shelter behind a rock, and it started to rain. Our dirty, wet clothes clung to us and there was no way to keep warm.

Mala said that it always rains at this time. Otherwise the young gulls in the cliffs, whose parents could bring them food but no drink, would suffer from thirst. If it did not rain they would never grow fat and delicious. Somehow this did not make me feel any better, and that night we were colder than ever. We lay together like spoons in a case, turning over when our outside layers became numb.

Next morning we walked out on the ice with more confidence, but when we had been walking for two hours we considered it worse than the land. But not worse than the clay—nothing could be.

There were seals on the ice, but there was also water. Mala had the first try at a seal and missed. Then I took the gun, and the seal spied me and flopped into the water.

We were both soaking wet, but, praise God! the sun came

out. We took my sealskin coat and, using it for a toboggan, threw our limited equipment upon it and dragged it behind us.

Mala tried his luck at another seal, but it sank. I shot and wounded one, but it got away. Mala missed another, I missed another, and several dived before we could get close to them.

At last we were down to four bullets. It would be impossible for us to go much longer without substantial food. If it had been winter we should have been dead long ago. It was my turn to crawl up to the next seal. Our bad luck had probably been due to the trumped-up sight we had attached to the gun, but now I was desperate.

The seal was no fool, and I put on such a performance as few actors have ever given an audience. I lay on my side, lifted my head and my legs like seal flippers. I rolled over and lay with my head in the wet snow on the ice—and I thought of what would happen if we died here of starvation after all our troubles. How silly we would look if we were found here on the ice . . . if a bear did not discover our bodies first.

Meanwhile the seal's head was up. It obviously distrusted me. Each time I crawled nearer it grew more uncertain of my kinship. I presume I played with that seal for three hours, wallowing in the wet snow, finally realizing that I was as close to it as I ever would get. The distance between us was still formidable, but I was in a rage by now and pulled up my gun and fired. The seal flopped over dead!

I dashed for it like a champion sprinter. It is said that seals often come to life and make for the blowhole, but this one did not. A dead seal never moves. Still, taking no chances, I pulled it far from the hole and shouted at Mala. He was dancing and leaping about like a madman! He had given up all hope of killing it, he said.

We were saved. Here was a whole big seal for us, and no dogs with which to share it. We lapped up the blood streaming from the bullet hole, we stroked the skin and considered where it would be best to start eating.

It was our big day, the day that gave us back our lives. We had cared for our matches all this time, and this was the first chance to use them. We used the blubber for fuel by chewing the fat and spewing it out over some turf. We found two flat stones, placed the meat between them over the fire and roasted it.

That is one dish I shall always remember. It was better than anything I have ever tasted in my life. I laid half the brain on a piece of blubber, and made a paste by chopping it with blubber oil. It was so delicious that the mere thought if it still excites my salivary glands.

The sun came out and the weather grew so warm that we took off our kamiks and dried them in the sun. The soles were worn completely through, but we tied the raw hide of the seal to our feet.

We had come down to Milne Inlet and not, as we had expected, to Eclipse Sound. We knew, however, that there were inhabitants at Toqujan and we headed straight for that community. It took us three more days, and when we finally came within sight of the village we were received with shrieks of joy and fright. Mala told the story of his people's starvation, and everyone sat down and wailed. Nearly all of them were related in some manner.

Mala tried to do his portion of the mourning, but he was too tired. Besides, it was an old story now, so he brought me inside his sister's house and showed me where to lie down. We both tumbled into bed and I only wakened to wind my watches, then turned over and slept again. For almost two days we lay on the ledge. The friendly Eskimos brought us tea and pancakes, and it was like heaven.

The women were fascinated at the sight of our bodies. We were so emaciated that we could have passed for freaks in a sideshow. All of them wanted to feel my ribs and made conjectures as to my probable appearance when well fed. I said I was not going to be butchered, and they thought that very, very funny, laughed uproariously and repeated the remark over and over.

We stayed with the natives for three days and then accompanied them to the trading station—Mitimatalik it is called in Eskimo (a place where a bird lights—in this case, the Hudson Bay Company was the bird). Mala and I rode the whole distance. I could not have walked. We were royally received, and I was invited to stay with the manager of the H.B.C. He was a fine man, but his hobby was a vulcanizing process, of all things. When he had a year in the outside world, he spent his time vulcanizing old tires, and his hope was to save enough money to set himself up in business. I listened to his plans with great interest until the fifth telling, then I knew all I wanted to know about vulcanizing.

The natives were going now to Button Point on the southeastern point of Bylot Island to hunt narwhales. I was still very weak and should not have gone, but I got a lift from a man with a

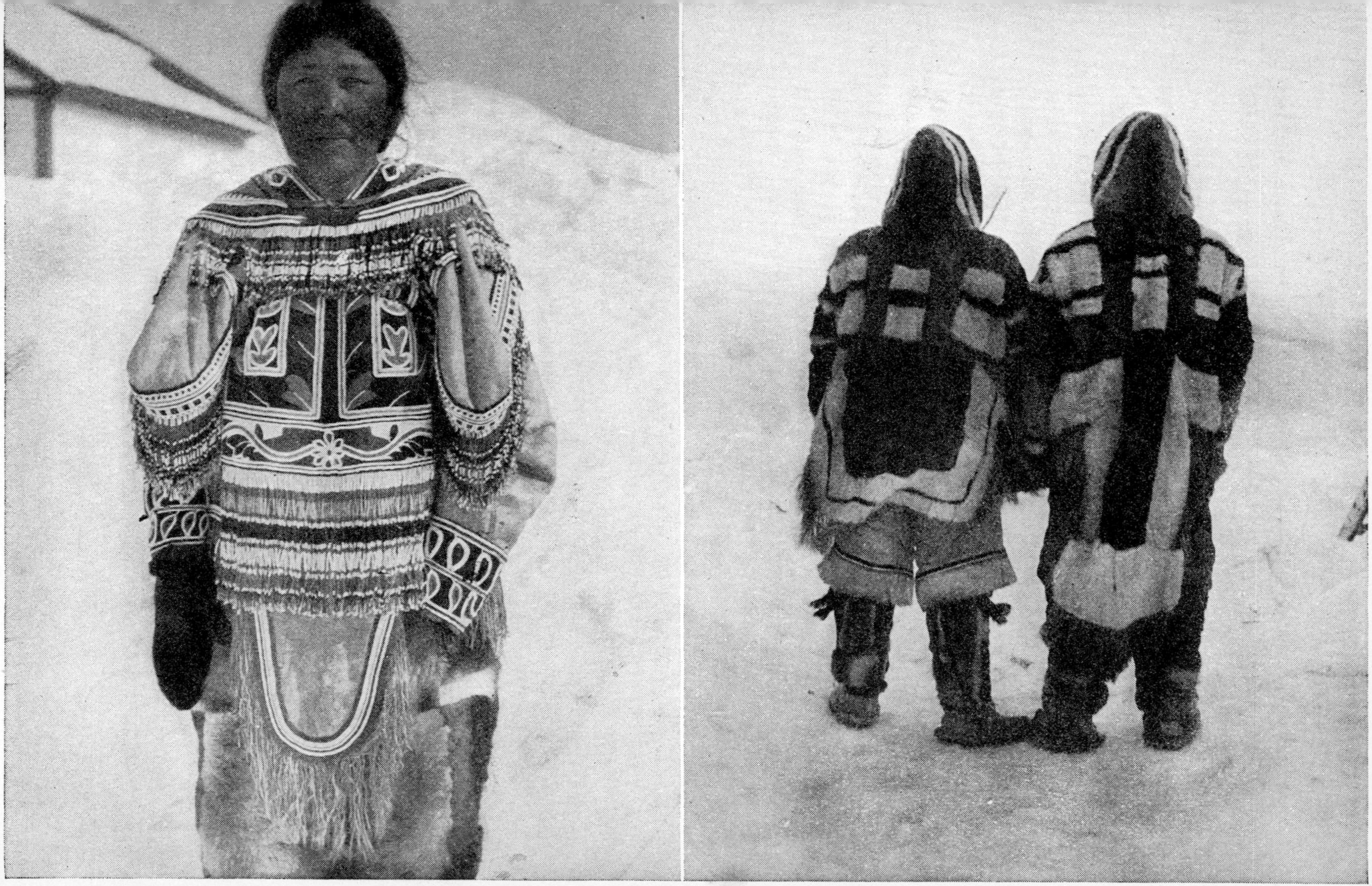

CONTRASTING COSTUMES OF AVILIK AND REINDEER WOMEN

good team, and it proved lucky. The man had a daughter and, although she was no great beauty, Mala took a shine to her—and I had promised to get him a wife.

We camped twice en route. Each night I used all my powers as lecturer, advocate and barker to convince the whole family that Mala was the one and only perfect man for a son-in-law. The father swayed like a reed in the wind. There was also a local widower after the girl—and he would give the girl a splendid wedding. The girl whispered this to me herself, and I told the family that if Mala married her while I was here, they should have such a wedding as none of them had ever imagined. From my ship would be brought box after box of presents. The kettles I would give to all the women related to the family would be miracles of beauty, and I would present Mala with a boat which the Hudson Bay Company would sell. That gave Mala the advantage over the widower.

When we landed at Button Point, Mala was informed that he was the lucky man. We did not see him, of course, until we reached our destination because he was still only guest and onlooker. He was tired, too, and would only ruin his new suit if he lent a hand with the dogs.

But now he was happier than he had ever been. He took his new wife into the tent I had given him, and I lived with them as long as we were at the point. When I finally left to walk back to Ponds Inlet, Mala said he was not yet through hunting, and would come along later. He needed more meat, he said, and his feet were not yet hungry for walking. Neither were mine, but it was August, and I knew I had to hurry.

I never saw Mala again, as he did not show up before I left Baffin Land. But at the 1934 annual dinner of the Circumnavigators Club in New York my good friend Reginald Orcutt screened some pictures he had filmed at Ponds Inlet. There was Mala in all the brilliant colors of the film. It was as if I enjoyed a visit with the fine boy again, and all the old memories of our struggles and companionship came back with a rush. It is to him that I owe my life—such as it is.

12

And finally there was our little ship, the *Soekongen*, rounding the cape. It was the most beautiful sight that has ever greeted my eyes. The police at the post donned their red coats to get through the formalities of customs, but Captain Pedersen was an old hand at cutting through red tape in the Arctic. He produced a few bottles and filled the glasses. No ship had been there that year, and the six bottles secured "for medical purposes" had long since disappeared.

I told Pedersen that we must go round to Admiralty Bay after my people. He was none too pleased, as the ice in Melville Bay had been bad to negotiate this year, and he was not sure that we could get back up to Thule again. Still Pedersen was not the man to give up without a trial, and immediately set about to get his crew ready for the trip. They had been invited to a dinner party on shore, and they talked of hunting next day. Pedersen poured liquor for them. He knew his sailors. He never drank himself.

Within four hours we were ready to go. We also gave the police officers a few bottles of the forbidden stuff so that they could taste for themselves how terrible it was, and we took care that they reached the beach safe afterward. Some of them were asleep. I gave the native storekeeper some gifts for Mala, and knew that he would receive them, for the man was honest as the soil.

And with that we sailed to the westward.

We could see immense flocks of snow geese feeding on the southwestern point of Bylot Island, and natives hunting them. We passed up through Eclipse Sound, and encountered no ice until we reached Lancaster Sound itself. And even that we managed to get through.

We found our friends at Adams Sound where I had arranged for them to be. They had had a hard time during the summer. There had been enough meat, but they had eaten little of it because they did not know when the ship might arrive and they wanted it to last. If I had not gone back for them there is no telling what might have happened. All the Canadian Eskimos had left on a caribou hunt, but the Greenlanders had faithfully remained at Adams Sound in the hope that the ship would come for them.

Now, of course, all the hardships were immediately forgotten. They had more than twenty puppies, sufficient to begin next year anew at Thule. Little Navarana had grown up and could run about merrily on the deck. She had certainly not forgotten how to eat bread and other ship delicacies.

We started back for Greenland immediately, and encountered

THE TEN-YEAR-OLD MEQUSAQ ON THE DAY HE FINALLY ARRIVED IN COPENHAGEN
FROM THULE

hard weather as soon as we hit Baffin Bay. It was impossible to get through even to Cape York, not to mention Thule. I asked Akrioq and Boatsman whether they wanted to be put ashore at Cape Seddon, if possible, or go on down to Danish Greenland. They all preferred Cape Seddon, since people of their own kin were there, and the two men and their wives had looked forward to seeing them for many years.

We made it safely, but I was disappointed. My son, Mequsaq, was still in Thule, and I would have to return to Denmark without him. My only consolation was in learning from the natives that he was in good health, and Akrioq and Boatsman would carry my presents to him. I would come back for him later. Since then he has lived about half the time in Greenland, the other half with me on my farm in Denmark and at school.

I gave Akrioq and Boatsman whatever we could spare from the *Soekongen* and I said good-bye to my friends there in Melville Bay to return to Denmark and become a civilized man once more, if possible.

If it had not been for my foot I would have gone up to get my boy, but that had to be attended to immediately.

At Upernivik we met the steamer *Hans Egede* with Director Daugaard-Jensen on board. I transferred to the faster boat, and everything was made pleasant for me. I was looked upon as a man raised from the dead. Rumors had been circulated at home that my body had been found, but the wreck of the *Bele,* our last sight on leaving Greenland years ago, had caused the building of several radio stations there, and I was able to send home word of my safe return.

Once again I visited Umanak Colony, and was offered new proof of the kindness of the Danes there. Uncle Jens greeted me, too, and our meeting was celebrated with party after party, and friendly, smiling faces.

But finally, after stopping at all the harbors, I felt the swells of the Atlantic under my feet, and it was fine to be rolled from side to side in my bunk.

On the way home I received shocking news. My old friend, Dr. Dreyer, manager of the Copenhagen Zoo, had died. Earlier in my life I had talked over the possibilities of becoming his successor, and he had promised to recommend me. I sent cables to the board of directors applying for the position. Handling animals had long been a hobby of mine, and I have always wanted to manage a zoo.

SAFE IN THE HARBOR AT COPENHAGEN AND GREETING PIPALUK, NOW SIX YEARS OLD

Fortunately for the zoo, however, the directors were wise men. They wanted a good man for the job, and of course the good man was not Peter Freuchen. I must be grateful to them now, I suppose, and the zoo must be thankful as well.

It is a long, monotonous trip home across the Atlantic in a small boat, but I was an honored guest and it was quite different from the time years ago when I had been a stoker on the same boat. For old times' sake I went down into the hold and took a shovel in my hands, but it was no good trying to stoke any more. My foot still pained too much.

I must be a very flighty person, easily affected by the advice of others. I am sure that, had I been forced to remain in Baffin Land and never reached Ponds Inlet, I would still have my foot. But now I had doctors about, telling me how bad the foot was, and spouting Latin terms at me. Consequently I was unable to do anything but limp from one place to another, and then sit down. I even considered learning to play cards during the trip. I was saved from that, thank God, and later I had no time to learn.

But everything must have an end, and on a certain day we passed old Kronborg castle, Hamlet's stomping ground. Two hours later we were in Copenhagen. The captain hoisted all his flags and stationed me on his bridge.

There was a great crowd. I saw my father and mother and little Pipaluk. Only now she was a big girl eight years old, and I hardly recognized her. There were dozens of journalists too, and I was overwhelmed by them and had to relate my story before I could go ashore. I started in on it, but soon asked them to excuse me. I would be back in a minute.

I ran up on deck and glanced about me. And there she was down on the dock—Magdalene. She stood quietly looking up at me, and I jumped onto the gangplank and rushed down to her.

I had better finish my speeches to everyone else, she said. She would go back to her hotel, and I could join her later.

I did as she bade me. Then I went back to her, and have remained with her ever since.

THE END